Shojo Beat

My love STORY!!

Story
KAZUNE
KAWAHARA

Art
ARUKO

13

MY love STORY!!

13

CONTENTS

STORY Thus Far...

Takeo Goda, a first-year high school student, is a hot-blooded guy who is 6'6" tall and weighs 265 pounds. Boys look up to him, but the girls he falls in love with all end up liking his handsome best friend, Makoto Sunakawa! But that all changes when Takeo saves Rinko Yamato from a groper on the train, and she becomes his girlfriend.

A transfer student named Tanaka starts to hang around Sunakawa, but he hides his true nature. Takeo doesn't think he's a bad guy, though, so he decides to take Tanaka day camping with him and Sunakawa. He manages to get Tanaka to express his true feelings, and they become friends! But then Tanaka ends up transferring schools once again...

Later, Yamato finds out that her father will be moving to Spain for work, and she has to go with him! She doesn't want to be separated from Takeo... Not knowing what to do, she runs away from home, and Takeo accompanies her all the way to Okinawa to bring her back!

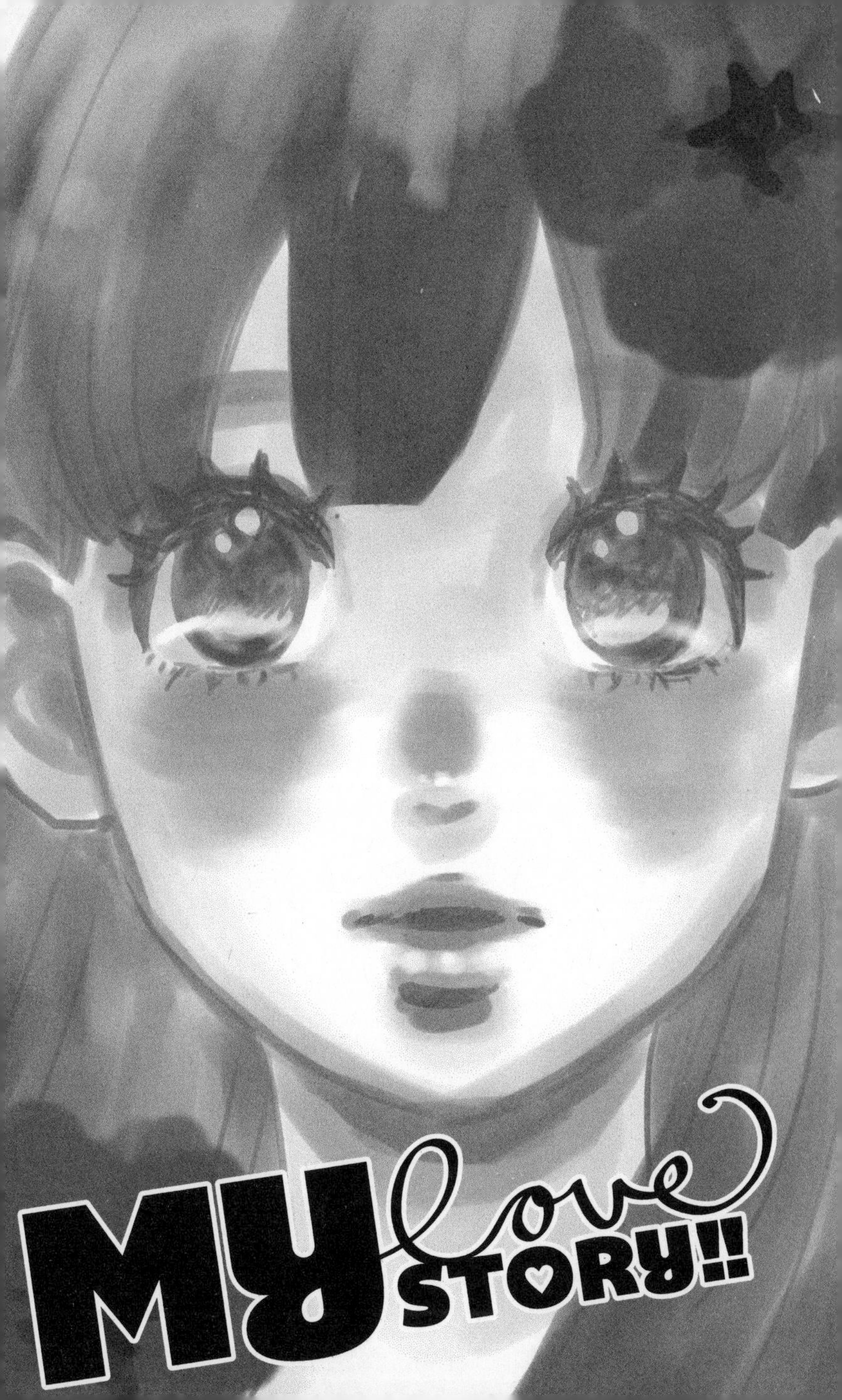
MY love STORY!!

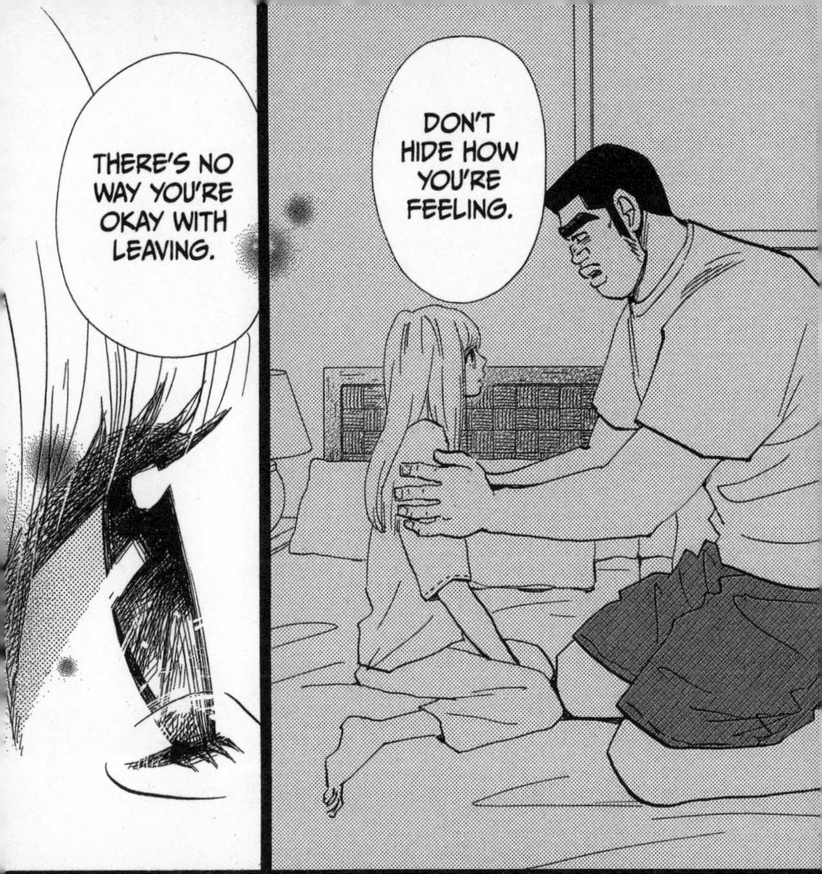
DON'T HIDE HOW YOU'RE FEELING.
THERE'S NO WAY YOU'RE OKAY WITH LEAVING.

MY love STORY!!

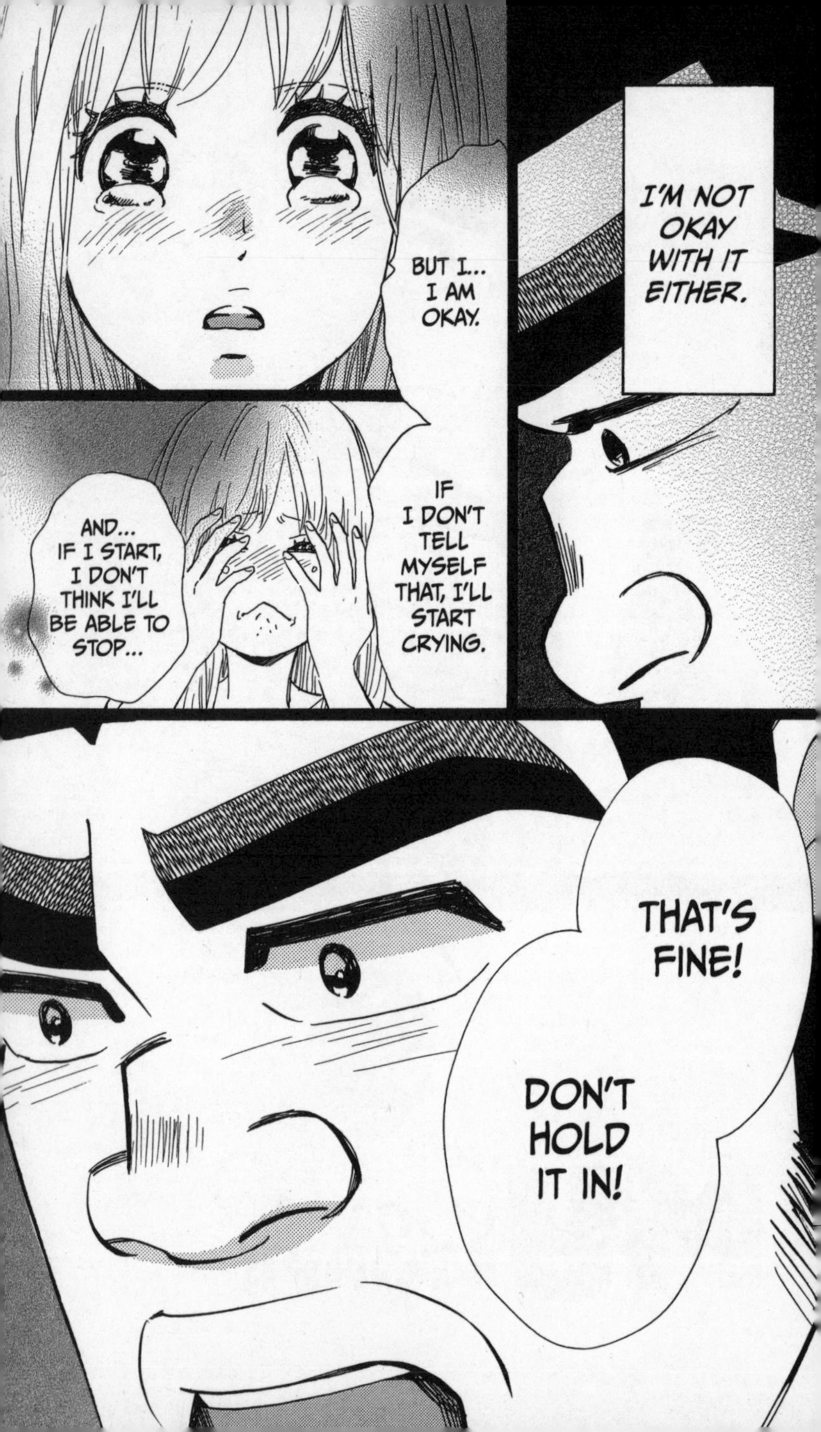
I'M NOT OKAY WITH IT EITHER.
BUT I... I AM OKAY.
IF I DON'T TELL MYSELF THAT, I'LL START CRYING.
AND... IF I START, I DON'T THINK I'LL BE ABLE TO STOP...
THAT'S FINE!
DON'T HOLD IT IN!

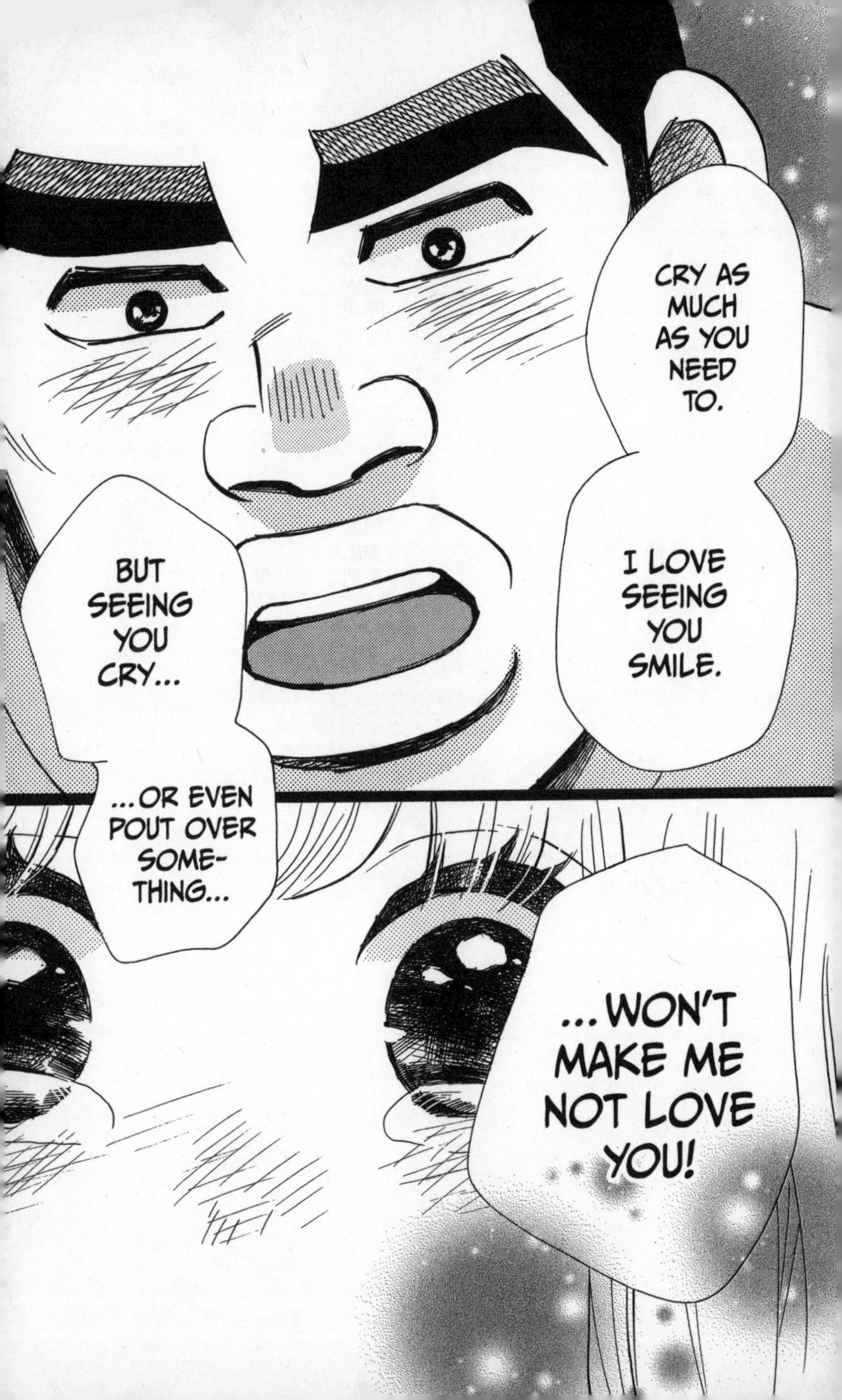
CRY AS MUCH AS YOU NEED TO.
I LOVE SEEING YOU SMILE.
BUT SEEING YOU CRY...
...OR EVEN POUT OVER SOME-THING...
...WON'T MAKE ME NOT LOVE YOU!

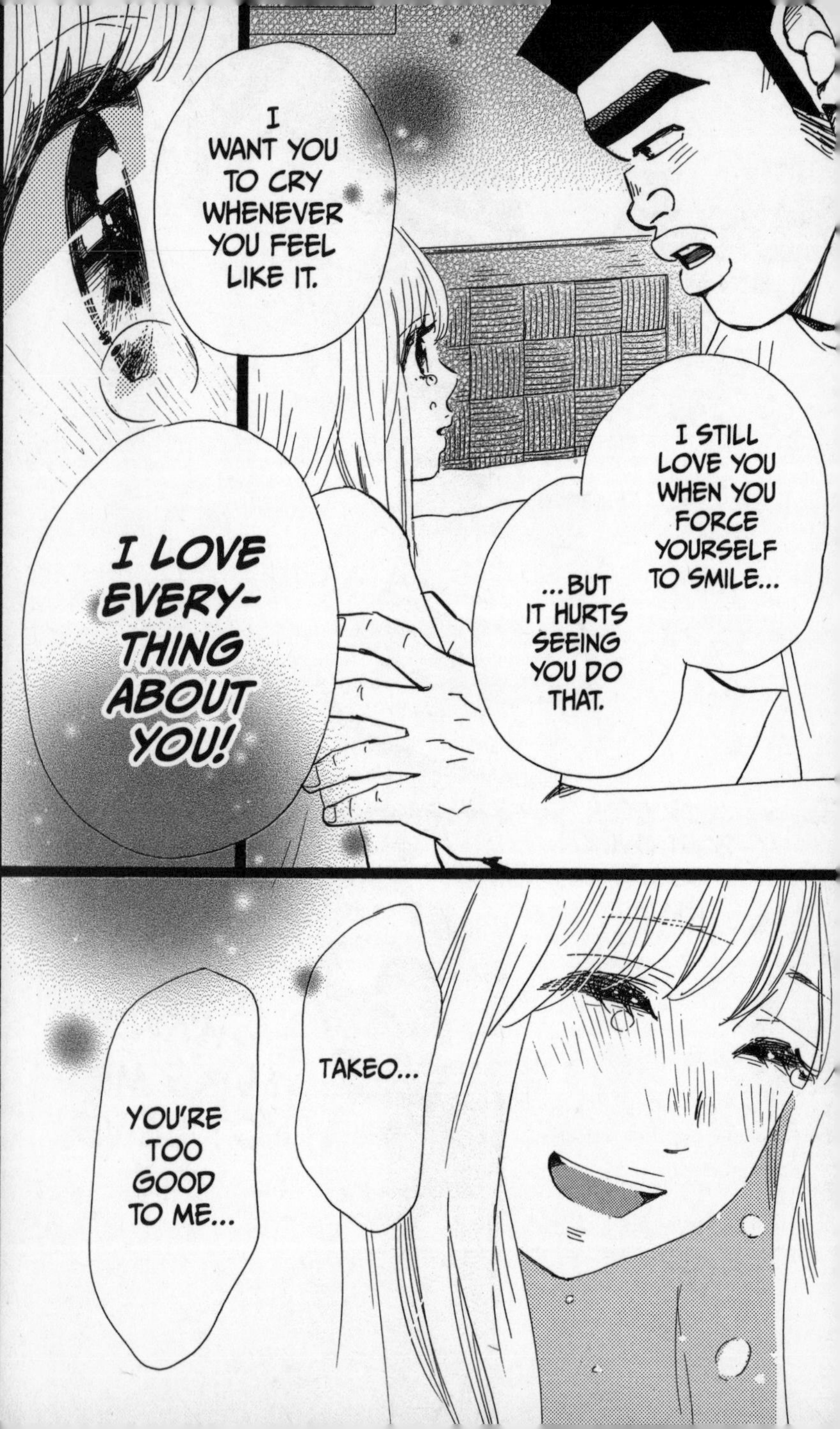
I STILL LOVE YOU WHEN YOU FORCE YOURSELF TO SMILE...
...BUT IT HURTS SEEING YOU DO THAT.
I WANT YOU TO CRY WHENEVER YOU FEEL LIKE IT.
I LOVE EVERY-THING ABOUT YOU!
TAKEO...
YOU'RE TOO GOOD TO ME...

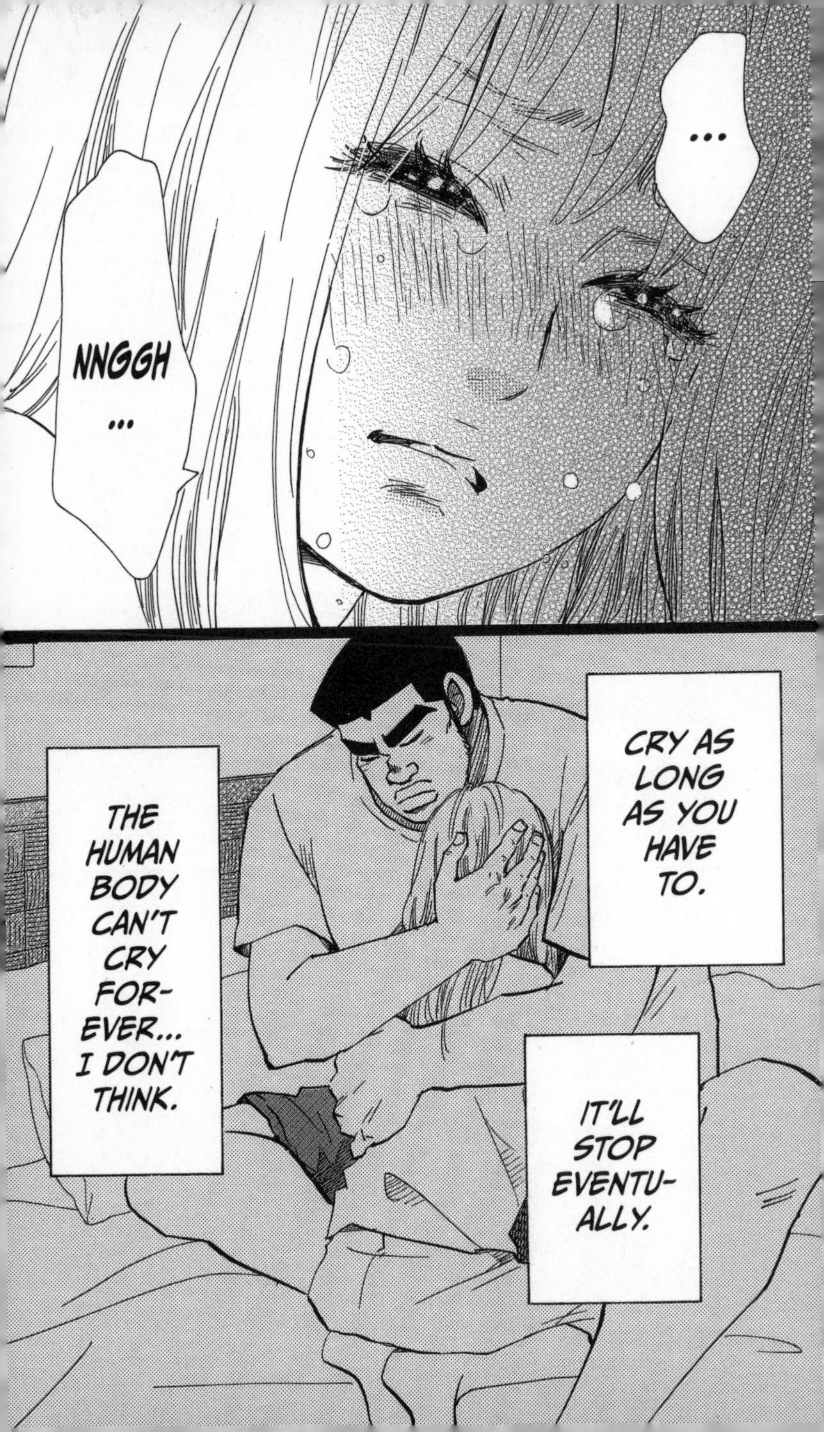
...
NNGGH ...
CRY AS LONG AS YOU HAVE TO.
THE HUMAN BODY CAN'T CRY FOR-EVER... I DON'T THINK.
IT'LL STOP EVENTU-ALLY.

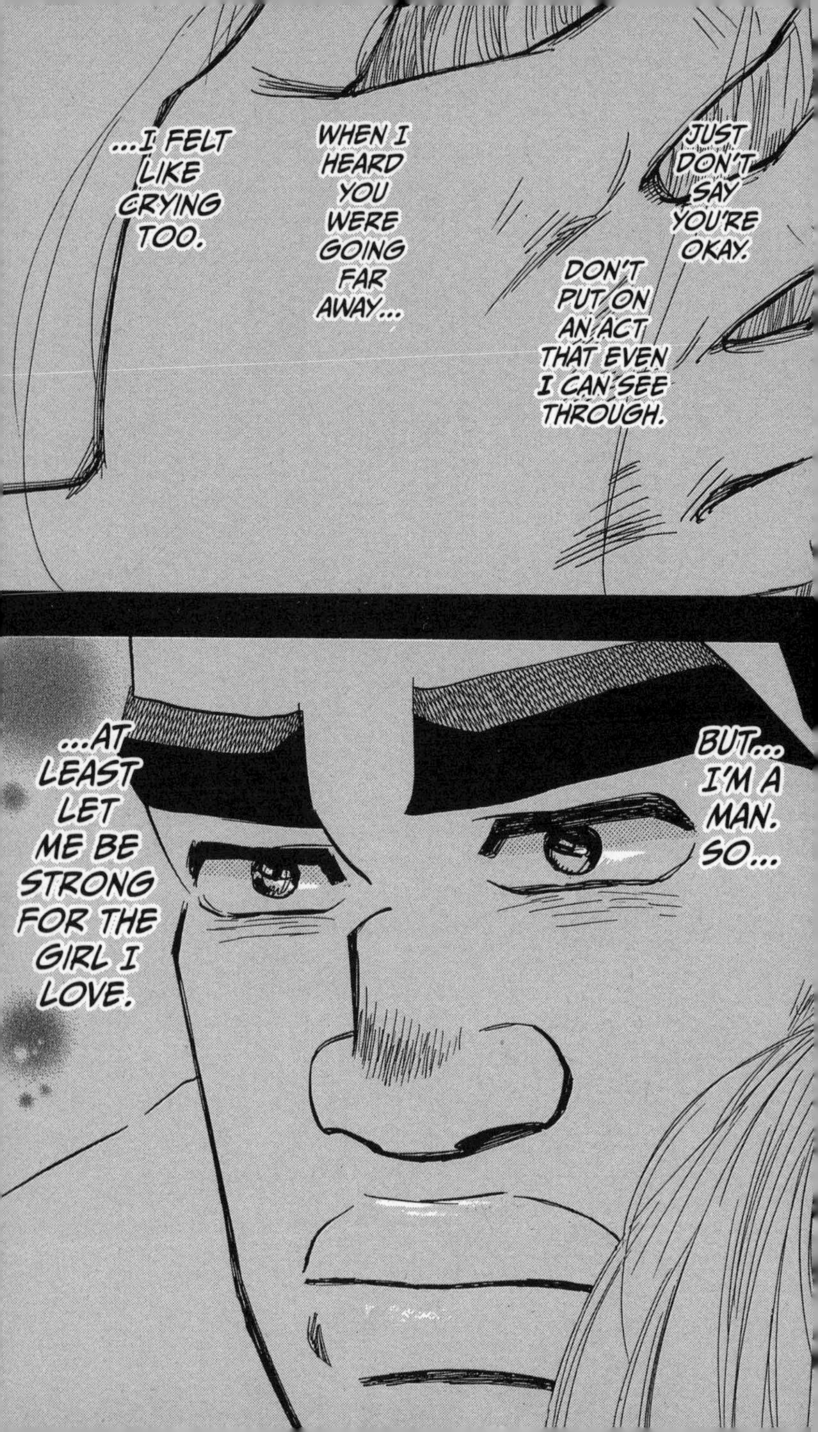
JUST DON'T SAY YOU'RE OKAY.
DON'T PUT ON AN ACT THAT EVEN I CAN SEE THROUGH.
WHEN I HEARD YOU WERE GOING FAR AWAY...
...I FELT LIKE CRYING TOO.
BUT... I'M A MAN. SO...
...AT LEAST LET ME BE STRONG FOR THE GIRL I LOVE.

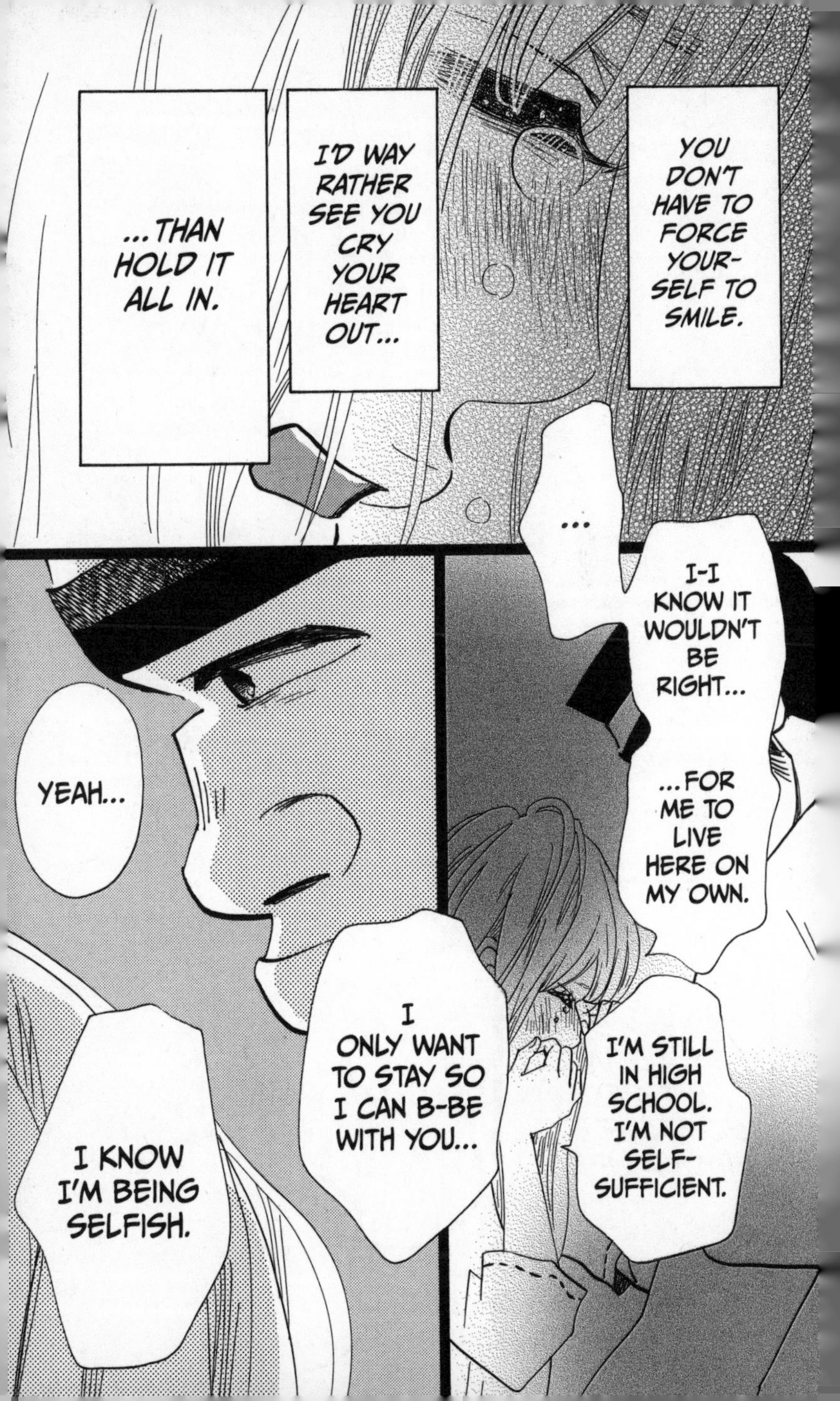
YOU DON'T HAVE TO FORCE YOUR-SELF TO SMILE.
I'D WAY RATHER SEE YOU CRY YOUR HEART OUT...
...THAN HOLD IT ALL IN.
...
I-I KNOW IT WOULDN'T BE RIGHT...
...FOR ME TO LIVE HERE ON MY OWN.
I'M STILL IN HIGH SCHOOL. I'M NOT SELF-SUFFICIENT.
I ONLY WANT TO STAY SO I CAN B-BE WITH YOU...
YEAH...
I KNOW I'M BEING SELFISH.

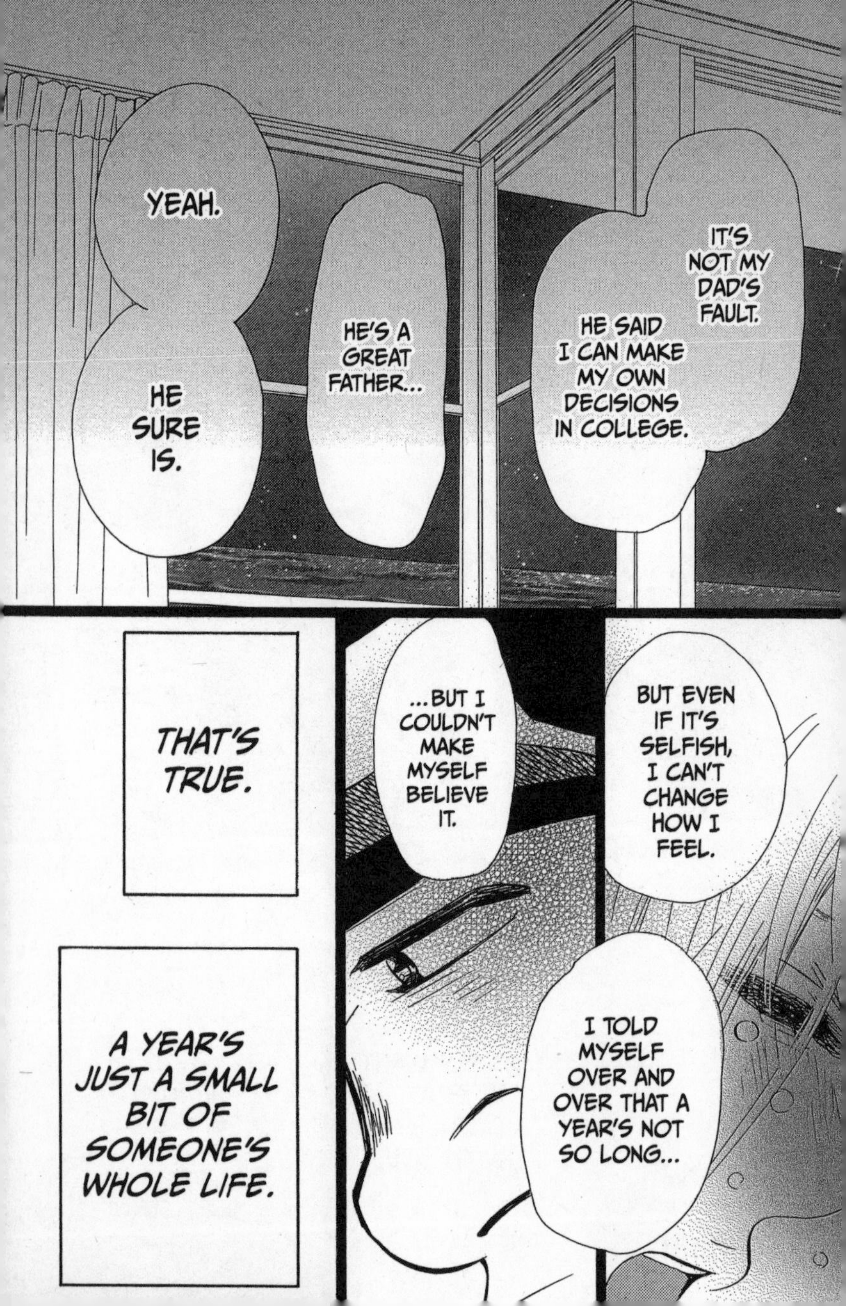
IT'S NOT MY DAD'S FAULT.
HE SAID I CAN MAKE MY OWN DECISIONS IN COLLEGE.
HE'S A GREAT FATHER...
YEAH.
HE SURE IS.
BUT EVEN IF IT'S SELFISH, I CAN'T CHANGE HOW I FEEL.
I TOLD MYSELF OVER AND OVER THAT A YEAR'S NOT SO LONG...
...BUT I COULDN'T MAKE MYSELF BELIEVE IT.
THAT'S TRUE.
A YEAR'S JUST A SMALL BIT OF SOMEONE'S WHOLE LIFE.

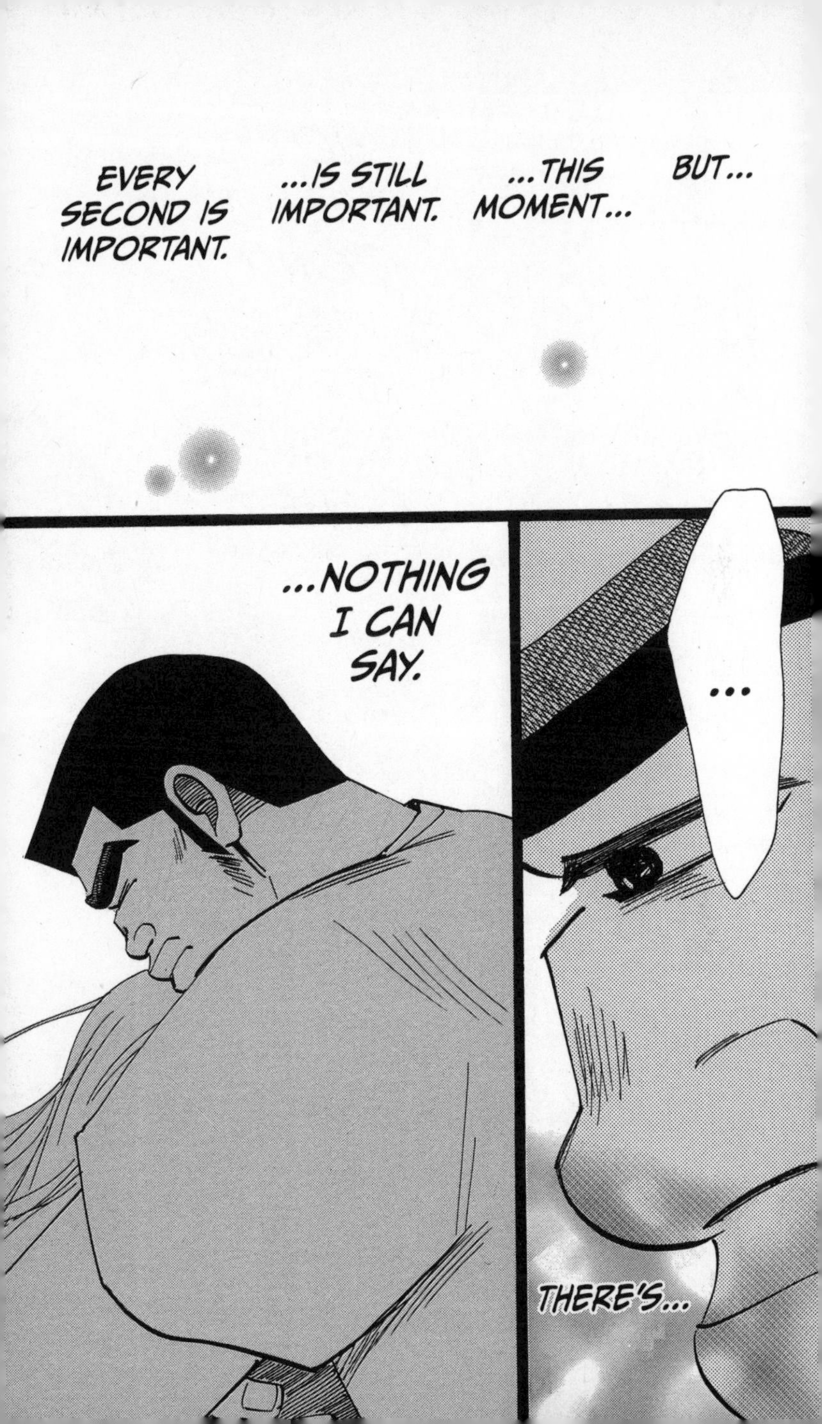
BUT...
...THIS MOMENT...
...IS STILL IMPORTANT.
EVERY SECOND IS IMPORTANT.
...
THERE'S...
...NOTHING I CAN SAY.

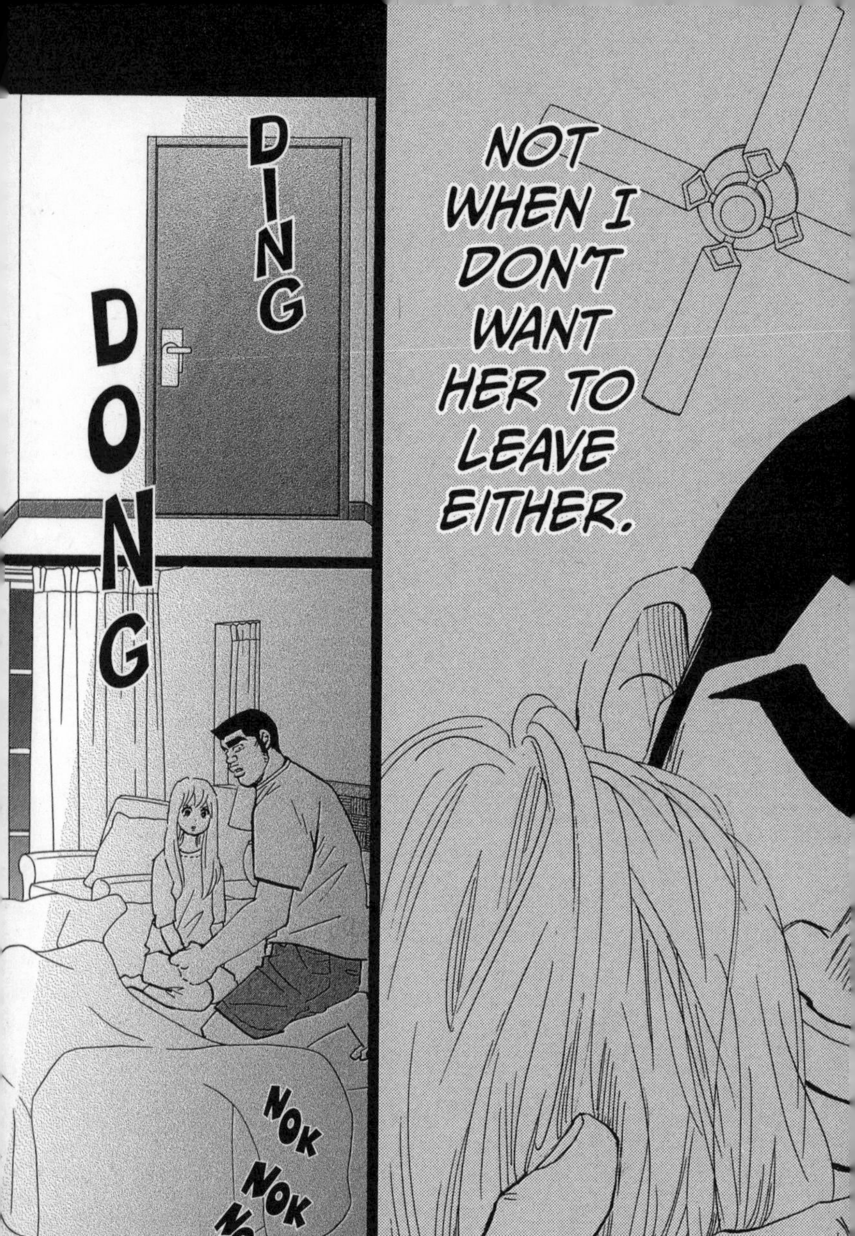
NOT WHEN I DON'T WANT HER TO LEAVE EITHER.
DING
DONG
NOK NOK NOK!

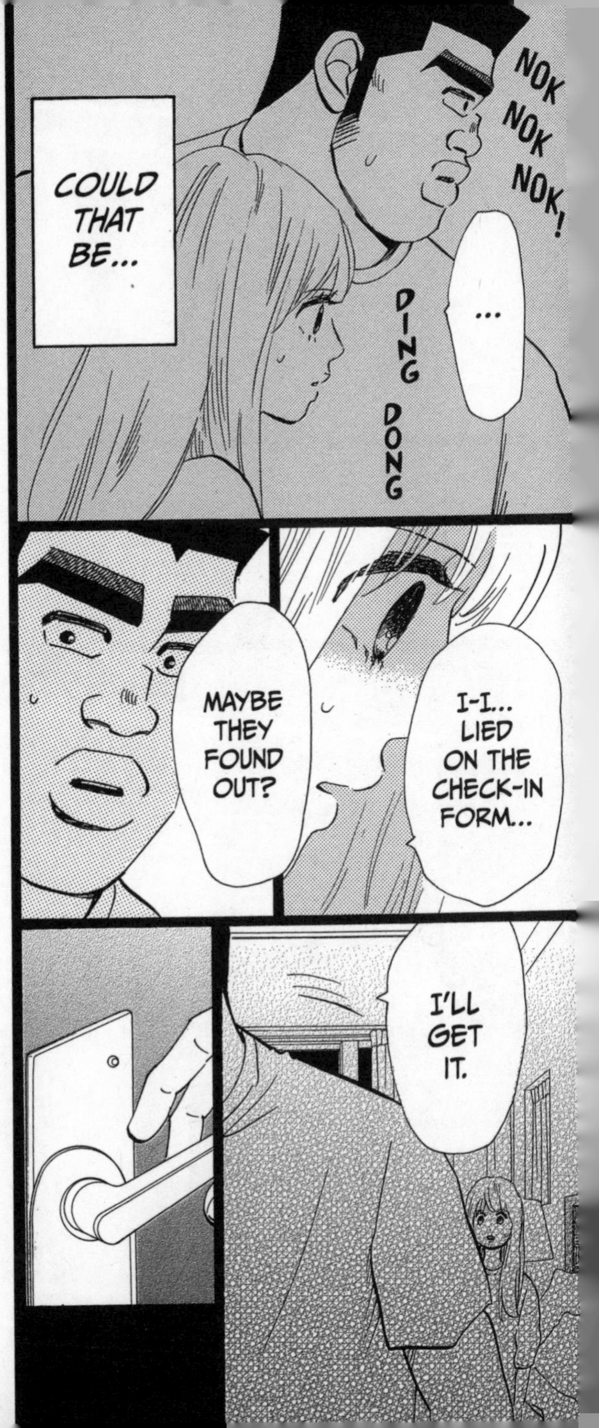
NOK NOK NOK!
...
DING DONG
COULD THAT BE...
I-I... LIED ON THE CHECK-IN FORM...
MAYBE THEY FOUND OUT?
I'LL GET IT.

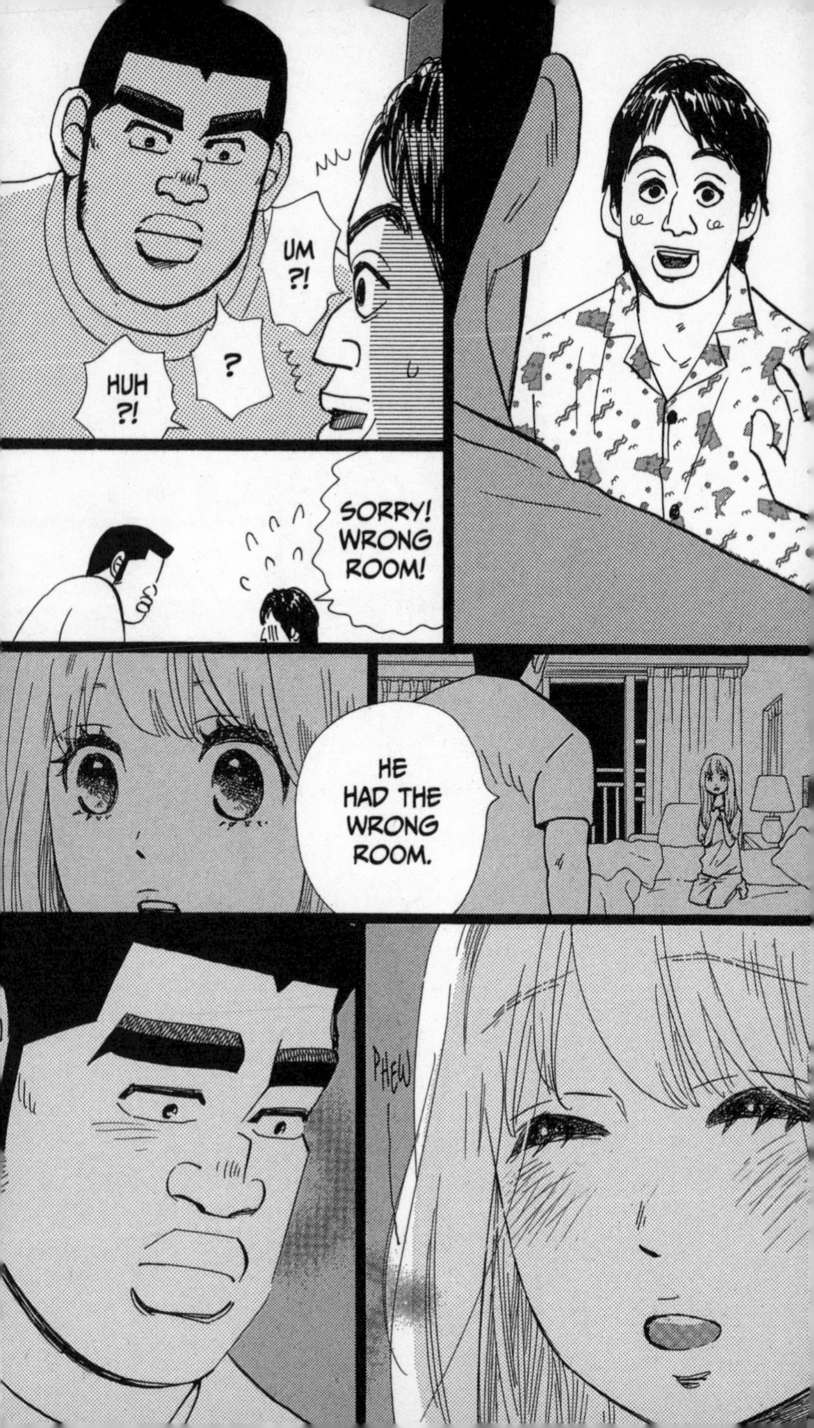
UM ?!
?
HUH ?!
SORRY! WRONG ROOM!
HE HAD THE WRONG ROOM.
PHEW

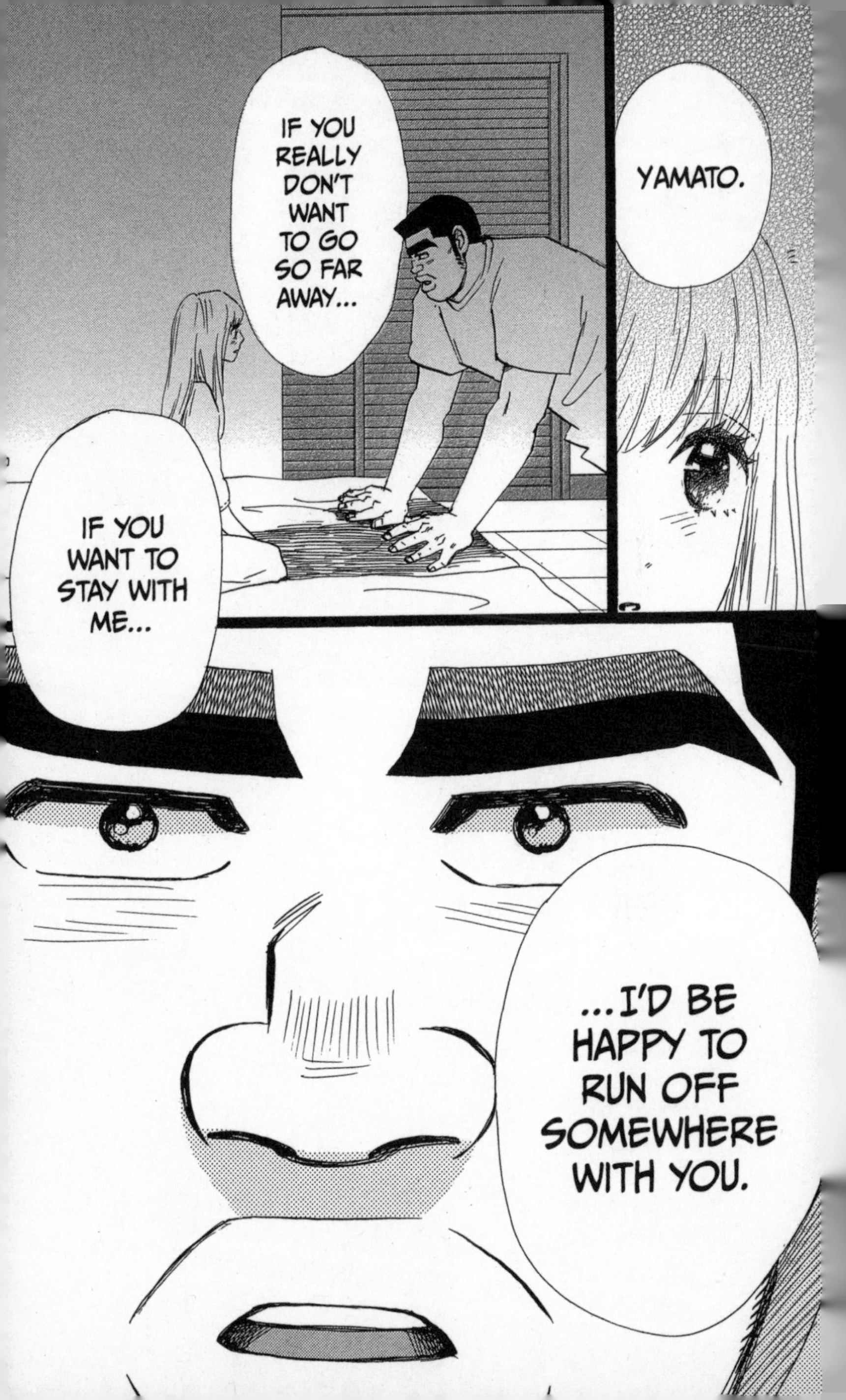
YAMATO.
IF YOU REALLY DON'T WANT TO GO SO FAR AWAY...
IF YOU WANT TO STAY WITH ME...
...I'D BE HAPPY TO RUN OFF SOMEWHERE WITH YOU.

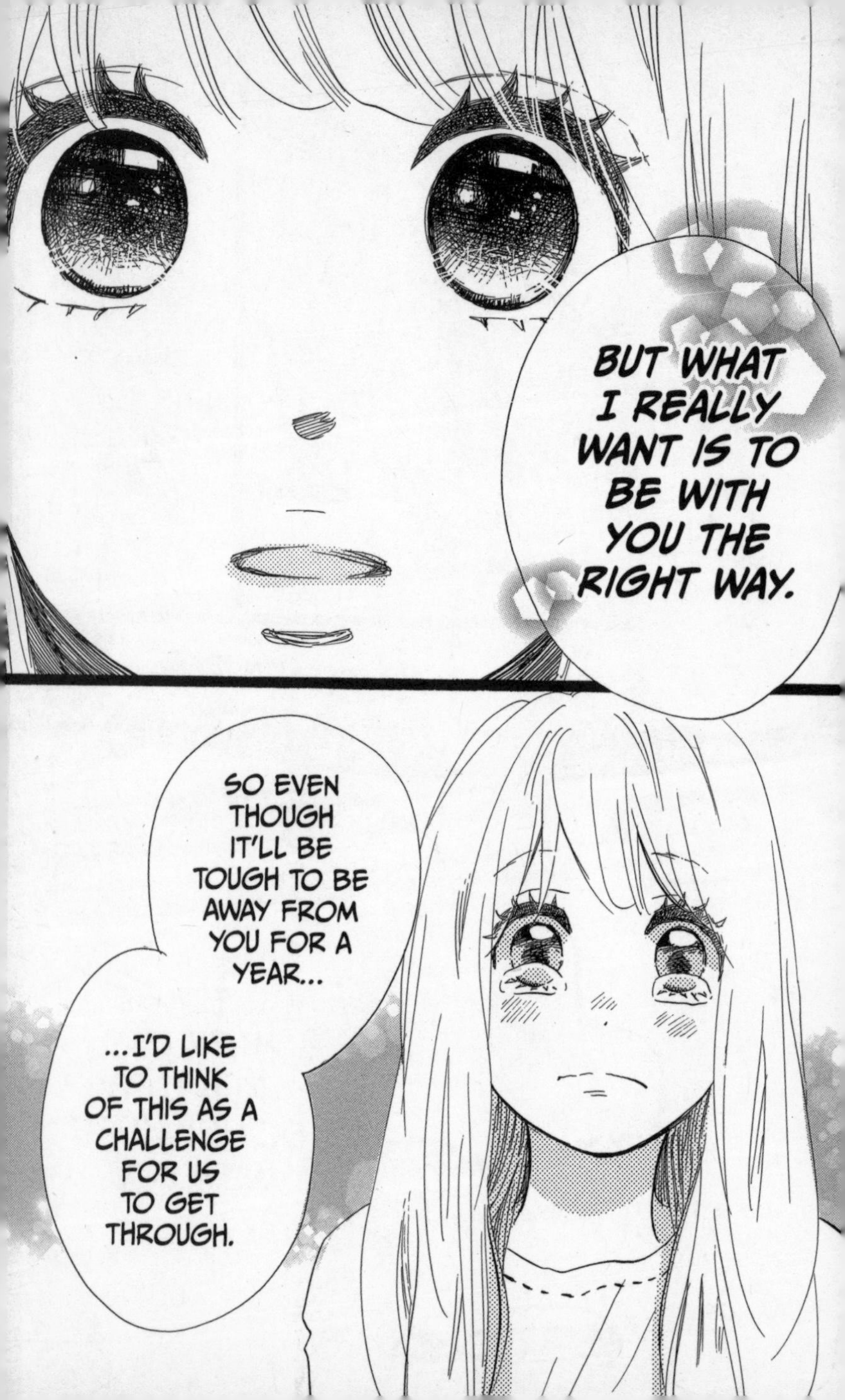
BUT WHAT I REALLY WANT IS TO BE WITH YOU THE RIGHT WAY.
SO EVEN THOUGH IT'LL BE TOUGH TO BE AWAY FROM YOU FOR A YEAR...
...I'D LIKE TO THINK OF THIS AS A CHALLENGE FOR US TO GET THROUGH.

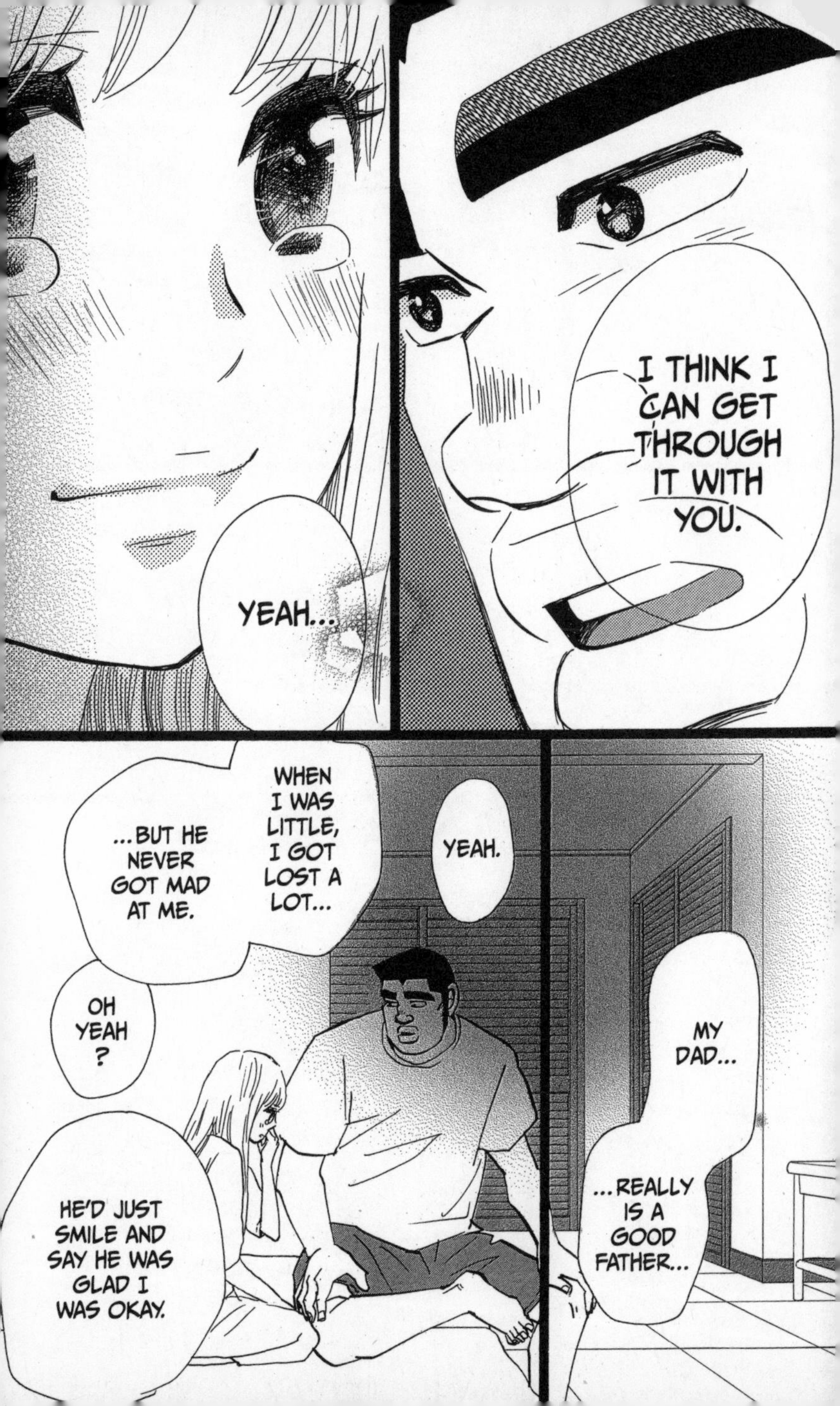

I THINK I CAN GET THROUGH IT WITH YOU.
YEAH...
MY DAD...
...REALLY IS A GOOD FATHER...
YEAH.
WHEN I WAS LITTLE, I GOT LOST A LOT...
...BUT HE NEVER GOT MAD AT ME.
OH YEAH?
HE'D JUST SMILE AND SAY HE WAS GLAD I WAS OKAY.

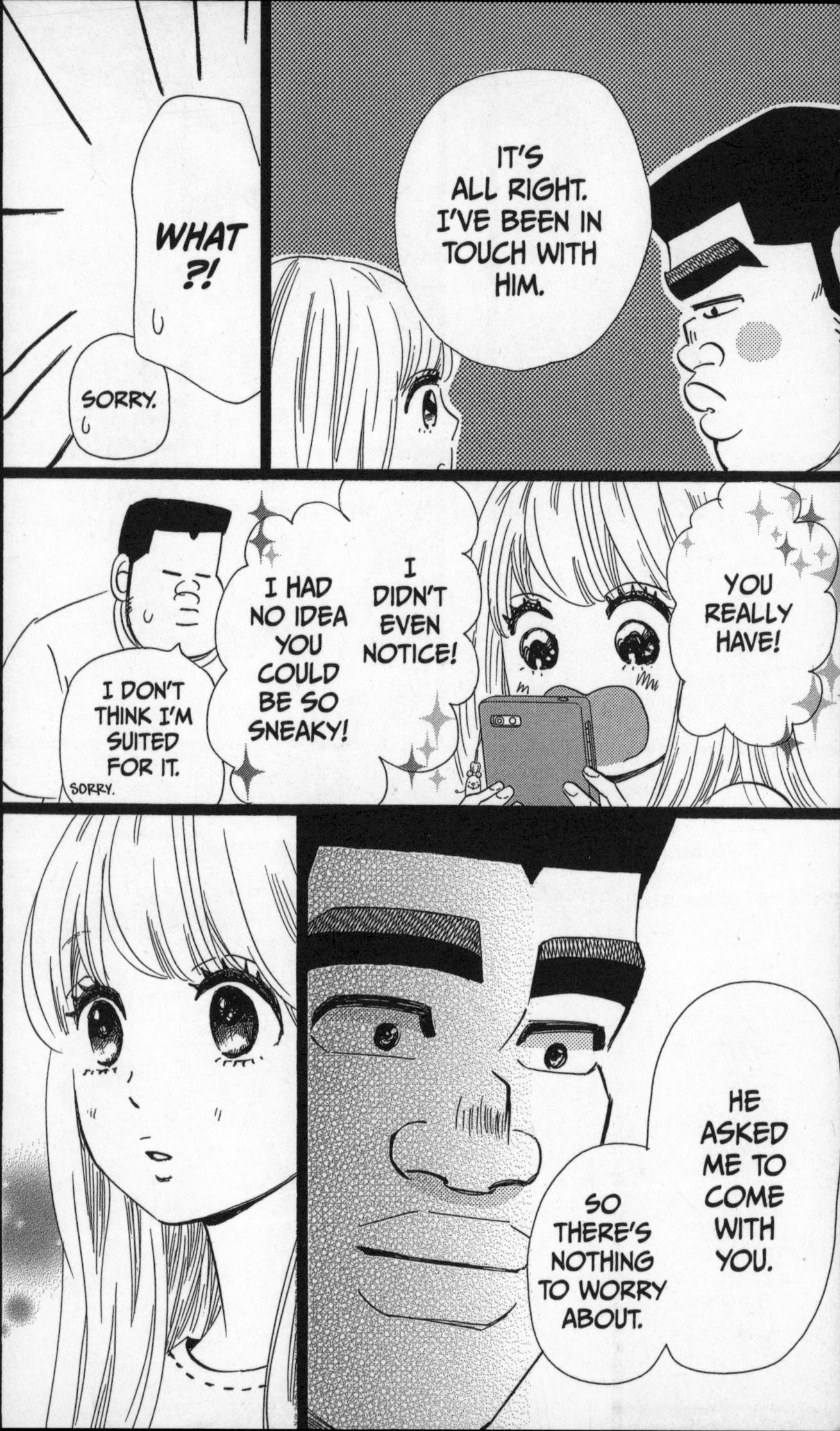
IT'S ALL RIGHT. I'VE BEEN IN TOUCH WITH HIM.
WHAT?!
SORRY.
YOU REALLY HAVE!
I DIDN'T EVEN NOTICE!
I HAD NO IDEA YOU COULD BE SO SNEAKY!
I DON'T THINK I'M SUITED FOR IT.
SORRY.
HE ASKED ME TO COME WITH YOU.
SO THERE'S NOTHING TO WORRY ABOUT.

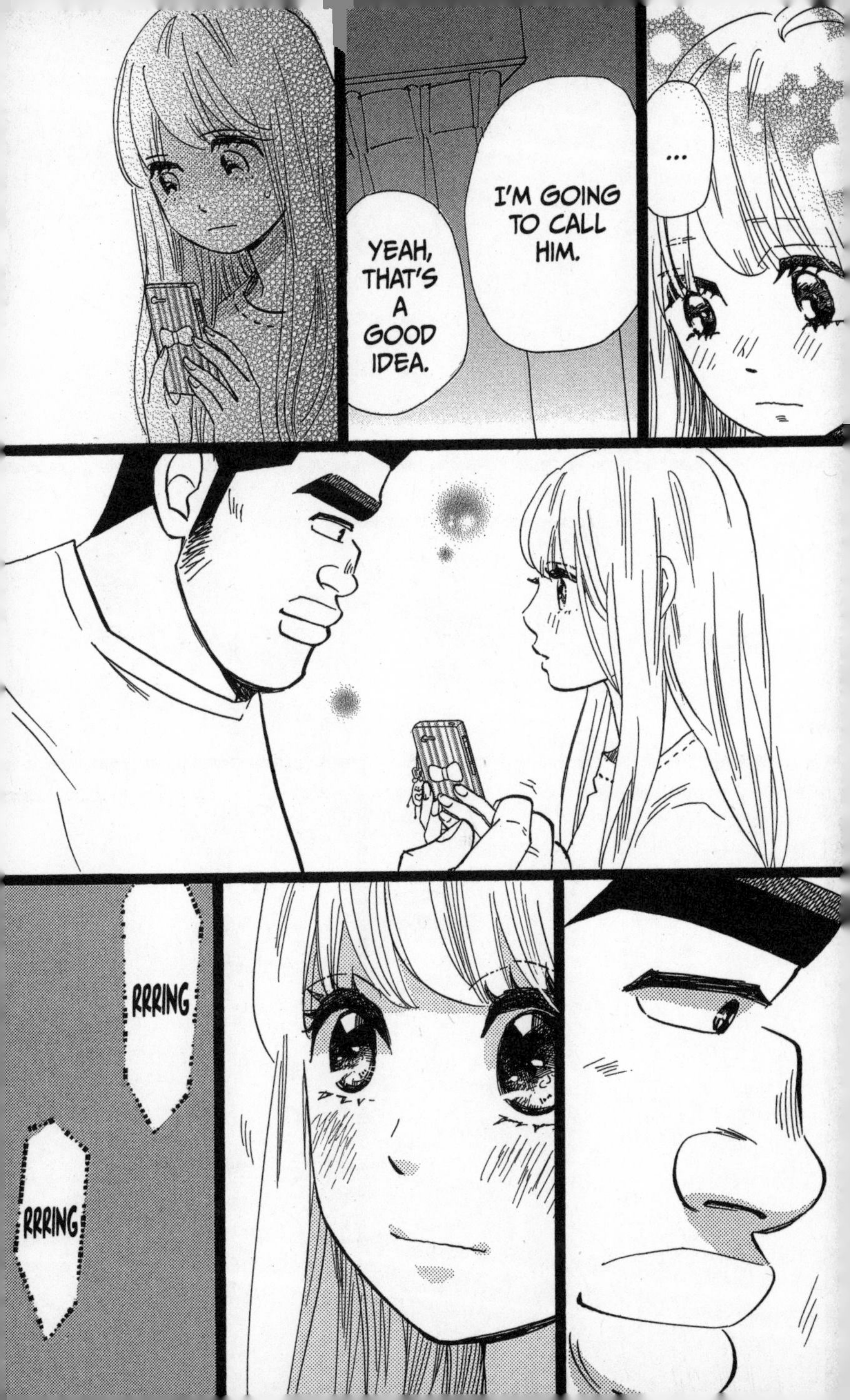
...
I'M GOING TO CALL HIM.
YEAH, THAT'S A GOOD IDEA.
RRRING
RRRING

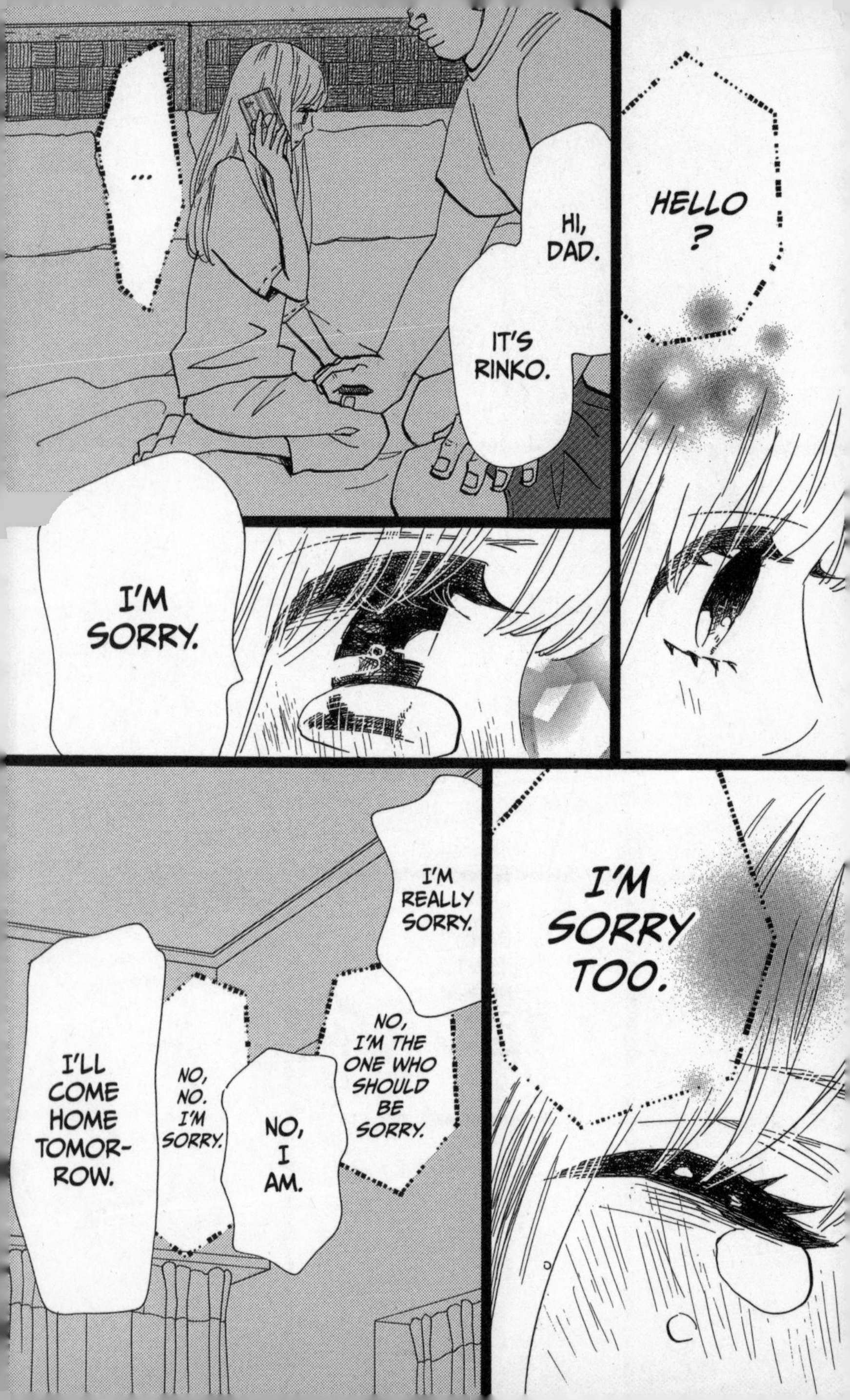
HELLO?
HI, DAD.
IT'S RINKO.
...
I'M SORRY.
I'M SORRY TOO.
I'M REALLY SORRY.
NO, I'M THE ONE WHO SHOULD BE SORRY.
NO, I AM.
NO, NO. I'M SORRY.
I'LL COME HOME TOMOR-ROW.

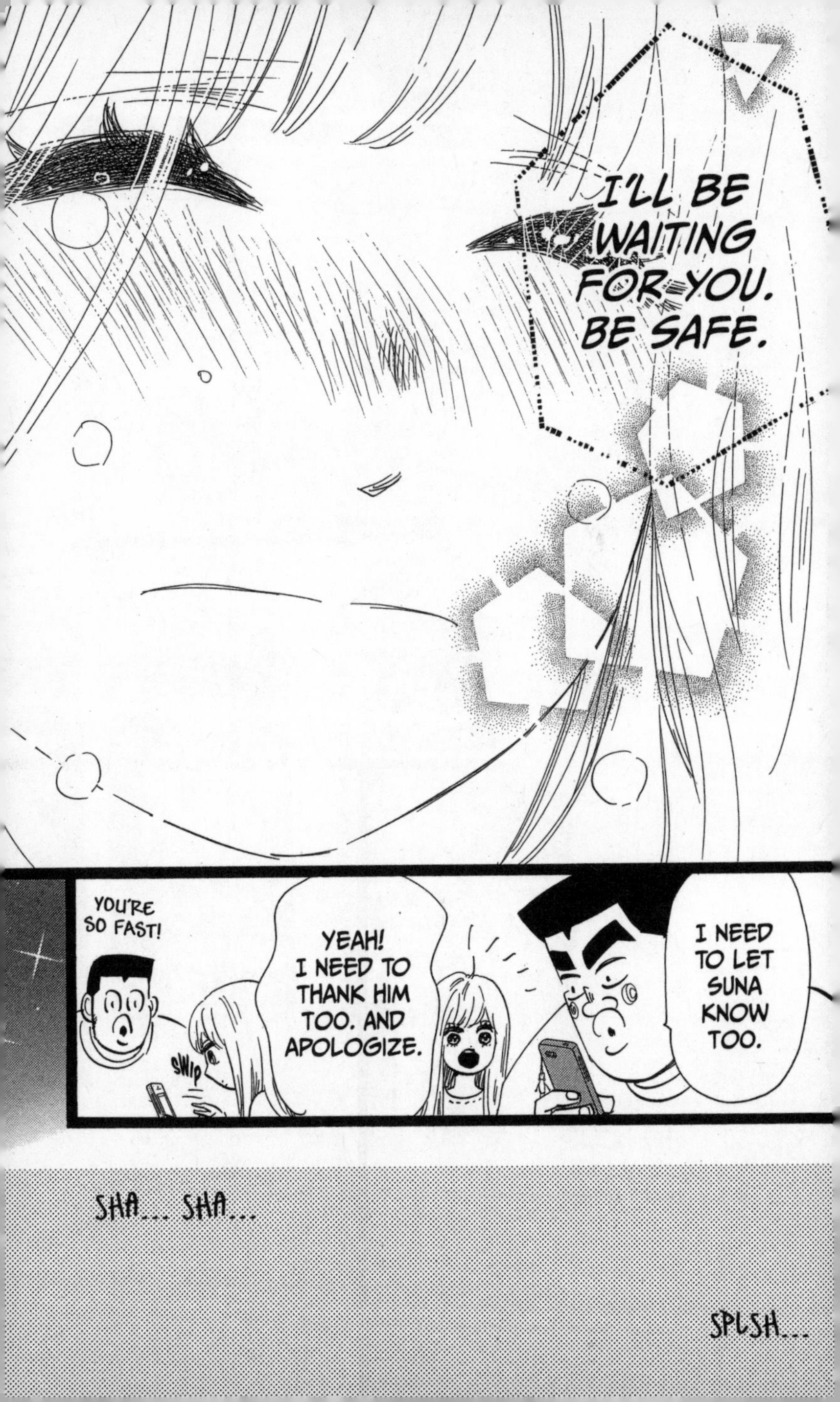
I'LL BE WAITING FOR YOU. BE SAFE.
I NEED TO LET SUNA KNOW TOO.
YEAH! I NEED TO THANK HIM TOO. AND APOLOGIZE.
SWIP
YOU'RE SO FAST!
SHA... SHA...
SPLSH...

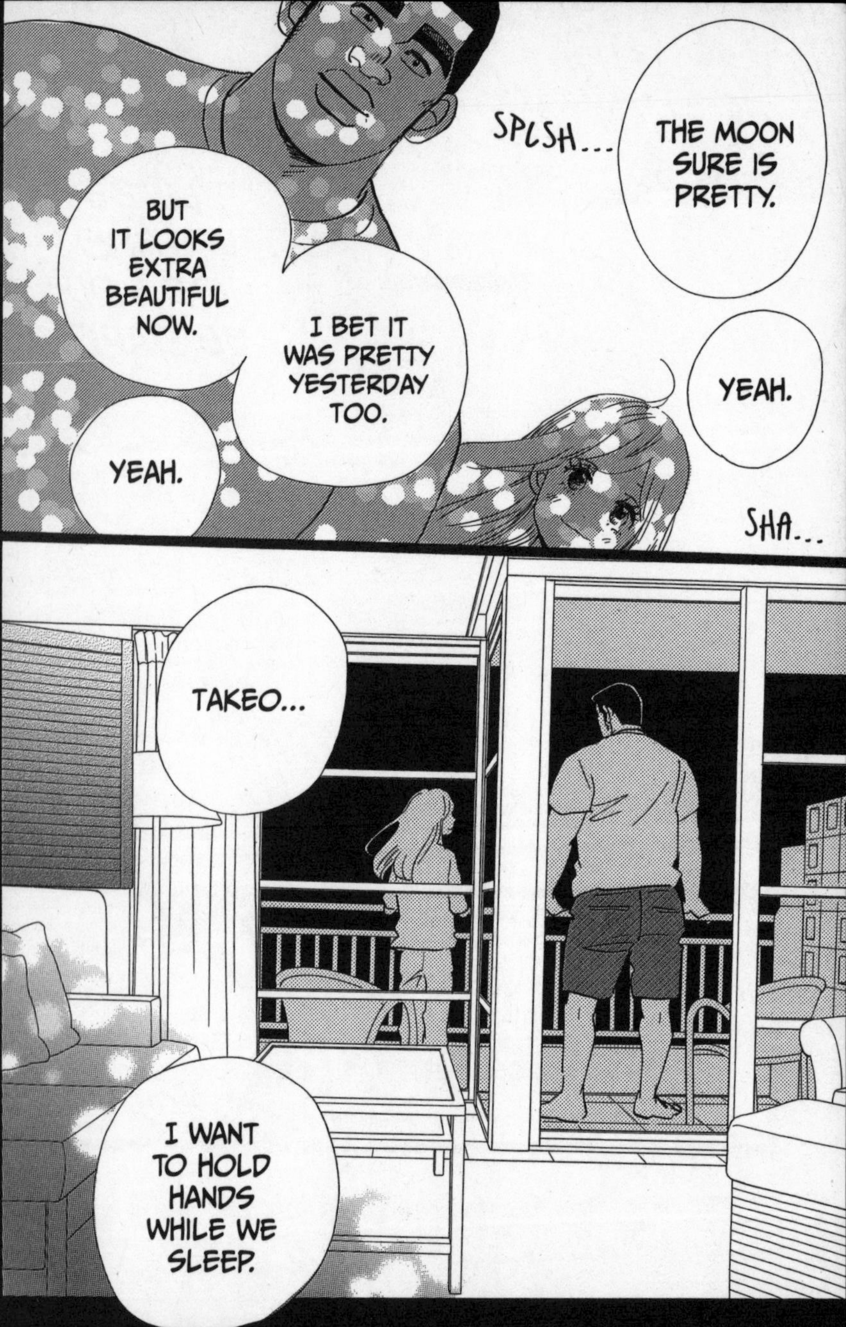
THE MOON SURE IS PRETTY.
SPLSH...
BUT IT LOOKS EXTRA BEAUTIFUL NOW.
YEAH.
I BET IT WAS PRETTY YESTERDAY TOO.
YEAH.
SHA...
TAKEO...
I WANT TO HOLD HANDS WHILE WE SLEEP.

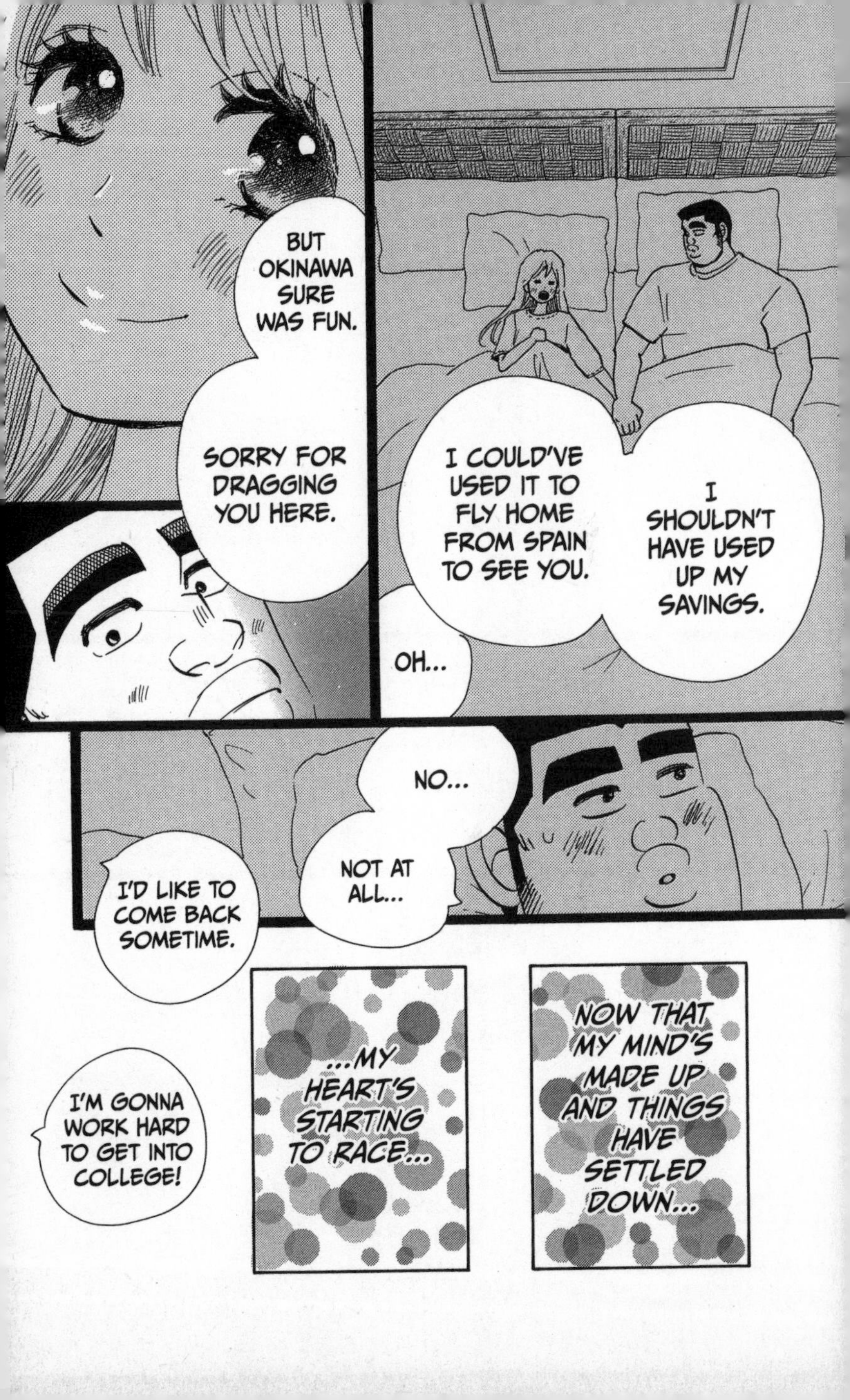
I SHOULDN'T HAVE USED UP MY SAVINGS.
I COULD'VE USED IT TO FLY HOME FROM SPAIN TO SEE YOU.
OH...
BUT OKINAWA SURE WAS FUN.
SORRY FOR DRAGGING YOU HERE.
NO...
NOT AT ALL...
I'D LIKE TO COME BACK SOMETIME.
NOW THAT MY MIND'S MADE UP AND THINGS HAVE SETTLED DOWN...
...MY HEART'S STARTING TO RACE...
I'M GONNA WORK HARD TO GET INTO COLLEGE!

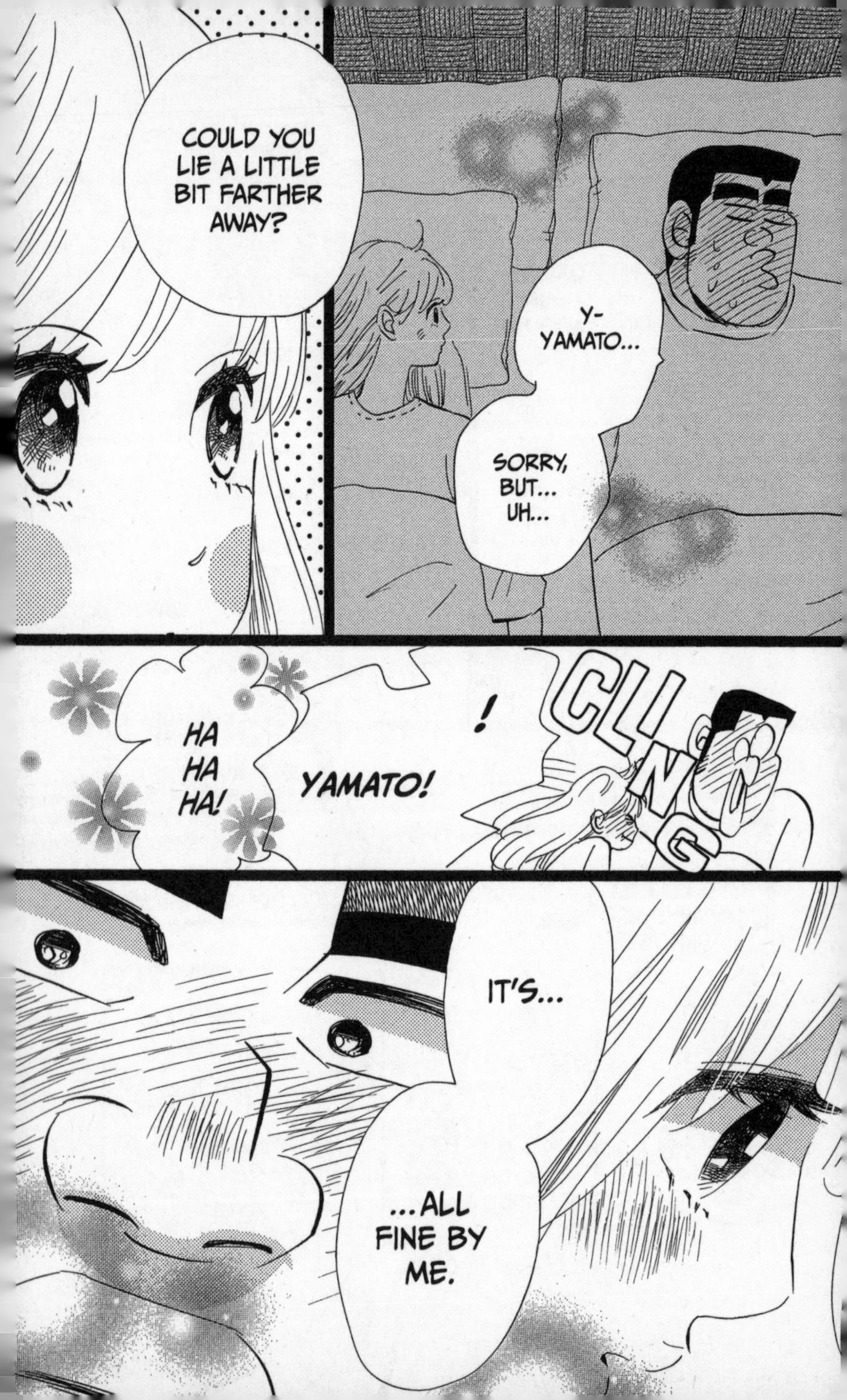
Y-YAMATO...
SORRY, BUT... UH...
COULD YOU LIE A LITTLE BIT FARTHER AWAY?
CLING
!
YAMATO!
HA HA HA!
IT'S...
...ALL FINE BY ME.

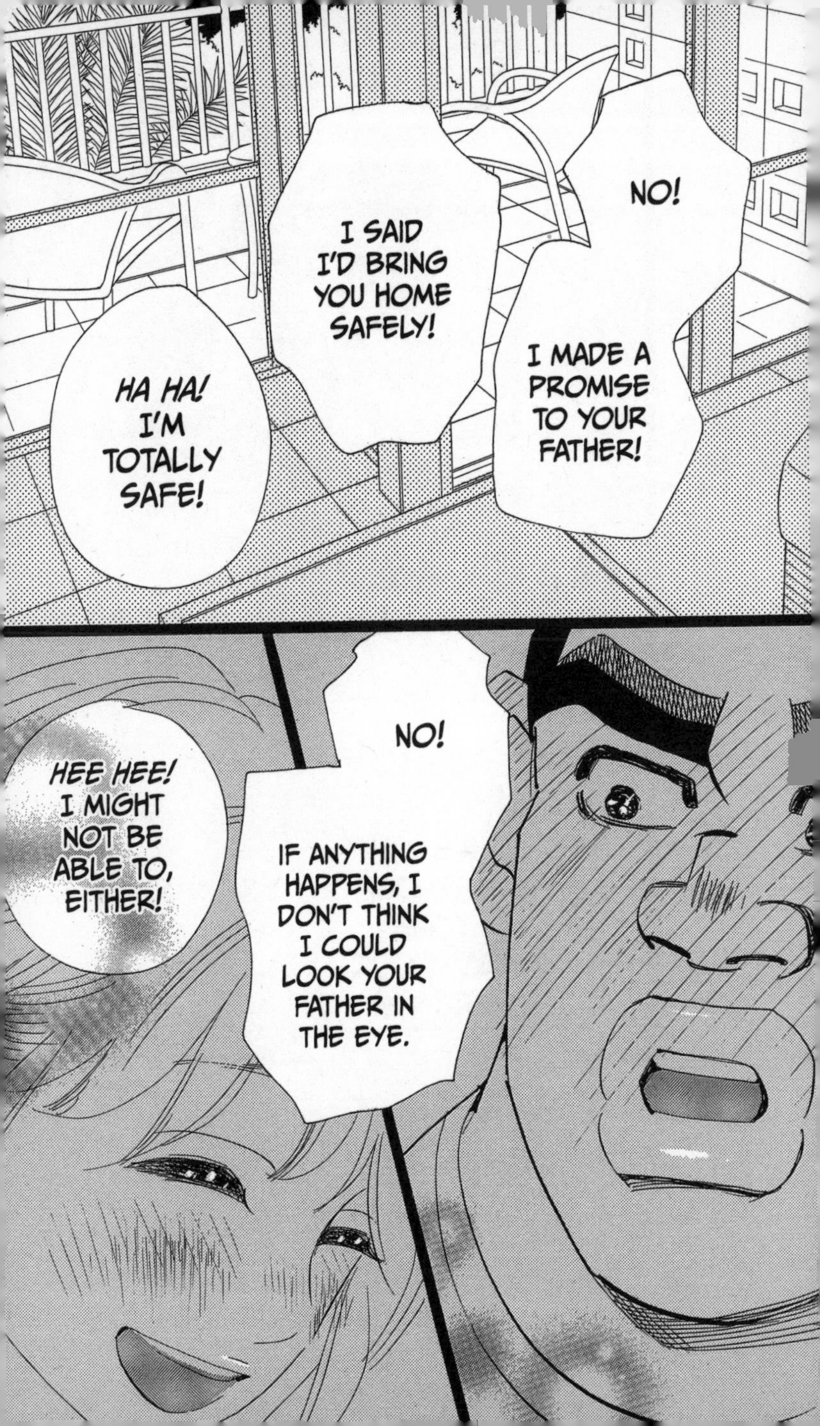
NO!
I MADE A PROMISE TO YOUR FATHER!
I SAID I'D BRING YOU HOME SAFELY!
HA HA! I'M TOTALLY SAFE!
NO!
IF ANYTHING HAPPENS, I DON'T THINK I COULD LOOK YOUR FATHER IN THE EYE.
HEE HEE! I MIGHT NOT BE ABLE TO, EITHER!

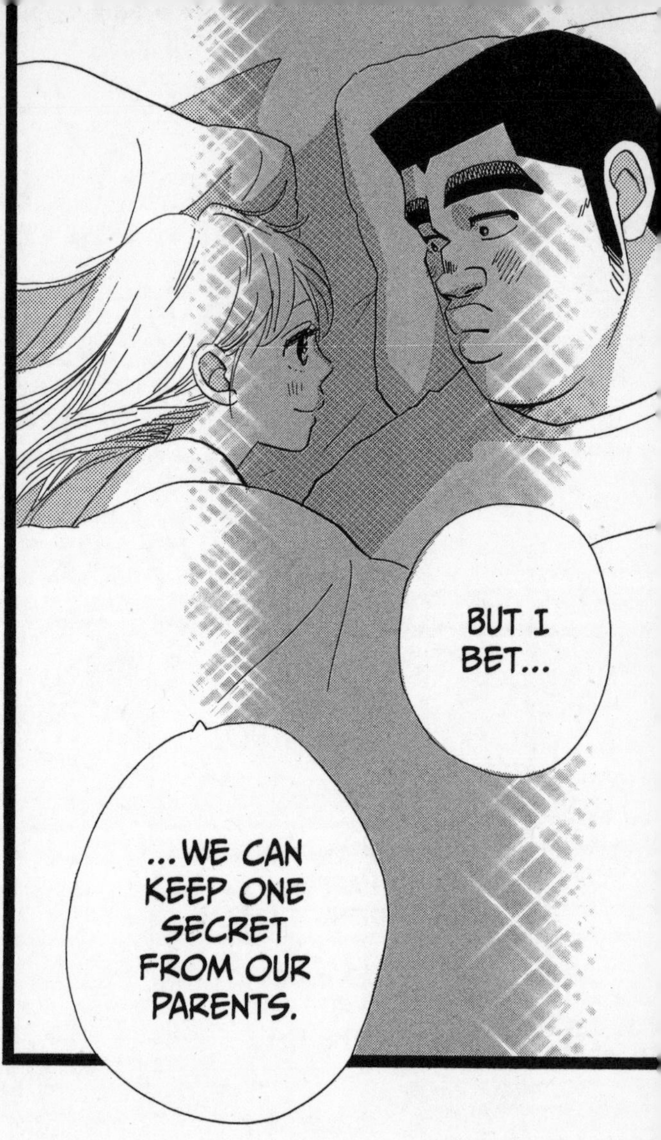
BUT I BET...
...WE CAN KEEP ONE SECRET FROM OUR PARENTS.

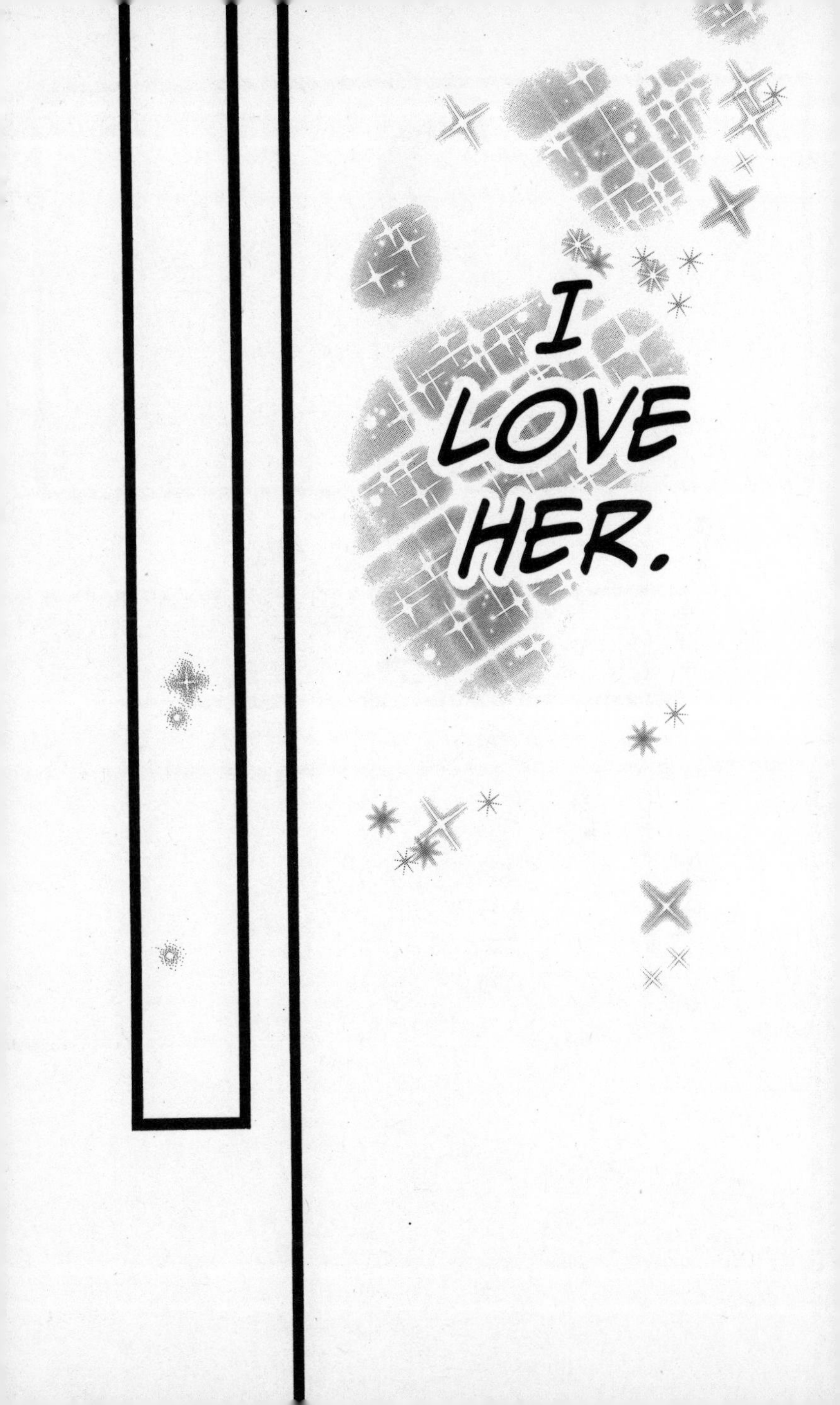
I LOVE HER.

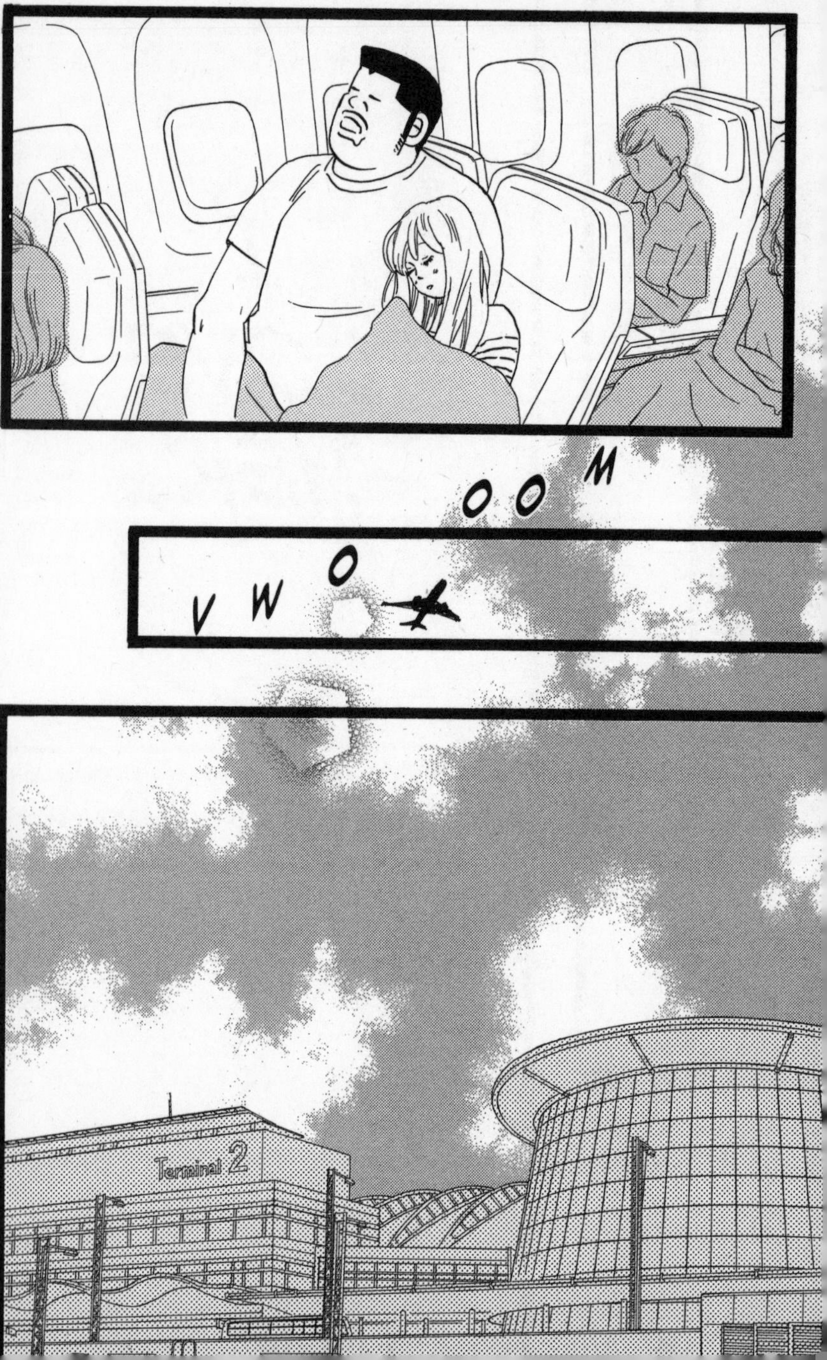
VWOOOM
Terminal 2

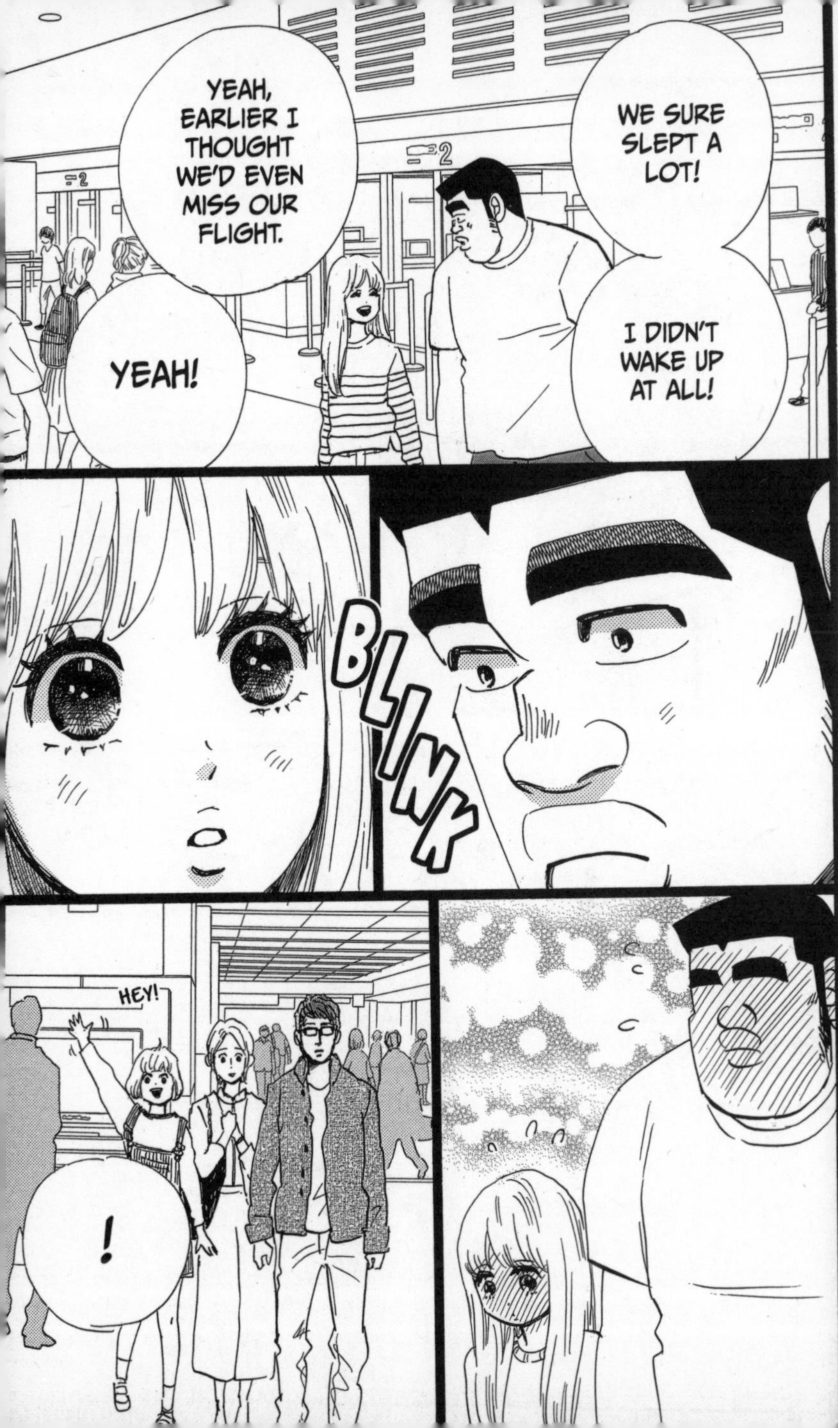
WE SURE SLEPT A LOT!
I DIDN'T WAKE UP AT ALL!
YEAH, EARLIER I THOUGHT WE'D EVEN MISS OUR FLIGHT.
YEAH!
BLINK
HEY!
!

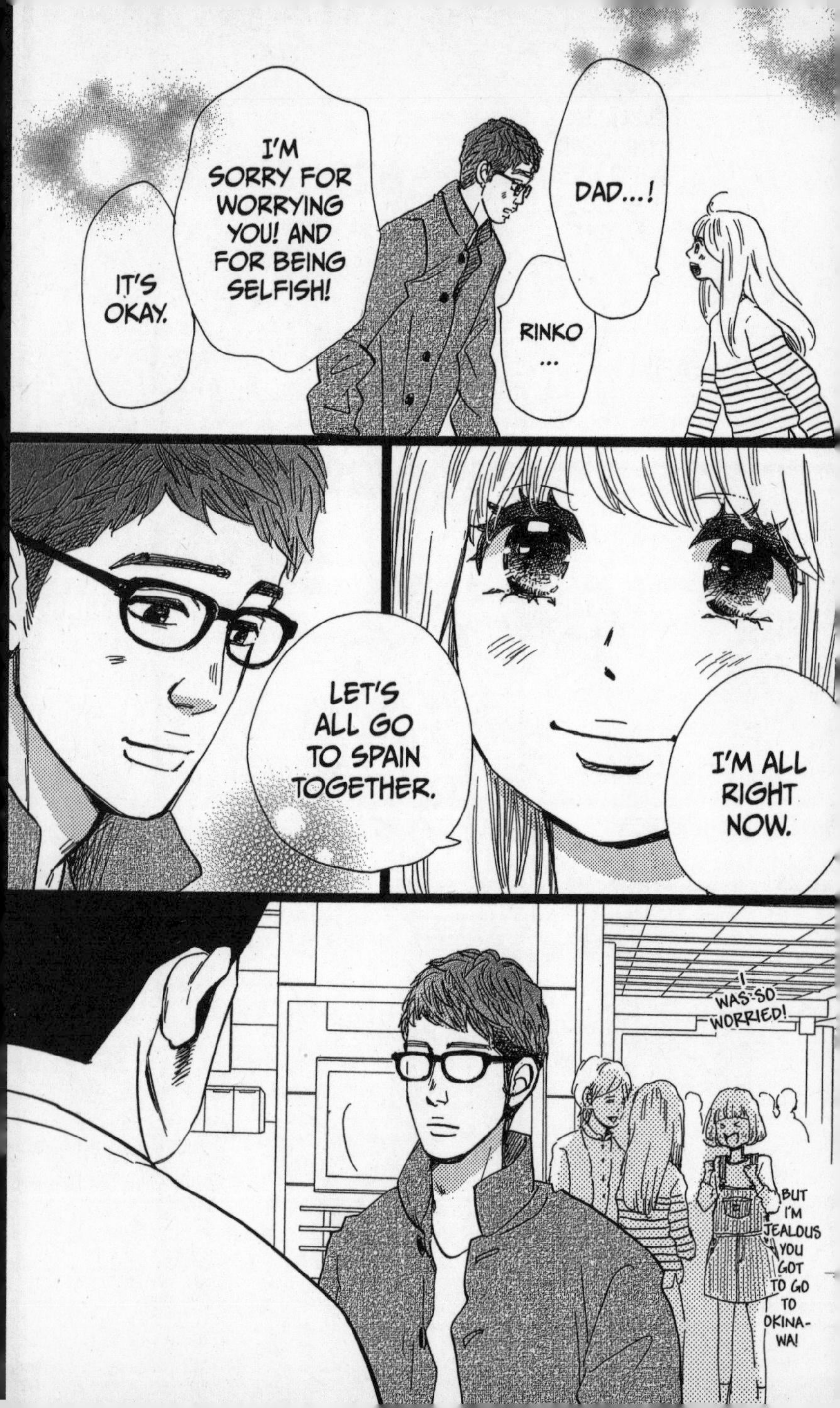

DAD...!
RINKO ...
I'M SORRY FOR WORRYING YOU! AND FOR BEING SELFISH!
IT'S OKAY.
I'M ALL RIGHT NOW.
LET'S ALL GO TO SPAIN TOGETHER.
I WAS SO WORRIED!
BUT I'M JEALOUS YOU GOT TO GO TO OKINA-WA!

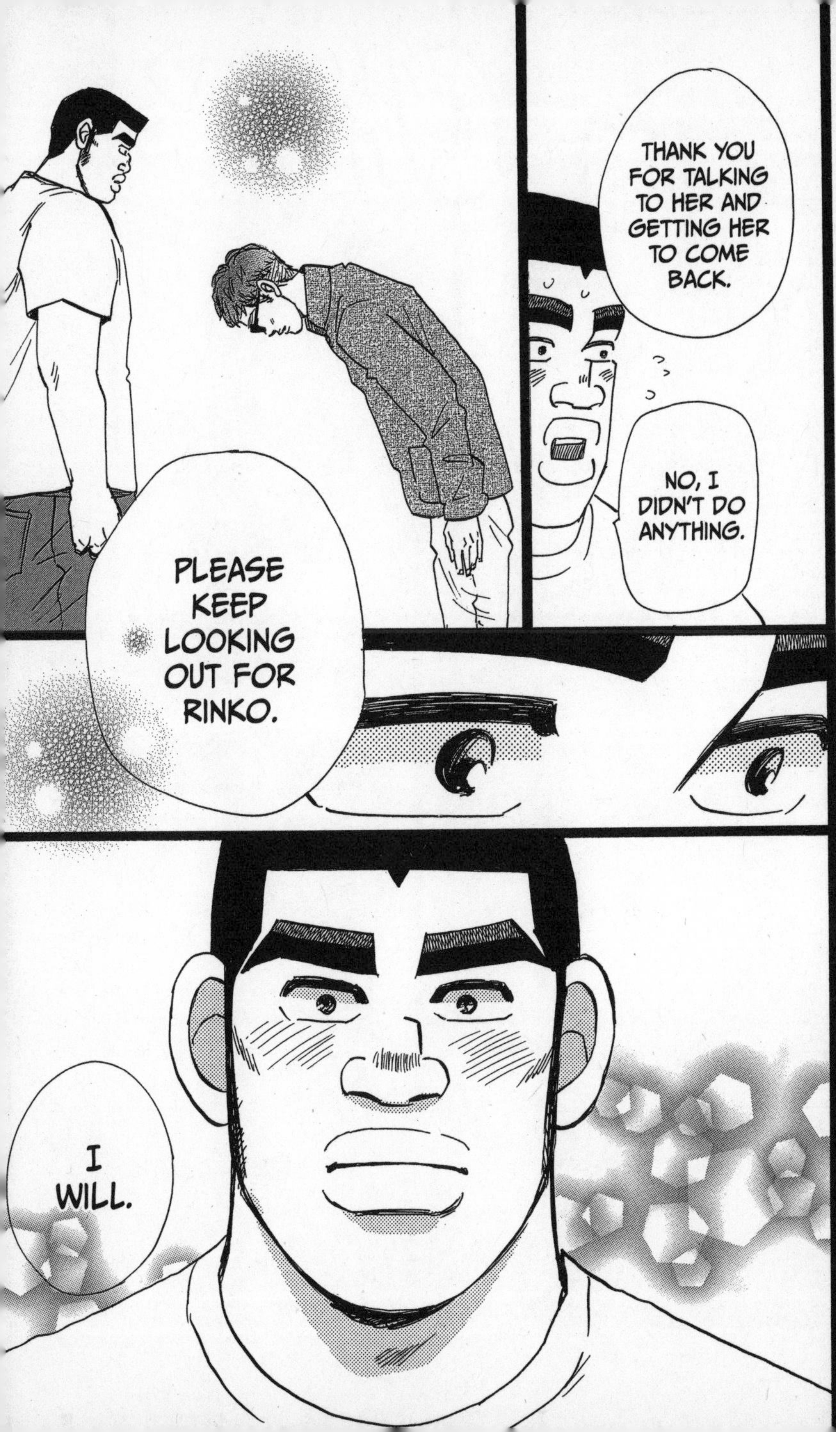
THANK YOU FOR TALKING TO HER AND GETTING HER TO COME BACK.
NO, I DIDN'T DO ANYTHING.
PLEASE KEEP LOOKING OUT FOR RINKO.
I WILL.

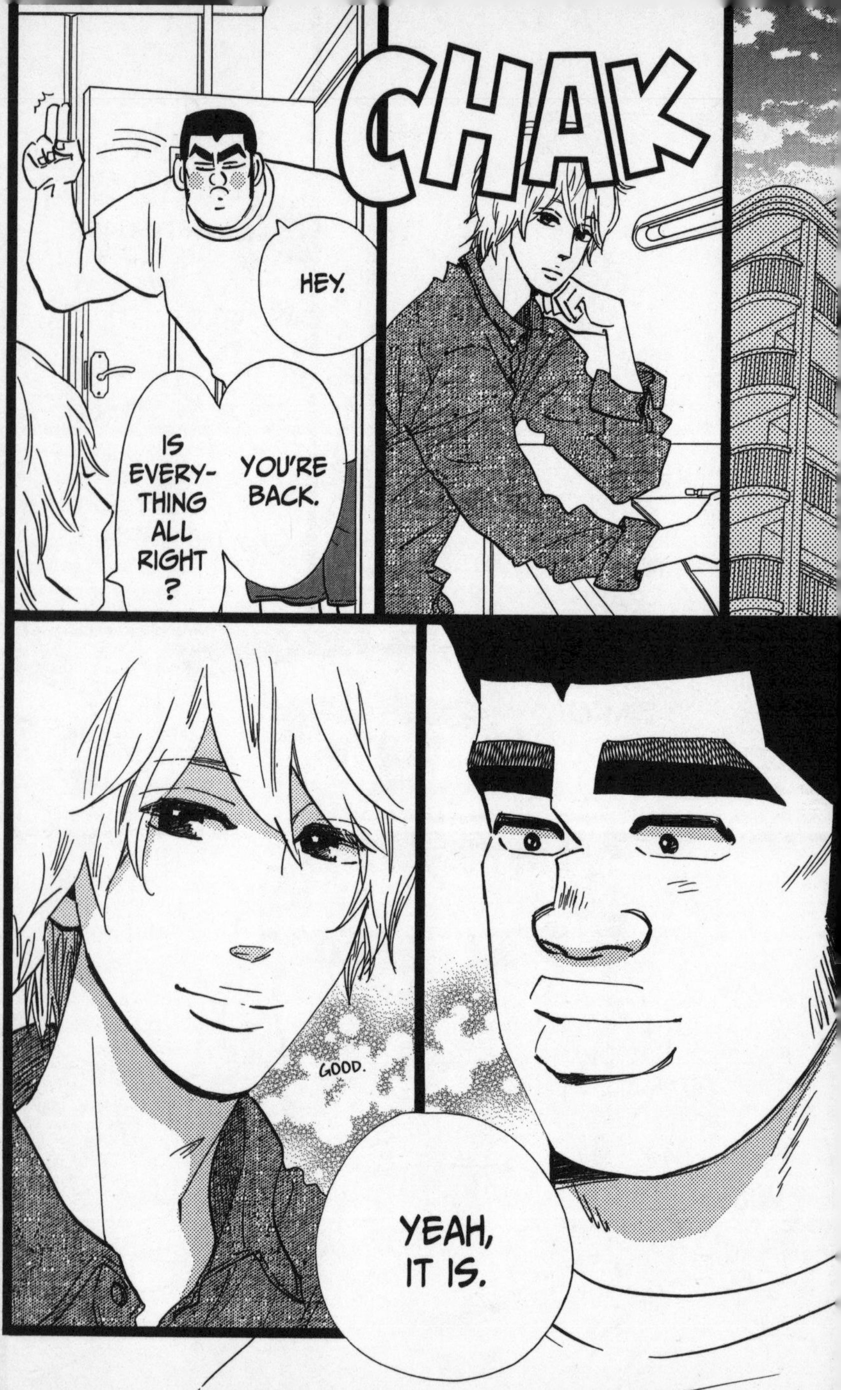

CHAK
HEY.
YOU'RE BACK.
IS EVERY-THING ALL RIGHT?
YEAH, IT IS.
GOOD.

EVERY-
THING...

...IS
ALL
RIGHT
NOW.

Narita Air

DEPAR-
TURE
DAY

THAT
WAS
FAST!

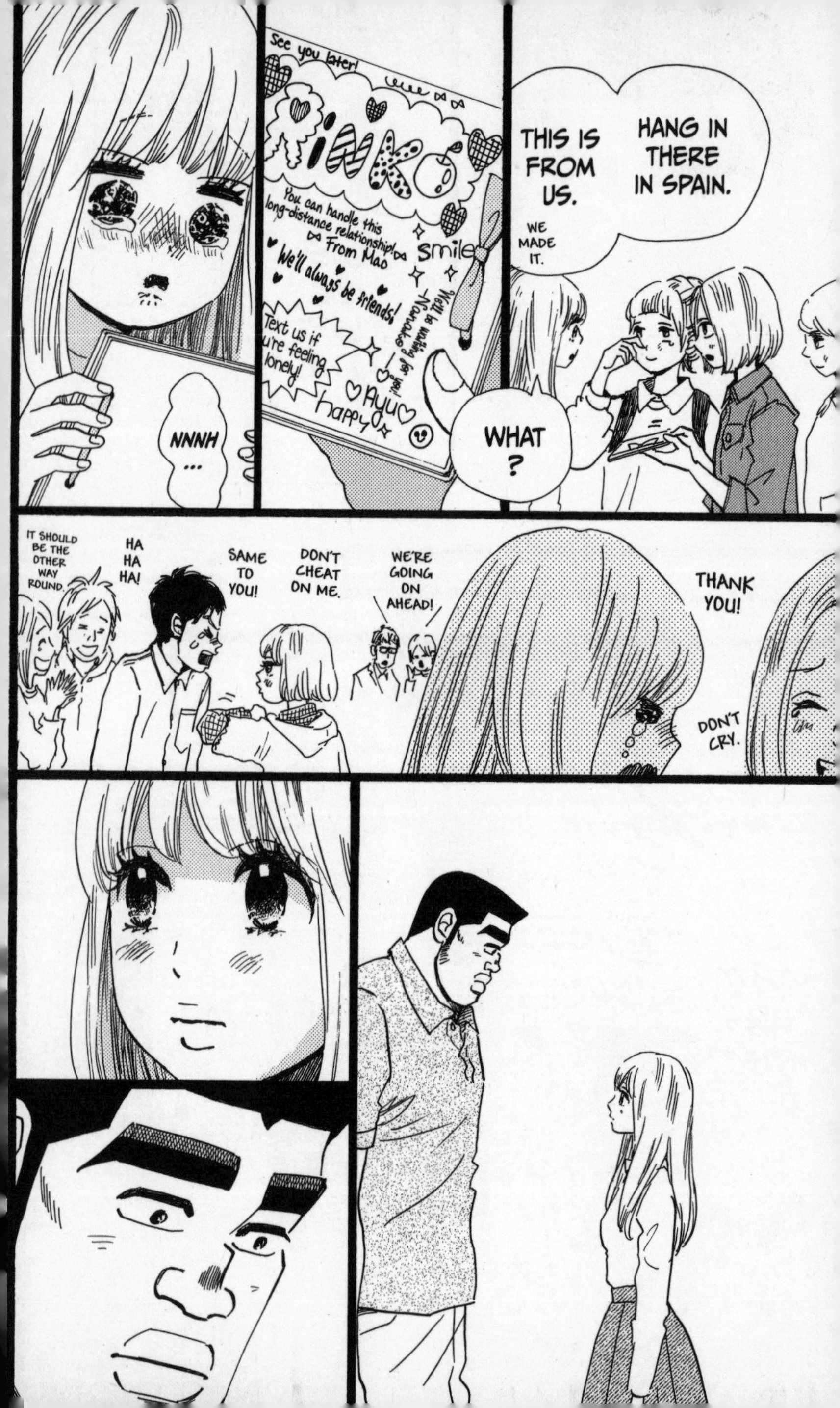
HANG IN THERE IN SPAIN.
THIS IS FROM US.
WE MADE IT.
WHAT?
See you later!
Rinko
You can handle this long-distance relationship! From Mao
smile
We'll always be friends!
We'll be waiting for you! -Nanako
Text us if u're feeling lonely!
Ayu
happy
NNNH...
THANK YOU!
DON'T CRY.
WE'RE GOING ON AHEAD!
DON'T CHEAT ON ME.
SAME TO YOU!
HA HA HA!
IT SHOULD BE THE OTHER WAY ROUND.

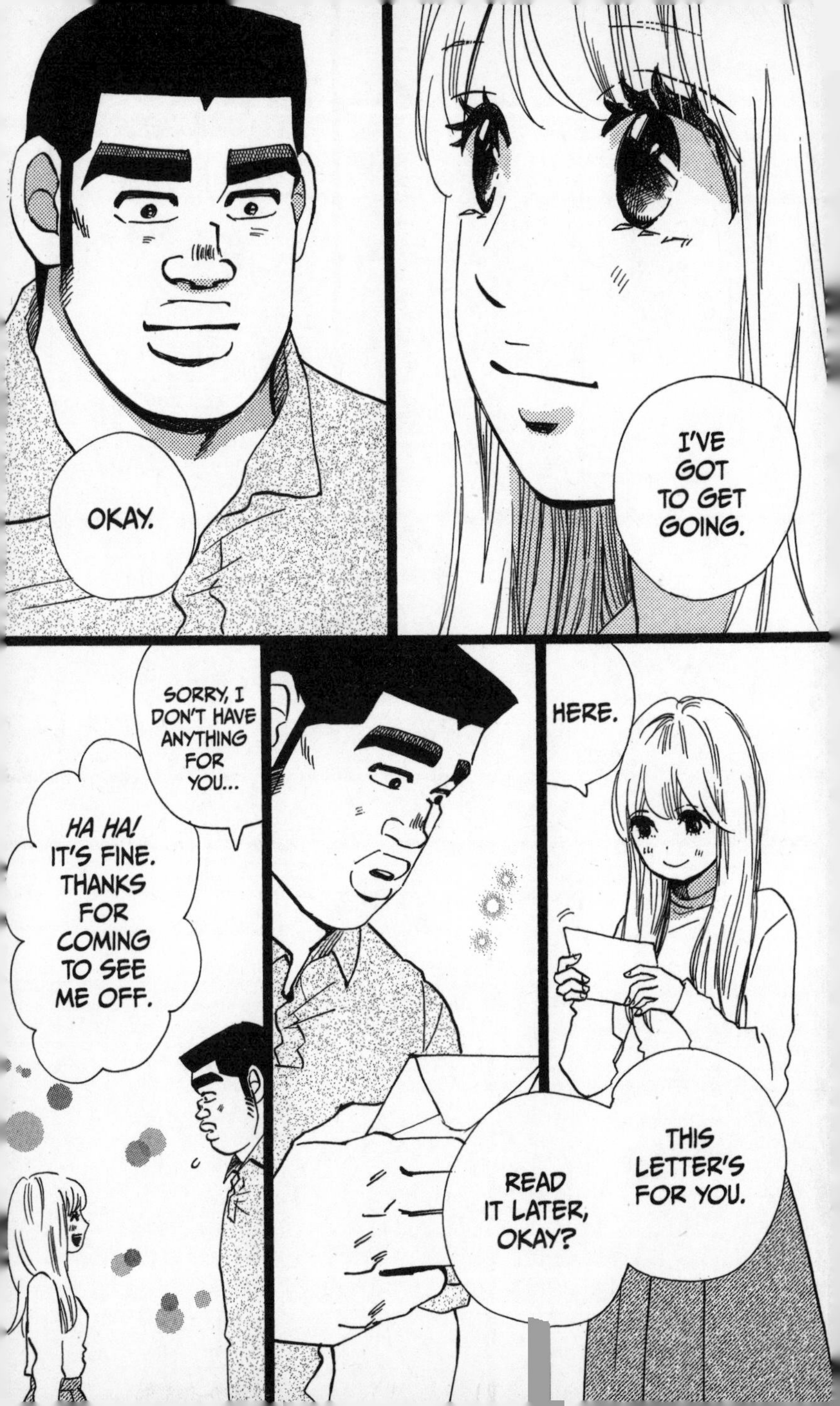
I'VE GOT TO GET GOING.
OKAY.
HERE.
THIS LETTER'S FOR YOU.
READ IT LATER, OKAY?
SORRY, I DON'T HAVE ANYTHING FOR YOU...
HA HA! IT'S FINE. THANKS FOR COMING TO SEE ME OFF.

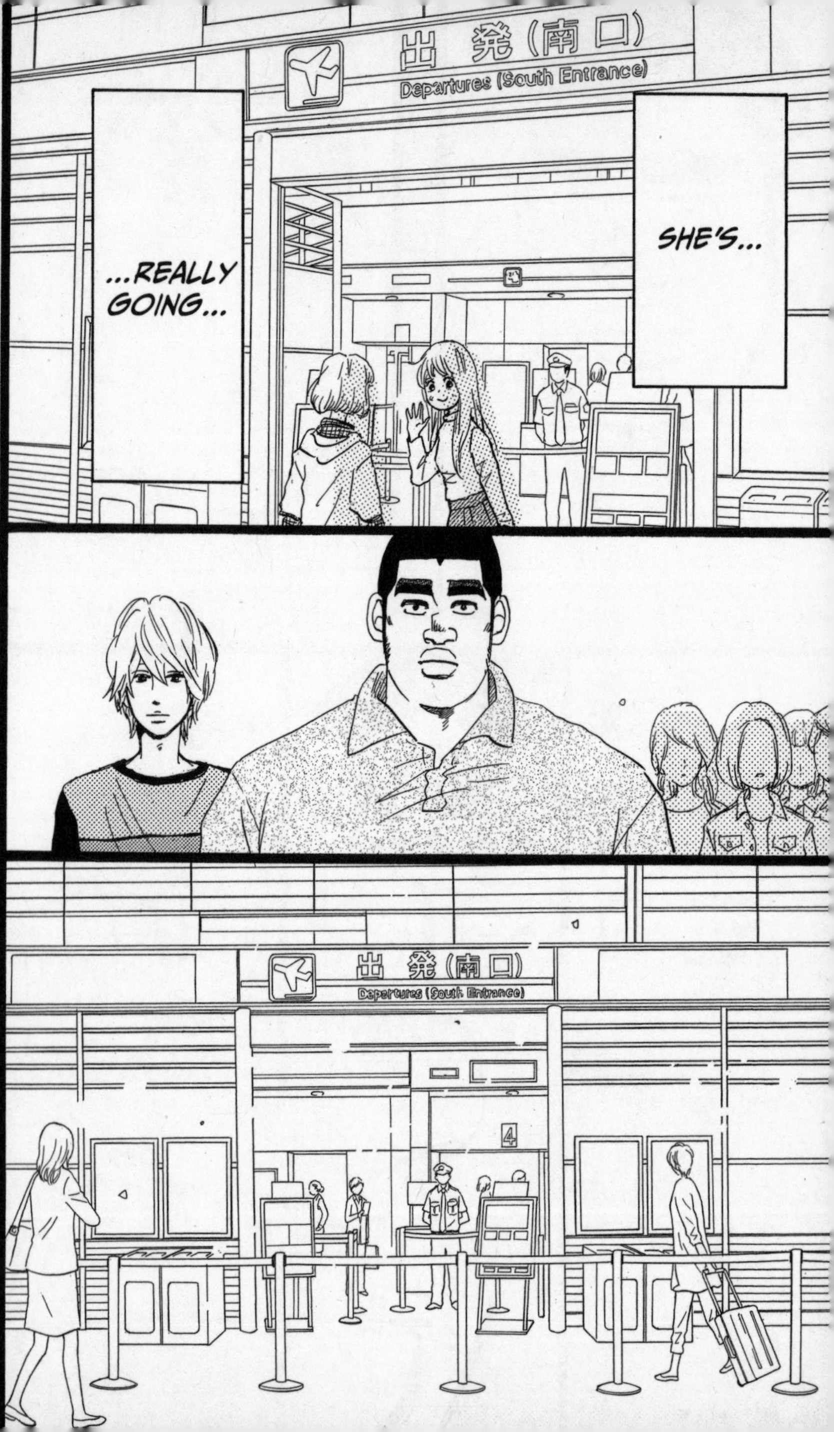
出発(南口)
Departures (South Entrance)
SHE'S...
...REALLY GOING...
出発(南口)
Departures (South Entrance)
4

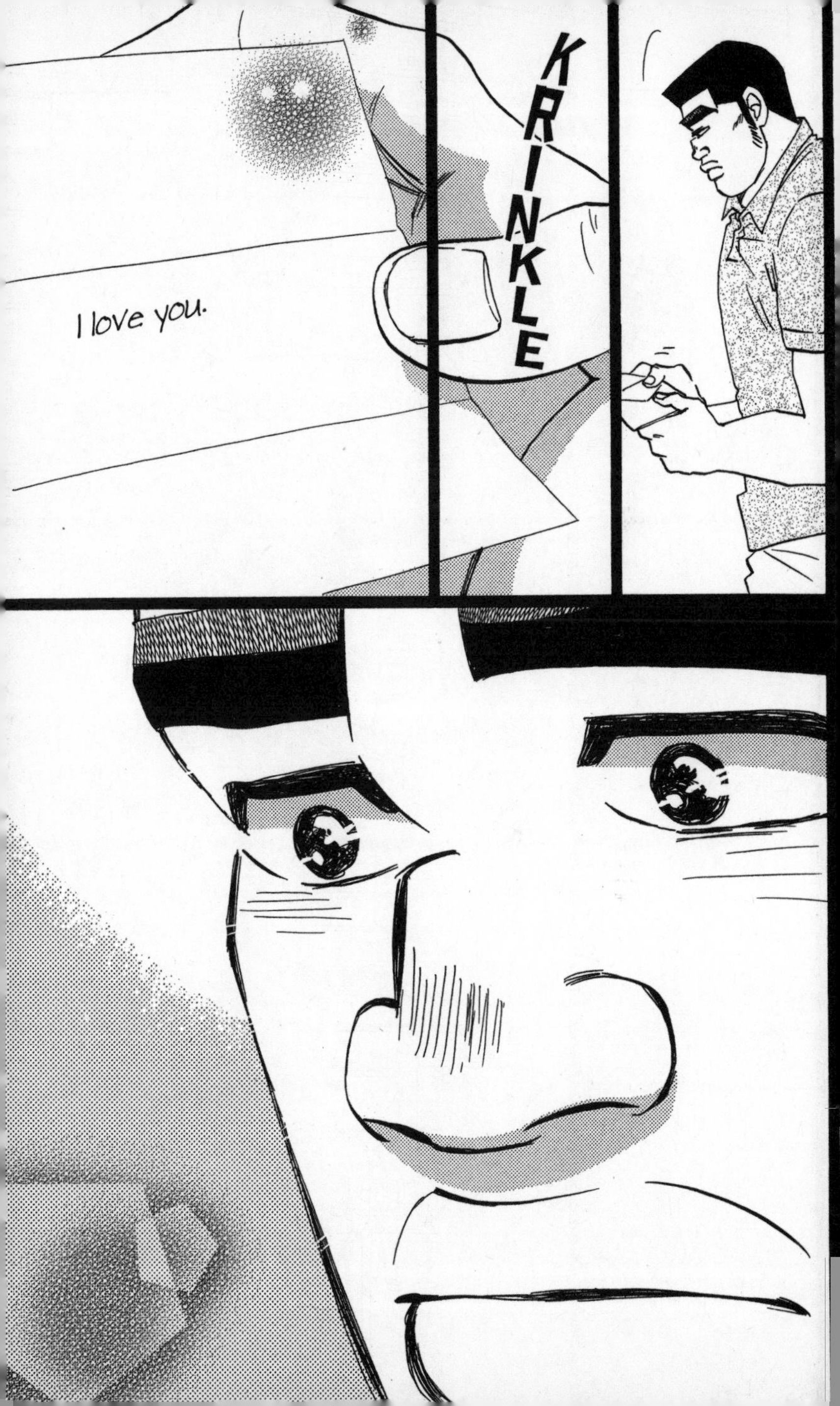
KRINKLE
I love you.

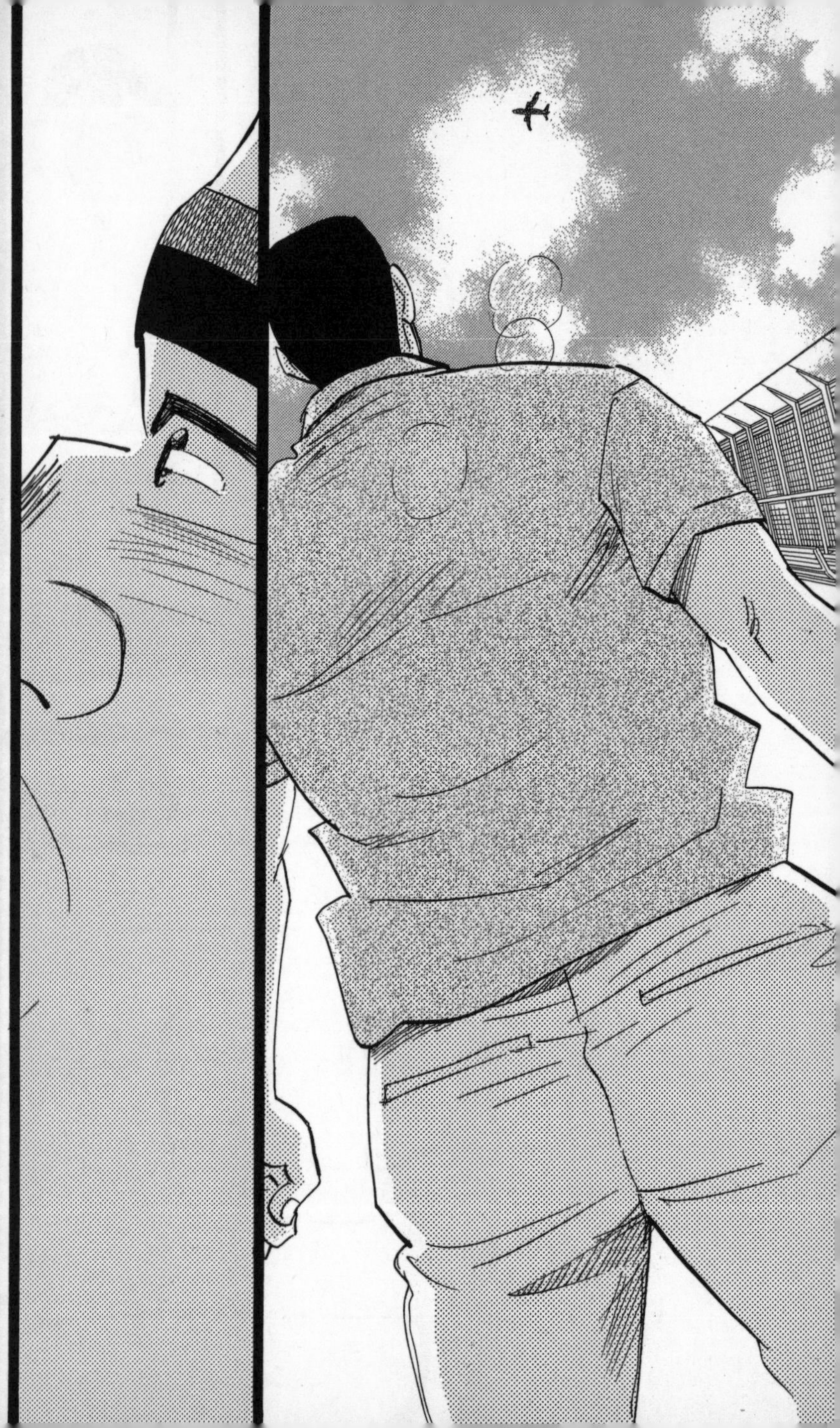

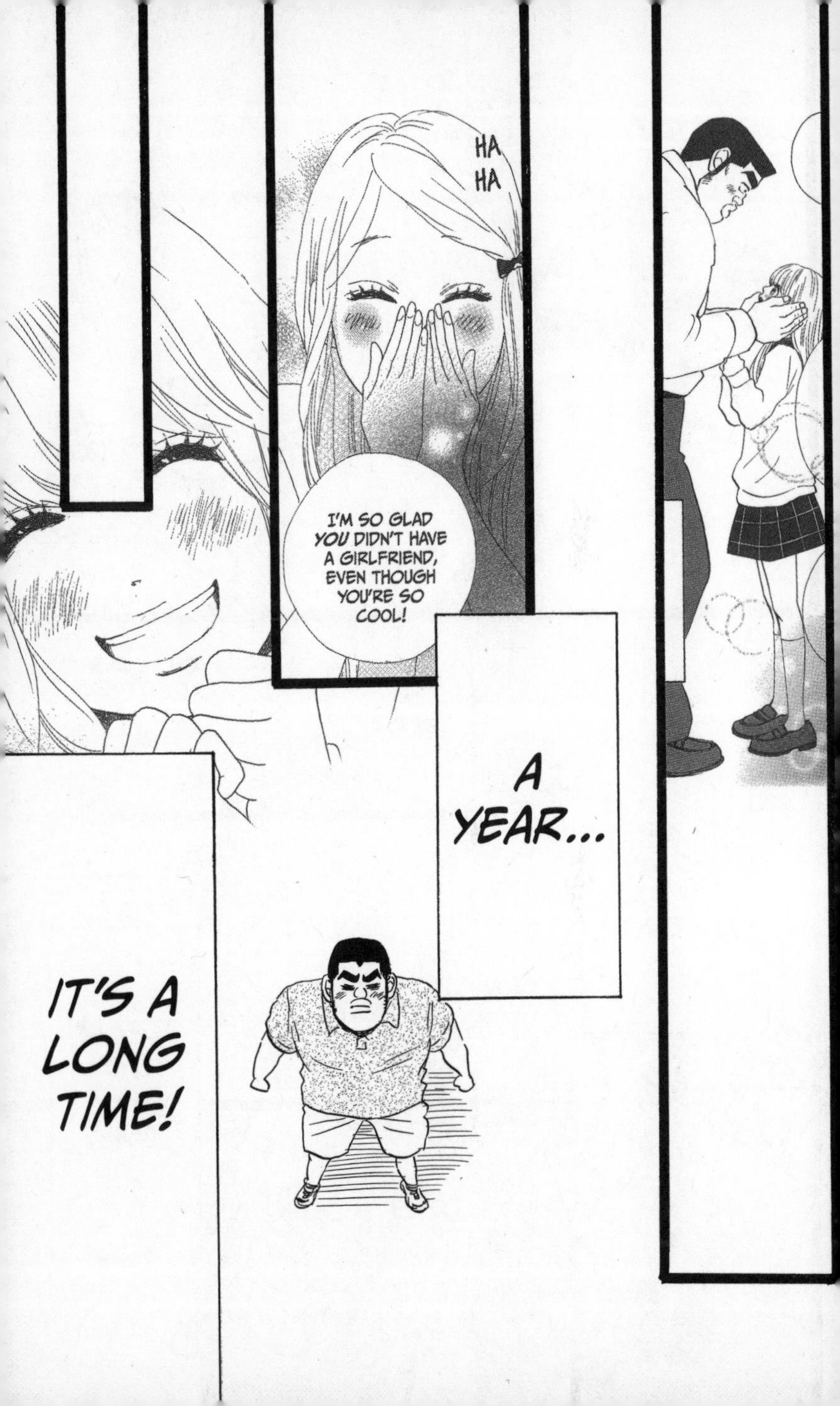
HA HA
I'M SO GLAD YOU DIDN'T HAVE A GIRLFRIEND, EVEN THOUGH YOU'RE SO COOL!
A YEAR...
IT'S A LONG TIME!

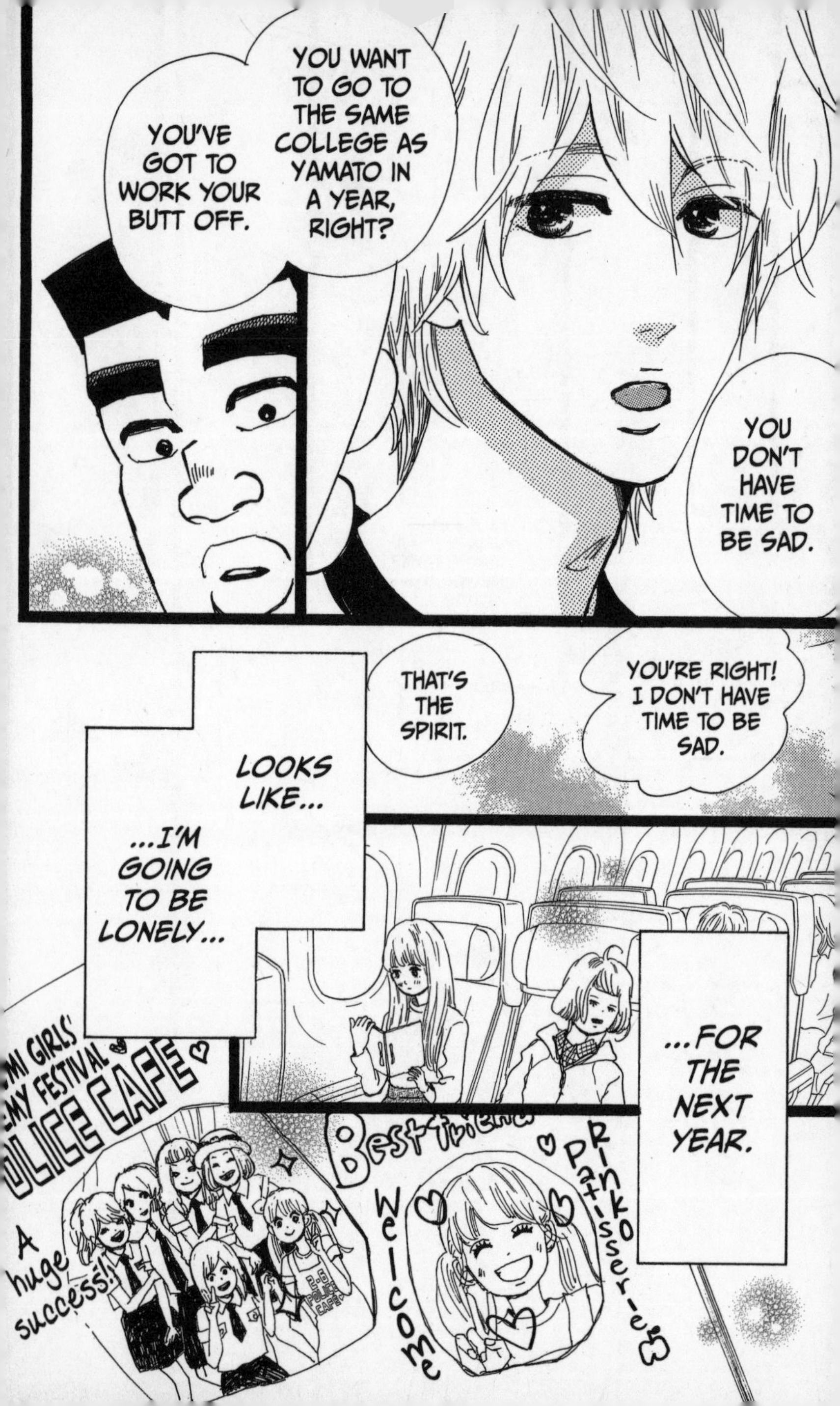
YOU WANT TO GO TO THE SAME COLLEGE AS YAMATO IN A YEAR, RIGHT?
YOU'VE GOT TO WORK YOUR BUTT OFF.
YOU DON'T HAVE TIME TO BE SAD.
YOU'RE RIGHT! I DON'T HAVE TIME TO BE SAD.
THAT'S THE SPIRIT.
LOOKS LIKE...
...I'M GOING TO BE LONELY...
...FOR THE NEXT YEAR.
Rinko Patisserie
Welcome
MI GIRLS'
MY FESTIVAL
OLICE CAFE
A huge success!
2-6 POLICE CAFE

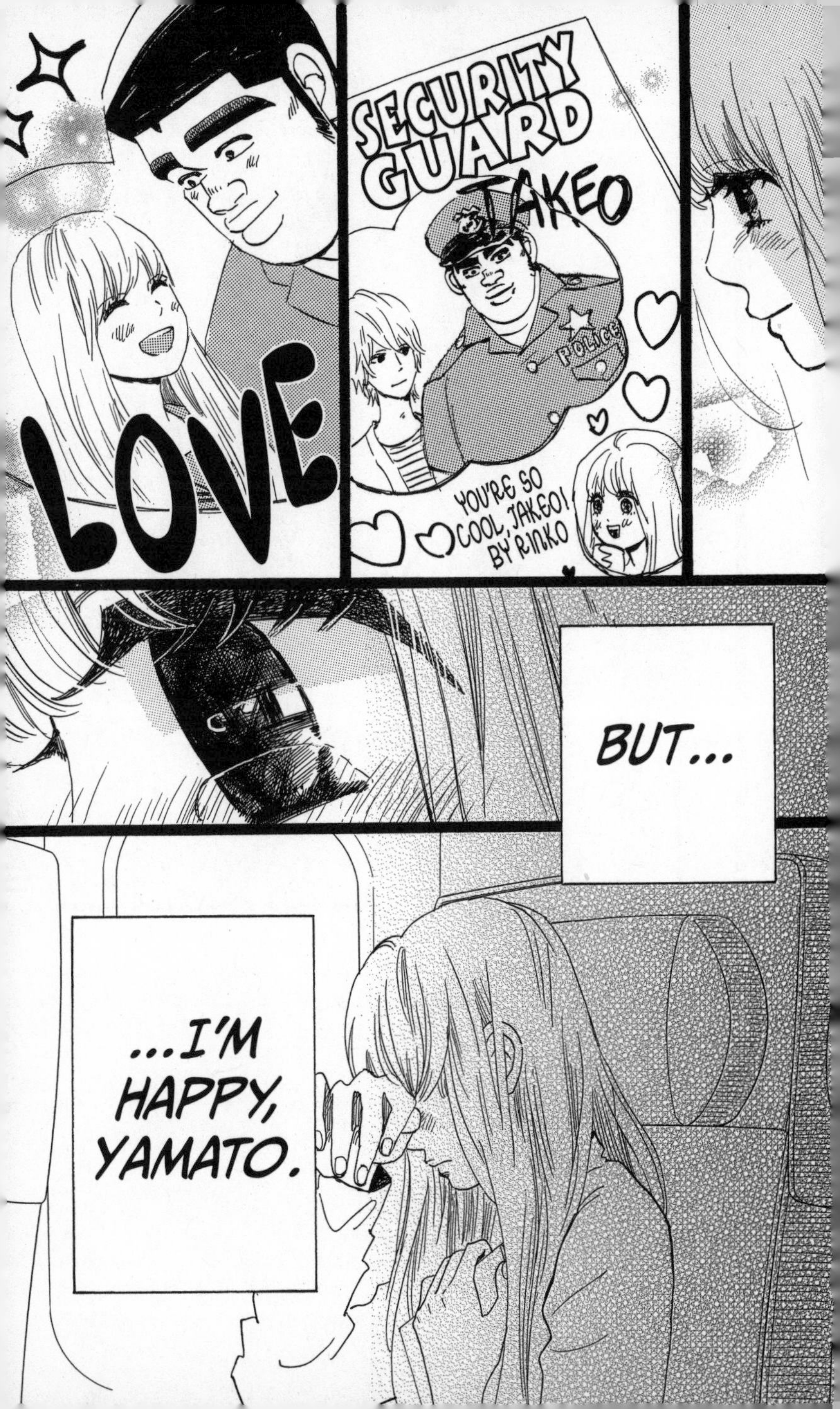
SECURITY GUARD TAKEO
POLICE
YOU'RE SO COOL, TAKEO! BY RINKO
LOVE
BUT...
...I'M HAPPY, YAMATO.

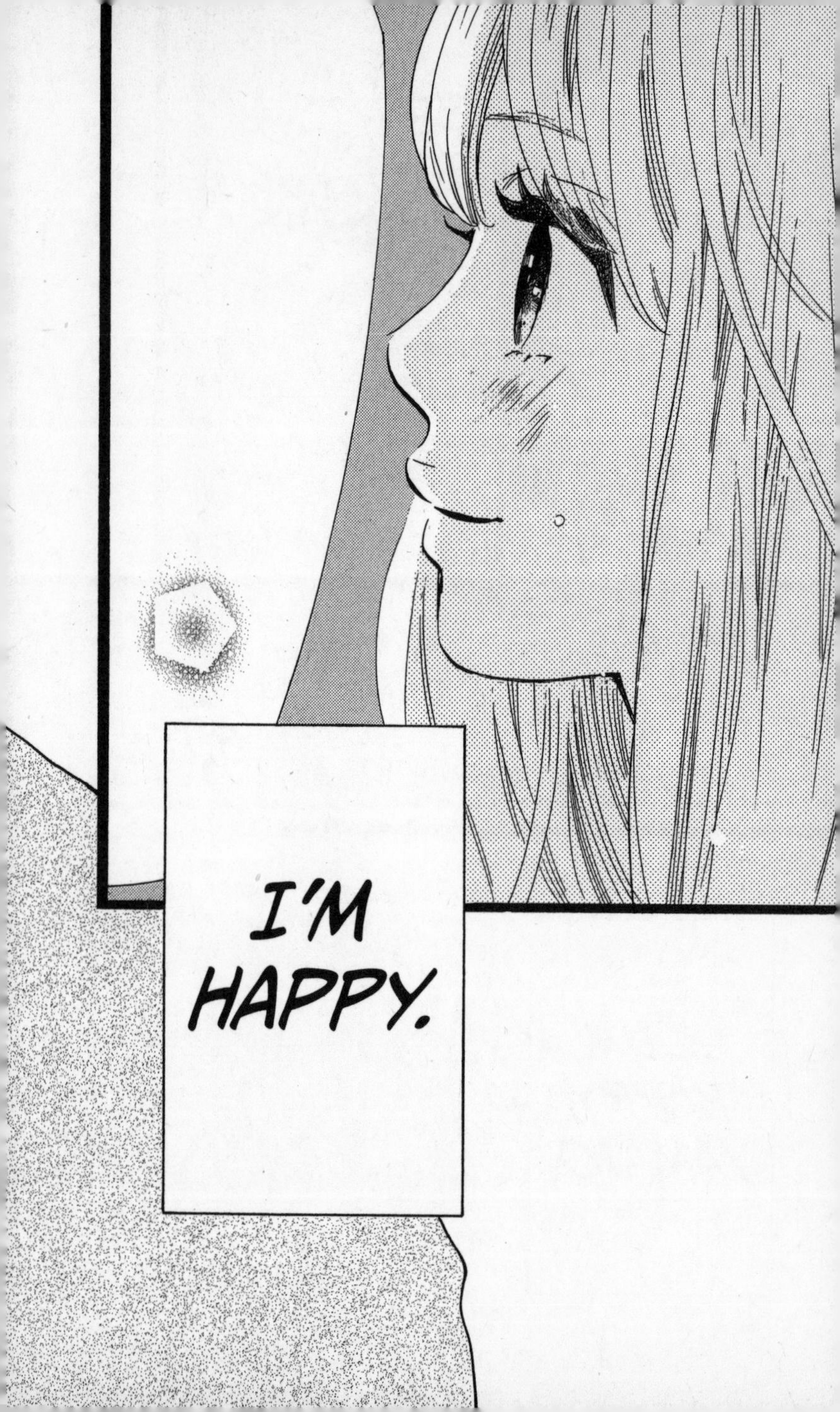
I'M HAPPY.

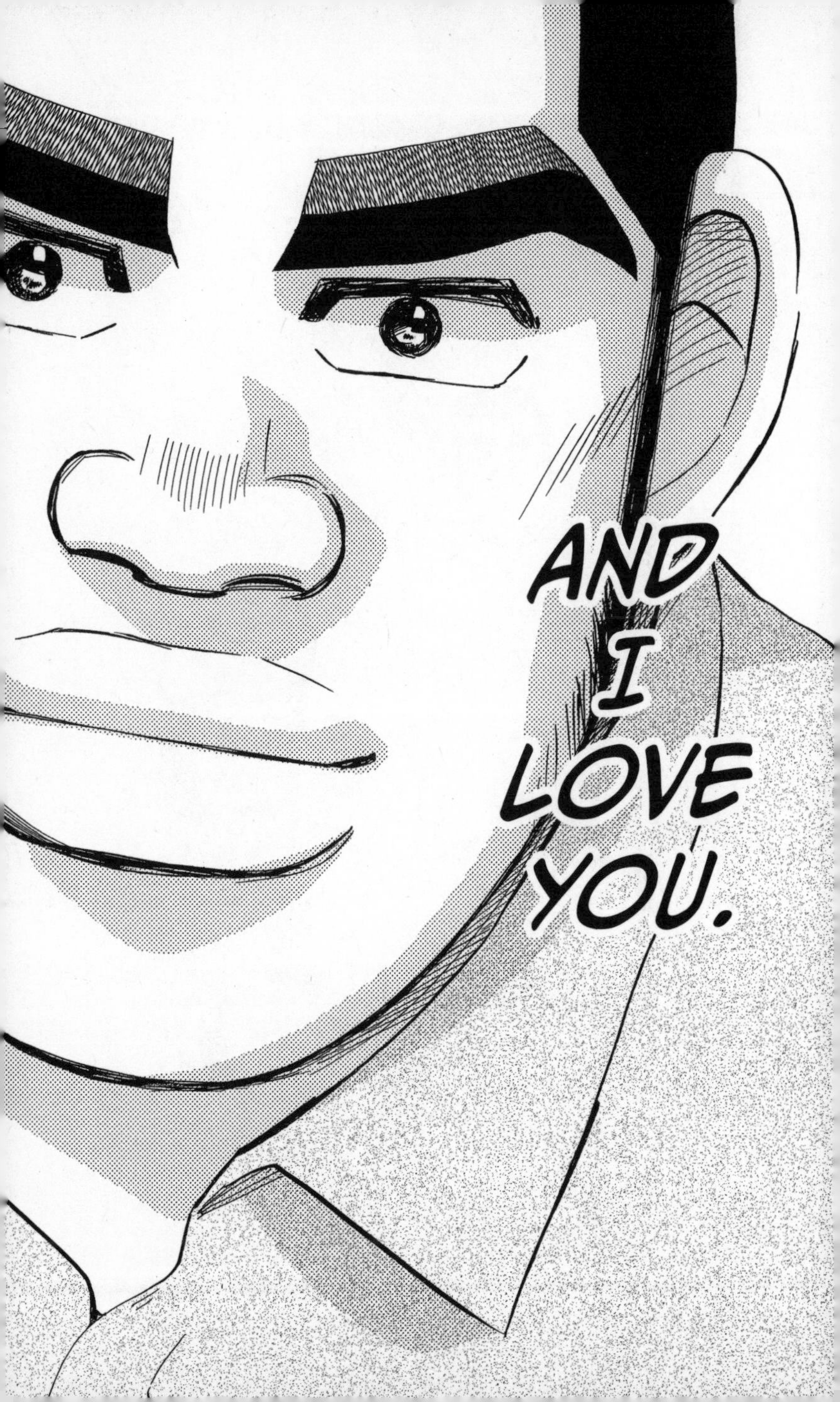
AND I LOVE YOU.

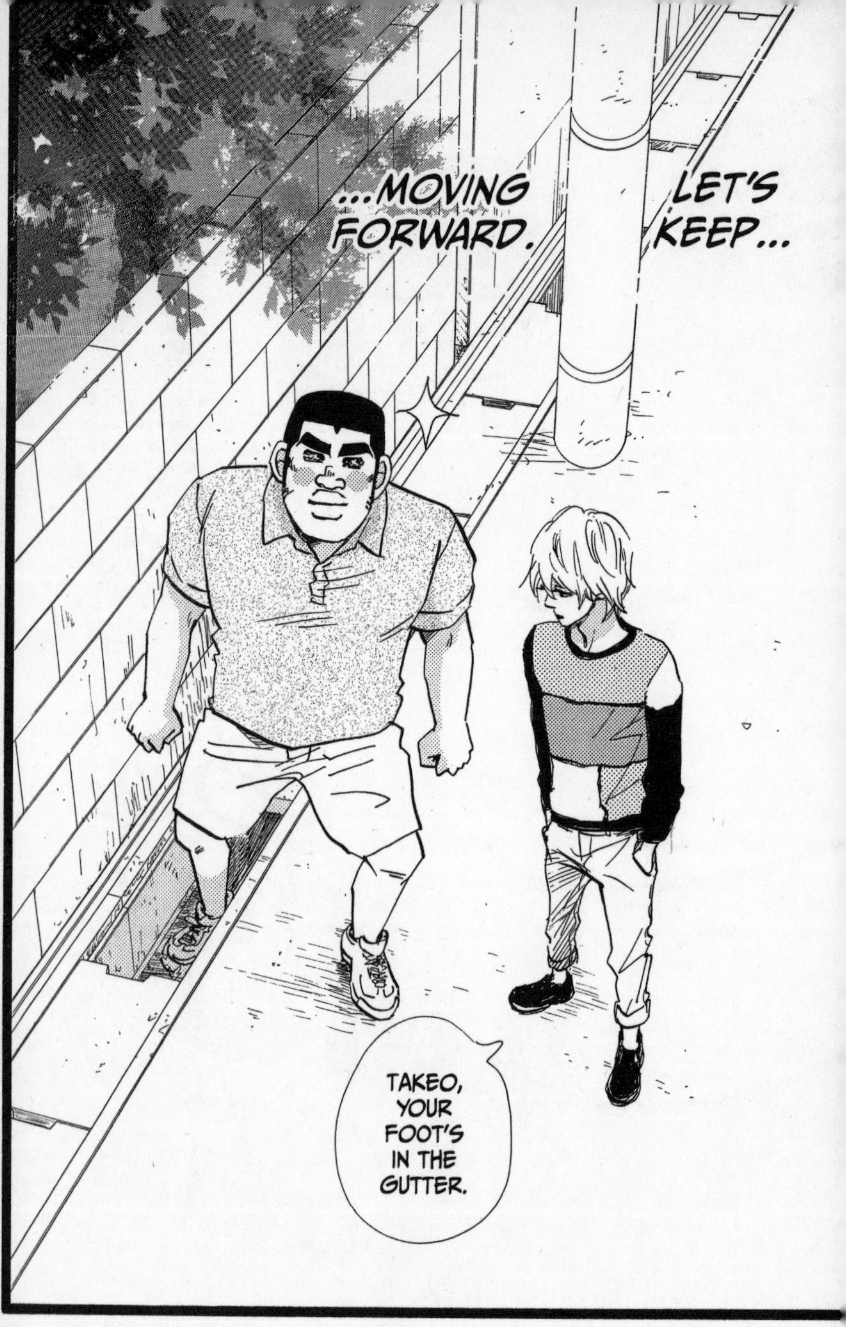
LET'S KEEP...
...MOVING FORWARD.
TAKEO, YOUR FOOT'S IN THE GUTTER.

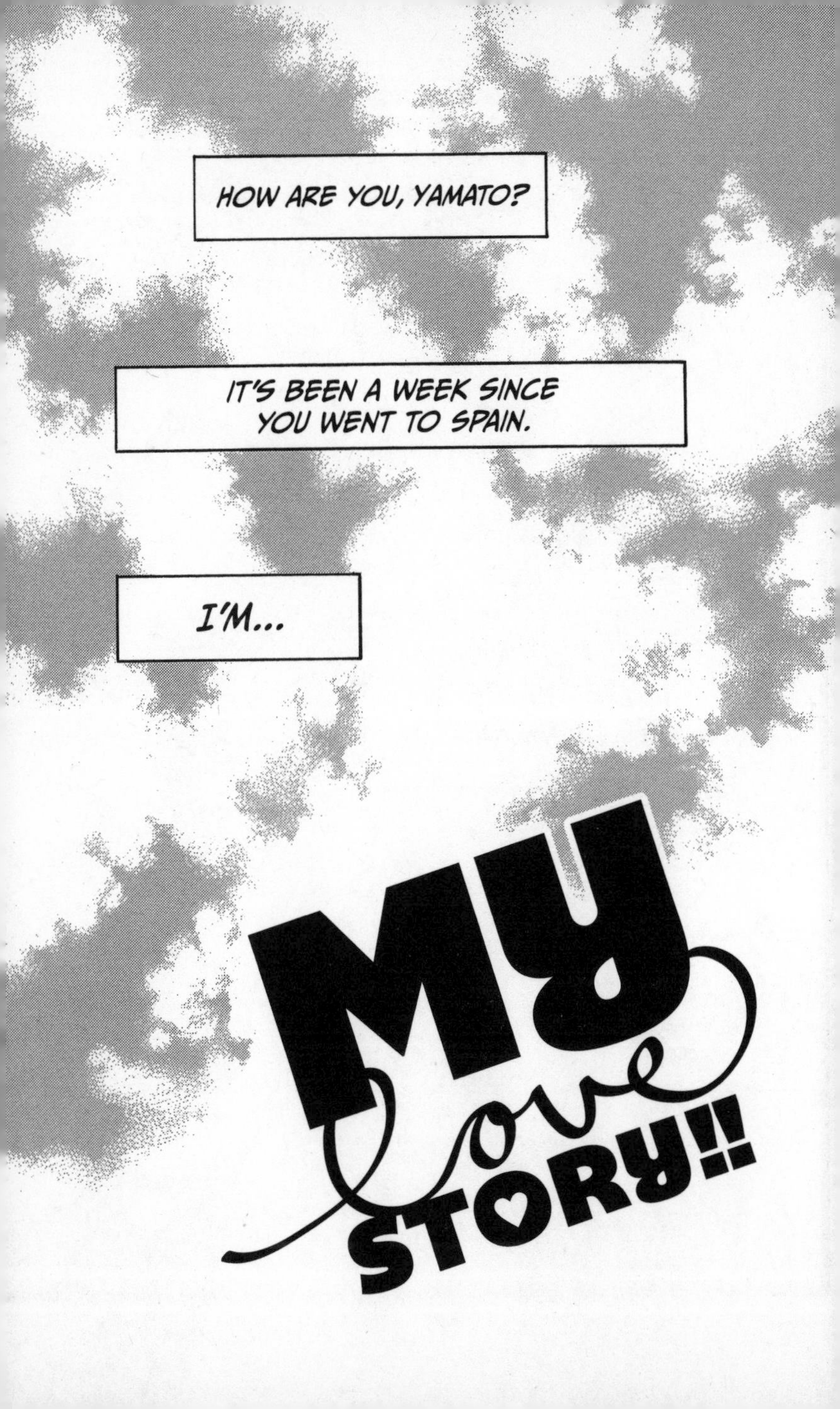
HOW ARE YOU, YAMATO?
IT'S BEEN A WEEK SINCE YOU WENT TO SPAIN.
I'M...
MY Love STORY!!

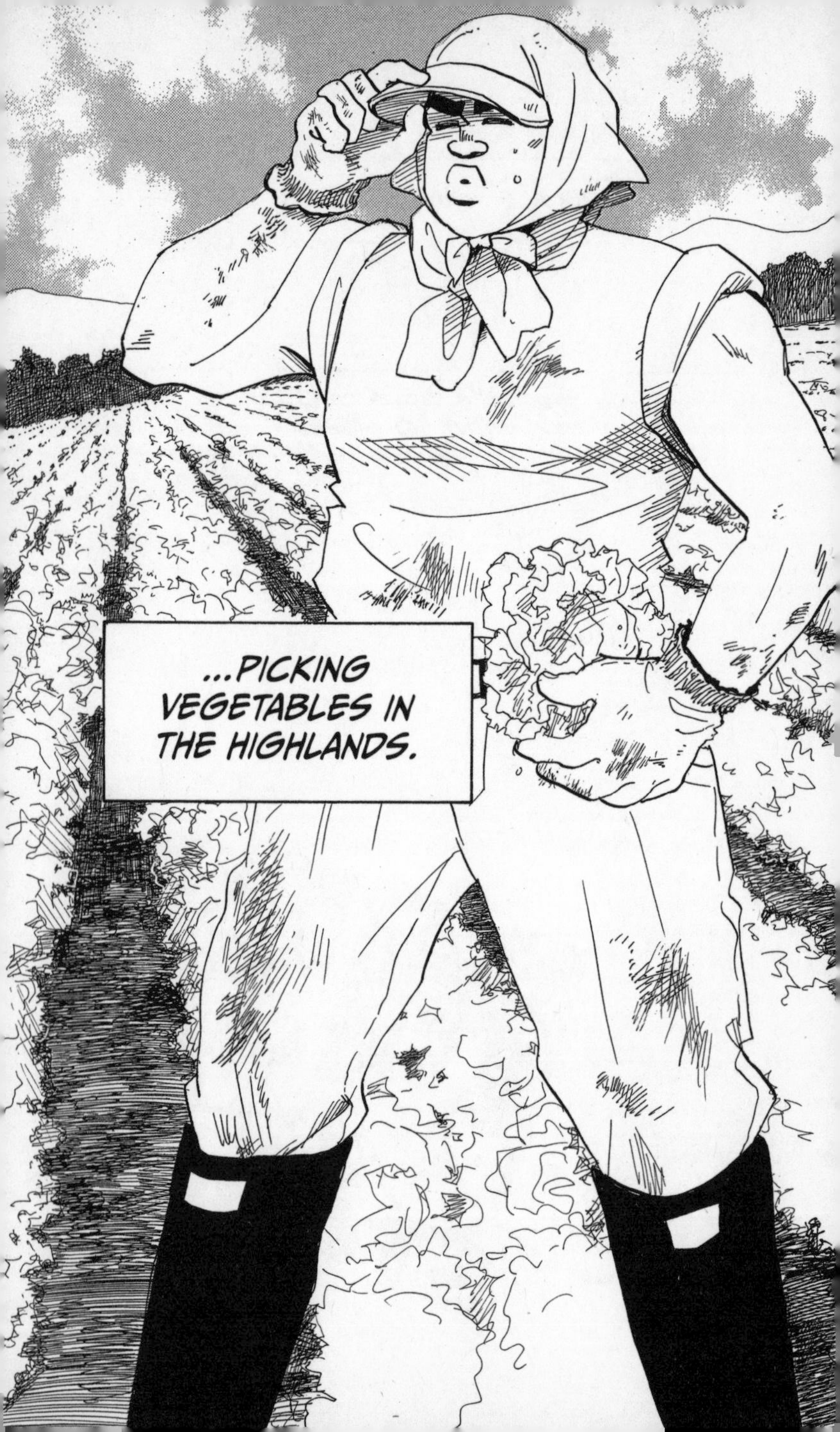
...PICKING VEGETABLES IN THE HIGHLANDS.

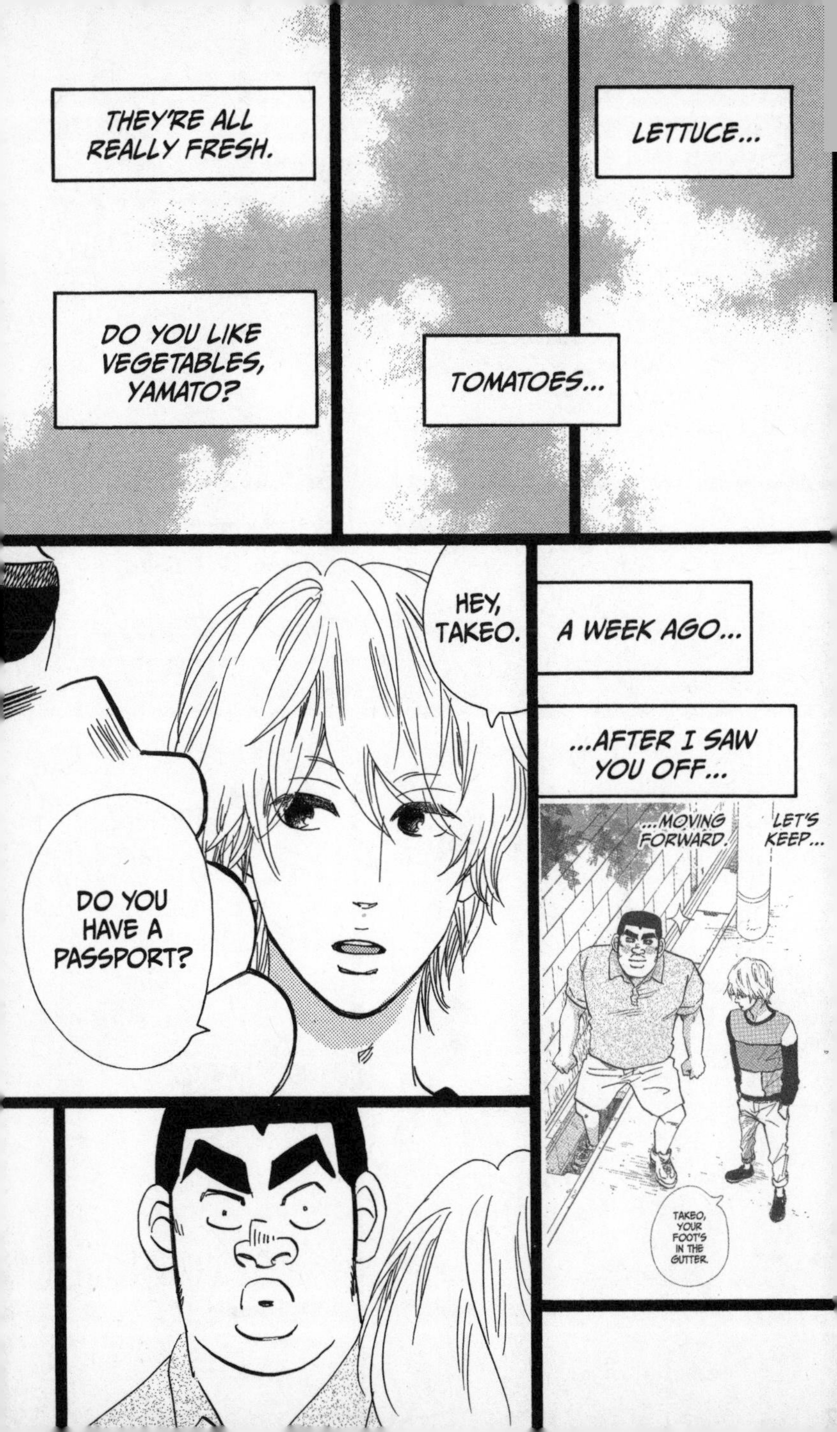
LETTUCE...
TOMATOES...
THEY'RE ALL REALLY FRESH.
DO YOU LIKE VEGETABLES, YAMATO?
A WEEK AGO...
...AFTER I SAW YOU OFF...
LET'S KEEP...
...MOVING FORWARD.
TAKEO, YOUR FOOT'S IN THE GUTTER.
HEY, TAKEO.
DO YOU HAVE A PASSPORT?

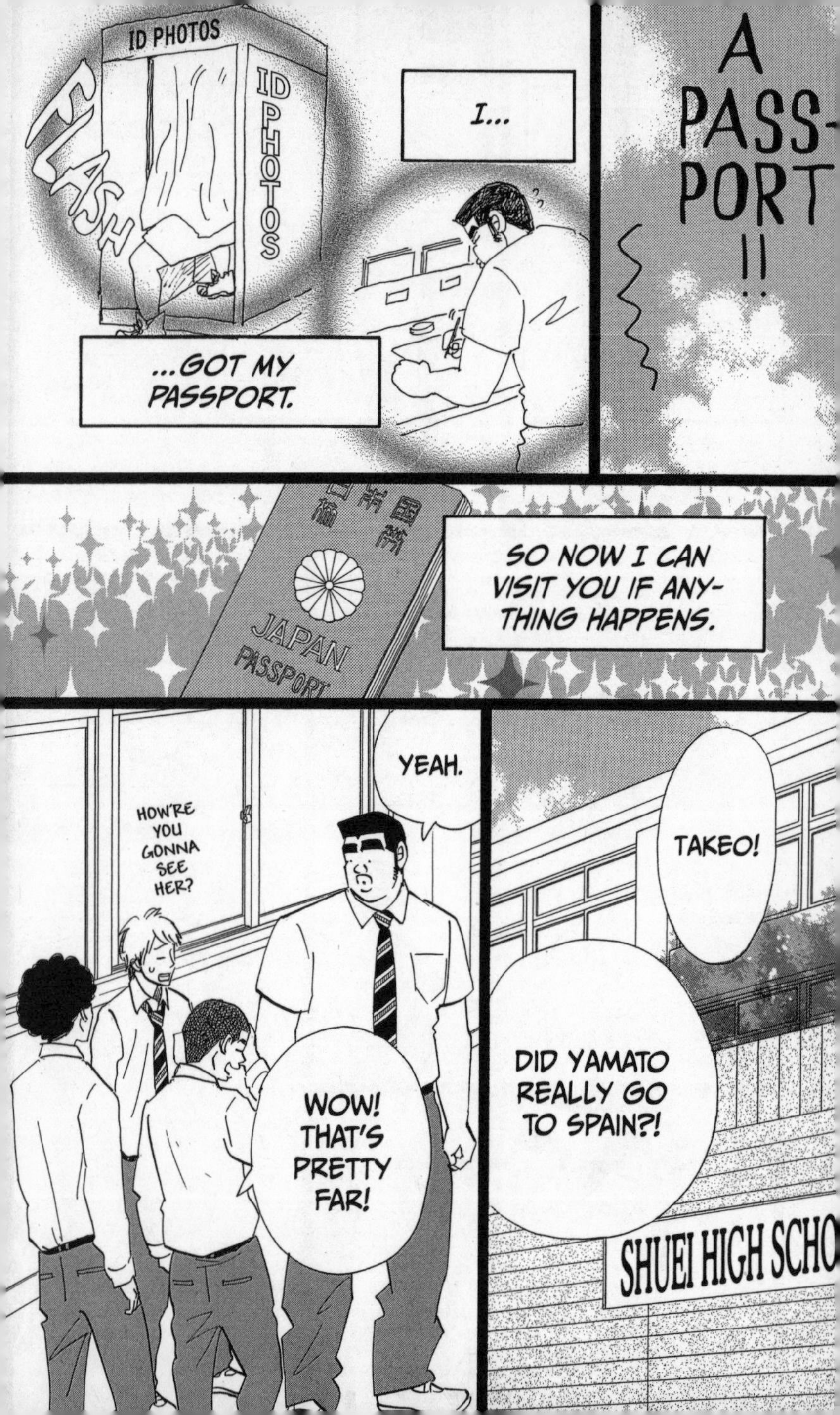
A PASSPORT!!
I...
ID PHOTOS
ID PHOTOS
FLASH
...GOT MY PASSPORT.
SO NOW I CAN VISIT YOU IF ANYTHING HAPPENS.
JAPAN
PASSPORT
TAKEO!
DID YAMATO REALLY GO TO SPAIN?!
SHUEI HIGH SCHO
YEAH.
WOW! THAT'S PRETTY FAR!
HOW'RE YOU GONNA SEE HER?

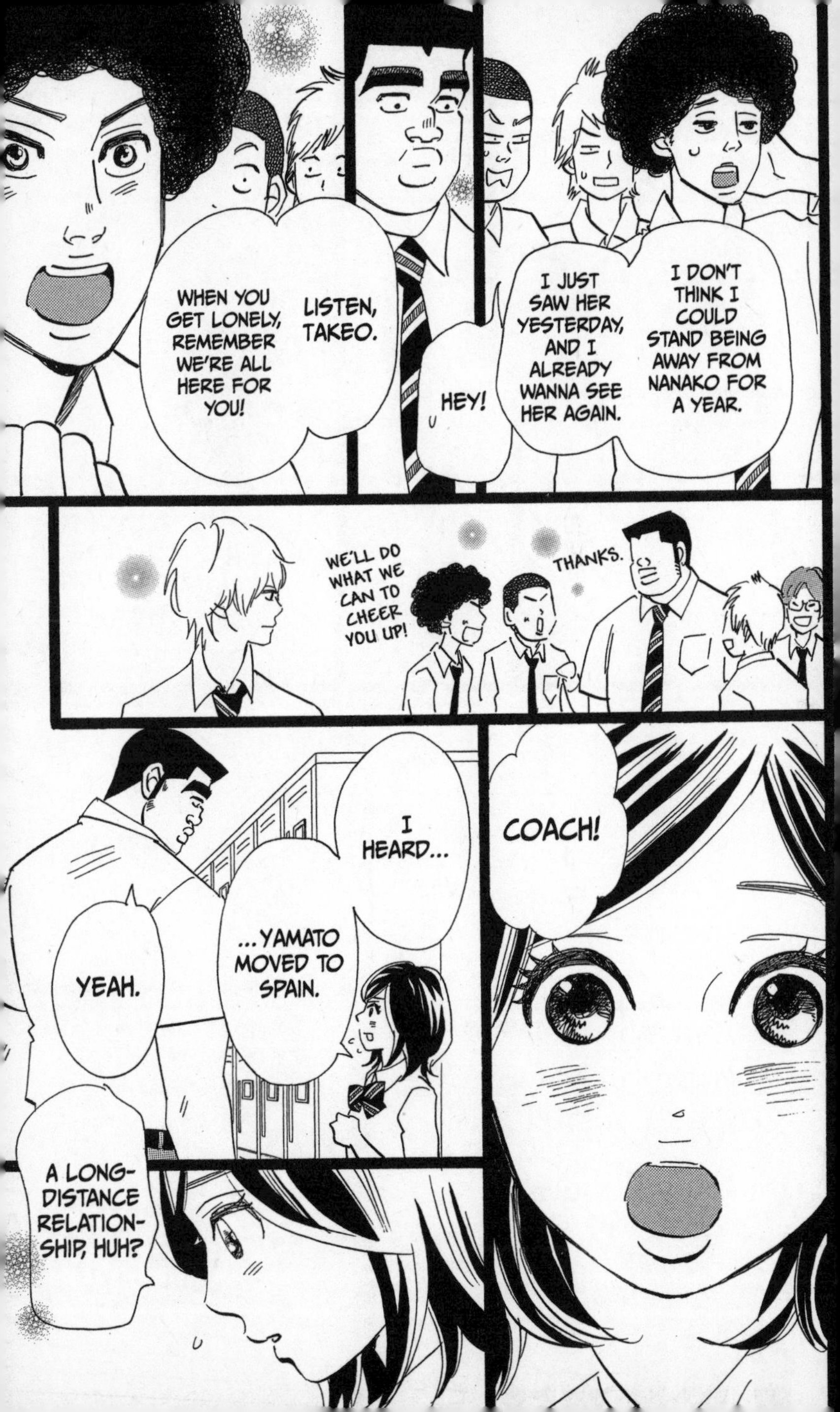
I DON'T THINK I COULD STAND BEING AWAY FROM NANAKO FOR A YEAR.
I JUST SAW HER YESTERDAY, AND I ALREADY WANNA SEE HER AGAIN.
HEY!
LISTEN, TAKEO.
WHEN YOU GET LONELY, REMEMBER WE'RE ALL HERE FOR YOU!
THANKS.
WE'LL DO WHAT WE CAN TO CHEER YOU UP!
COACH!
I HEARD...
...YAMATO MOVED TO SPAIN.
YEAH.
A LONG-DISTANCE RELATIONSHIP, HUH?

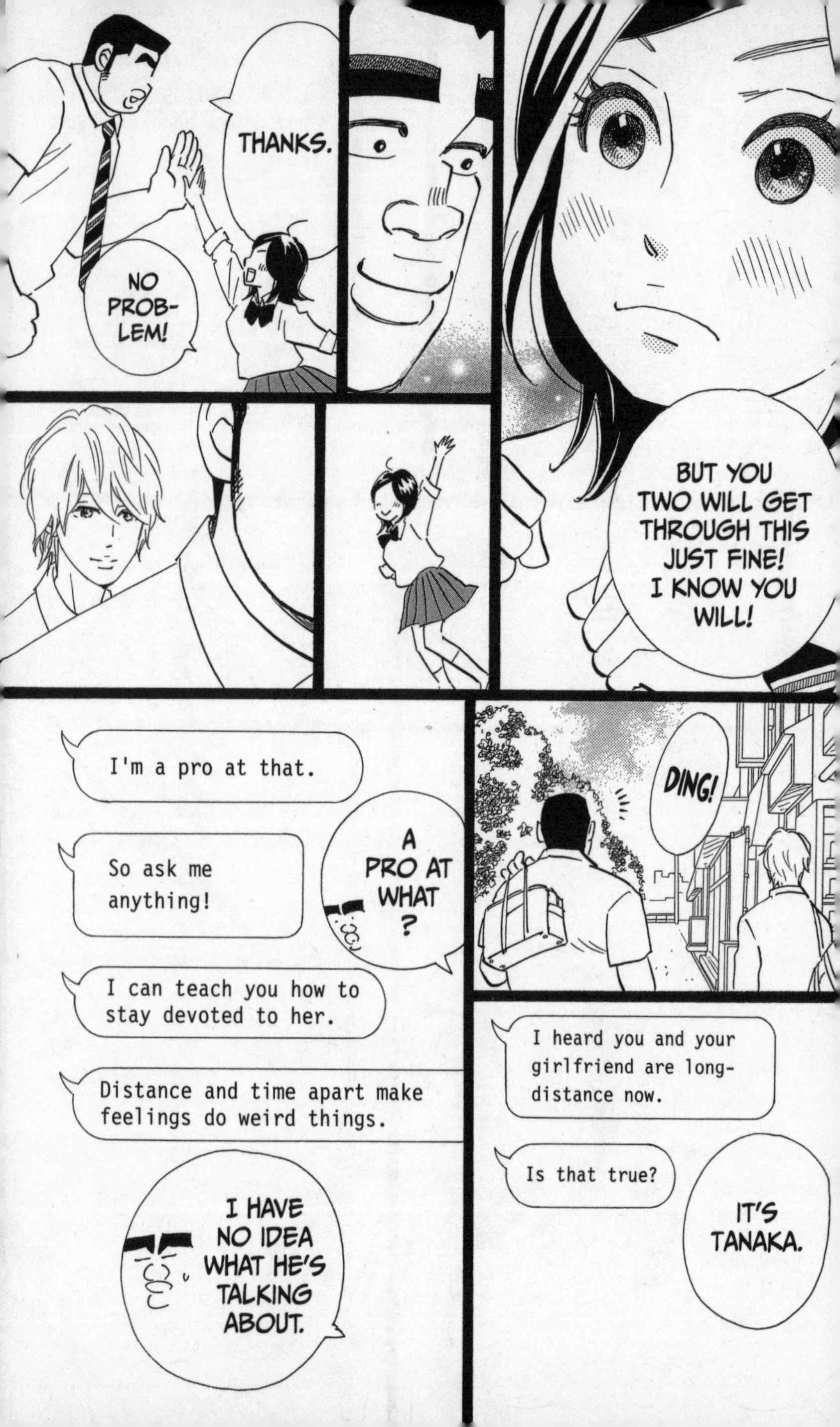
BUT YOU TWO WILL GET THROUGH THIS JUST FINE! I KNOW YOU WILL!
THANKS.
NO PROB-LEM!
DING!
IT'S TANAKA.
I heard you and your girlfriend are long-distance now.
Is that true?
I'm a pro at that.
So ask me anything!
A PRO AT WHAT?
I can teach you how to stay devoted to her.
Distance and time apart make feelings do weird things.
I HAVE NO IDEA WHAT HE'S TALKING ABOUT.

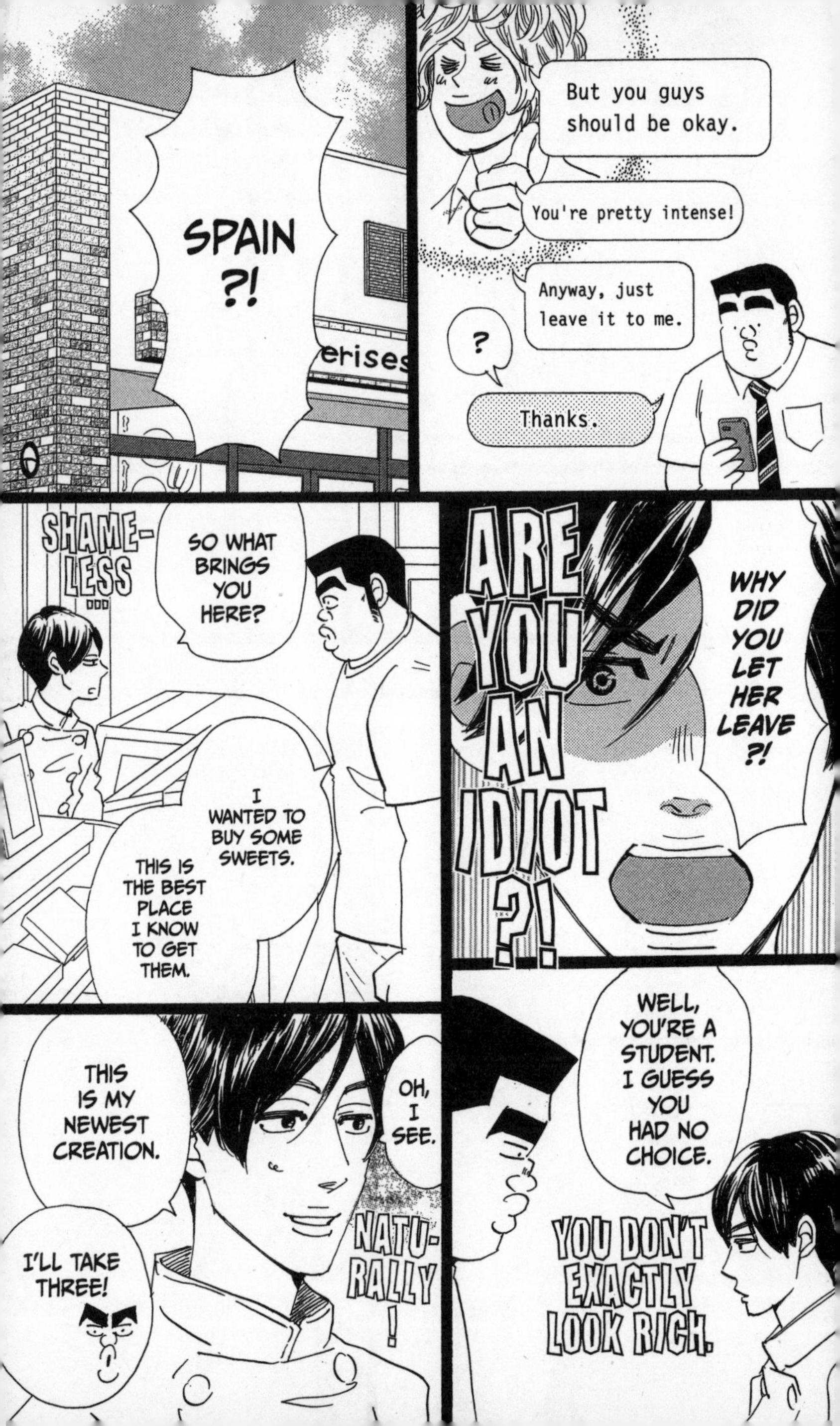

But you guys should be okay.
You're pretty intense!
Anyway, just leave it to me.
?
Thanks.
SPAIN ?!
erises
ARE YOU AN IDIOT ?!
WHY DID YOU LET HER LEAVE ?!
SO WHAT BRINGS YOU HERE?
SHAME-LESS...
I WANTED TO BUY SOME SWEETS.
THIS IS THE BEST PLACE I KNOW TO GET THEM.
WELL, YOU'RE A STUDENT. I GUESS YOU HAD NO CHOICE.
YOU DON'T EXACTLY LOOK RICH.
OH, I SEE.
THIS IS MY NEWEST CREATION.
NATU-RALLY!
I'LL TAKE THREE!

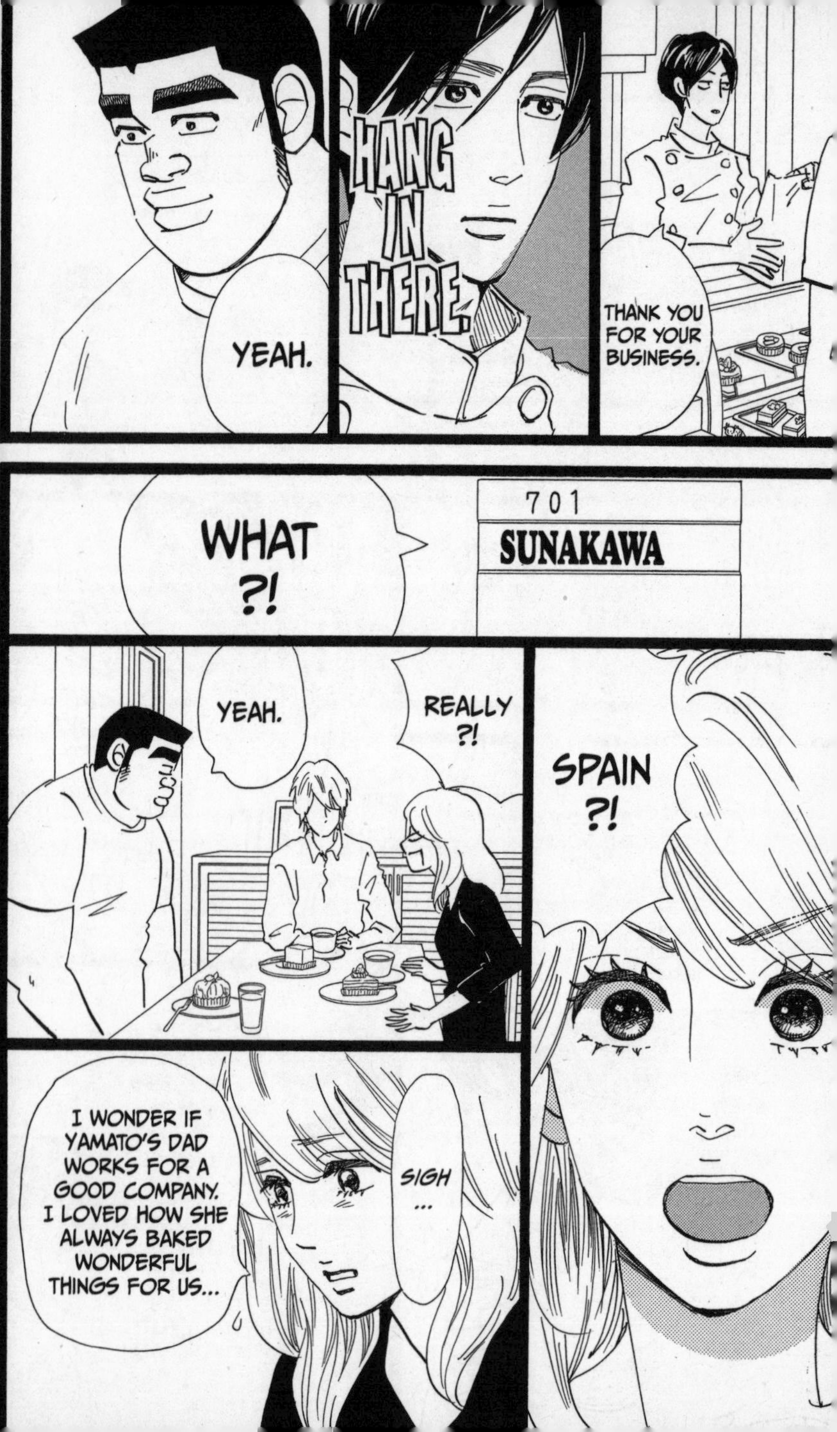
THANK YOU FOR YOUR BUSINESS.
HANG IN THERE.
YEAH.
701
SUNAKAWA
WHAT ?!
SPAIN ?!
REALLY ?!
YEAH.
SIGH ...
I WONDER IF YAMATO'S DAD WORKS FOR A GOOD COMPANY. I LOVED HOW SHE ALWAYS BAKED WONDERFUL THINGS FOR US...

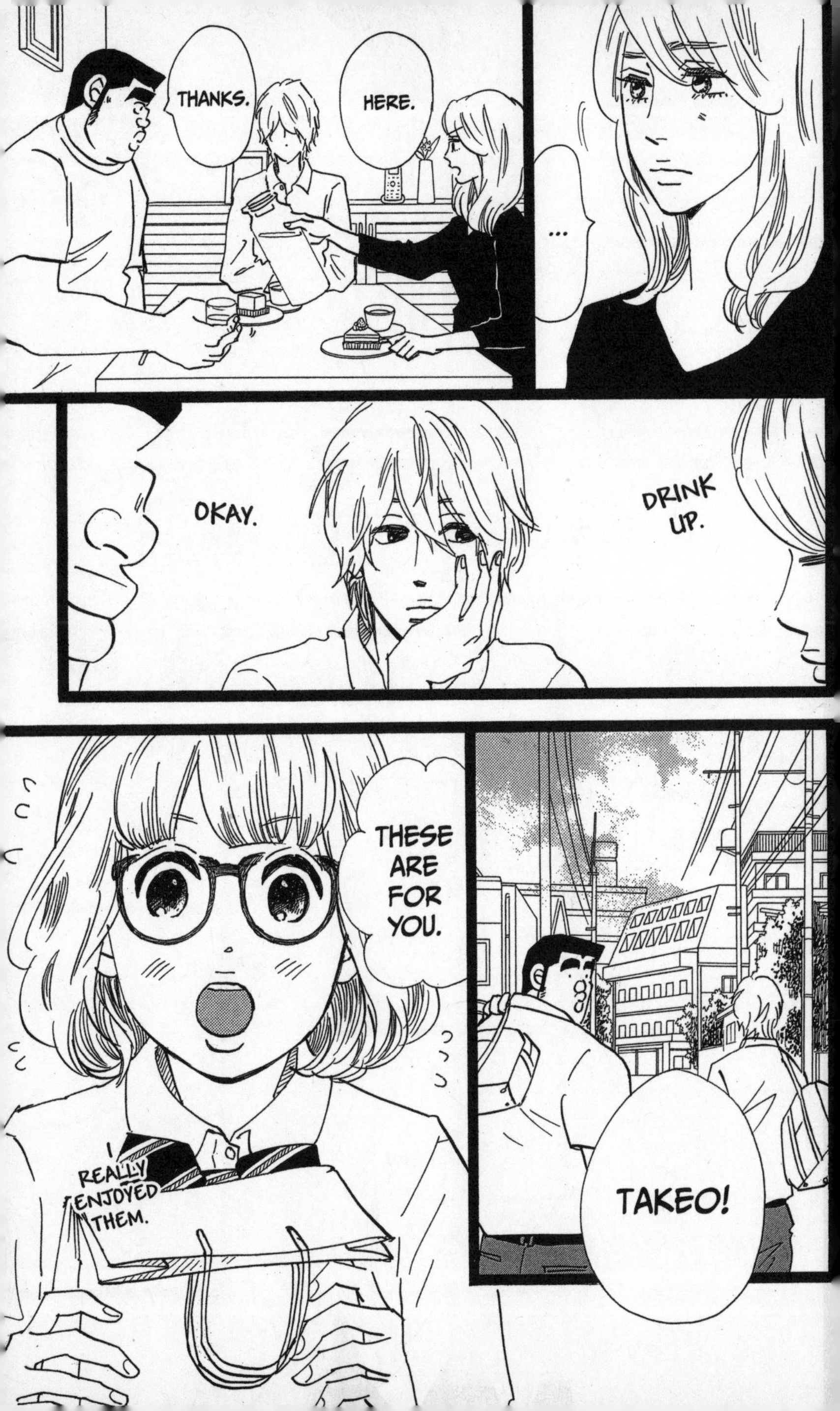
...
HERE.
THANKS.
DRINK UP.
OKAY.
TAKEO!
THESE ARE FOR YOU.
I REALLY ENJOYED THEM.

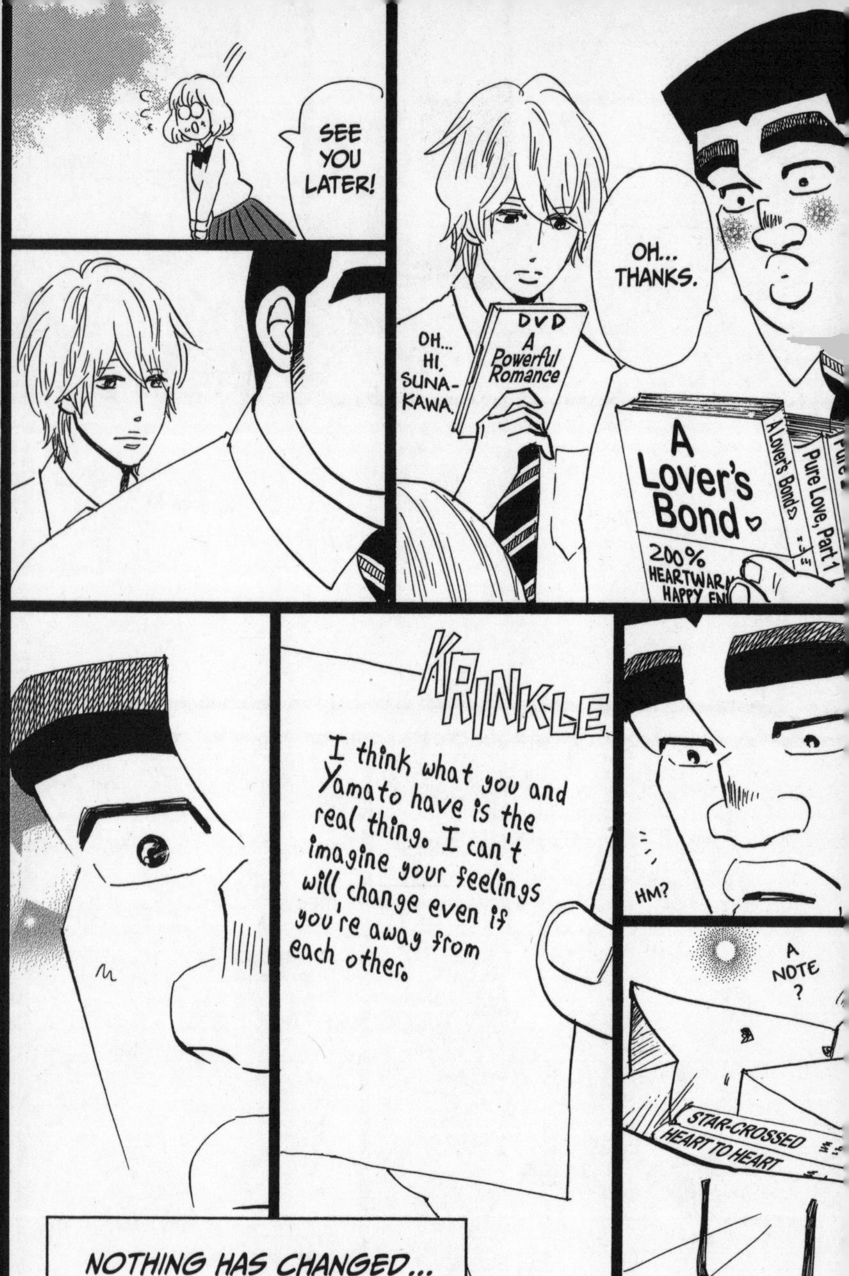
OH... THANKS.
OH... HI, SUNA-KAWA.
DVD A Powerful Romance
A Lover's Bond
200% HEARTWARM HAPPY EN
A Lover's Bond
Pure Love, Part 1
SEE YOU LATER!
HM?
A NOTE ?
STAR-CROSSED
HEART TO HEART
KRINKLE
I think what you and Yamato have is the real thing. I can't imagine your feelings will change even if you're away from each other.
NOTHING HAS CHANGED...

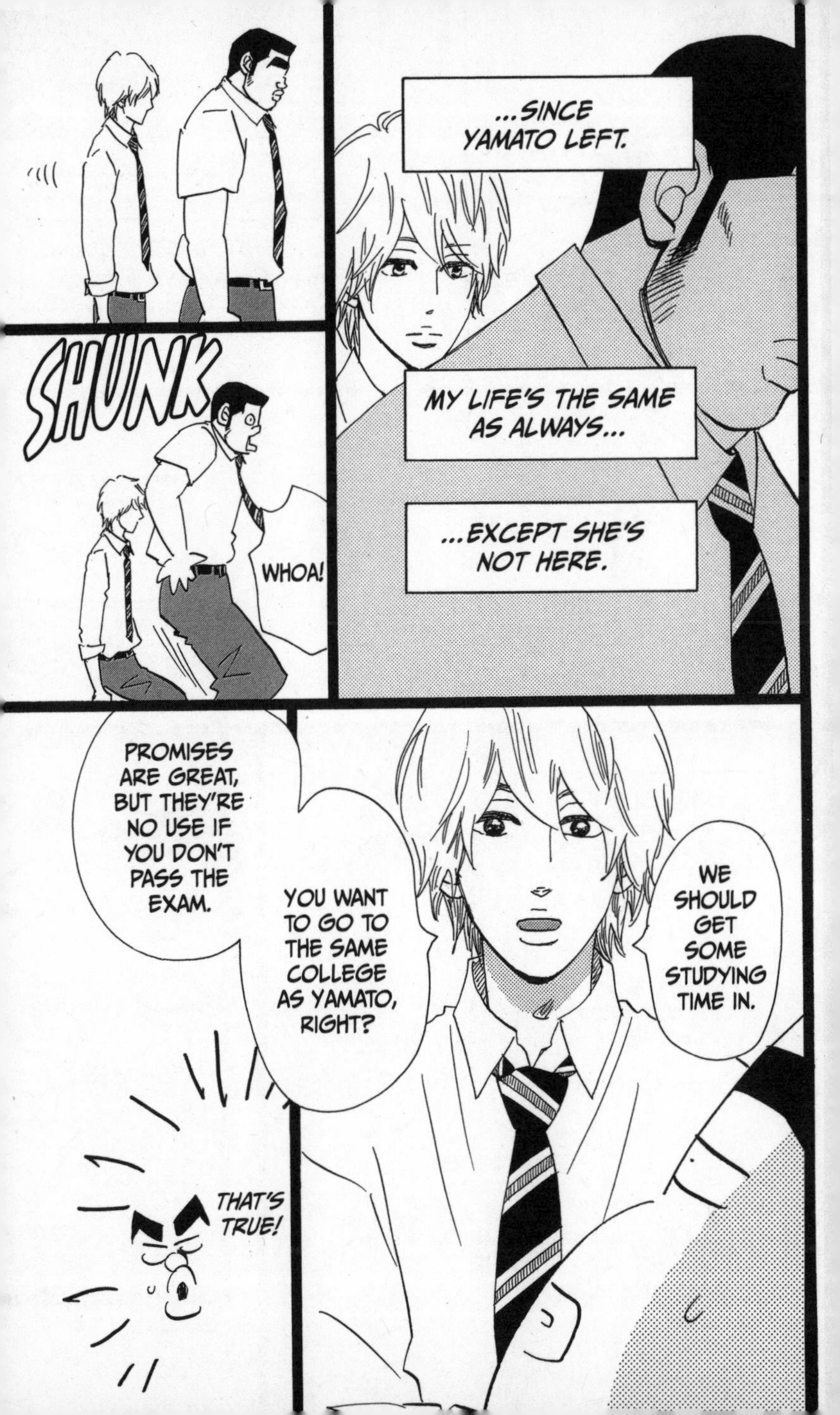
...SINCE YAMATO LEFT.
MY LIFE'S THE SAME AS ALWAYS...
...EXCEPT SHE'S NOT HERE.
SHUNK
WHOA!
WE SHOULD GET SOME STUDYING TIME IN.
YOU WANT TO GO TO THE SAME COLLEGE AS YAMATO, RIGHT?
PROMISES ARE GREAT, BUT THEY'RE NO USE IF YOU DON'T PASS THE EXAM.
THAT'S TRUE!

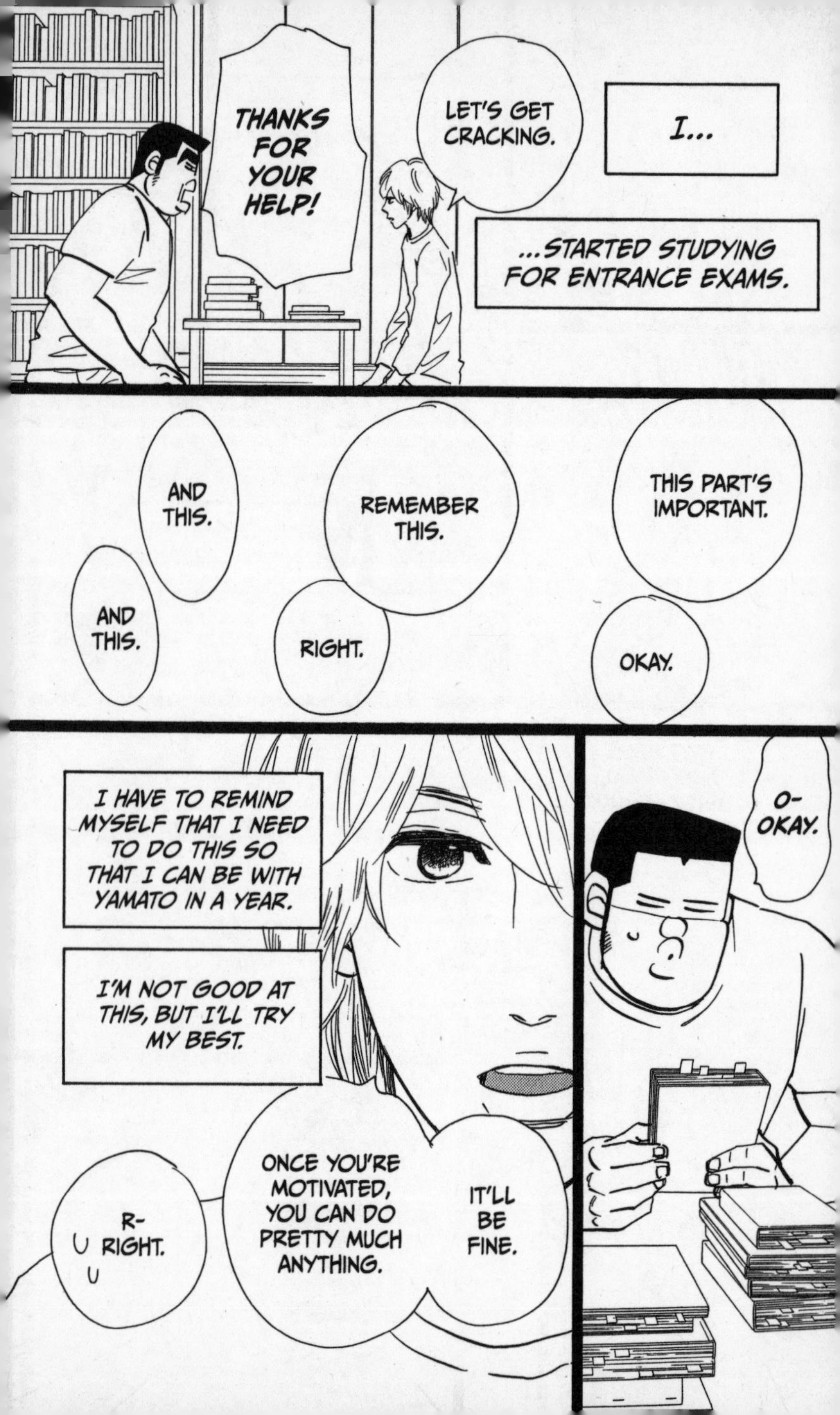
I...
...STARTED STUDYING FOR ENTRANCE EXAMS.
LET'S GET CRACKING.
THANKS FOR YOUR HELP!
THIS PART'S IMPORTANT.
OKAY.
REMEMBER THIS.
RIGHT.
AND THIS.
AND THIS.
O-OKAY.
I HAVE TO REMIND MYSELF THAT I NEED TO DO THIS SO THAT I CAN BE WITH YAMATO IN A YEAR.
I'M NOT GOOD AT THIS, BUT I'LL TRY MY BEST.
IT'LL BE FINE.
ONCE YOU'RE MOTIVATED, YOU CAN DO PRETTY MUCH ANYTHING.
R-RIGHT.

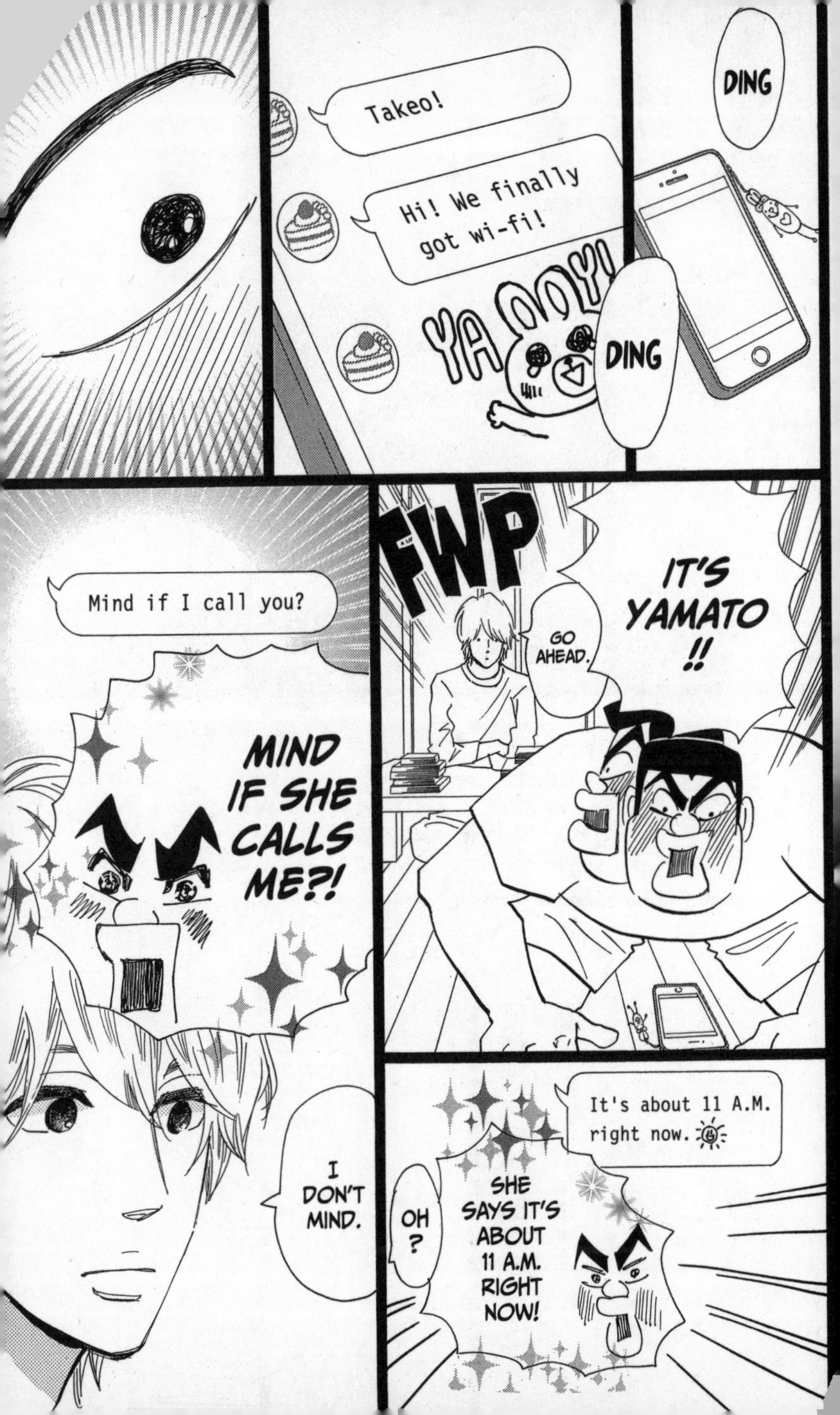
DING
DING
Takeo!
Hi! We finally got wi-fi!
YAAAY!
FWP
IT'S YAMATO!!
GO AHEAD.
It's about 11 A.M. right now.
SHE SAYS IT'S ABOUT 11 A.M. RIGHT NOW!
OH?
Mind if I call you?
MIND IF SHE CALLS ME?!
I DON'T MIND.

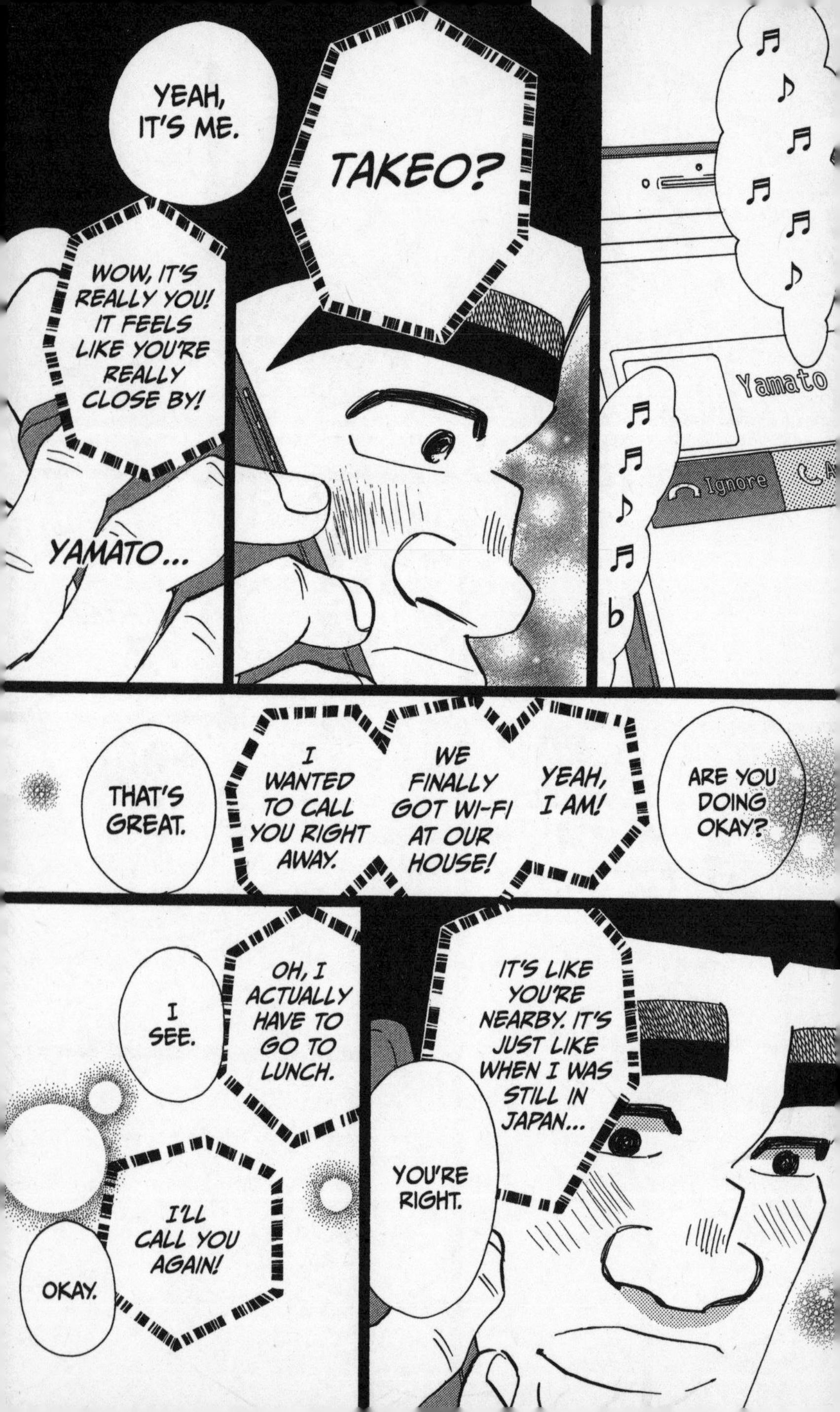
Yamato
Ignore
TAKEO?
YEAH, IT'S ME.
WOW, IT'S REALLY YOU! IT FEELS LIKE YOU'RE REALLY CLOSE BY!
YAMATO...
ARE YOU DOING OKAY?
YEAH, I AM!
WE FINALLY GOT WI-FI AT OUR HOUSE!
I WANTED TO CALL YOU RIGHT AWAY.
THAT'S GREAT.
IT'S LIKE YOU'RE NEARBY. IT'S JUST LIKE WHEN I WAS STILL IN JAPAN...
YOU'RE RIGHT.
OH, I ACTUALLY HAVE TO GO TO LUNCH.
I SEE.
I'LL CALL YOU AGAIN!
OKAY.

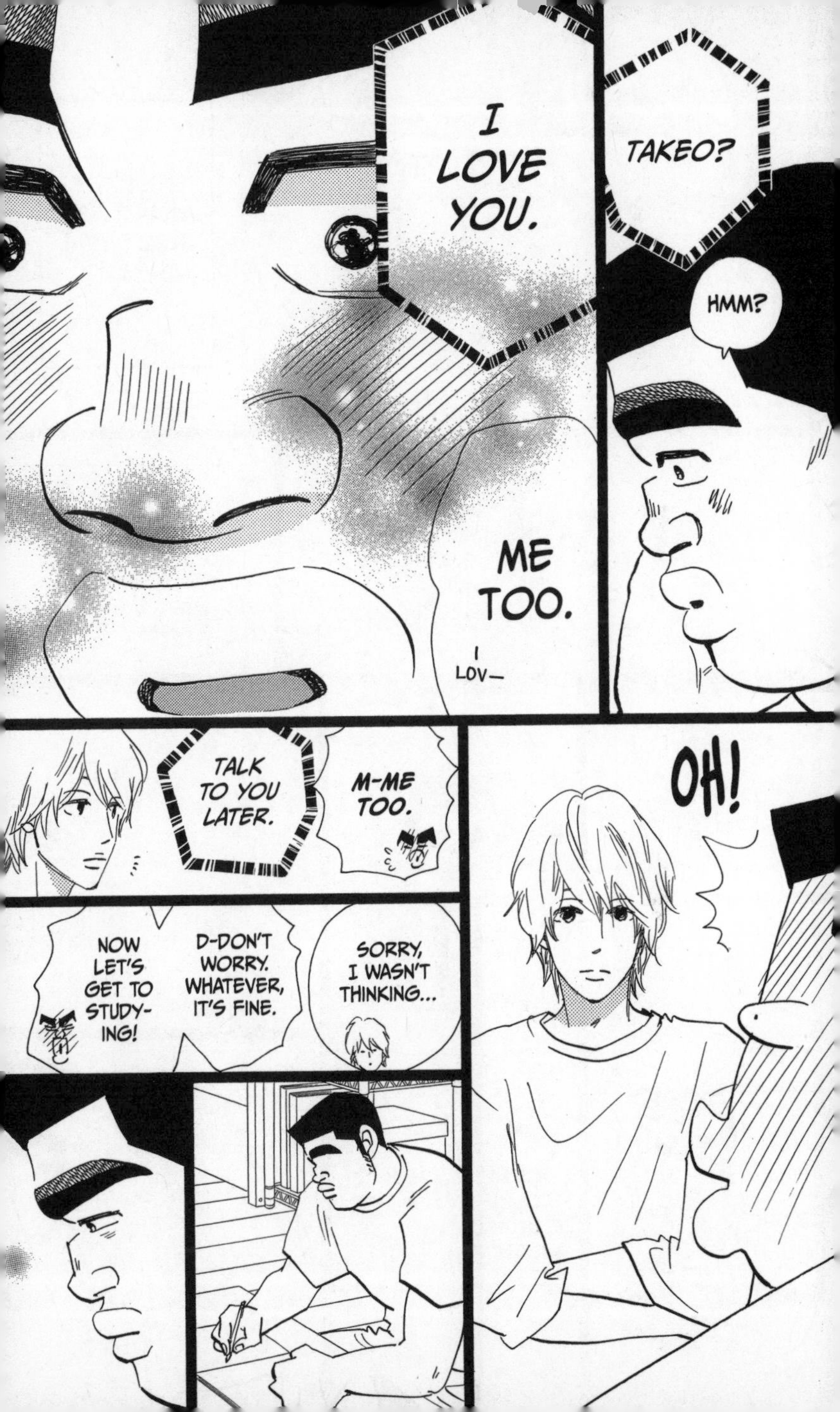
TAKEO?
HMM?
I LOVE YOU.
ME TOO.
I LOV—
OH!
M-ME TOO.
TALK TO YOU LATER.
SORRY, I WASN'T THINKING...
D-DON'T WORRY. WHATEVER, IT'S FINE.
NOW LET'S GET TO STUDY-ING!

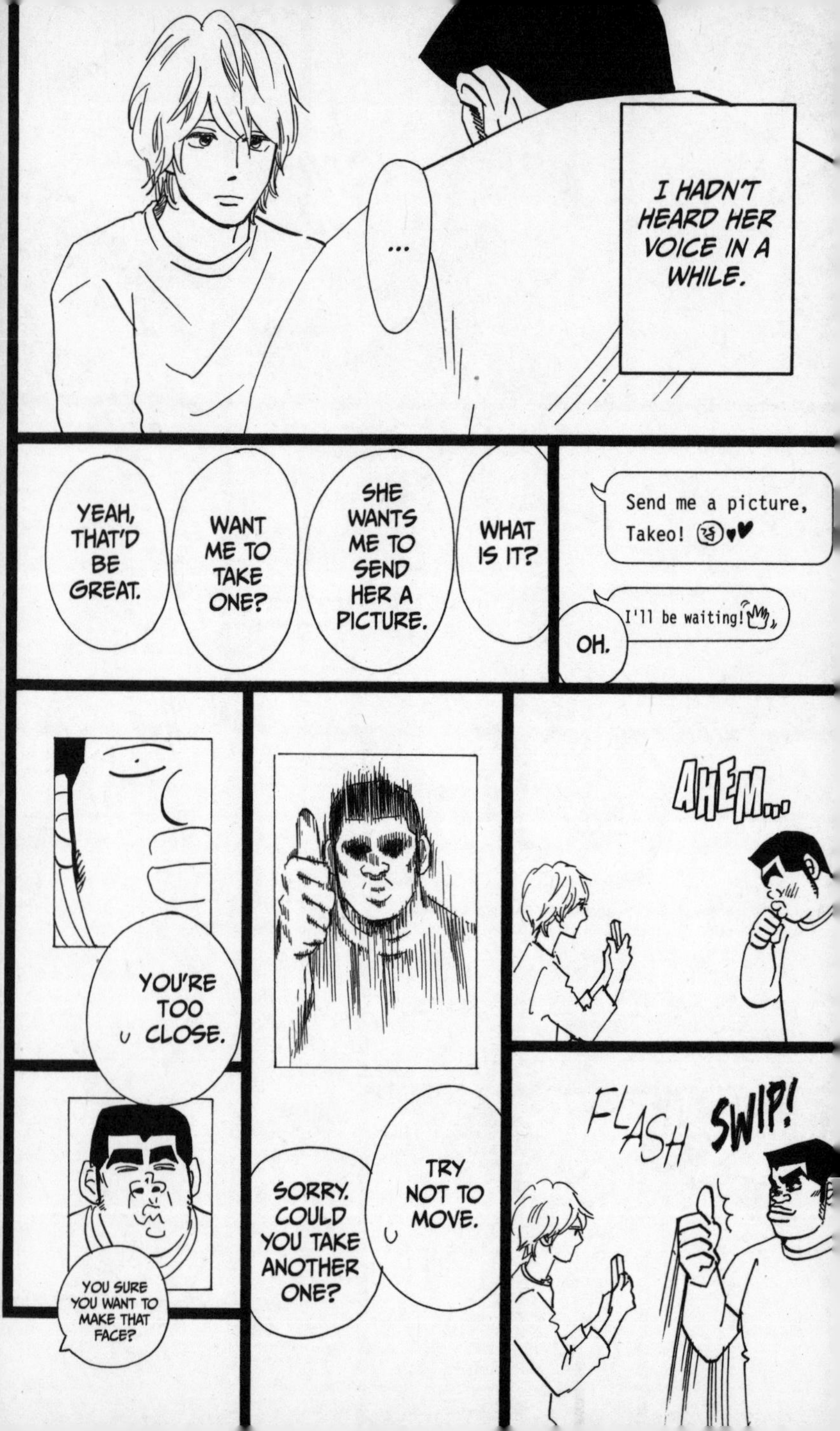

I HADN'T HEARD HER VOICE IN A WHILE.
...
Send me a picture, Takeo!
I'll be waiting!
OH.
WHAT IS IT?
SHE WANTS ME TO SEND HER A PICTURE.
WANT ME TO TAKE ONE?
YEAH, THAT'D BE GREAT.
AHEM...
FLASH
SWIP!
TRY NOT TO MOVE.
SORRY. COULD YOU TAKE ANOTHER ONE?
YOU'RE TOO CLOSE.
YOU SURE YOU WANT TO MAKE THAT FACE?

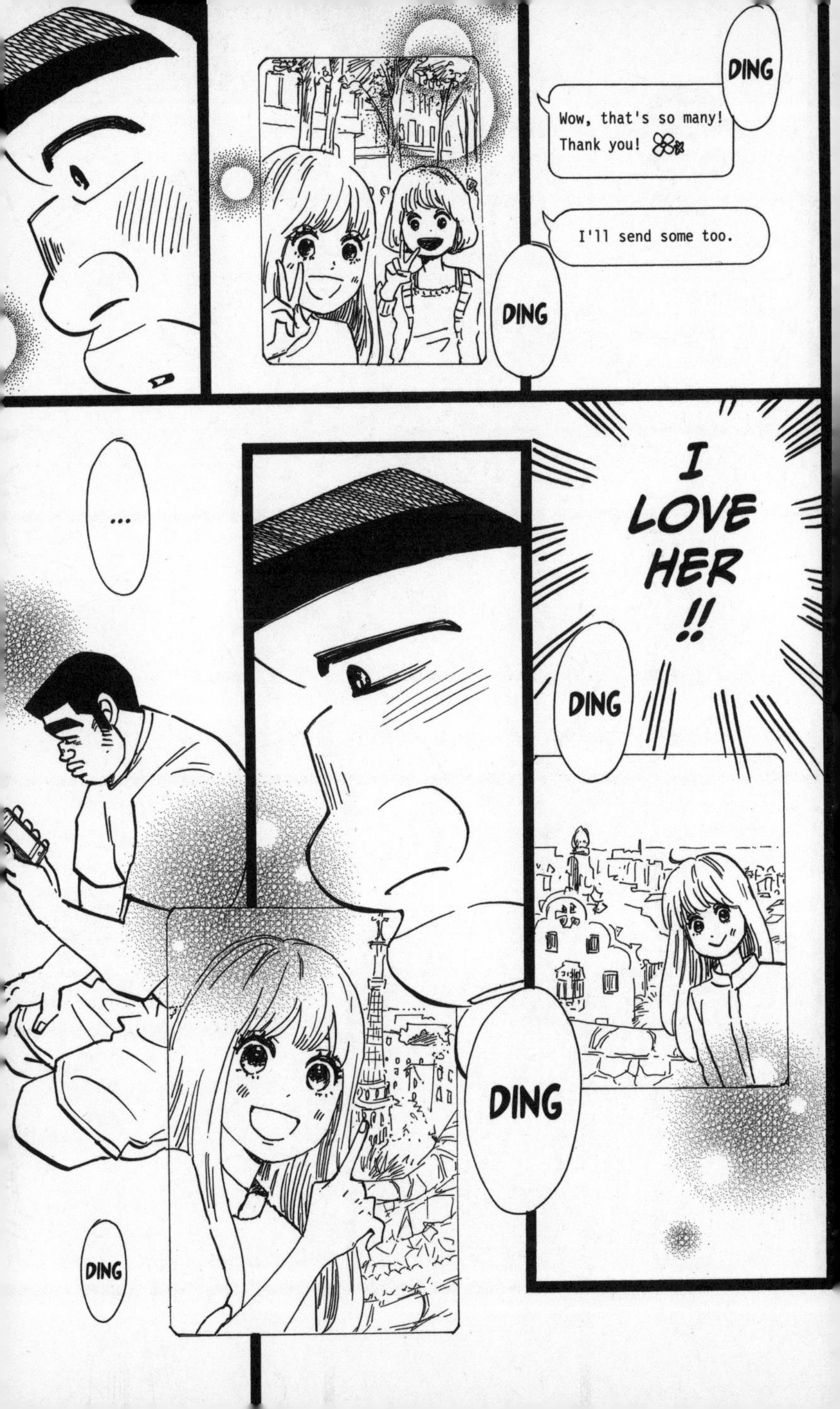

DING
Wow, that's so many! Thank you!
I'll send some too.
DING
I LOVE HER!!
DING
DING
...
DING

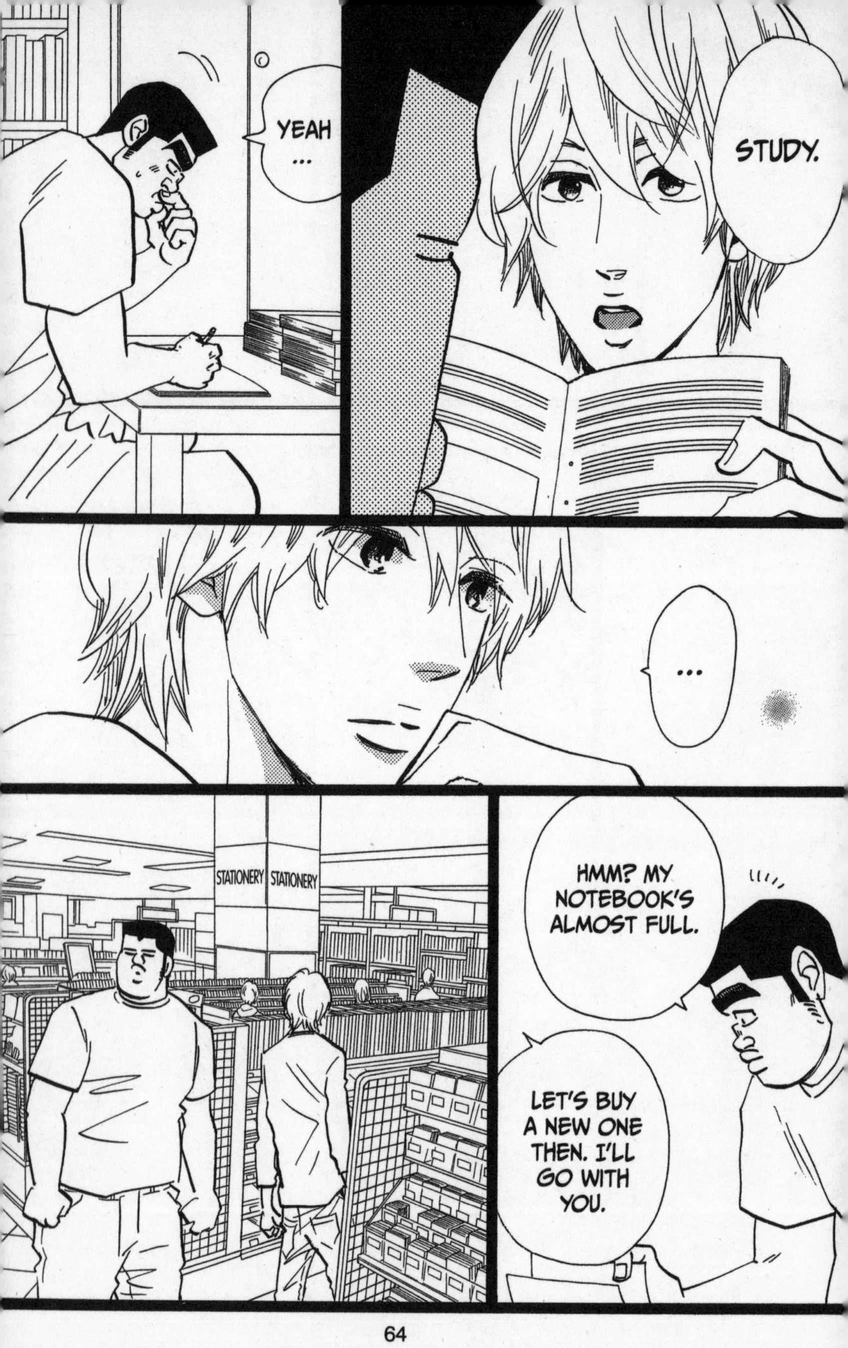
STUDY.
YEAH ...
...
HMM? MY NOTEBOOK'S ALMOST FULL.
LET'S BUY A NEW ONE THEN. I'LL GO WITH YOU.
STATIONERY
STATIONERY

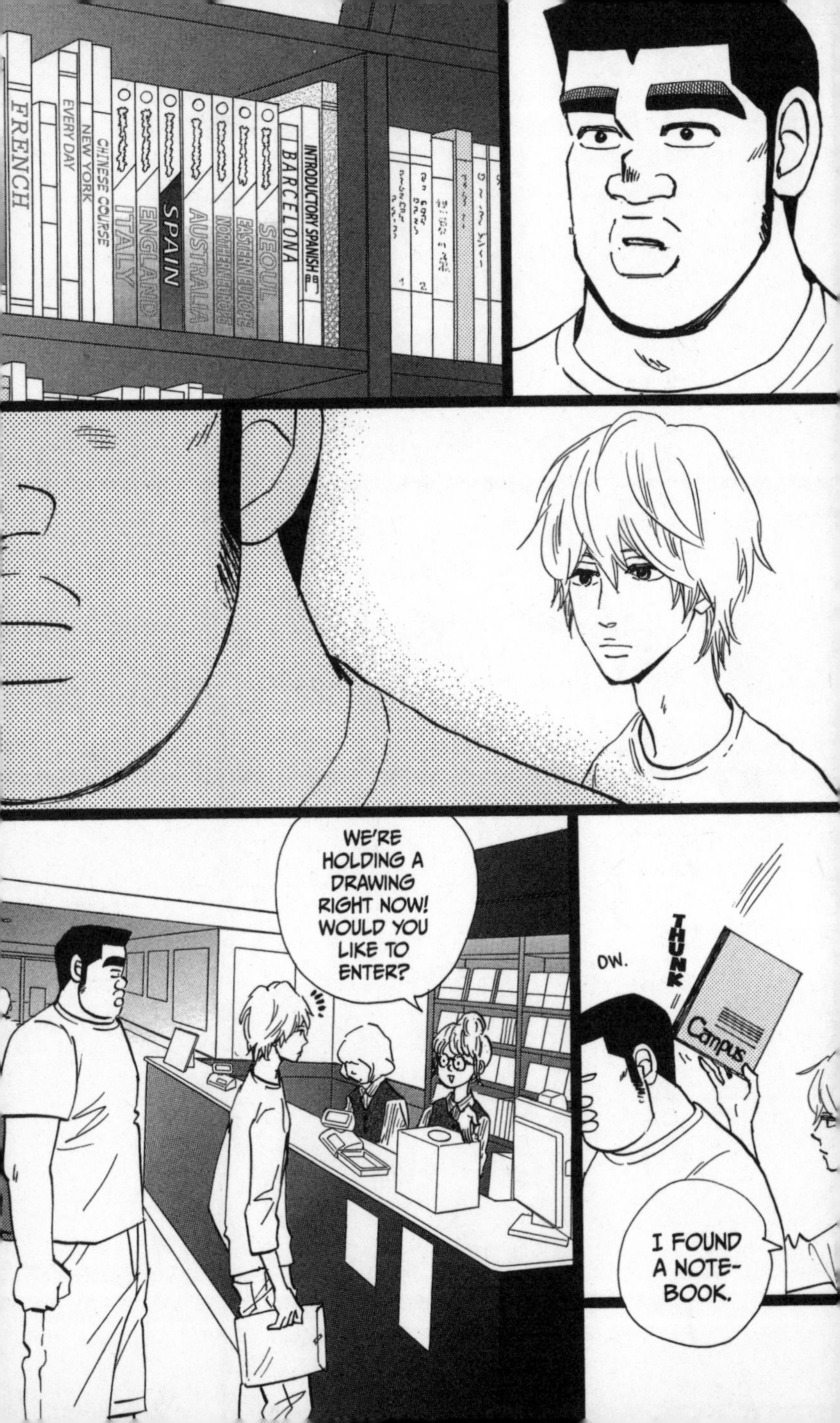
FRENCH
EVERY DAY
NEW YORK
CHINESE COURSE
ITALY
ENGLAND
SPAIN
AUSTRALIA
NORTHERN EUROPE
EASTERN EUROPE
SEOUL
BARCELONA
INTRODUCTORY SPANISH
OW.
THUNK
Campus
I FOUND A NOTE-BOOK.
WE'RE HOLDING A DRAWING RIGHT NOW! WOULD YOU LIKE TO ENTER?

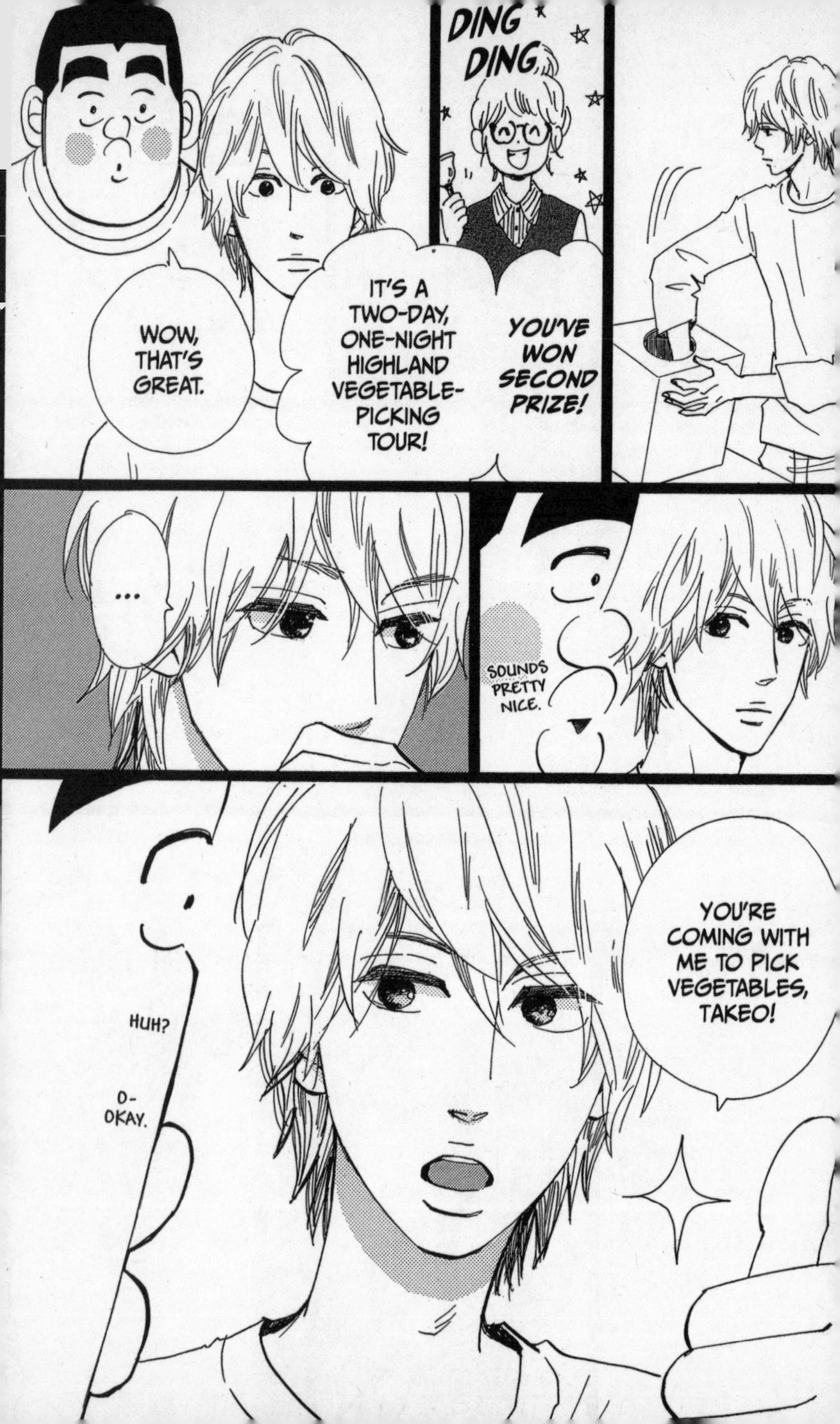
DING DING
YOU'VE WON SECOND PRIZE!
IT'S A TWO-DAY, ONE-NIGHT HIGHLAND VEGETABLE-PICKING TOUR!
WOW, THAT'S GREAT.
SOUNDS PRETTY NICE.
...
YOU'RE COMING WITH ME TO PICK VEGETABLES, TAKEO!
HUH?
O-OKAY.

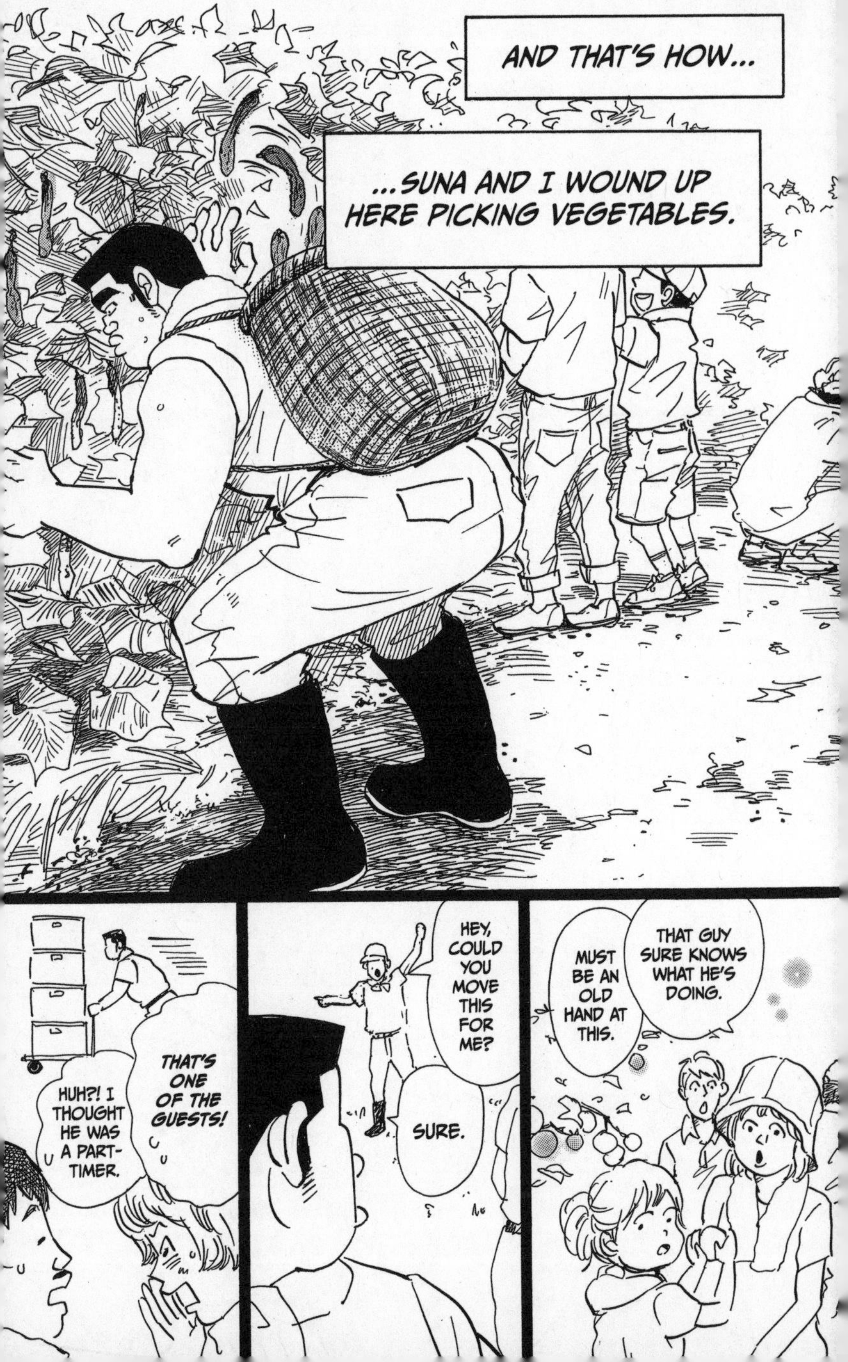
AND THAT'S HOW...
...SUNA AND I WOUND UP HERE PICKING VEGETABLES.
THAT GUY SURE KNOWS WHAT HE'S DOING.
MUST BE AN OLD HAND AT THIS.
HEY, COULD YOU MOVE THIS FOR ME?
SURE.
THAT'S ONE OF THE GUESTS!
HUH?! I THOUGHT HE WAS A PART-TIMER.

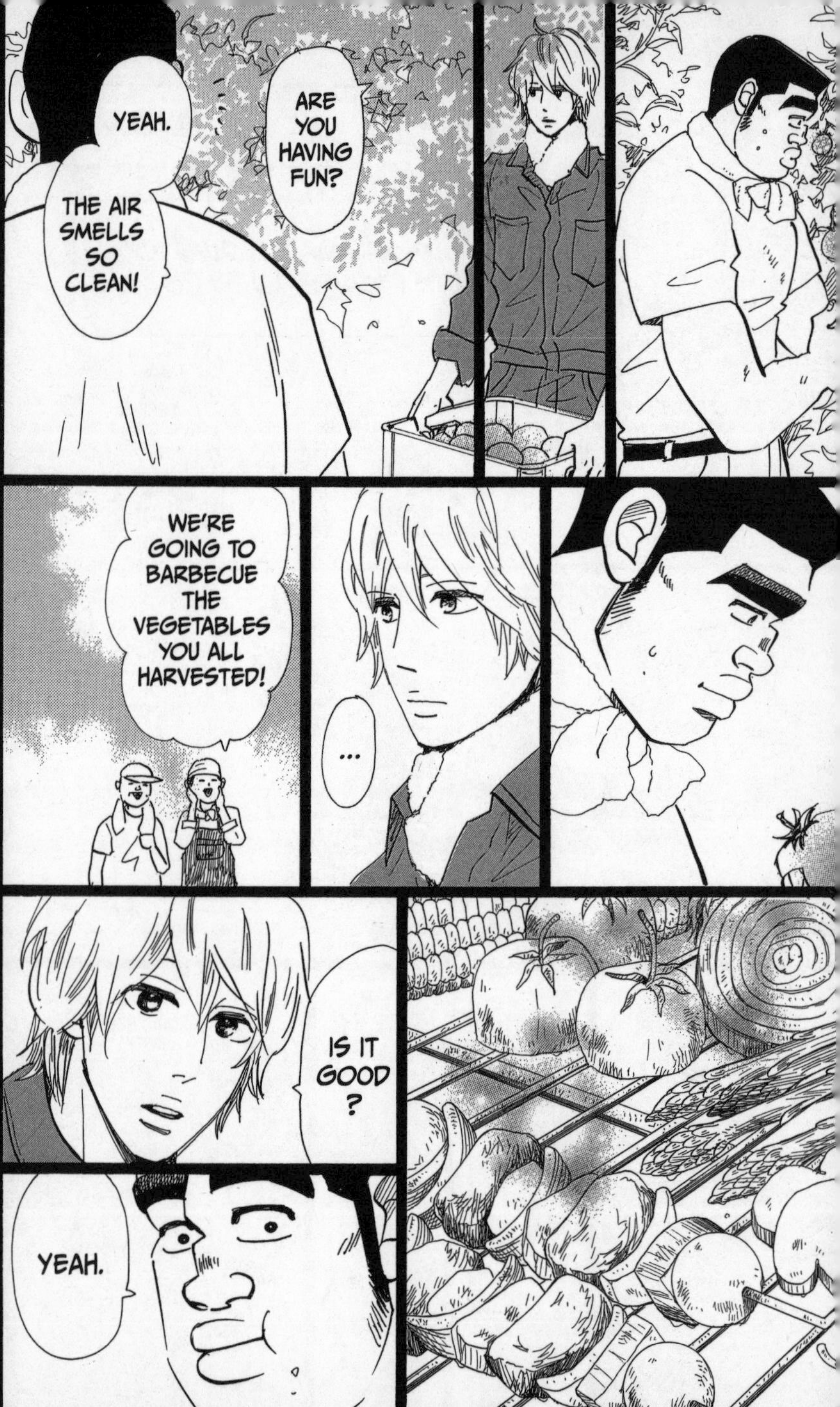
ARE YOU HAVING FUN?
YEAH.
THE AIR SMELLS SO CLEAN!
...
WE'RE GOING TO BARBECUE THE VEGETABLES YOU ALL HARVESTED!
IS IT GOOD?
YEAH.

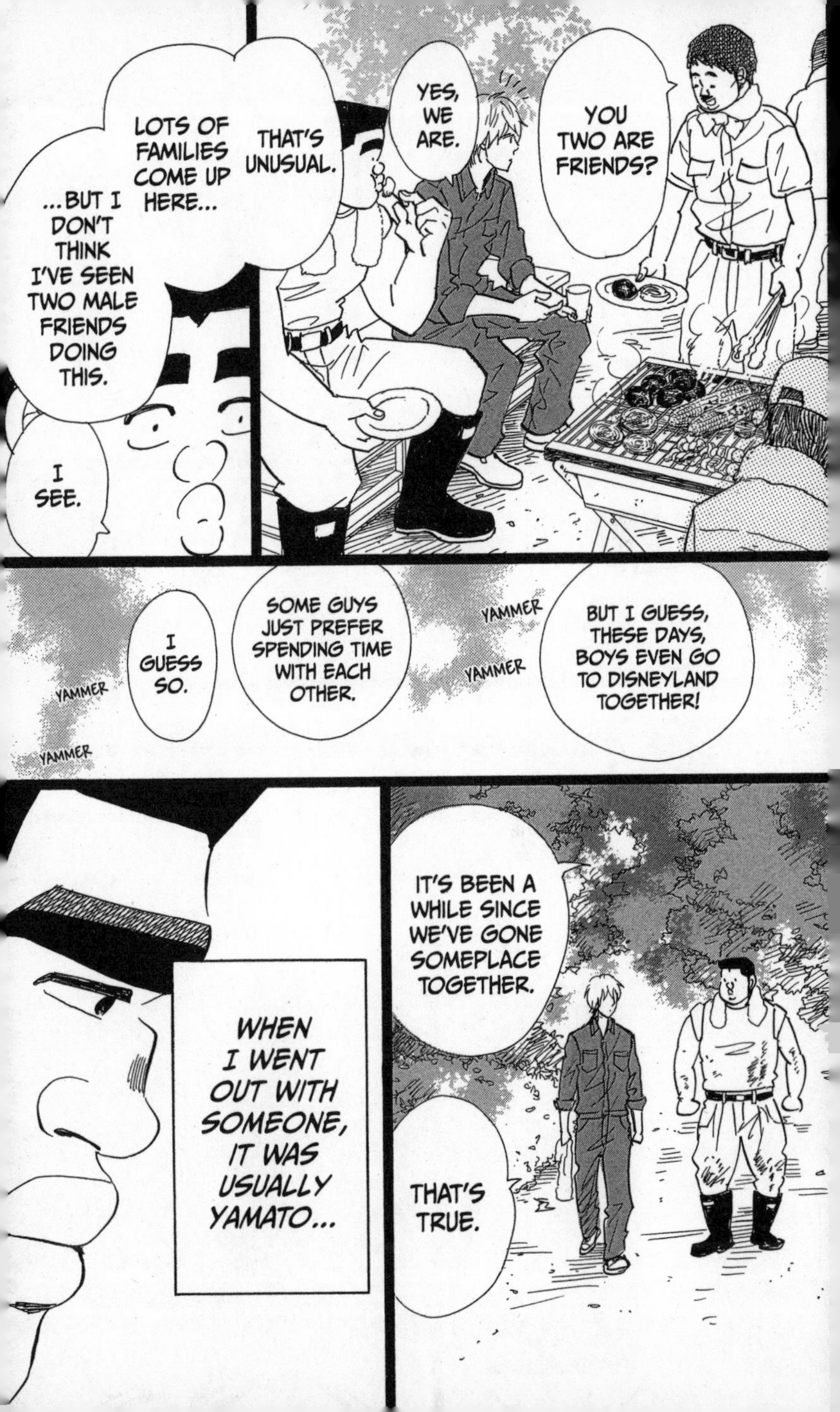
YOU TWO ARE FRIENDS?
YES, WE ARE.
THAT'S UNUSUAL.
LOTS OF FAMILIES COME UP HERE...
...BUT I DON'T THINK I'VE SEEN TWO MALE FRIENDS DOING THIS.
I SEE.
BUT I GUESS, THESE DAYS, BOYS EVEN GO TO DISNEYLAND TOGETHER!
YAMMER
YAMMER
SOME GUYS JUST PREFER SPENDING TIME WITH EACH OTHER.
I GUESS SO.
YAMMER
YAMMER
IT'S BEEN A WHILE SINCE WE'VE GONE SOMEPLACE TOGETHER.
THAT'S TRUE.
WHEN I WENT OUT WITH SOMEONE, IT WAS USUALLY YAMATO...

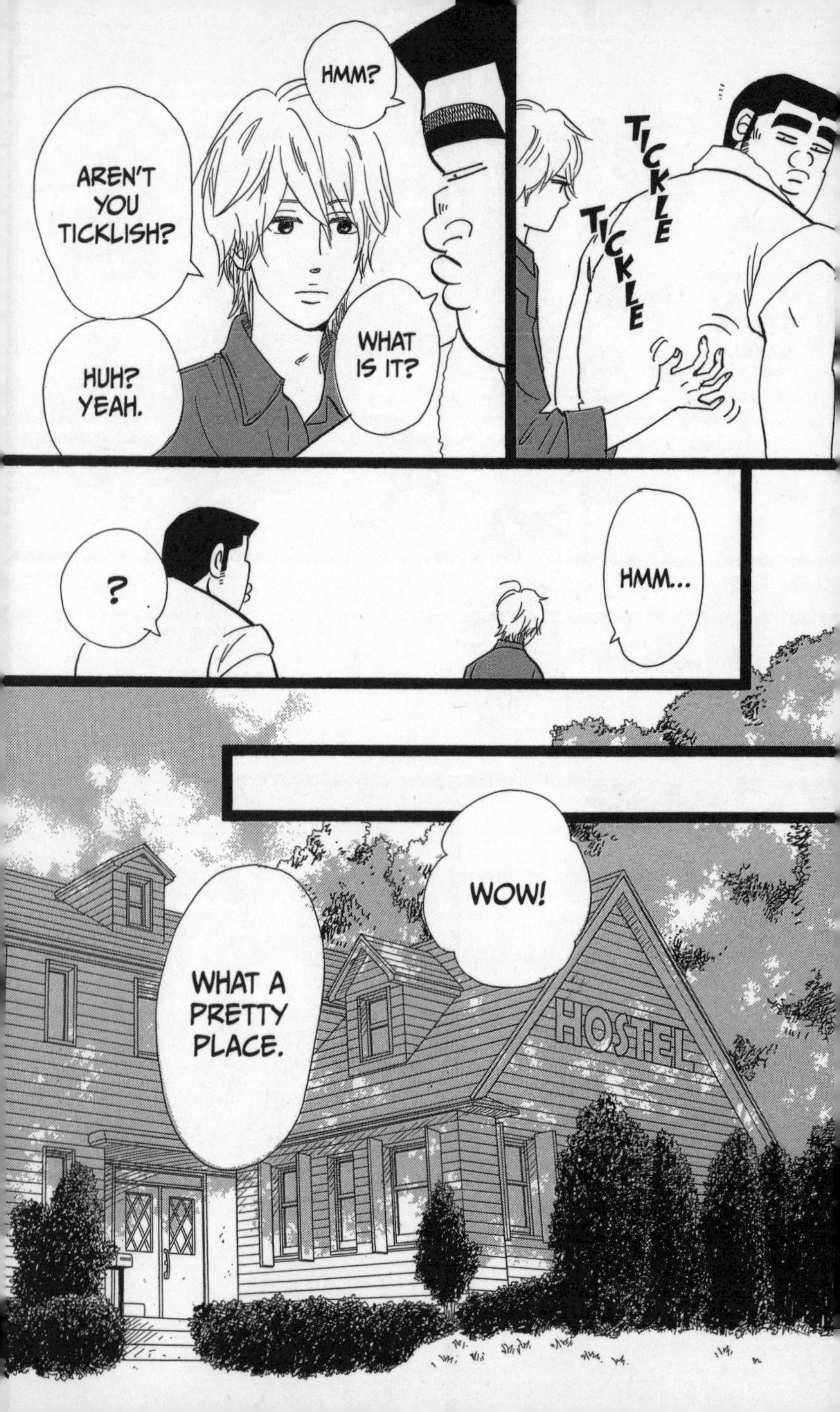
TICKLE
TICKLE
HMM?
WHAT IS IT?
AREN'T YOU TICKLISH?
HUH? YEAH.
HMM...
?
WOW!
WHAT A PRETTY PLACE.
HOSTEL

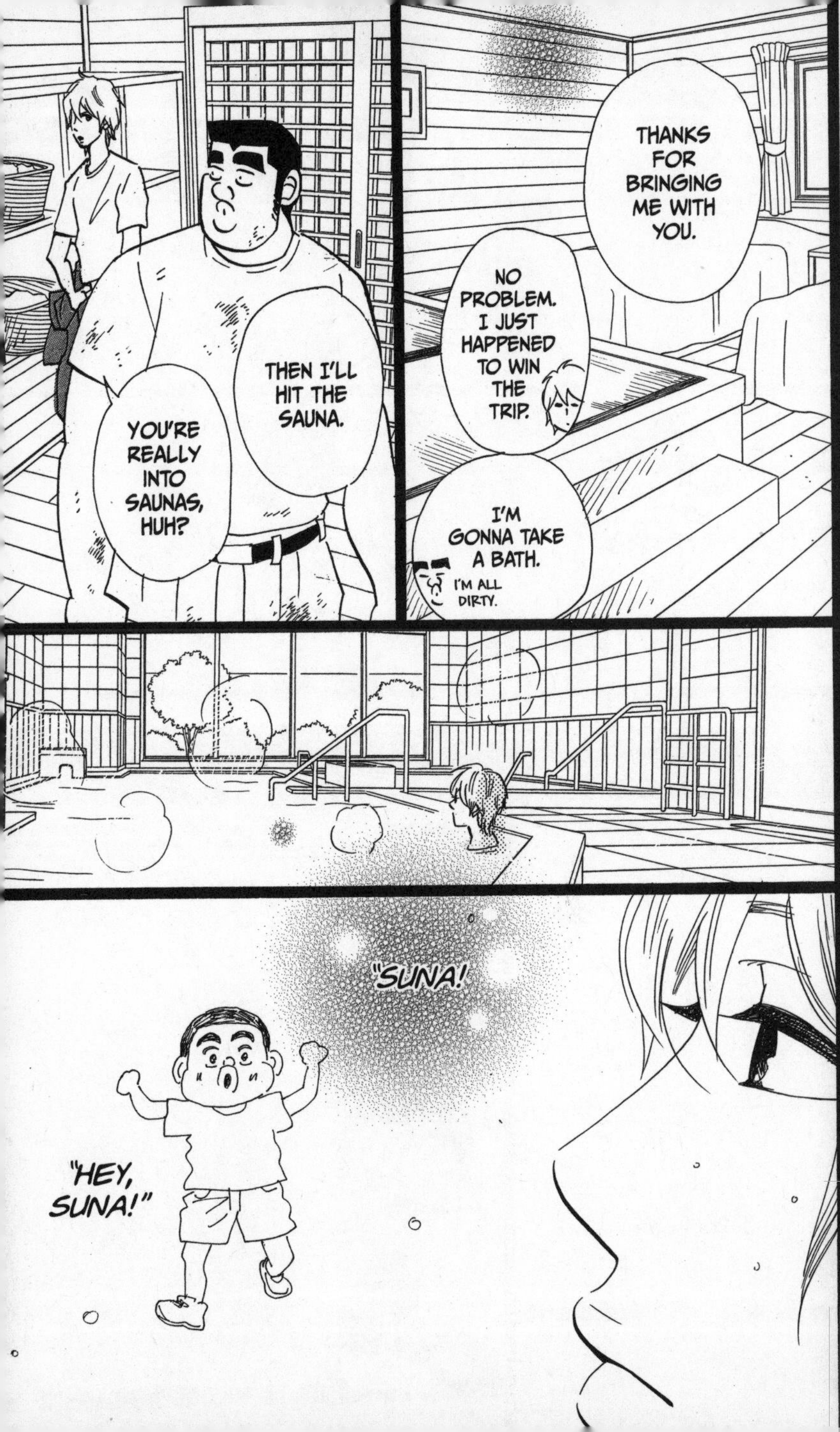
THANKS FOR BRINGING ME WITH YOU.
NO PROBLEM. I JUST HAPPENED TO WIN THE TRIP.
I'M GONNA TAKE A BATH.
I'M ALL DIRTY.
THEN I'LL HIT THE SAUNA.
YOU'RE REALLY INTO SAUNAS, HUH?
"SUNA!
"HEY, SUNA!"

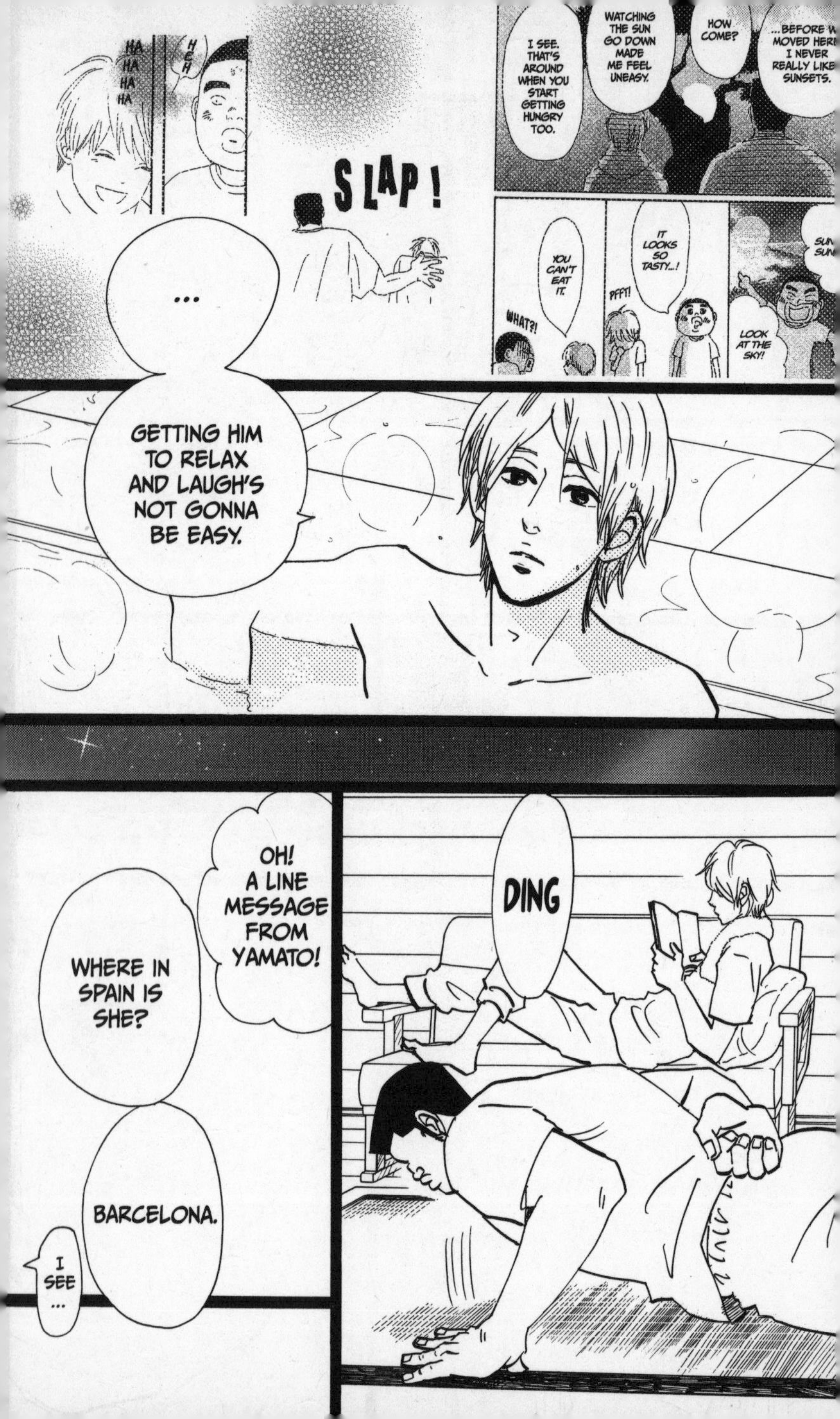
...BEFORE W MOVED HER I NEVER REALLY LIKE SUNSETS.
HOW COME?
WATCHING THE SUN GO DOWN MADE ME FEEL UNEASY.
I SEE. THAT'S AROUND WHEN YOU START GETTING HUNGRY TOO.
LOOK AT THE SKY!
IT LOOKS SO TASTY...!
PFFT!
YOU CAN'T EAT IT.
WHAT?!
HEH
HA HA HA HA
SLAP!
...
GETTING HIM TO RELAX AND LAUGH'S NOT GONNA BE EASY.
DING
OH! A LINE MESSAGE FROM YAMATO!
WHERE IN SPAIN IS SHE?
BARCELONA.
I SEE...

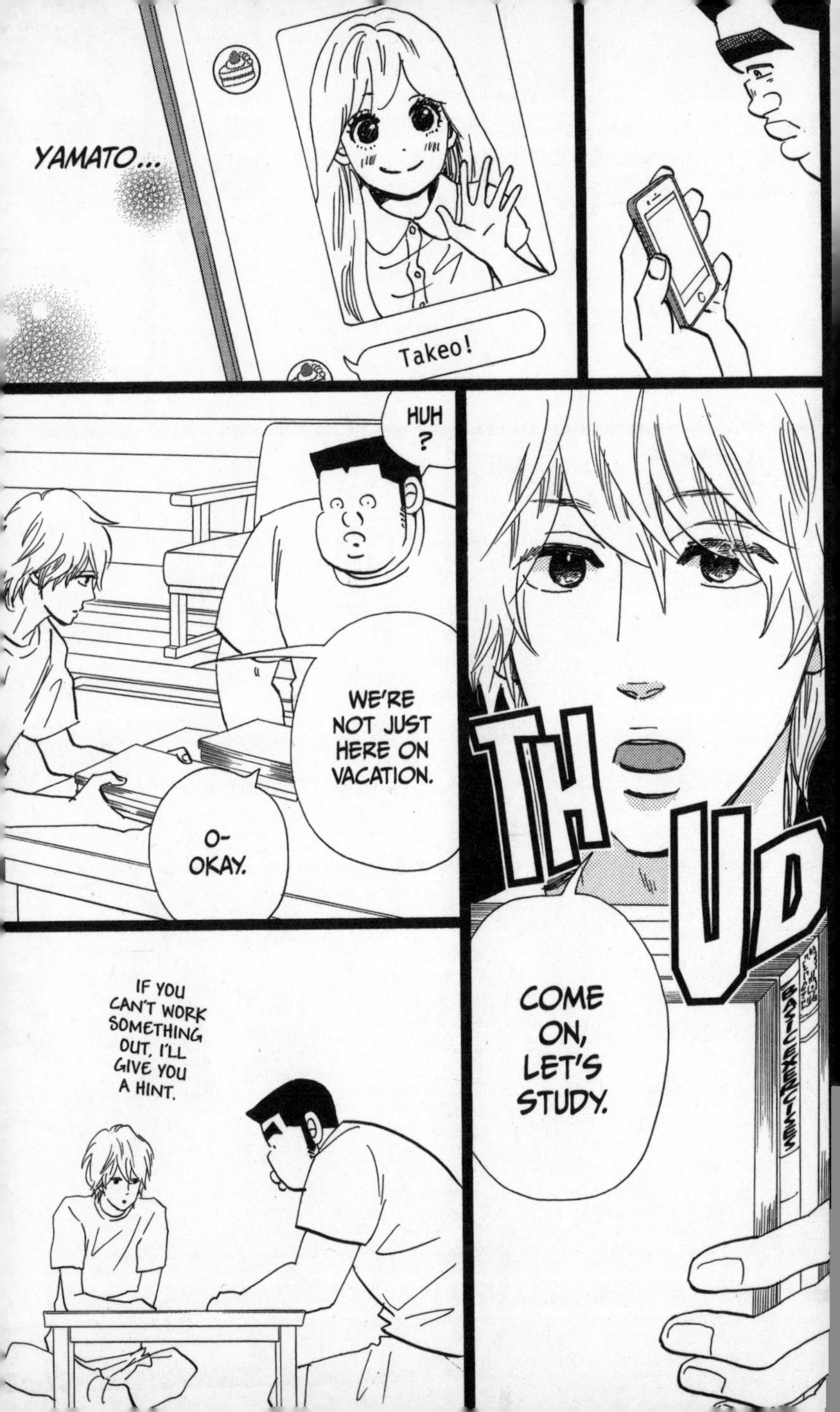
Takeo!
YAMATO...
THUD
COME ON, LET'S STUDY.
BASIC EXERCISES
HUH?
WE'RE NOT JUST HERE ON VACATION.
O-OKAY.
IF YOU CAN'T WORK SOMETHING OUT, I'LL GIVE YOU A HINT.

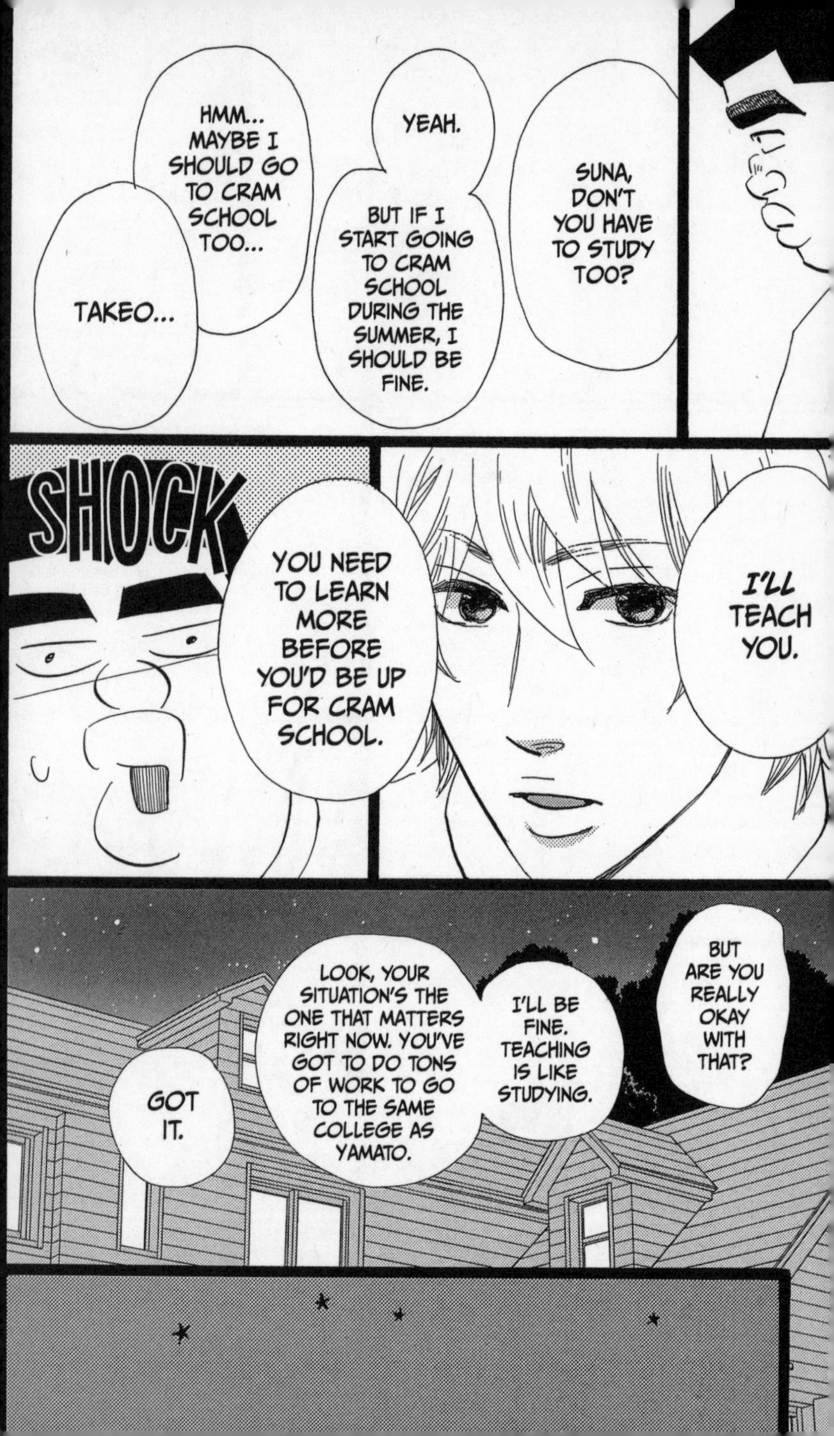
SUNA, DON'T YOU HAVE TO STUDY TOO?
YEAH.
BUT IF I START GOING TO CRAM SCHOOL DURING THE SUMMER, I SHOULD BE FINE.
HMM... MAYBE I SHOULD GO TO CRAM SCHOOL TOO...
TAKEO...
I'LL TEACH YOU.
YOU NEED TO LEARN MORE BEFORE YOU'D BE UP FOR CRAM SCHOOL.
SHOCK
BUT ARE YOU REALLY OKAY WITH THAT?
I'LL BE FINE. TEACHING IS LIKE STUDYING.
LOOK, YOUR SITUATION'S THE ONE THAT MATTERS RIGHT NOW. YOU'VE GOT TO DO TONS OF WORK TO GO TO THE SAME COLLEGE AS YAMATO.
GOT IT.

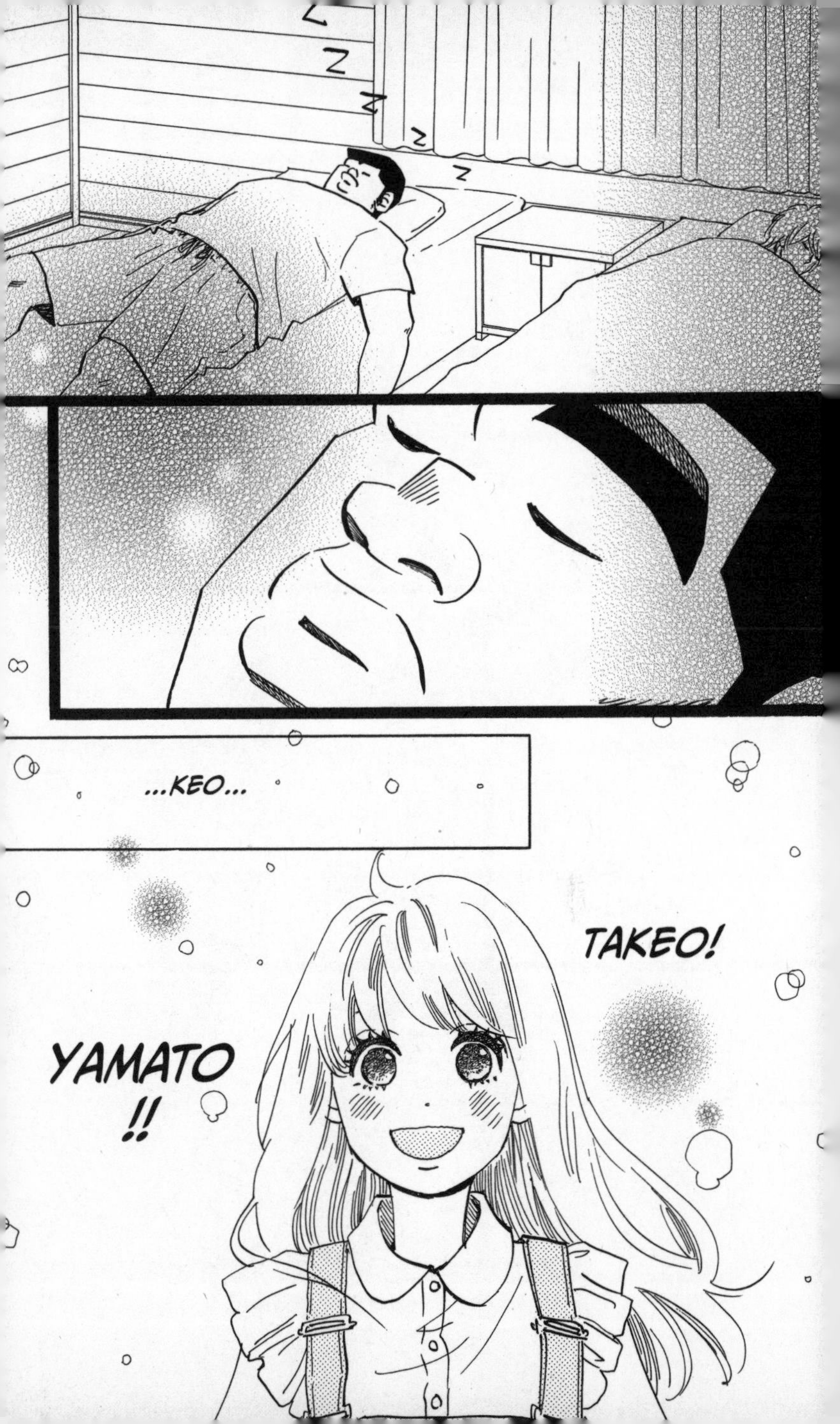
Z Z Z Z Z
...KEO...
TAKEO!
YAMATO !!

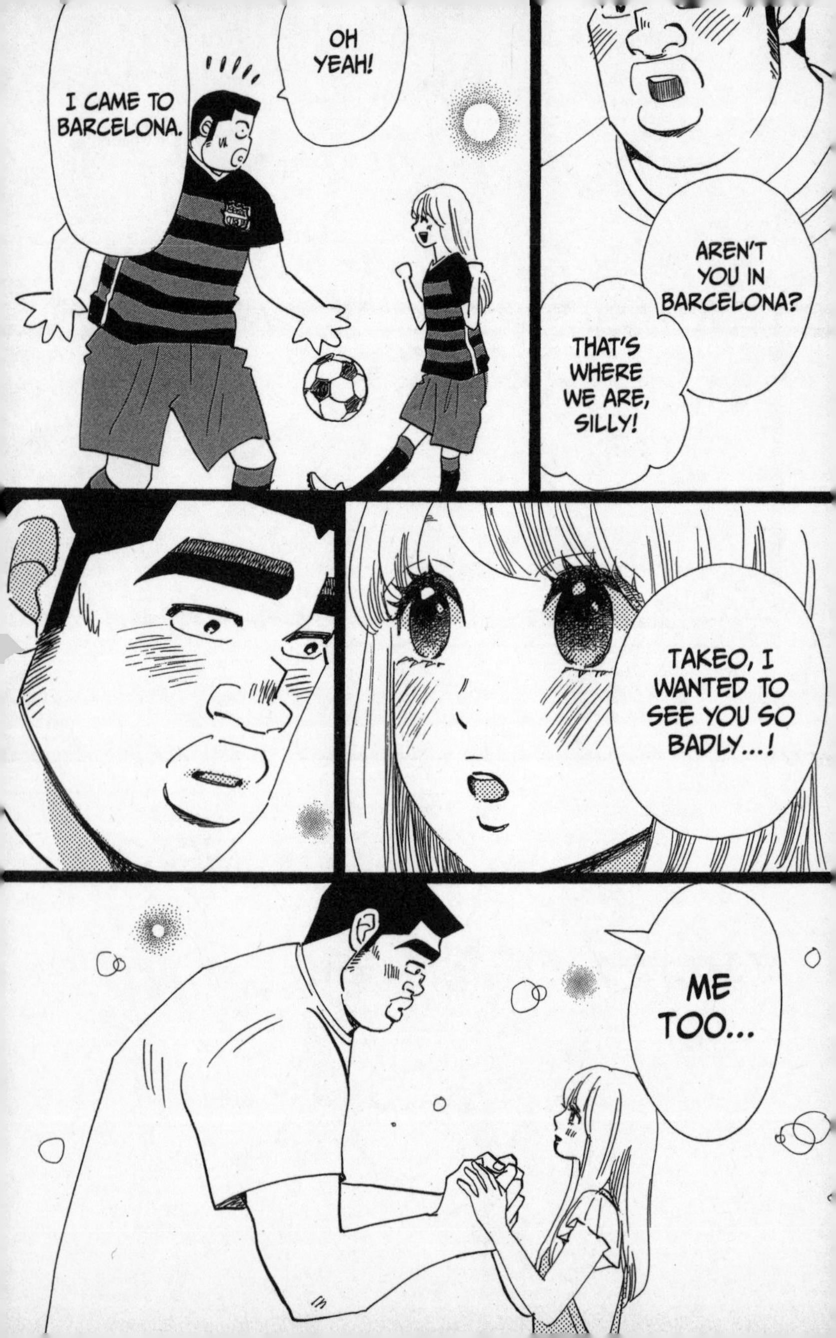
AREN'T YOU IN BARCELONA?
THAT'S WHERE WE ARE, SILLY!
OH YEAH!
I CAME TO BARCELONA.
TAKEO, I WANTED TO SEE YOU SO BADLY...!
ME TOO...

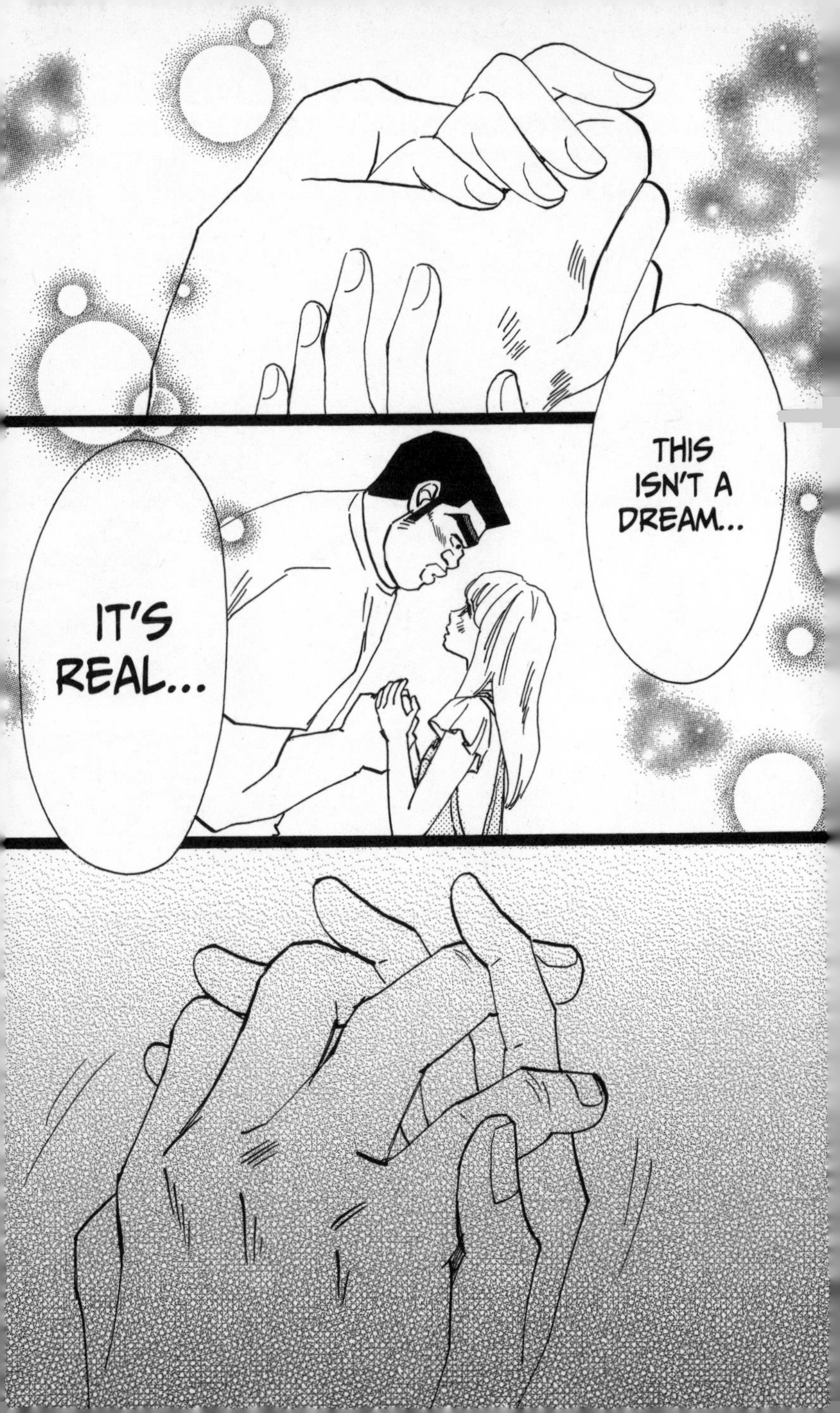
THIS ISN'T A DREAM...
IT'S REAL...

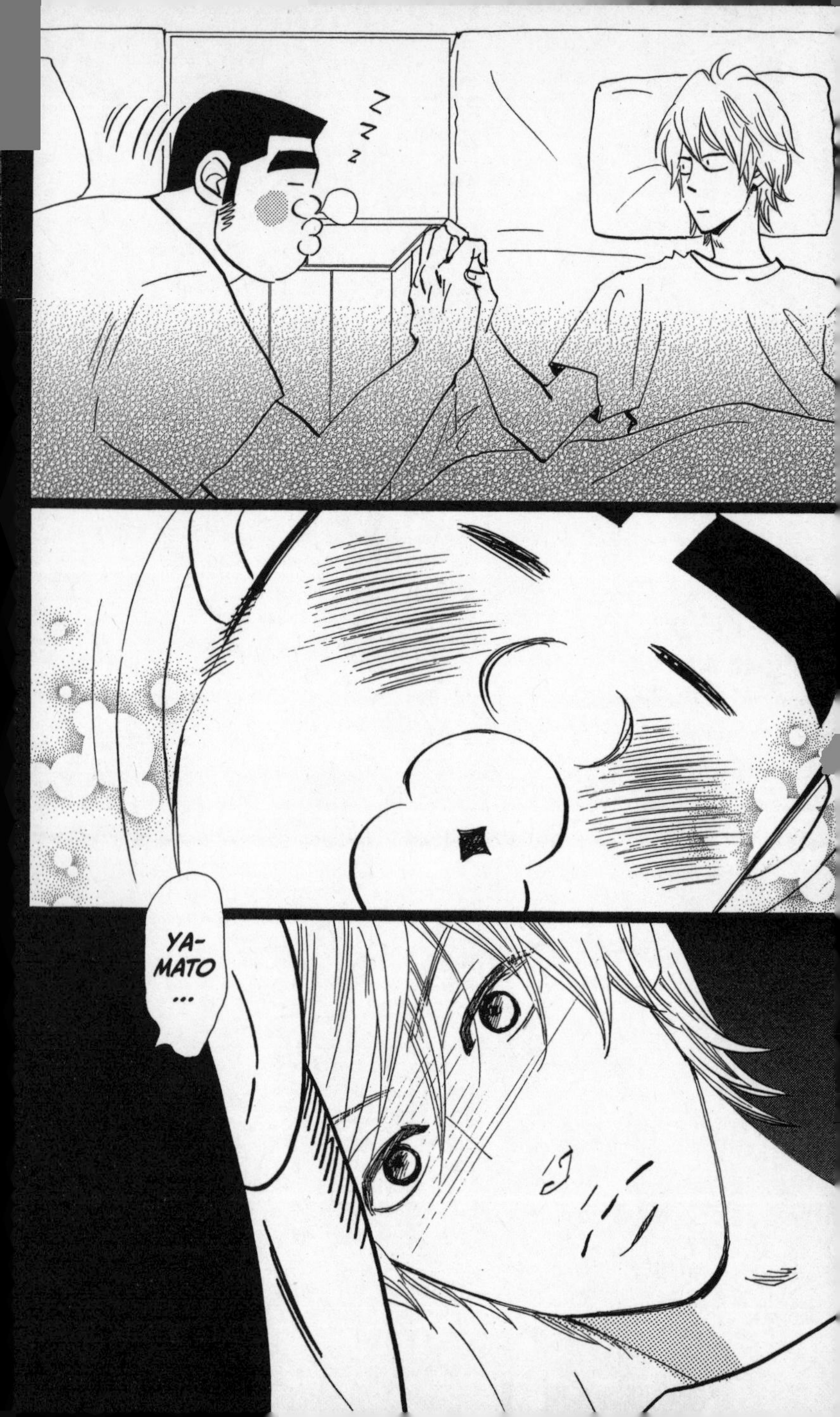
ZZZ
YA-MATO ...

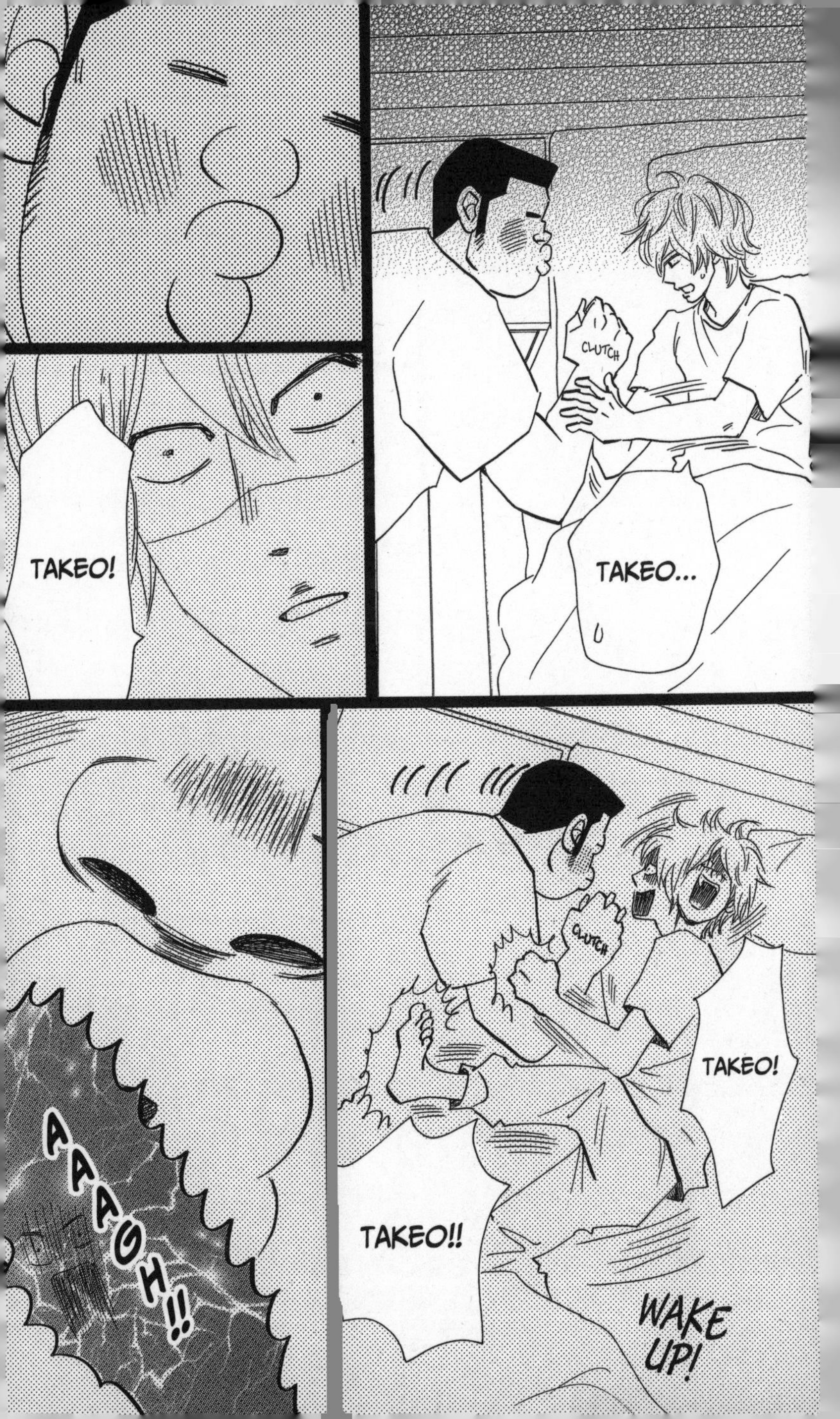

CLUTCH
TAKEO...
TAKEO!
CLUTCH
TAKEO!
TAKEO!!
WAKE UP!
AAAGH!!

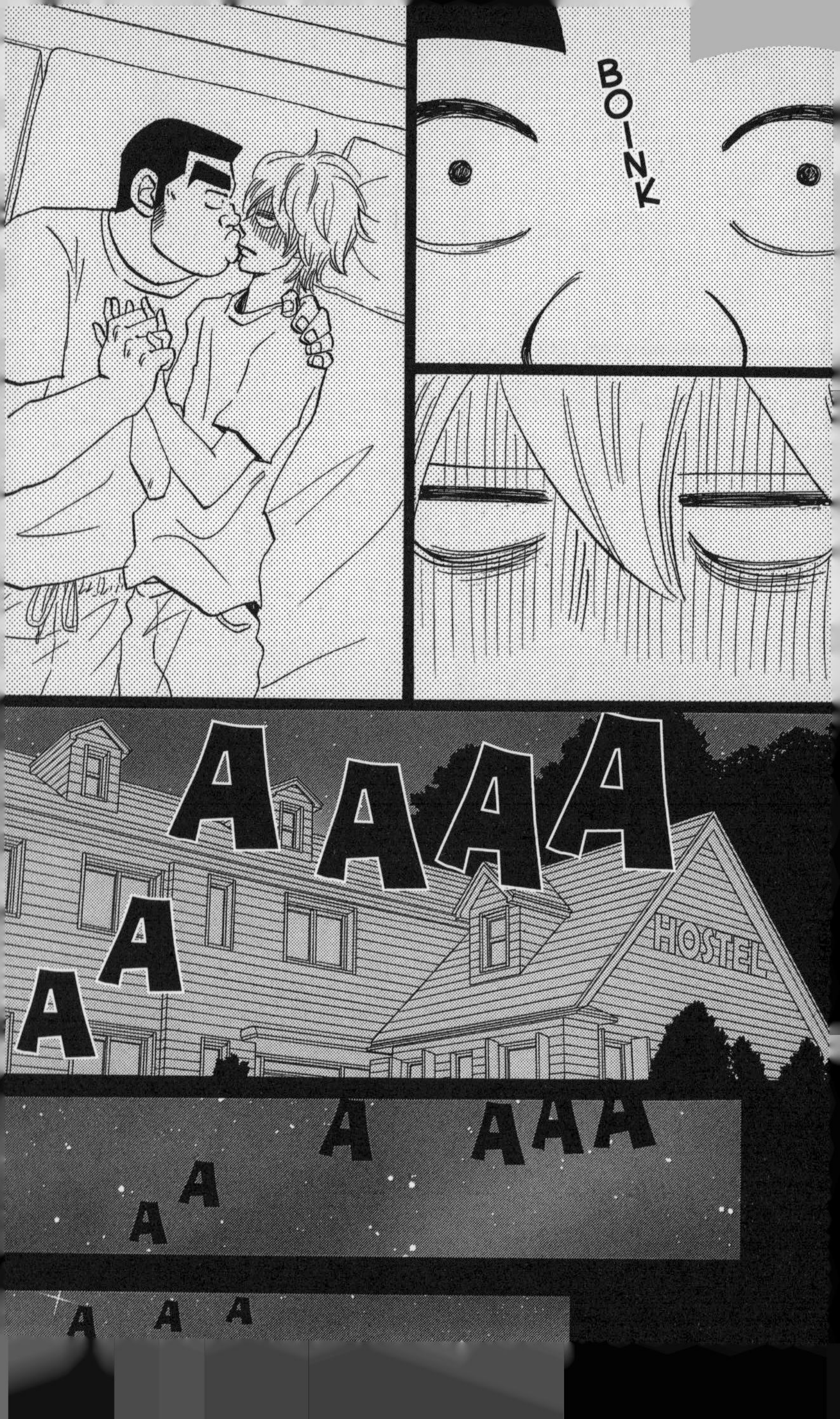

BOINK
AAAAAA
HOSTEL
AAAAAA
AAA

THANK YOU FOR JOINING OUR TOUR!

HERE ARE SOME VEGE-TABLES TO TAKE HOME WITH YOU!

CHIRP CHIRP CHIRP

...

KA-SHUNK

KA-SHUNK

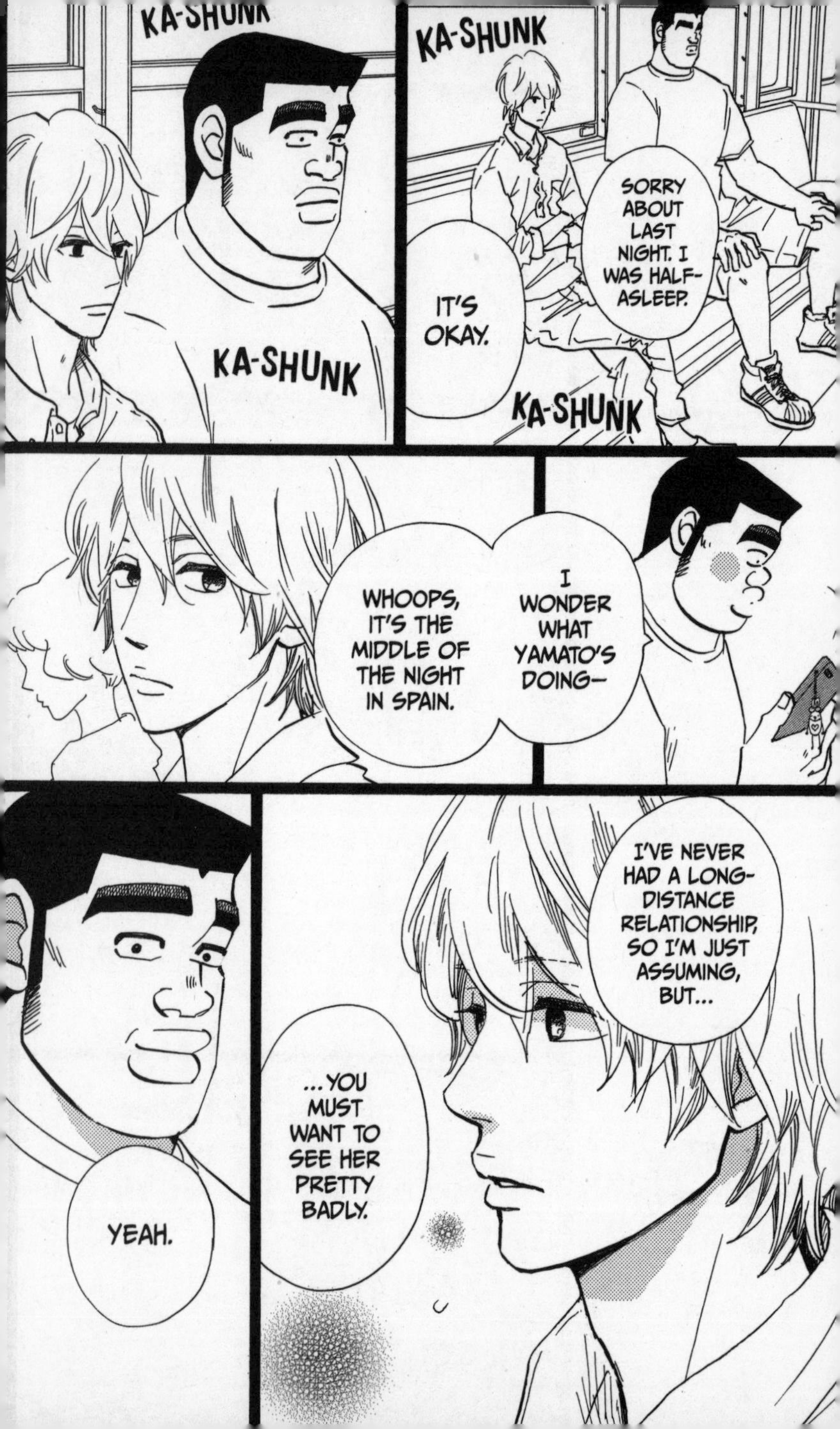
KA-SHUNK
SORRY ABOUT LAST NIGHT. I WAS HALF-ASLEEP.
IT'S OKAY.
KA-SHUNK
KA-SHUNK
KA-SHUNK
I WONDER WHAT YAMATO'S DOING—
WHOOPS, IT'S THE MIDDLE OF THE NIGHT IN SPAIN.
I'VE NEVER HAD A LONG-DISTANCE RELATIONSHIP, SO I'M JUST ASSUMING, BUT...
...YOU MUST WANT TO SEE HER PRETTY BADLY.
YEAH.

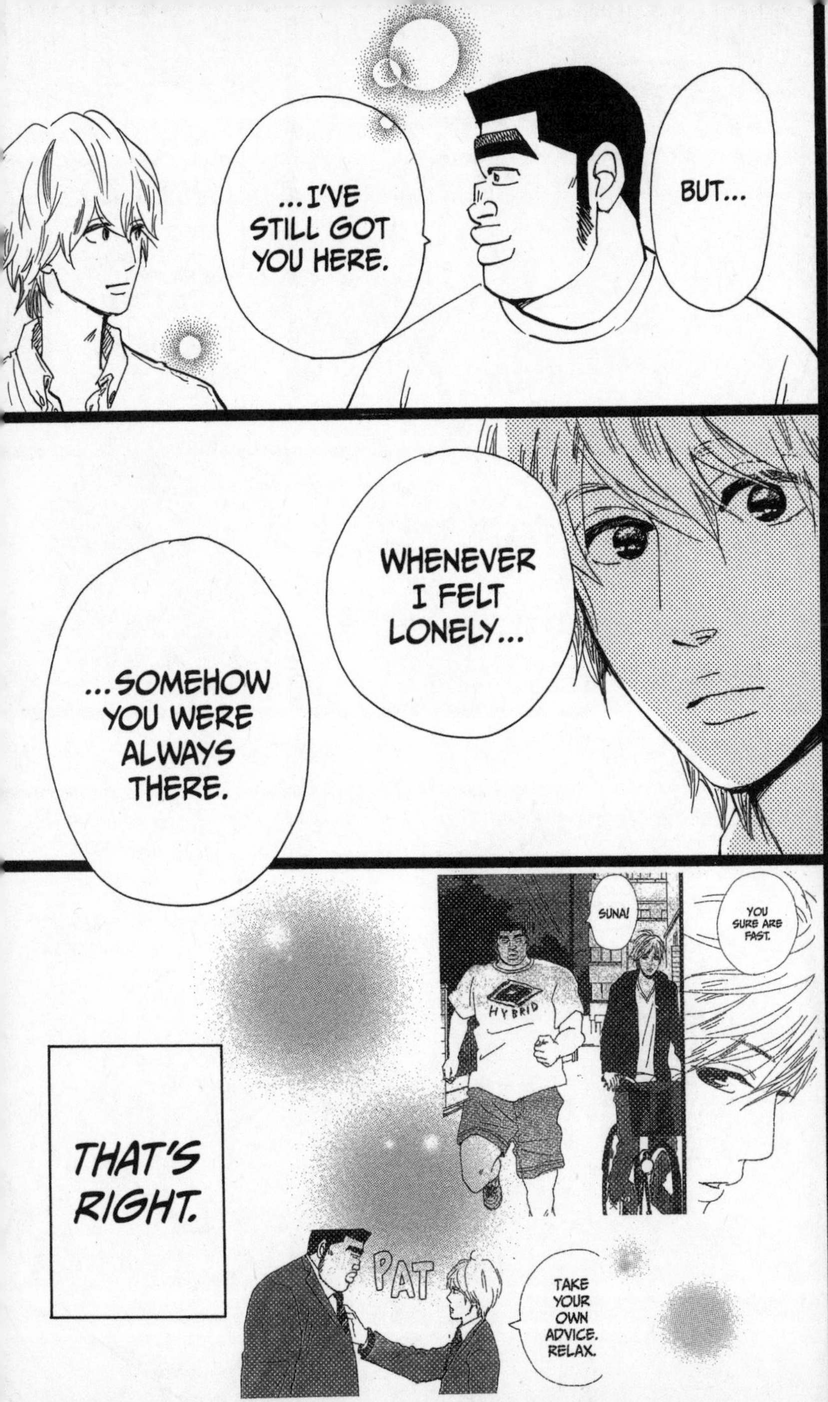
BUT...
...I'VE STILL GOT YOU HERE.
WHENEVER I FELT LONELY...
...SOMEHOW YOU WERE ALWAYS THERE.
YOU SURE ARE FAST.
SUNA!
HYBRID
TAKE YOUR OWN ADVICE. RELAX.
PAT
THAT'S RIGHT.

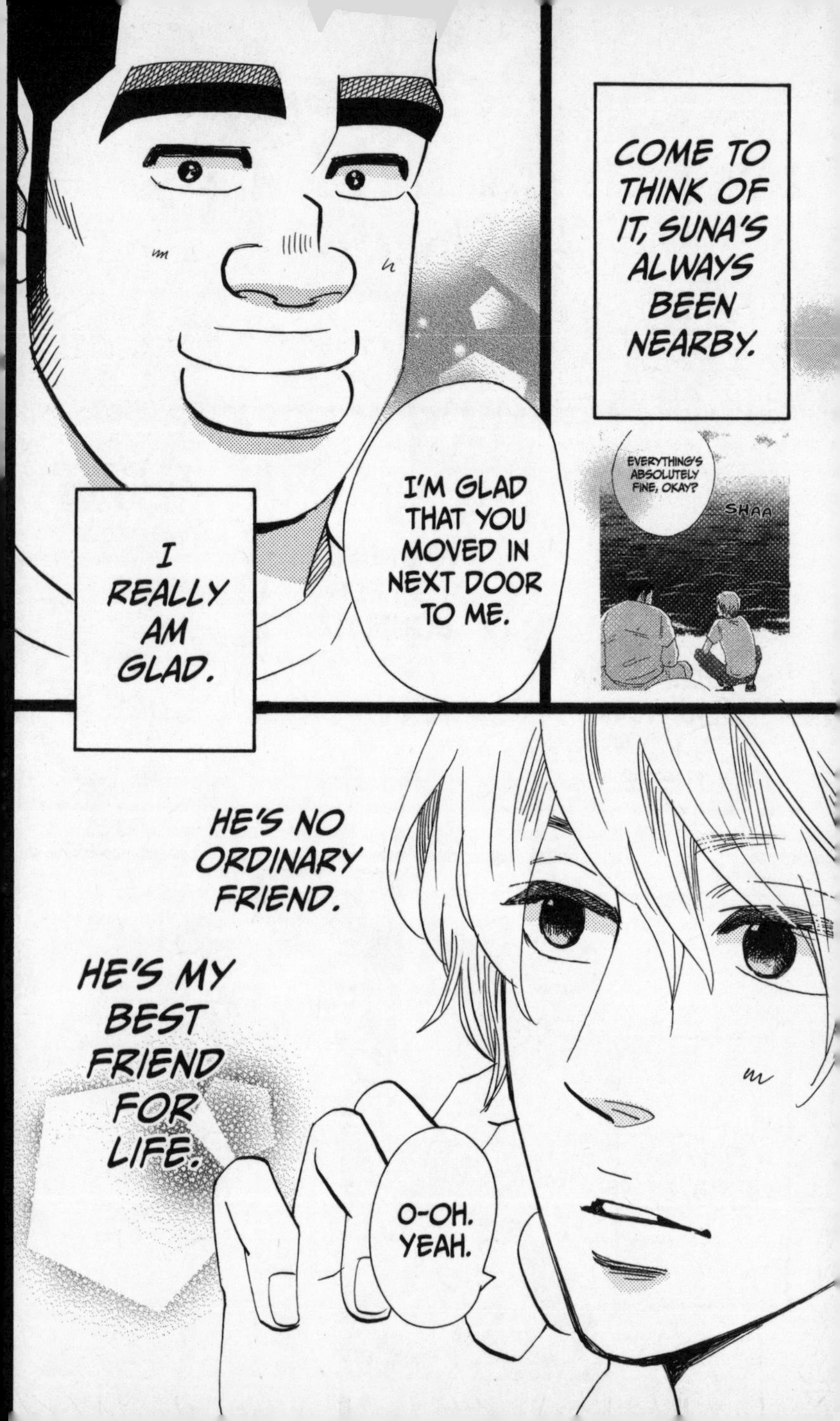
COME TO THINK OF IT, SUNA'S ALWAYS BEEN NEARBY.
EVERYTHING'S ABSOLUTELY FINE, OKAY?
SHAA
I'M GLAD THAT YOU MOVED IN NEXT DOOR TO ME.
I REALLY AM GLAD.
HE'S NO ORDINARY FRIEND.
HE'S MY BEST FRIEND FOR LIFE.
O-OH. YEAH.

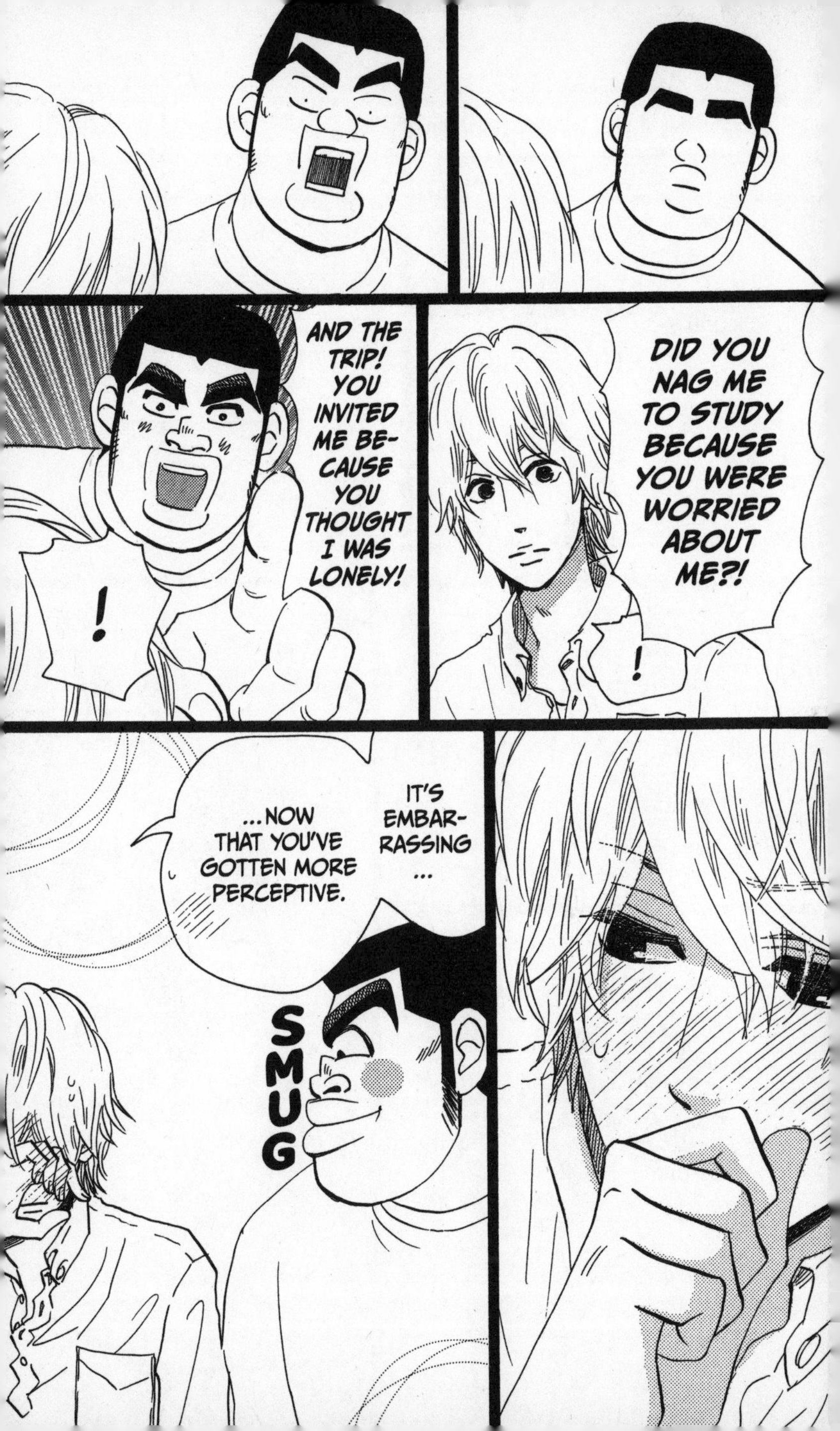
DID YOU NAG ME TO STUDY BECAUSE YOU WERE WORRIED ABOUT ME?!
!
AND THE TRIP! YOU INVITED ME BE-CAUSE YOU THOUGHT I WAS LONELY!
!
IT'S EMBAR-RASSING ...
...NOW THAT YOU'VE GOTTEN MORE PERCEPTIVE.
SMUG

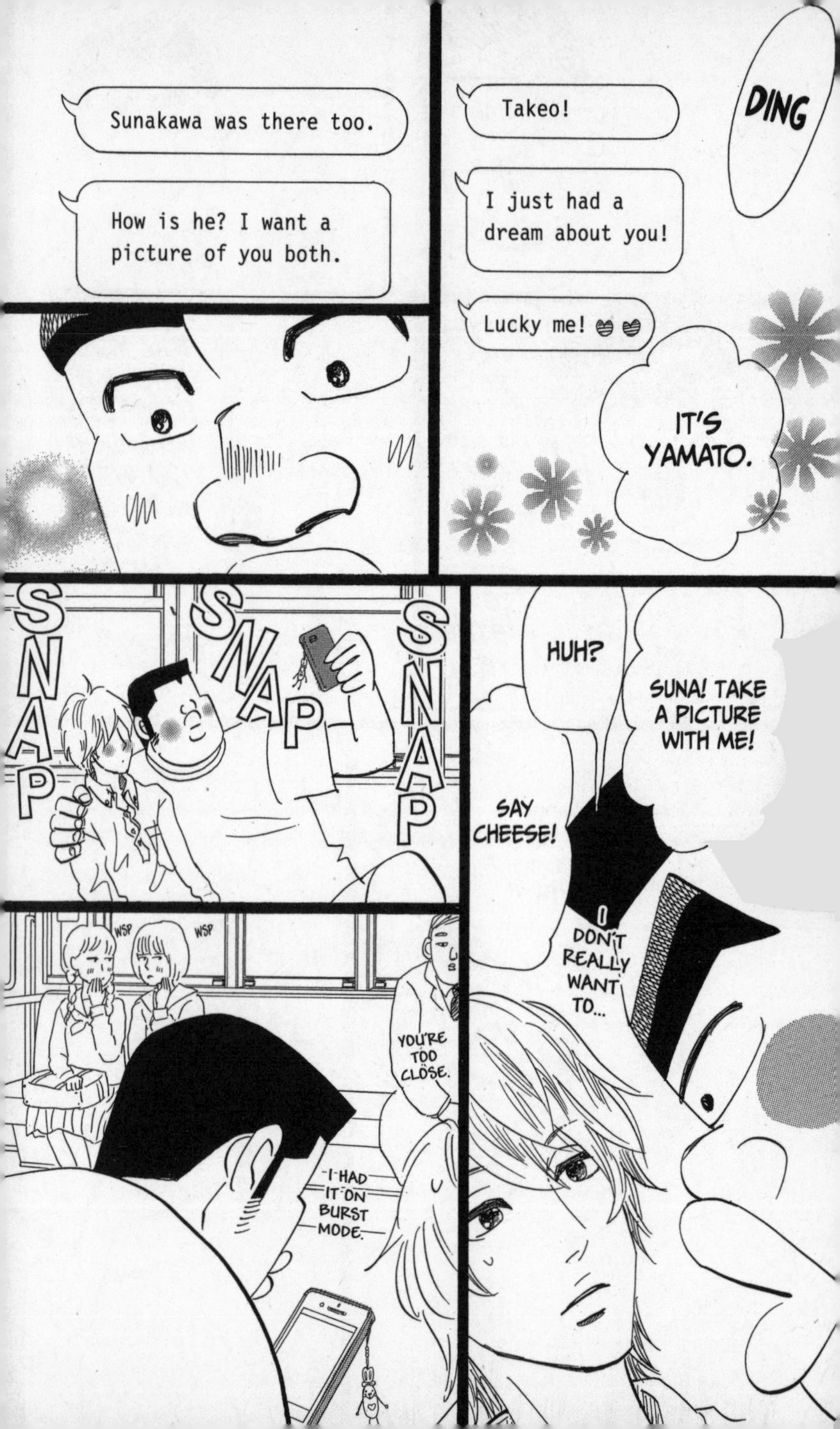
DING
Takeo!
I just had a dream about you!
Lucky me!
IT'S YAMATO.
Sunakawa was there too.
How is he? I want a picture of you both.
SUNA! TAKE A PICTURE WITH ME!
HUH?
SAY CHEESE!
I DON'T REALLY WANT TO...
SNAP
SNAP
SNAP
WSP
WSP
YOU'RE TOO CLOSE.
I HAD IT ON BURST MODE.

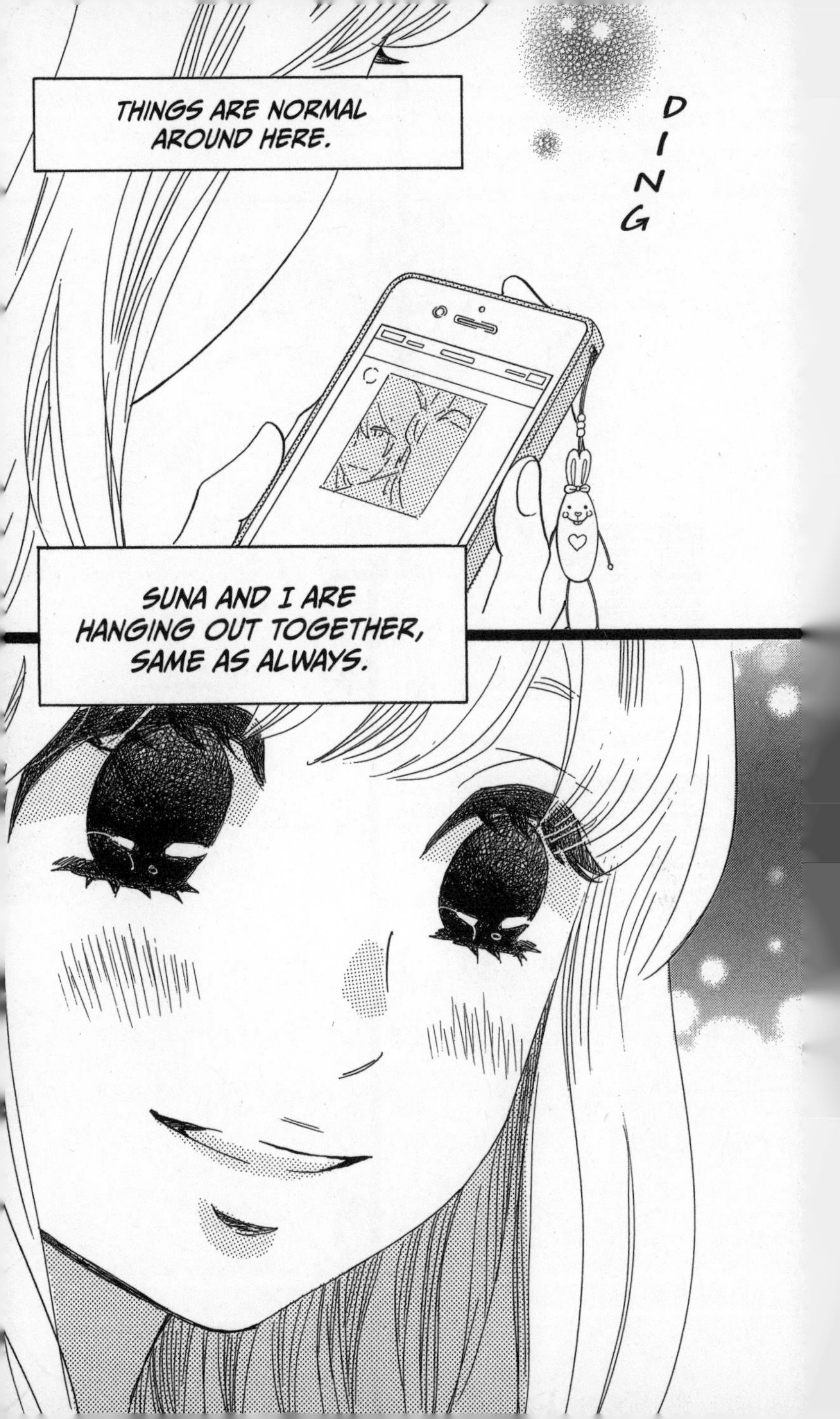
DING
THINGS ARE NORMAL AROUND HERE.
SUNA AND I ARE HANGING OUT TOGETHER, SAME AS ALWAYS.

 You both look great!

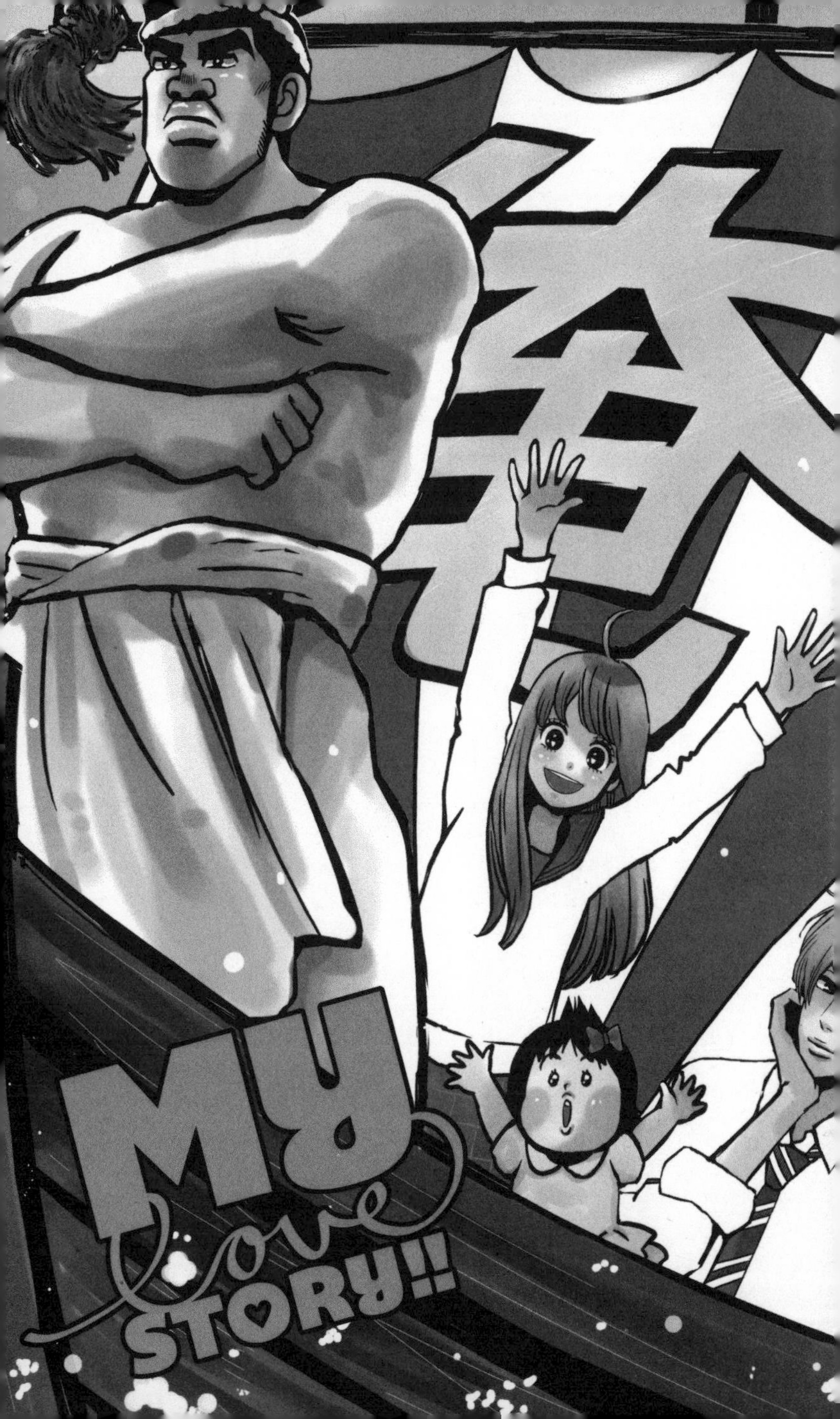
My Love STORY!!

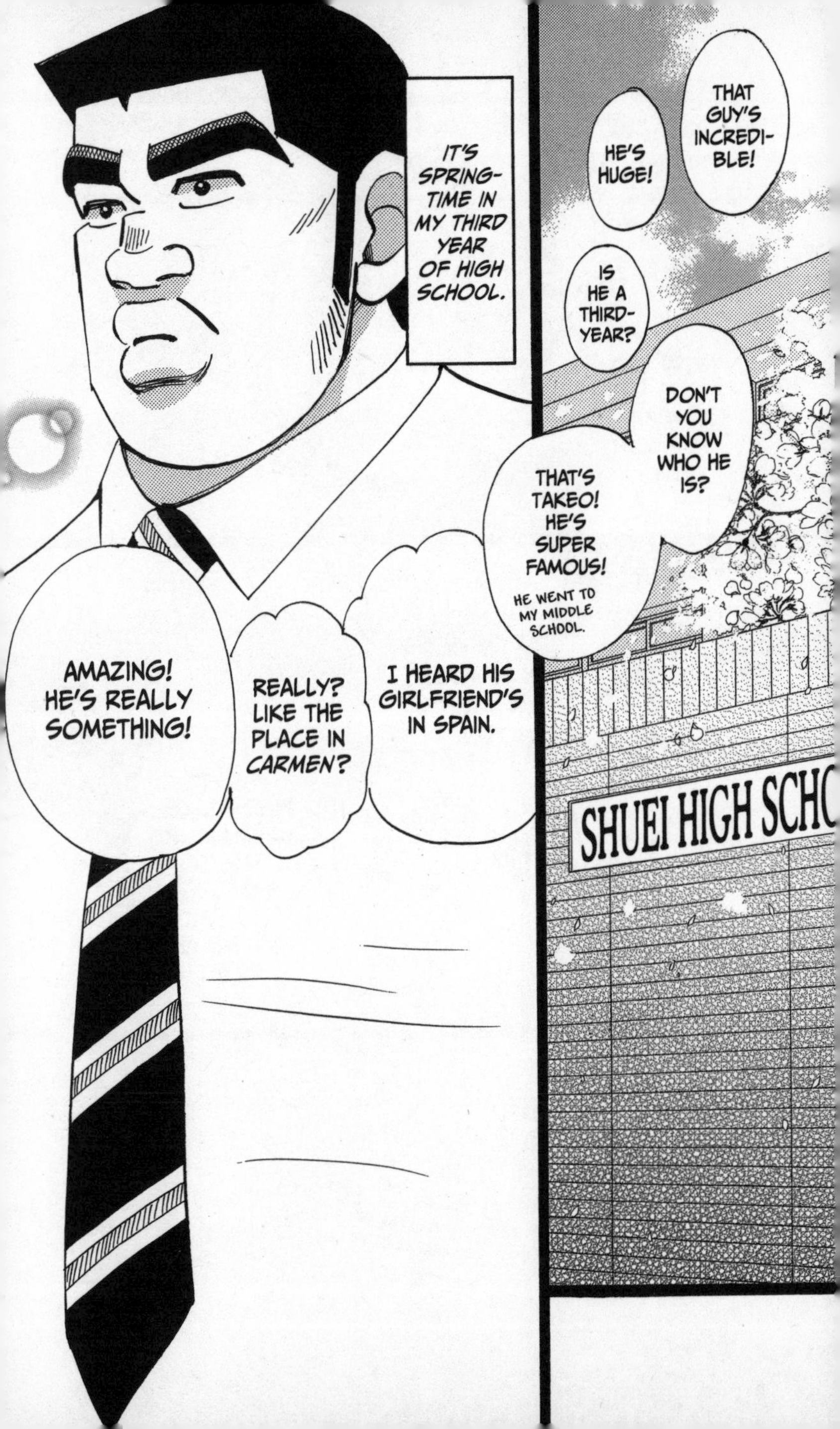
THAT GUY'S INCREDI-BLE!
HE'S HUGE!
IS HE A THIRD-YEAR?
DON'T YOU KNOW WHO HE IS?
THAT'S TAKEO! HE'S SUPER FAMOUS!
HE WENT TO MY MIDDLE SCHOOL.
SHUEI HIGH SCHO
IT'S SPRING-TIME IN MY THIRD YEAR OF HIGH SCHOOL.
I HEARD HIS GIRLFRIEND'S IN SPAIN.
REALLY? LIKE THE PLACE IN CARMEN?
AMAZING! HE'S REALLY SOMETHING!

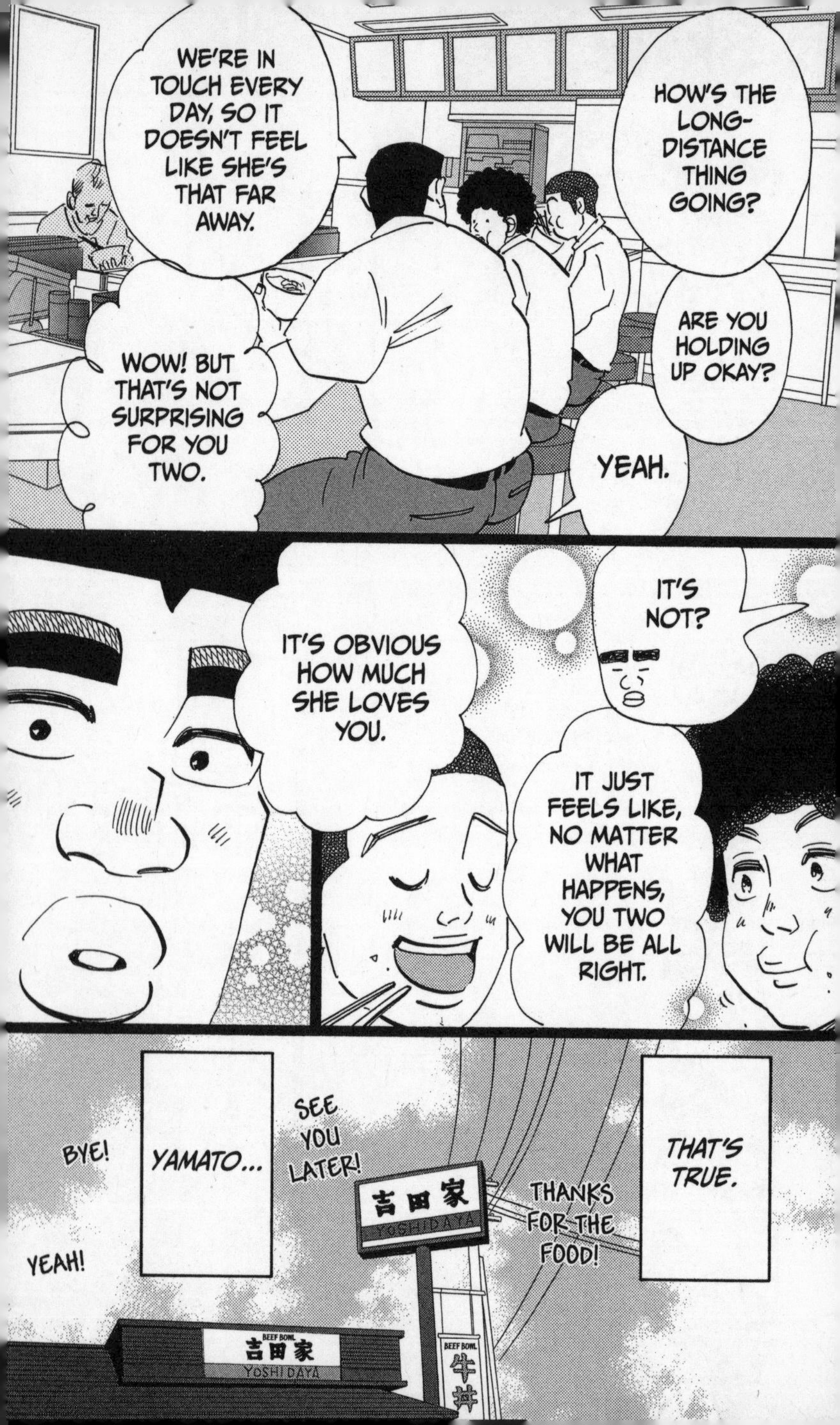
HOW'S THE LONG-DISTANCE THING GOING?
ARE YOU HOLDING UP OKAY?
YEAH.
WE'RE IN TOUCH EVERY DAY, SO IT DOESN'T FEEL LIKE SHE'S THAT FAR AWAY.
WOW! BUT THAT'S NOT SURPRISING FOR YOU TWO.
IT'S NOT?
IT JUST FEELS LIKE, NO MATTER WHAT HAPPENS, YOU TWO WILL BE ALL RIGHT.
IT'S OBVIOUS HOW MUCH SHE LOVES YOU.
THAT'S TRUE.
THANKS FOR THE FOOD!
吉田家
YOSHIDAYA
SEE YOU LATER!
YAMATO...
BYE!
YEAH!
BEEF BOWL
吉田家
YOSHIDAYA
BEEF BOWL
牛丼

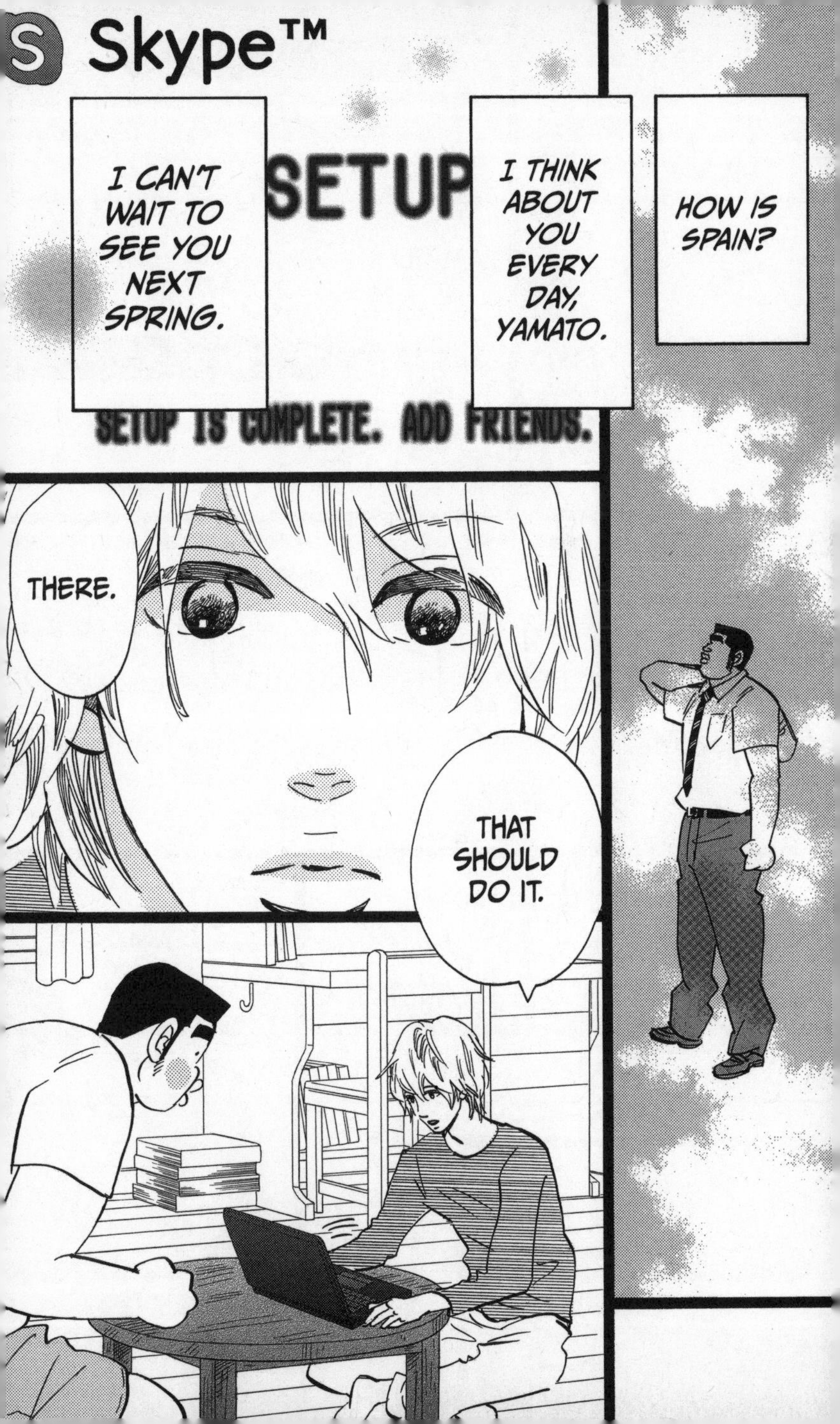
HOW IS SPAIN?
I THINK ABOUT YOU EVERY DAY, YAMATO.
I CAN'T WAIT TO SEE YOU NEXT SPRING.
Skype™
SETUP
SETUP IS COMPLETE. ADD FRIENDS.
THERE.
THAT SHOULD DO IT.

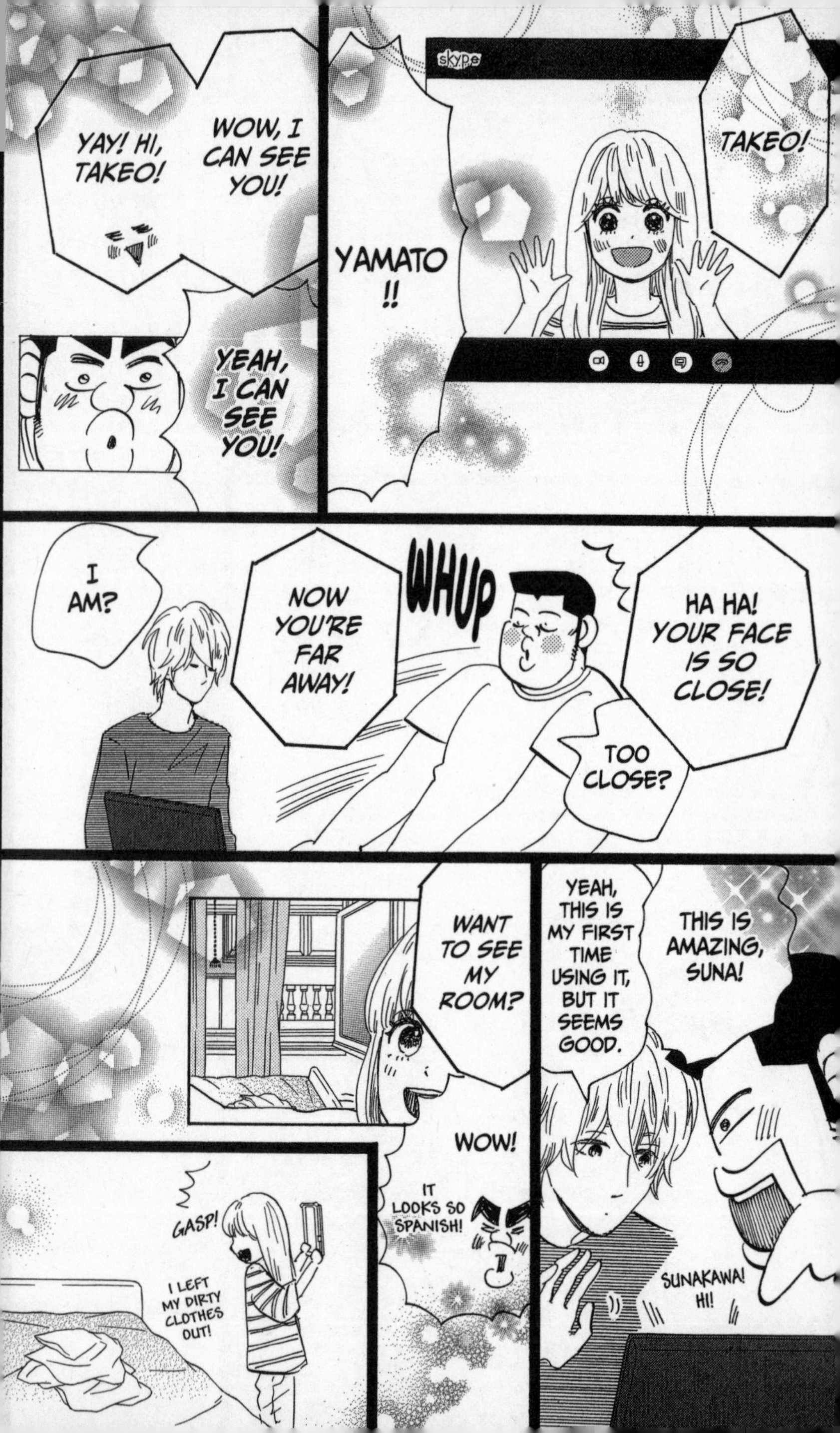
skype
TAKEO!
YAMATO !!
WOW, I CAN SEE YOU!
YAY! HI, TAKEO!
YEAH, I CAN SEE YOU!
HA HA! YOUR FACE IS SO CLOSE!
TOO CLOSE?
WHUP
NOW YOU'RE FAR AWAY!
I AM?
THIS IS AMAZING, SUNA!
YEAH, THIS IS MY FIRST TIME USING IT, BUT IT SEEMS GOOD.
SUNAKAWA! HI!
WANT TO SEE MY ROOM?
WOW!
IT LOOKS SO SPANISH!
GASP!
I LEFT MY DIRTY CLOTHES OUT!

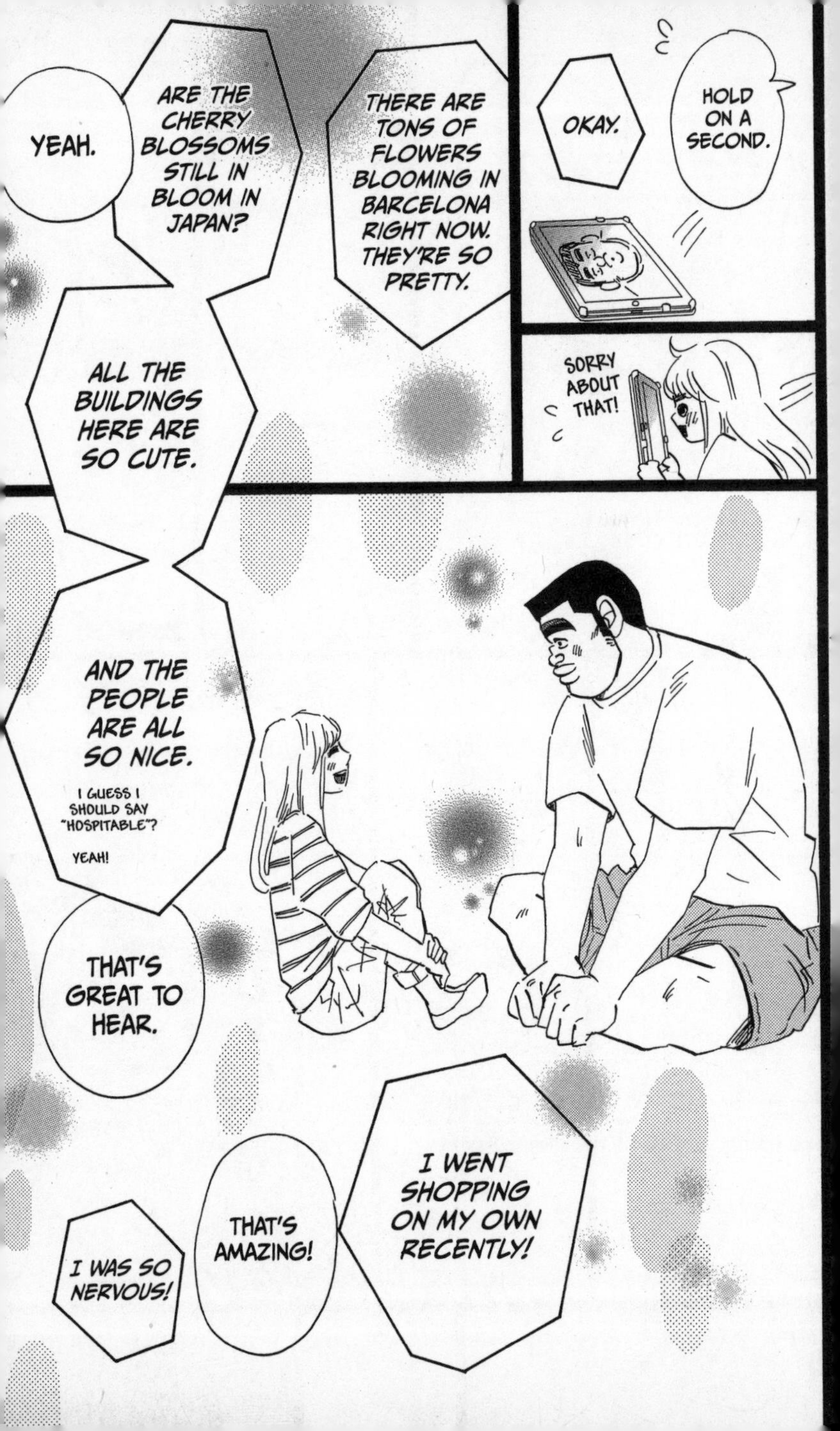
HOLD ON A SECOND.
OKAY.
SORRY ABOUT THAT!
THERE ARE TONS OF FLOWERS BLOOMING IN BARCELONA RIGHT NOW. THEY'RE SO PRETTY.
ARE THE CHERRY BLOSSOMS STILL IN BLOOM IN JAPAN?
YEAH.
ALL THE BUILDINGS HERE ARE SO CUTE.
AND THE PEOPLE ARE ALL SO NICE.
I GUESS I SHOULD SAY "HOSPITABLE"?
YEAH!
THAT'S GREAT TO HEAR.
I WENT SHOPPING ON MY OWN RECENTLY!
THAT'S AMAZING!
I WAS SO NERVOUS!

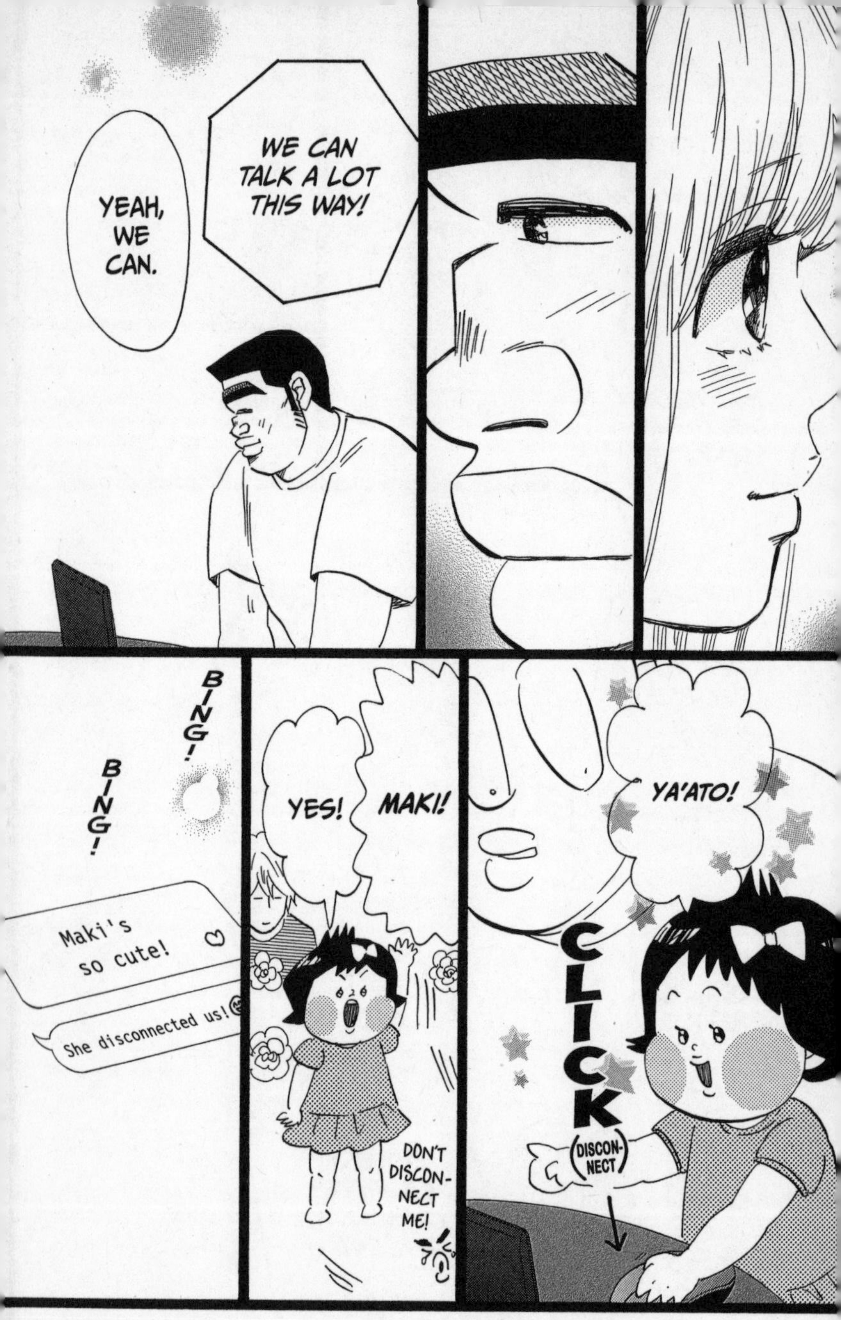
WE CAN TALK A LOT THIS WAY!
YEAH, WE CAN.
YA'ATO!
CLICK
(DISCON-NECT)
MAKI!
YES!
DON'T DISCON-NECT ME!
BING!
BING!
Maki's so cute!
She disconnected us!

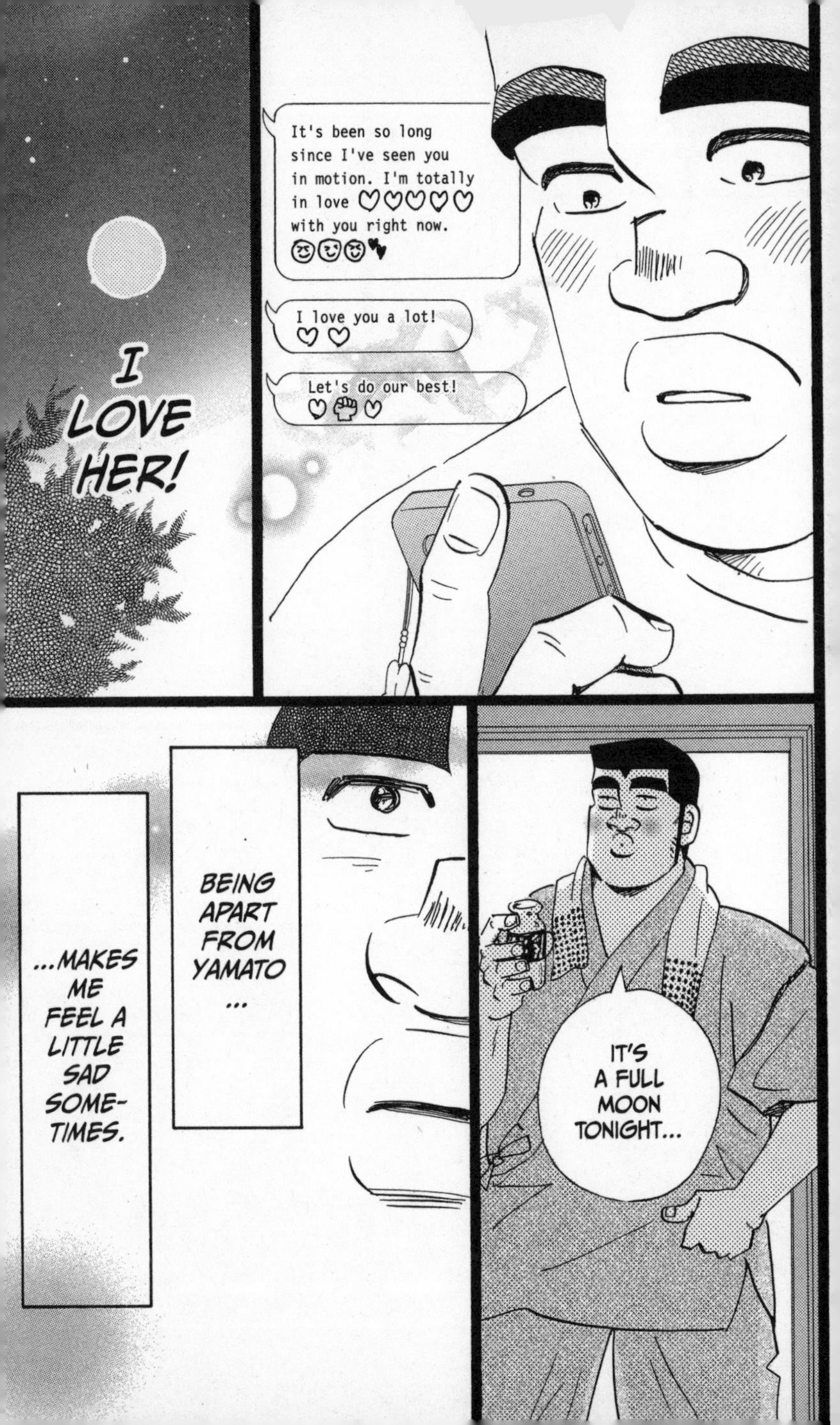

It's been so long since I've seen you in motion. I'm totally in love ♡♡♡♡♡ with you right now.
I love you a lot! ♡ ♡
Let's do our best! ♡ ♡
I LOVE HER!
IT'S A FULL MOON TONIGHT...
BEING APART FROM YAMATO...
...MAKES ME FEEL A LITTLE SAD SOME-TIMES.

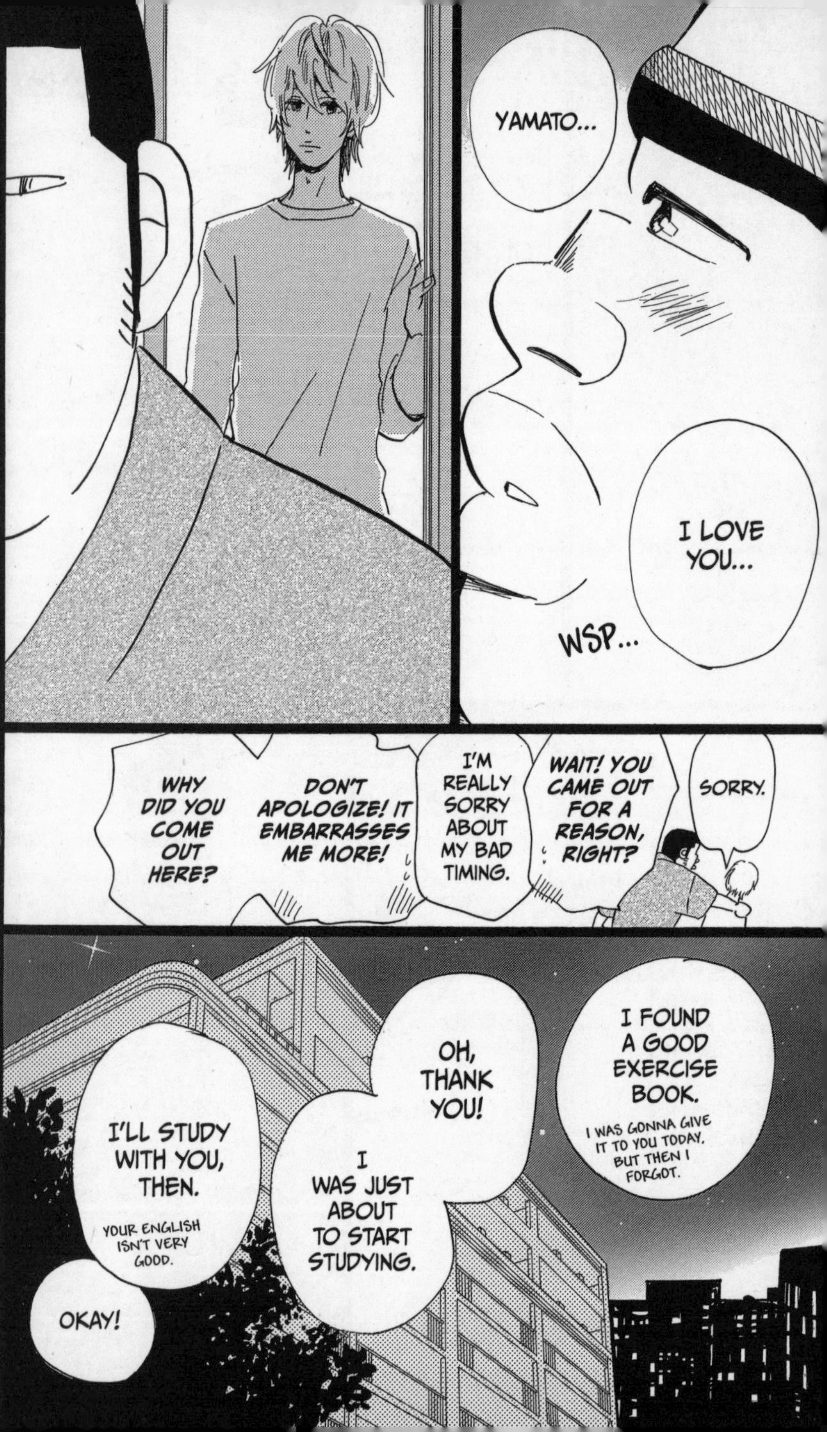
YAMATO...
I LOVE YOU...
WSP...
SORRY.
WAIT! YOU CAME OUT FOR A REASON, RIGHT?
I'M REALLY SORRY ABOUT MY BAD TIMING.
DON'T APOLOGIZE! IT EMBARRASSES ME MORE!
WHY DID YOU COME OUT HERE?
I FOUND A GOOD EXERCISE BOOK.
I WAS GONNA GIVE IT TO YOU TODAY, BUT THEN I FORGOT.
OH, THANK YOU!
I WAS JUST ABOUT TO START STUDYING.
I'LL STUDY WITH YOU, THEN.
YOUR ENGLISH ISN'T VERY GOOD.
OKAY!

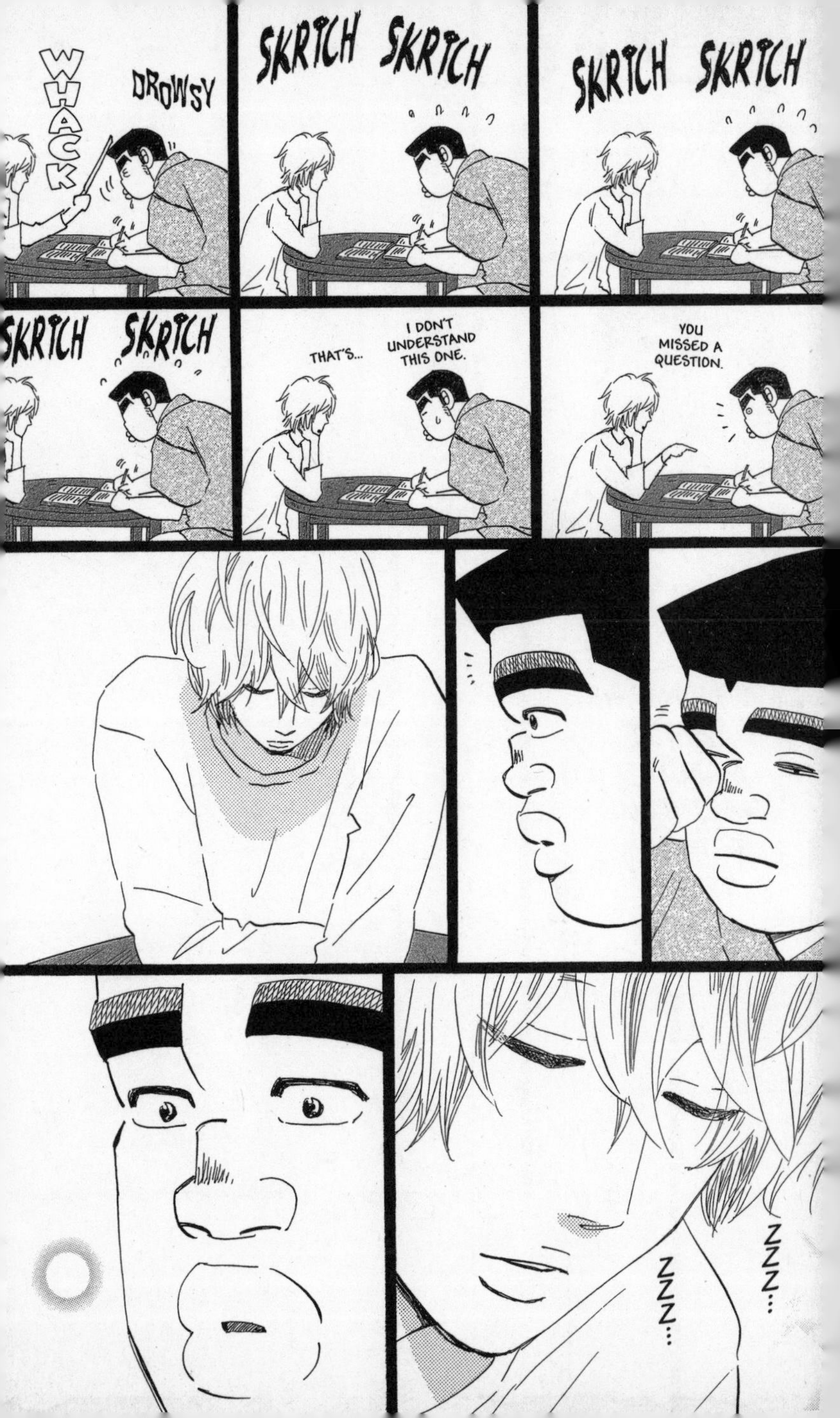
SKRTCH SKRTCH
SKRTCH SKRTCH
DROWSY
WHACK
YOU MISSED A QUESTION.
I DON'T UNDERSTAND THIS ONE.
THAT'S...
SKRTCH SKRTCH
ZZZ...
ZZZ...

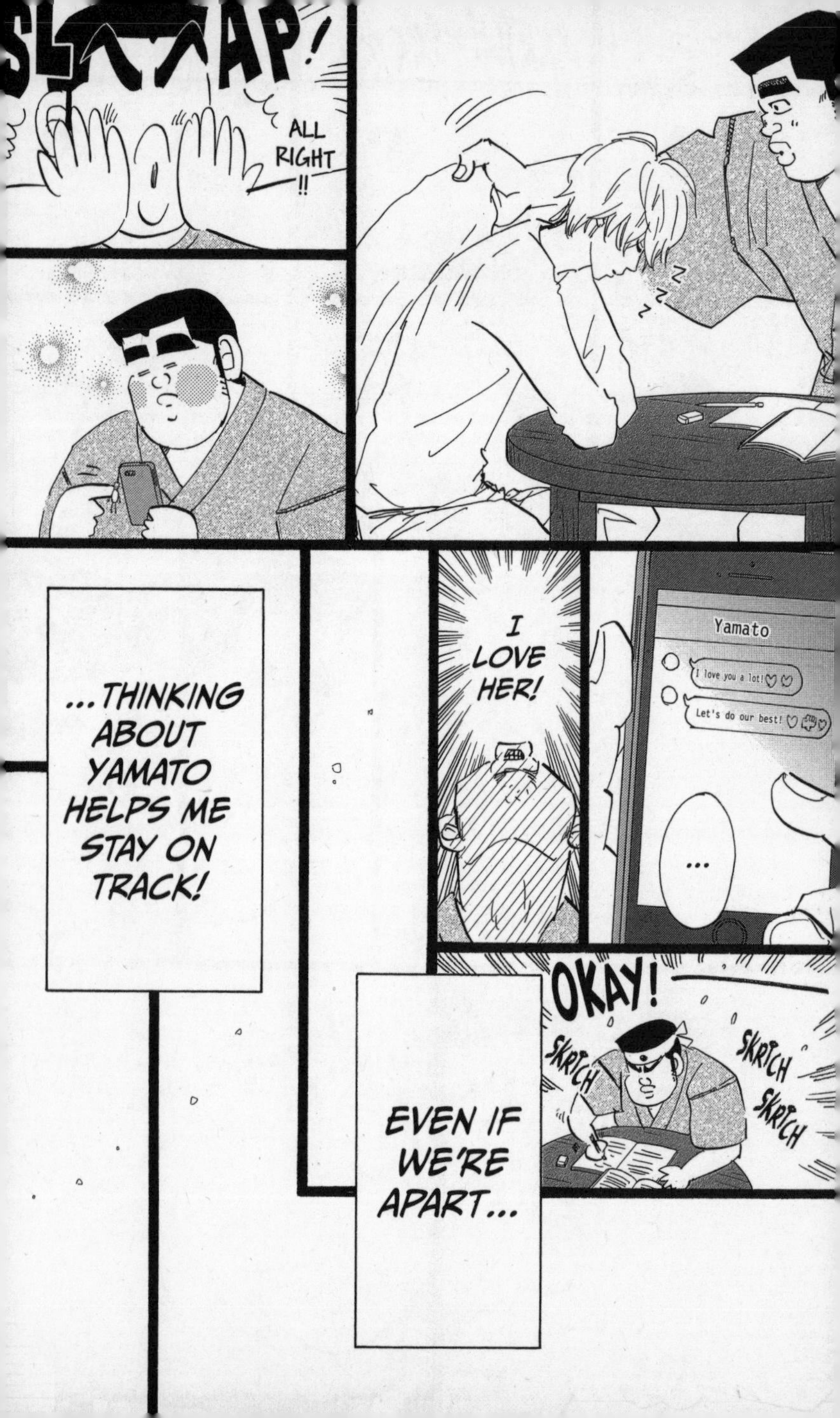
SLAP!
ALL RIGHT!!
Yamato
I love you a lot!
Let's do our best!
...
I LOVE HER!
OKAY!
SKRITCH
SKRITCH
SKRITCH
EVEN IF WE'RE APART...
...THINKING ABOUT YAMATO HELPS ME STAY ON TRACK!

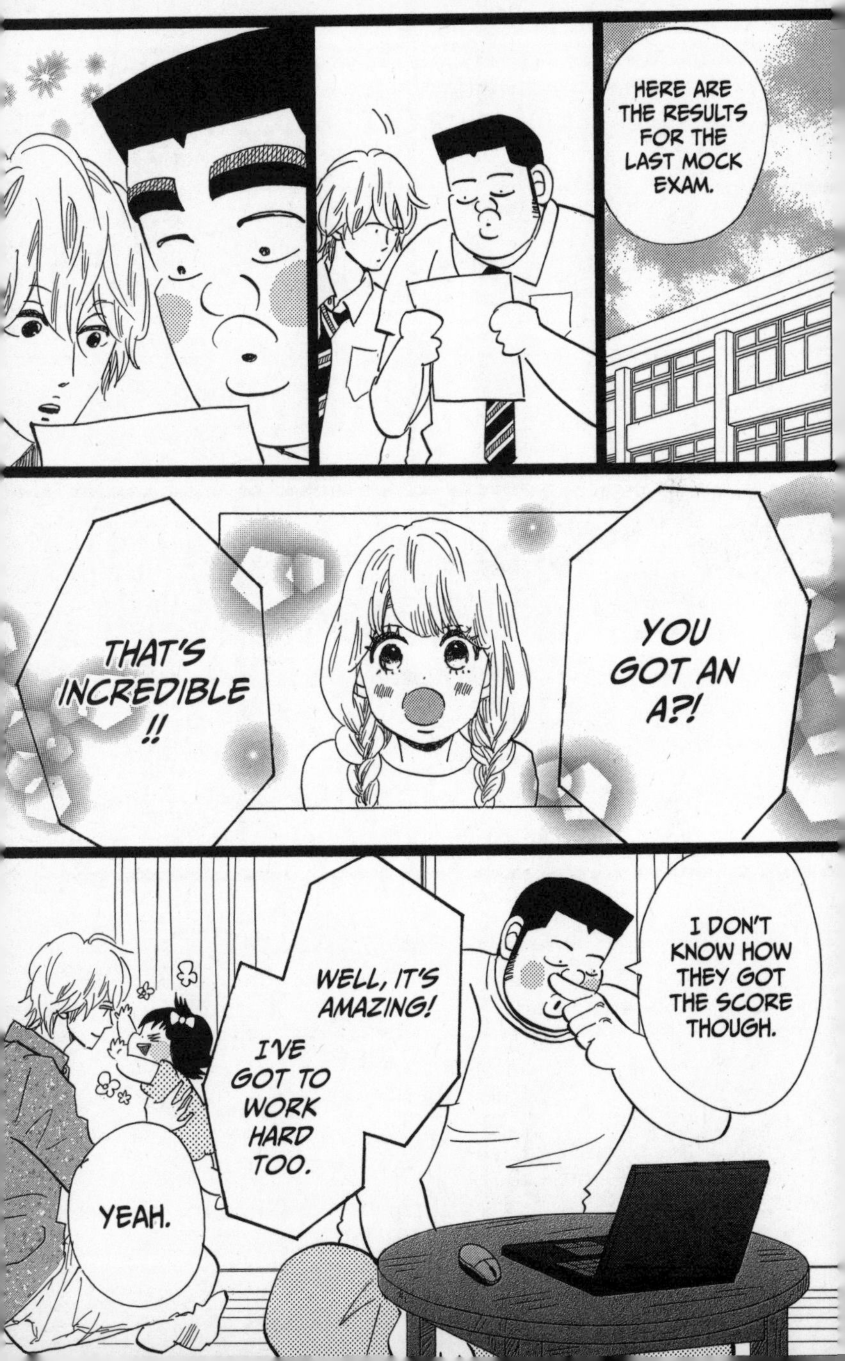
HERE ARE THE RESULTS FOR THE LAST MOCK EXAM.
YOU GOT AN A?!
THAT'S INCREDIBLE!!
I DON'T KNOW HOW THEY GOT THE SCORE THOUGH.
WELL, IT'S AMAZING!
I'VE GOT TO WORK HARD TOO.
YEAH.

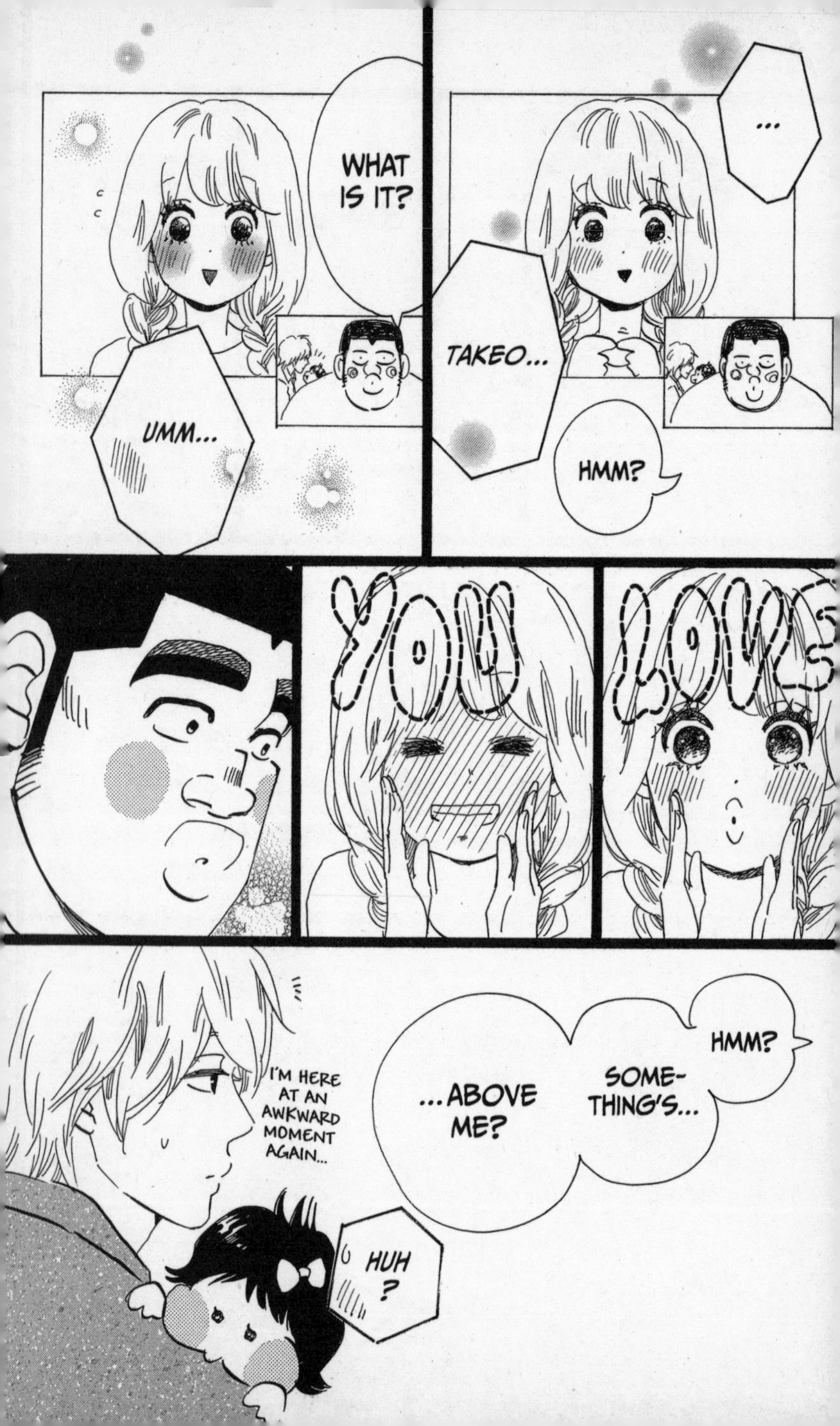
...
TAKEO...
HMM?
WHAT IS IT?
UMM...
LOVES
YOU
HMM?
SOME-THING'S...
...ABOVE ME?
I'M HERE AT AN AWKWARD MOMENT AGAIN...
HUH ?

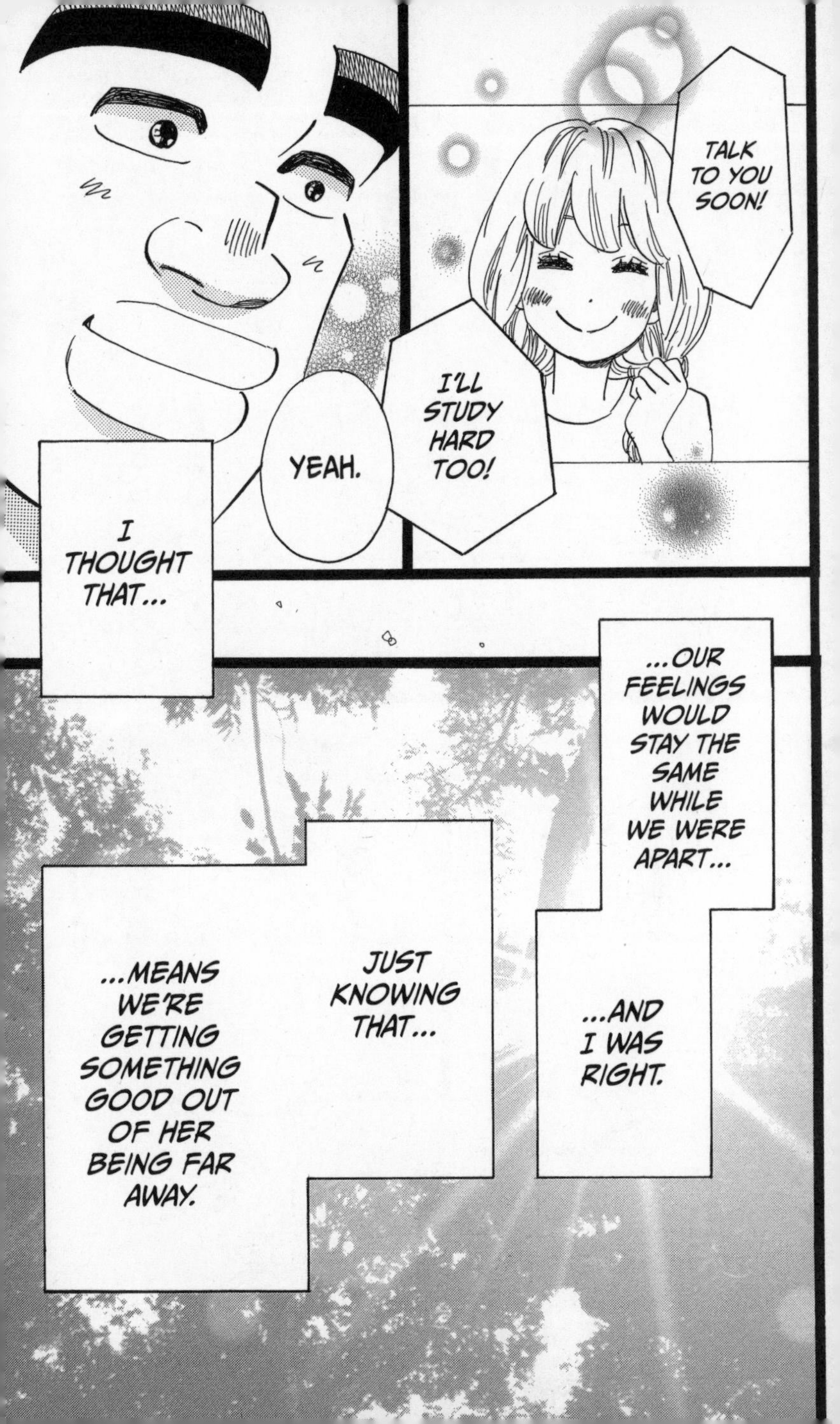
TALK TO YOU SOON!
I'LL STUDY HARD TOO!
YEAH.
I THOUGHT THAT...
...OUR FEELINGS WOULD STAY THE SAME WHILE WE WERE APART...
...AND I WAS RIGHT.
JUST KNOWING THAT...
...MEANS WE'RE GETTING SOMETHING GOOD OUT OF HER BEING FAR AWAY.

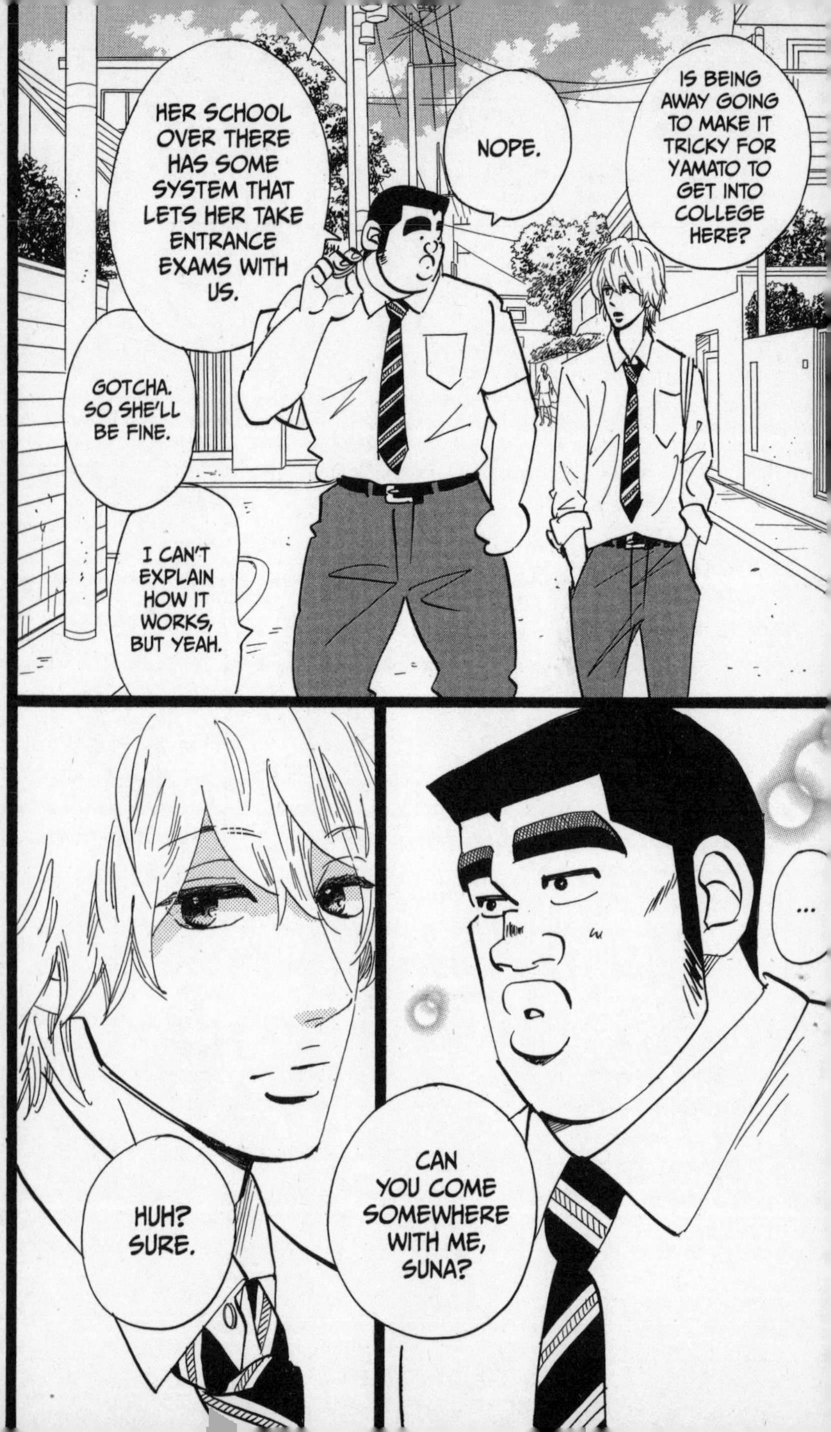
IS BEING AWAY GOING TO MAKE IT TRICKY FOR YAMATO TO GET INTO COLLEGE HERE?
NOPE.
HER SCHOOL OVER THERE HAS SOME SYSTEM THAT LETS HER TAKE ENTRANCE EXAMS WITH US.
GOTCHA. SO SHE'LL BE FINE.
I CAN'T EXPLAIN HOW IT WORKS, BUT YEAH.
...
CAN YOU COME SOMEWHERE WITH ME, SUNA?
HUH? SURE.

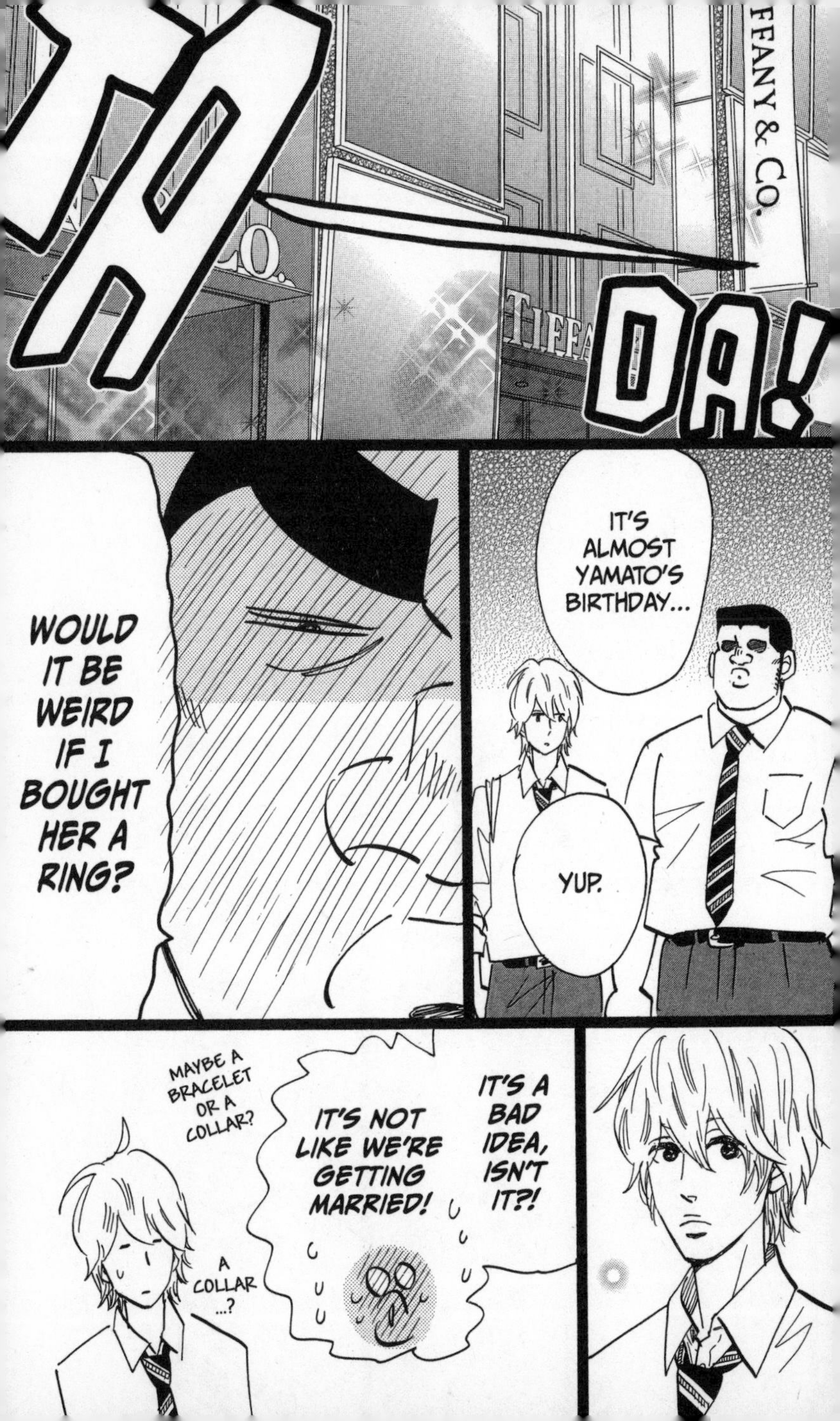
FFANY & CO.
TIFFA
DA!
IT'S ALMOST YAMATO'S BIRTHDAY...
YUP.
WOULD IT BE WEIRD IF I BOUGHT HER A RING?
IT'S A BAD IDEA, ISN'T IT?!
IT'S NOT LIKE WE'RE GETTING MARRIED!
MAYBE A BRACELET OR A COLLAR?
A COLLAR ...?

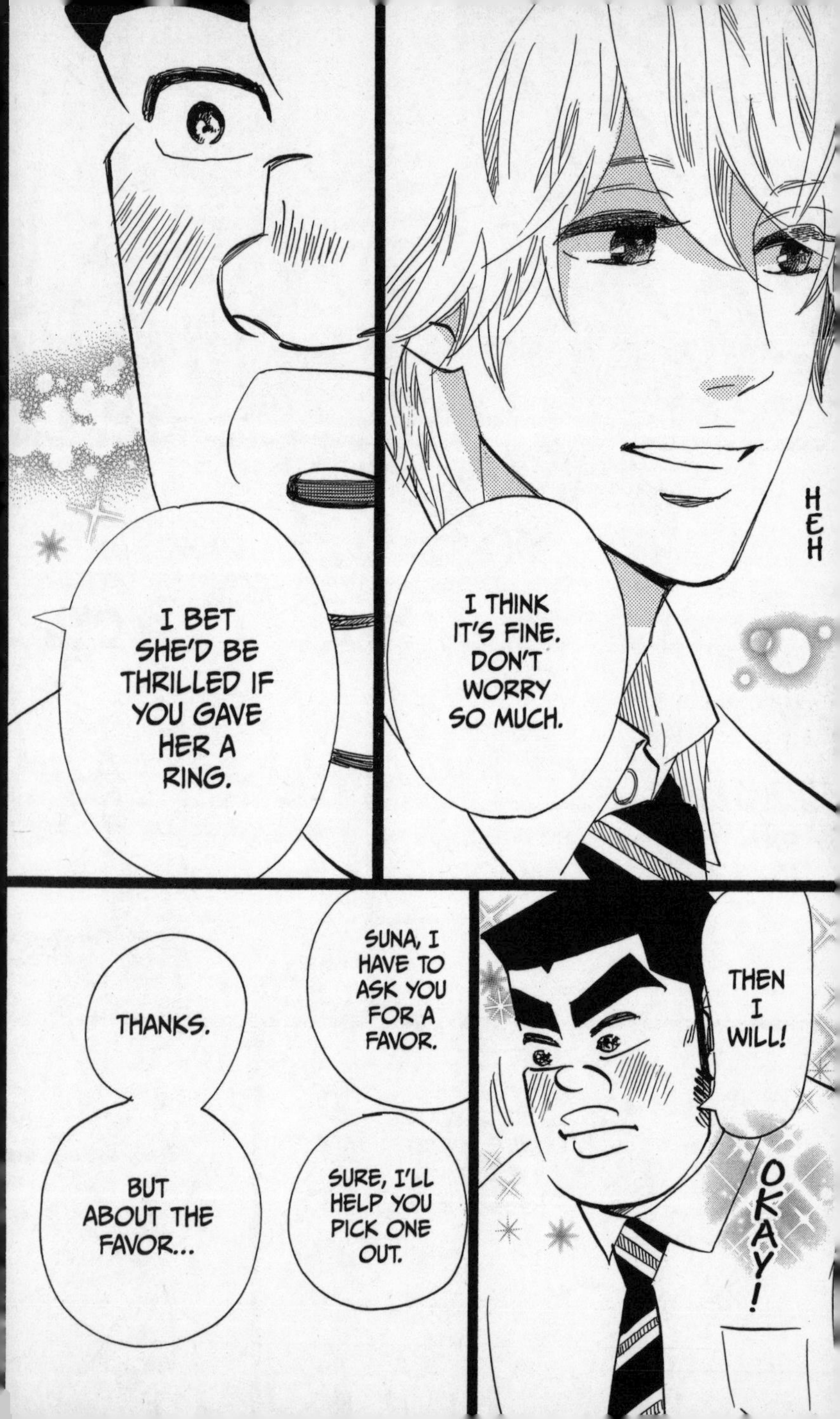
HEH
I THINK IT'S FINE. DON'T WORRY SO MUCH.
I BET SHE'D BE THRILLED IF YOU GAVE HER A RING.
THEN I WILL!
OKAY!
SUNA, I HAVE TO ASK YOU FOR A FAVOR.
SURE, I'LL HELP YOU PICK ONE OUT.
THANKS.
BUT ABOUT THE FAVOR...

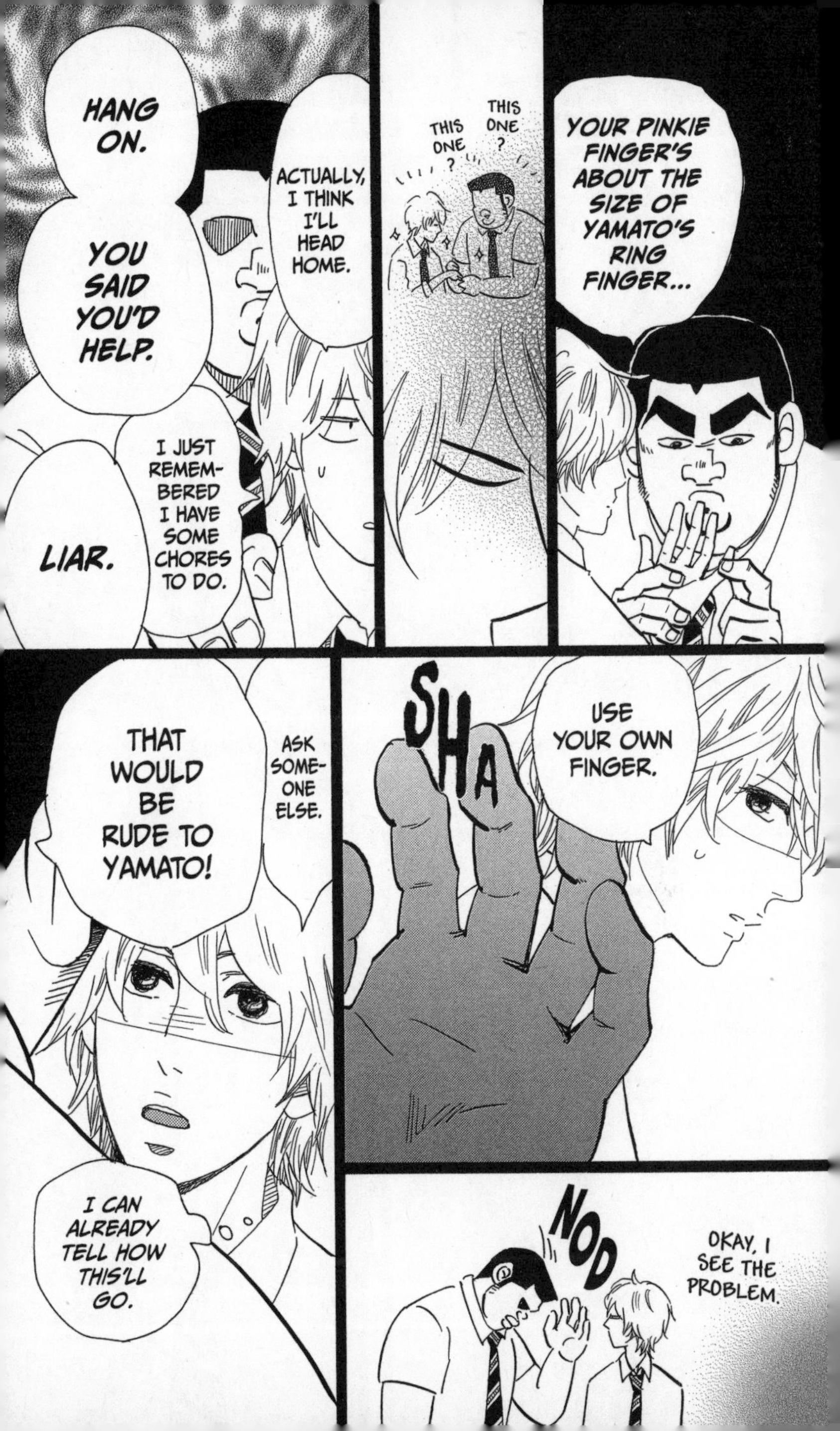
YOUR PINKIE FINGER'S ABOUT THE SIZE OF YAMATO'S RING FINGER...
THIS ONE ?
THIS ONE ?
ACTUALLY, I THINK I'LL HEAD HOME.
HANG ON.
YOU SAID YOU'D HELP.
I JUST REMEMBERED I HAVE SOME CHORES TO DO.
LIAR.
USE YOUR OWN FINGER.
SHA
OKAY, I SEE THE PROBLEM.
NOD
ASK SOMEONE ELSE.
THAT WOULD BE RUDE TO YAMATO!
I CAN ALREADY TELL HOW THIS'LL GO.

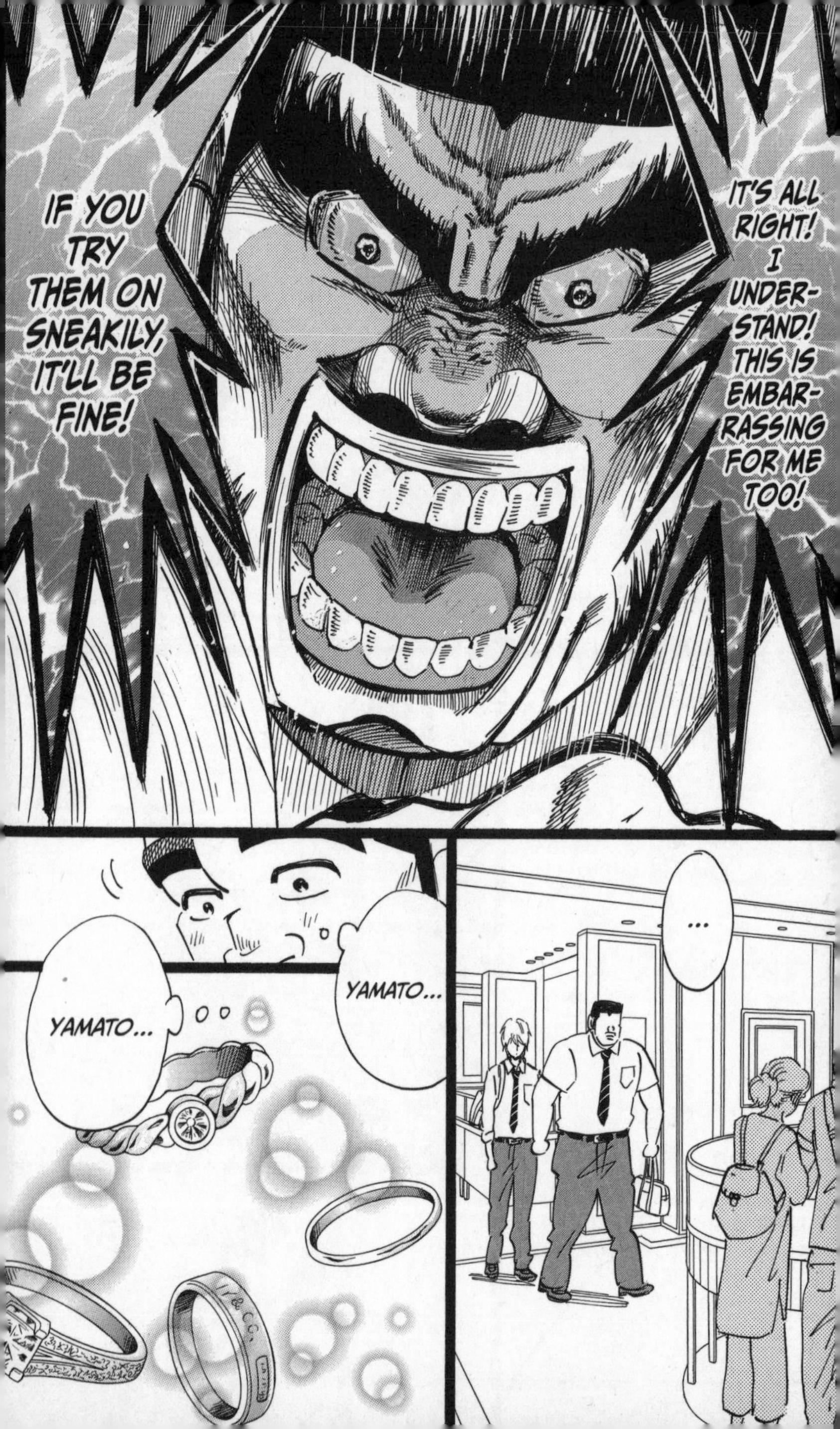
IT'S ALL RIGHT! I UNDERSTAND! THIS IS EMBARRASSING FOR ME TOO!
IF YOU TRY THEM ON SNEAKILY, IT'LL BE FINE!
...
YAMATO...
YAMATO...

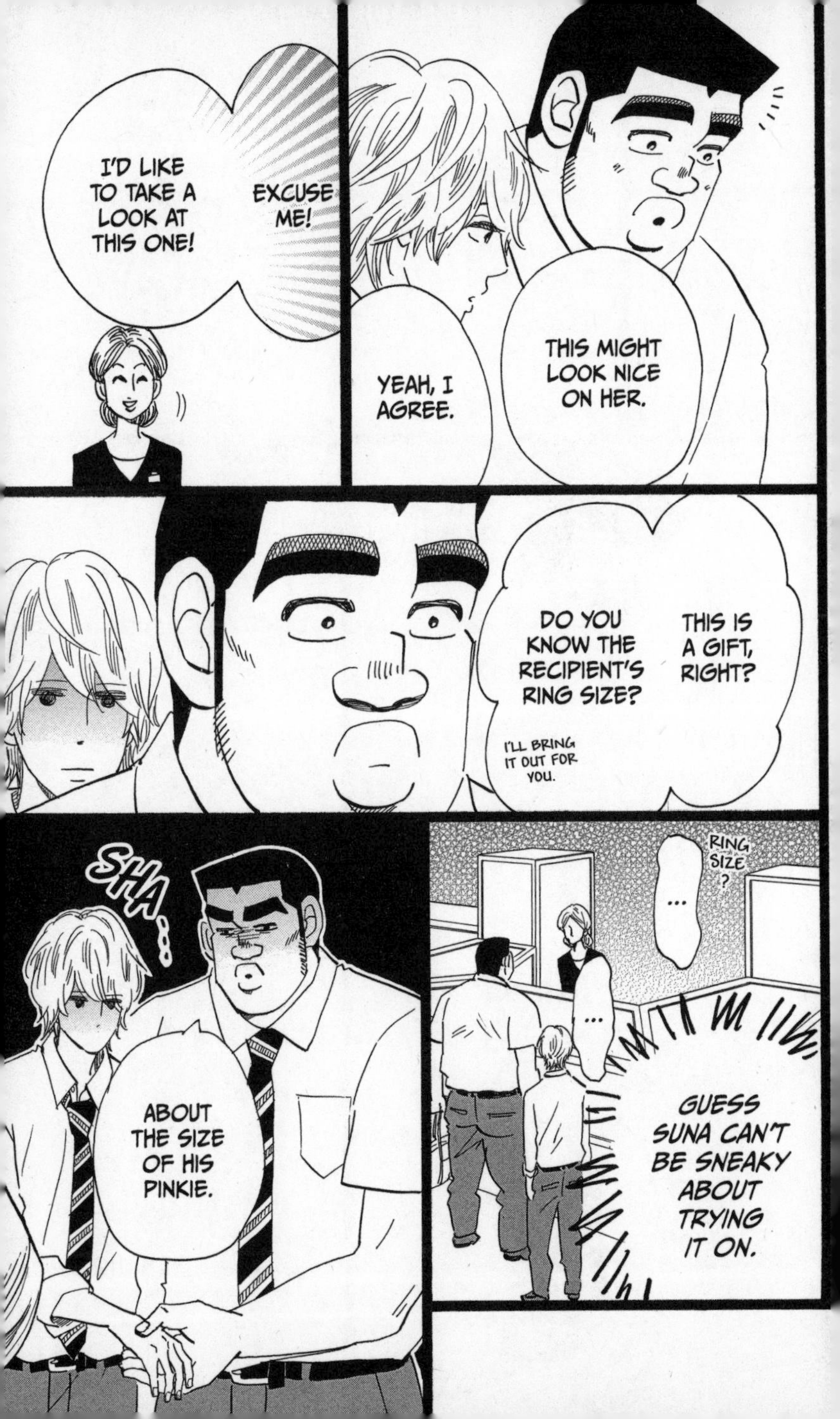
THIS MIGHT LOOK NICE ON HER.
YEAH, I AGREE.
EXCUSE ME!
I'D LIKE TO TAKE A LOOK AT THIS ONE!
THIS IS A GIFT, RIGHT?
DO YOU KNOW THE RECIPIENT'S RING SIZE?
I'LL BRING IT OUT FOR YOU.
RING SIZE?
...
...
GUESS SUNA CAN'T BE SNEAKY ABOUT TRYING IT ON.
SHA...
ABOUT THE SIZE OF HIS PINKIE.

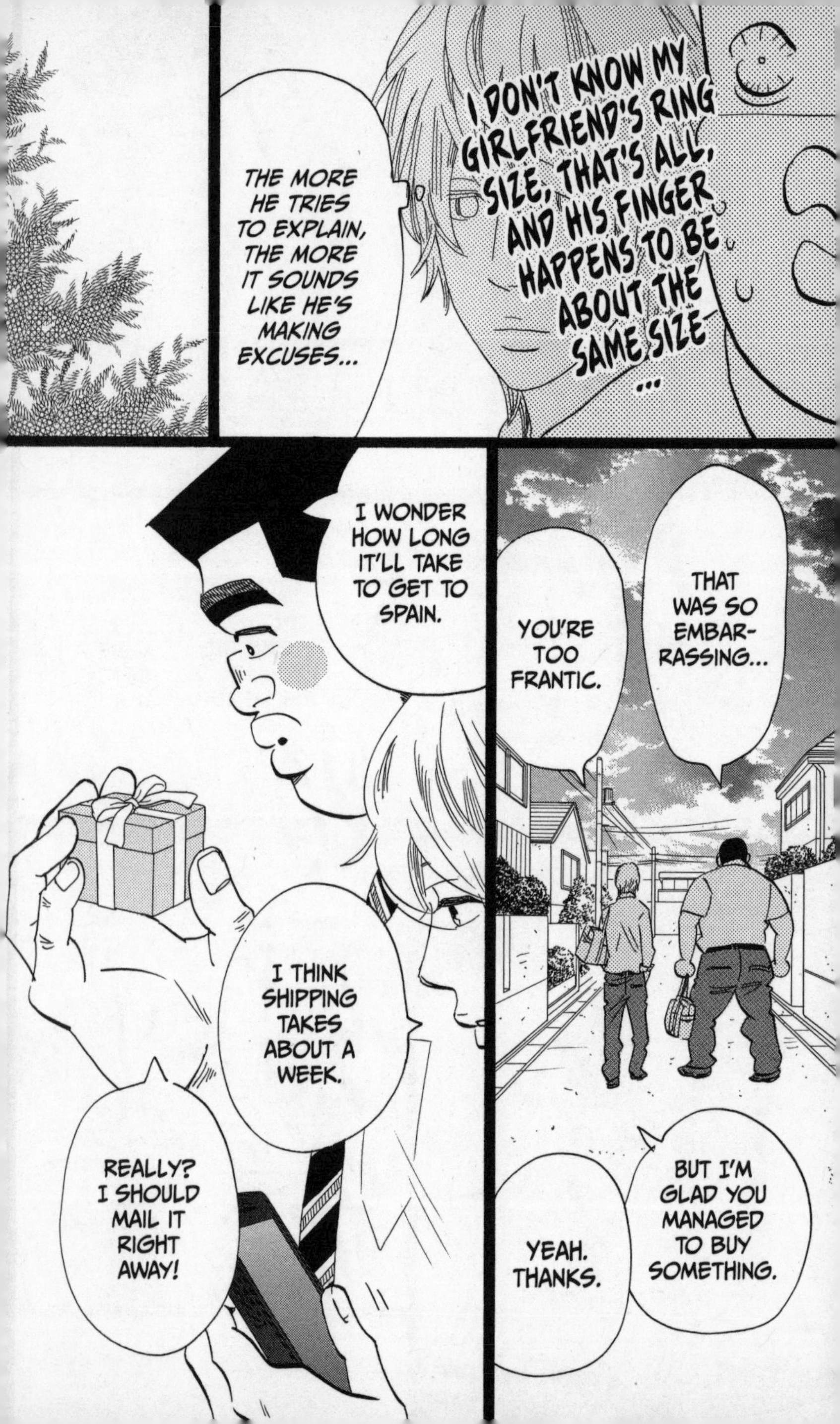
I DON'T KNOW MY GIRLFRIEND'S RING SIZE, THAT'S ALL, AND HIS FINGER HAPPENS TO BE ABOUT THE SAME SIZE ...
THE MORE HE TRIES TO EXPLAIN, THE MORE IT SOUNDS LIKE HE'S MAKING EXCUSES...
THAT WAS SO EMBARRASSING...
YOU'RE TOO FRANTIC.
BUT I'M GLAD YOU MANAGED TO BUY SOMETHING.
YEAH. THANKS.
I WONDER HOW LONG IT'LL TAKE TO GET TO SPAIN.
I THINK SHIPPING TAKES ABOUT A WEEK.
REALLY? I SHOULD MAIL IT RIGHT AWAY!

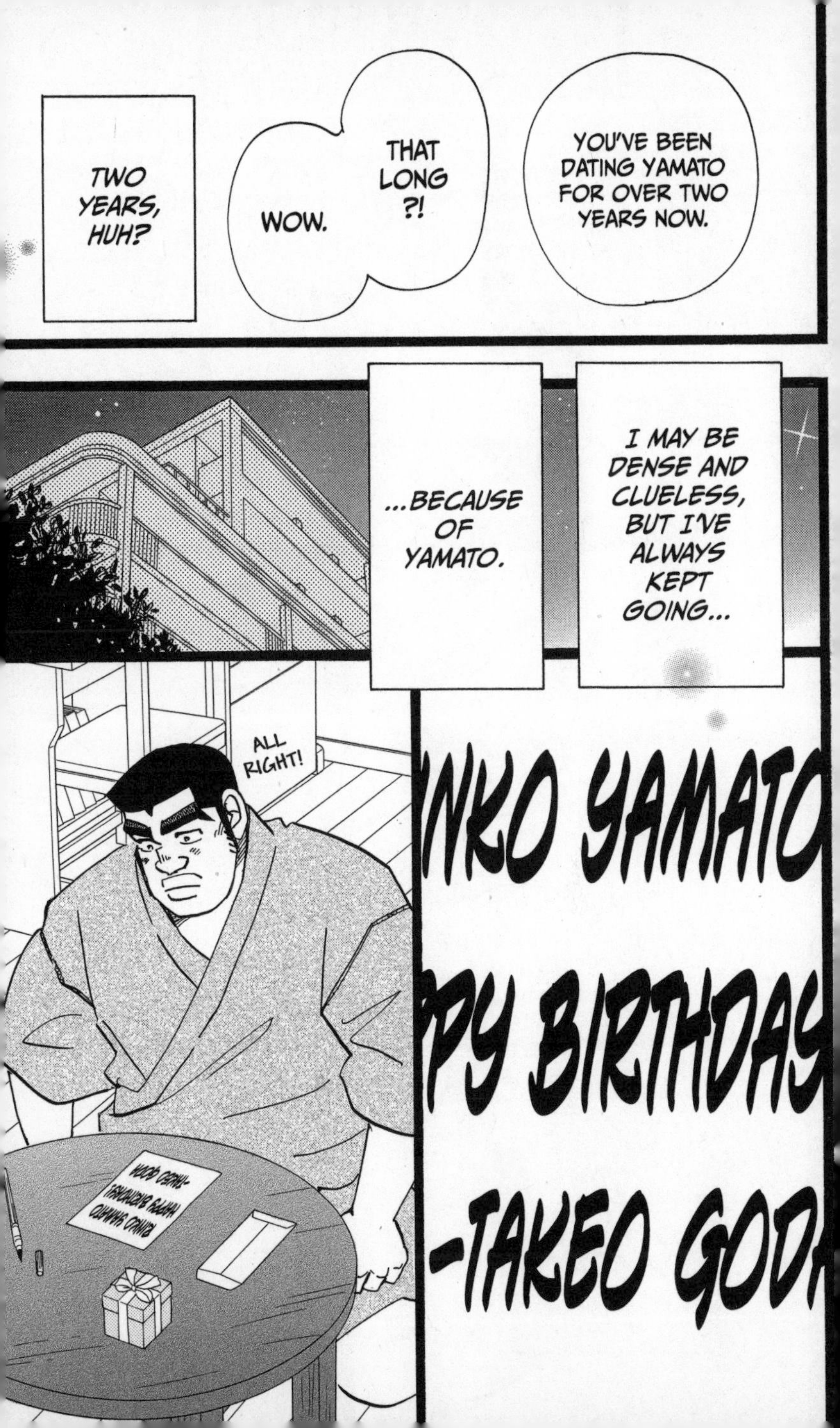
YOU'VE BEEN DATING YAMATO FOR OVER TWO YEARS NOW.
WOW. THAT LONG?!
TWO YEARS, HUH?
I MAY BE DENSE AND CLUELESS, BUT I'VE ALWAYS KEPT GOING...
...BECAUSE OF YAMATO.
NKO YAMATO
PY BIRTHDA
-TAKEO GOD
ALL RIGHT!

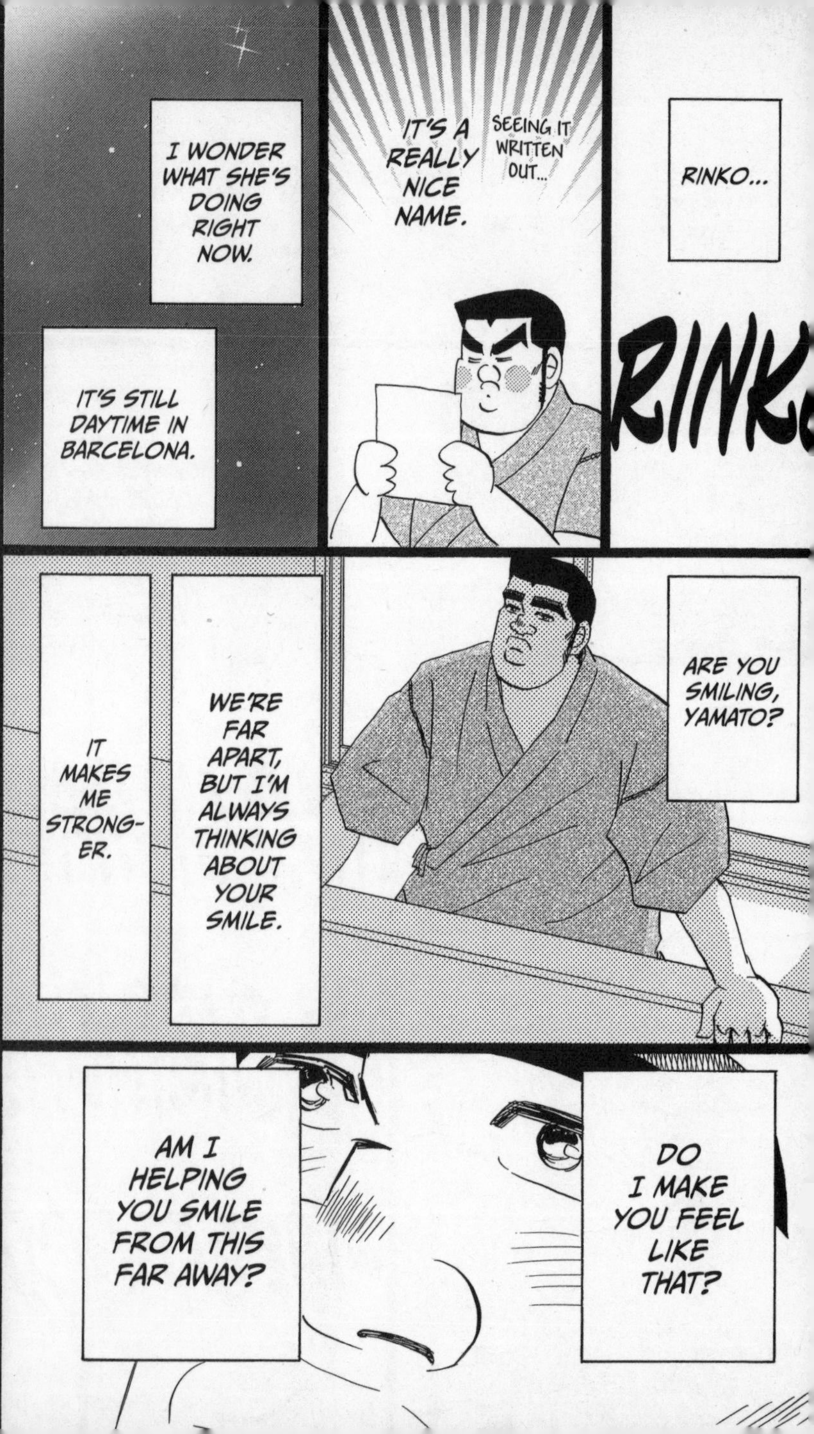
RINKO...
RINKO
SEEING IT WRITTEN OUT...
IT'S A REALLY NICE NAME.
I WONDER WHAT SHE'S DOING RIGHT NOW.
IT'S STILL DAYTIME IN BARCELONA.
ARE YOU SMILING, YAMATO?
WE'RE FAR APART, BUT I'M ALWAYS THINKING ABOUT YOUR SMILE.
IT MAKES ME STRONG-ER.
DO I MAKE YOU FEEL LIKE THAT?
AM I HELPING YOU SMILE FROM THIS FAR AWAY?

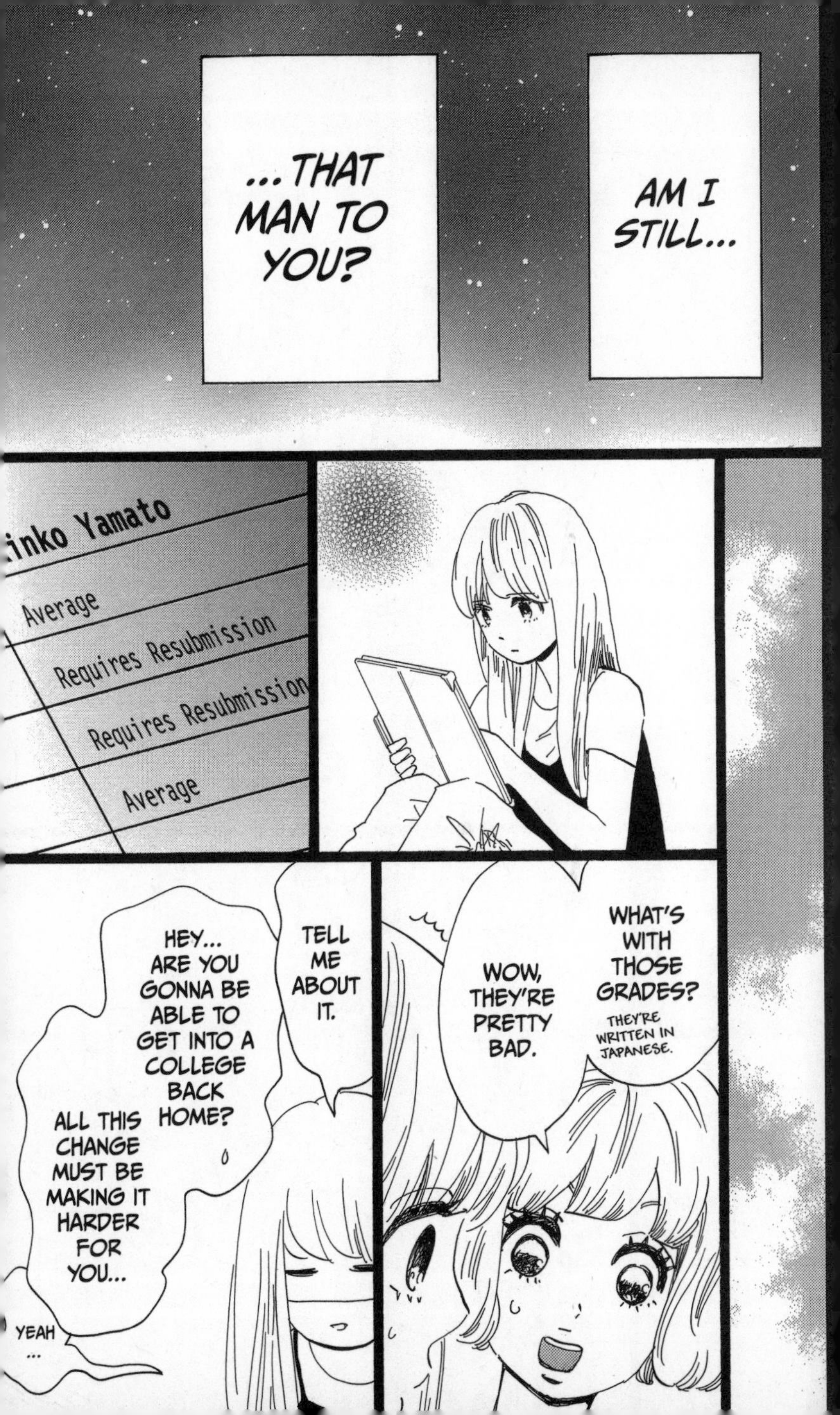
AM I STILL...
...THAT MAN TO YOU?
inko Yamato
Average
Requires Resubmission
Requires Resubmission
Average
WHAT'S WITH THOSE GRADES?
THEY'RE WRITTEN IN JAPANESE.
WOW, THEY'RE PRETTY BAD.
TELL ME ABOUT IT.
HEY... ARE YOU GONNA BE ABLE TO GET INTO A COLLEGE BACK HOME?
ALL THIS CHANGE MUST BE MAKING IT HARDER FOR YOU...
YEAH ...

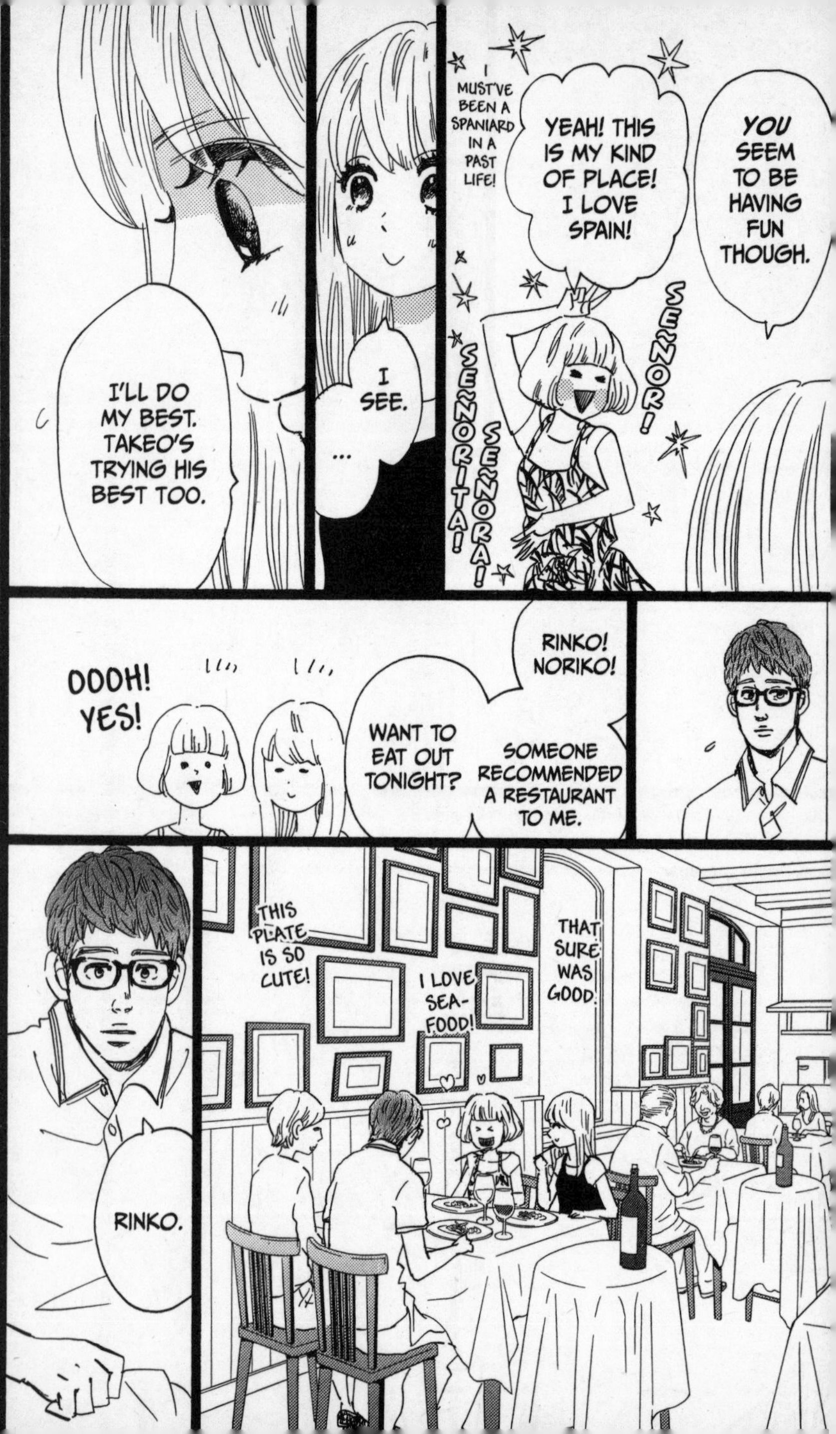
YOU SEEM TO BE HAVING FUN THOUGH.
YEAH! THIS IS MY KIND OF PLACE! I LOVE SPAIN!
I MUST'VE BEEN A SPANIARD IN A PAST LIFE!
SEÑOR!
SEÑORA!
SEÑORITA!
I SEE.
...
I'LL DO MY BEST. TAKEO'S TRYING HIS BEST TOO.
RINKO! NORIKO!
SOMEONE RECOMMENDED A RESTAURANT TO ME.
WANT TO EAT OUT TONIGHT?
OOOH! YES!
THAT SURE WAS GOOD.
I LOVE SEA-FOOD!
THIS PLATE IS SO CUTE!
RINKO.

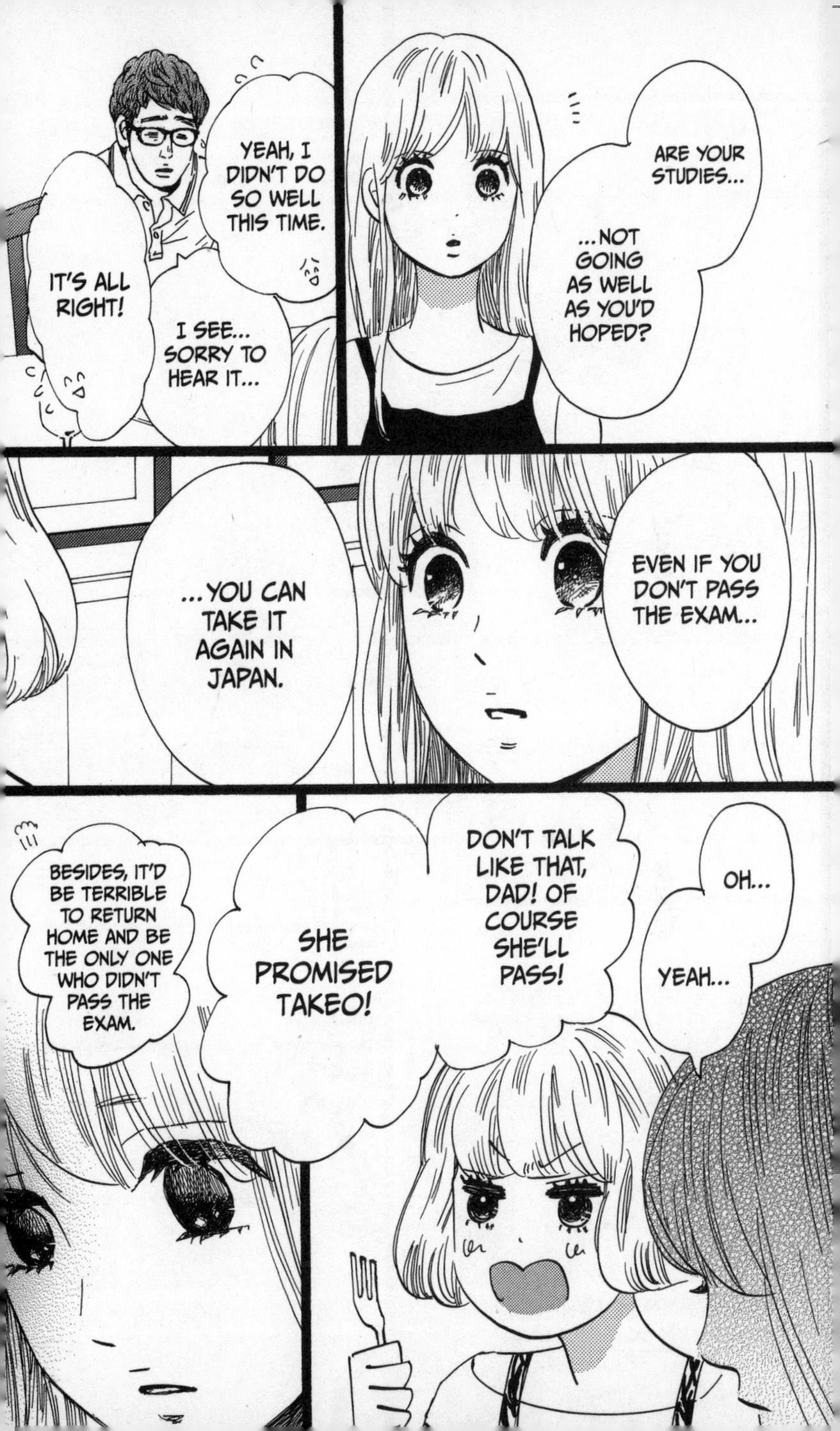
ARE YOUR STUDIES...
...NOT GOING AS WELL AS YOU'D HOPED?
YEAH, I DIDN'T DO SO WELL THIS TIME.
I SEE... SORRY TO HEAR IT...
IT'S ALL RIGHT!
EVEN IF YOU DON'T PASS THE EXAM...
...YOU CAN TAKE IT AGAIN IN JAPAN.
OH...
YEAH...
DON'T TALK LIKE THAT, DAD! OF COURSE SHE'LL PASS!
SHE PROMISED TAKEO!
BESIDES, IT'D BE TERRIBLE TO RETURN HOME AND BE THE ONLY ONE WHO DIDN'T PASS THE EXAM.

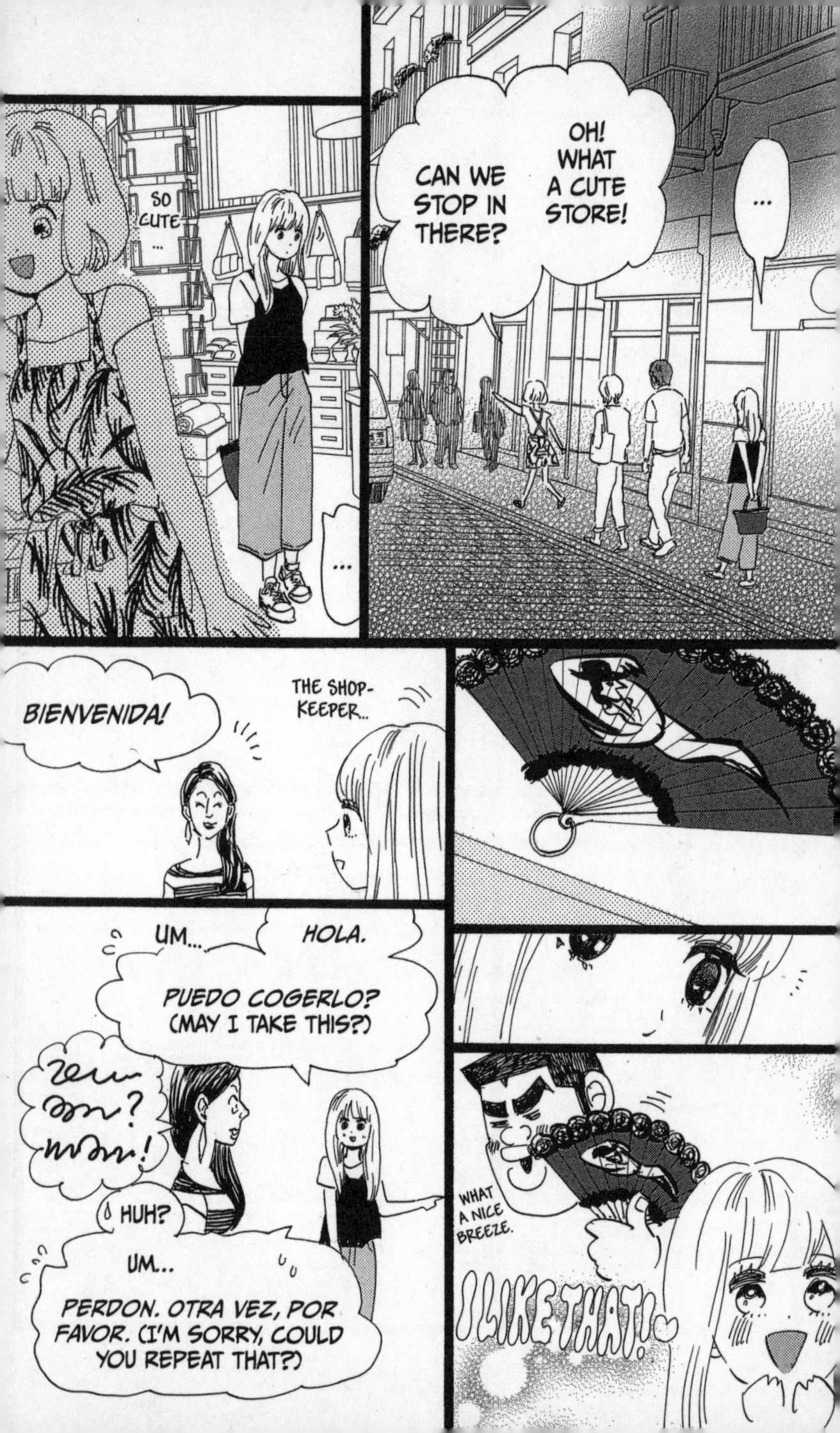
...
OH! WHAT A CUTE STORE!
CAN WE STOP IN THERE?
SO CUTE...
...
THE SHOP-KEEPER...
BIENVENIDA!
WHAT A NICE BREEZE.
I LIKE THAT!
UM... HOLA. PUEDO COGERLO? (MAY I TAKE THIS?)
HUH?
UM... PERDON. OTRA VEZ, POR FAVOR. (I'M SORRY, COULD YOU REPEAT THAT?)

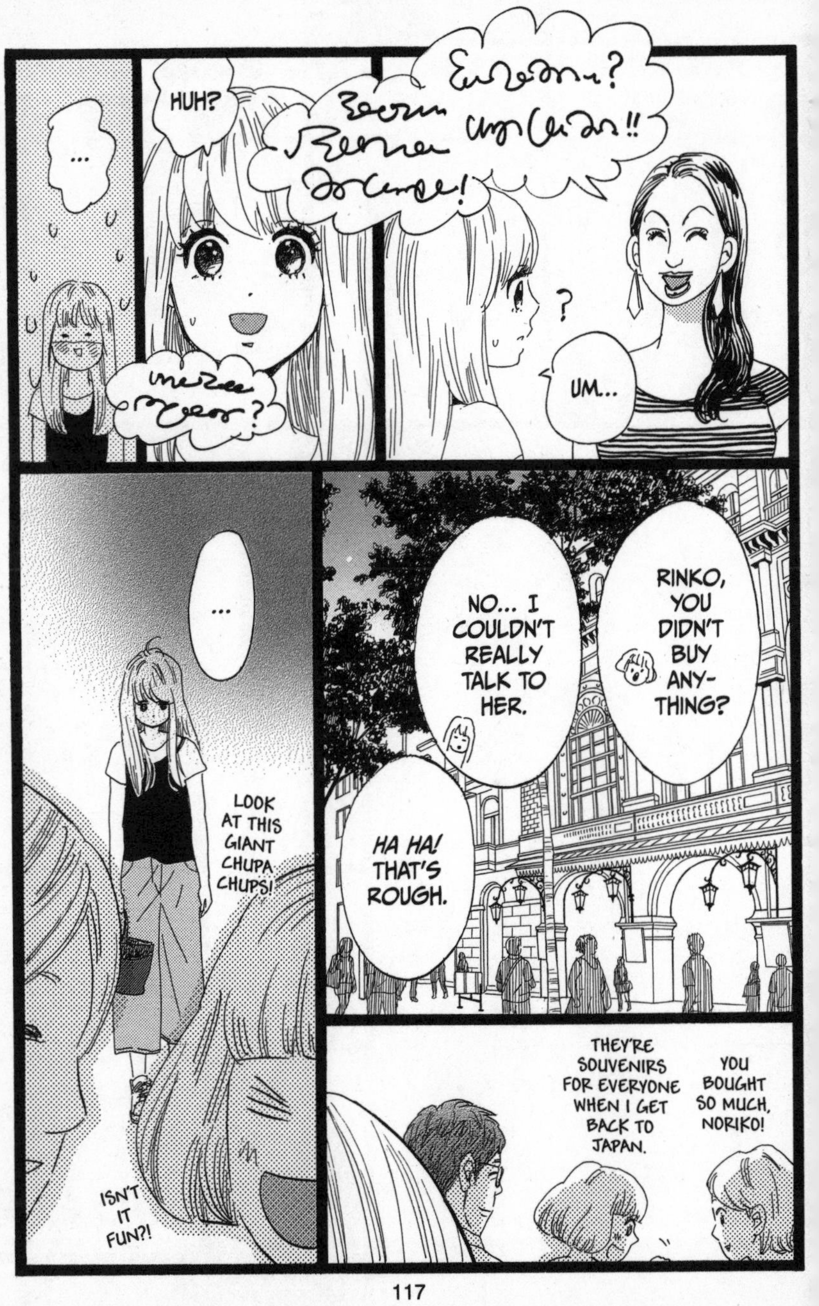
?
UM...
HUH?
...
RINKO, YOU DIDN'T BUY ANYTHING?
NO... I COULDN'T REALLY TALK TO HER.
HA HA! THAT'S ROUGH.
YOU BOUGHT SO MUCH, NORIKO!
THEY'RE SOUVENIRS FOR EVERYONE WHEN I GET BACK TO JAPAN.
...
LOOK AT THIS GIANT CHUPA CHUPS!
ISN'T IT FUN?!

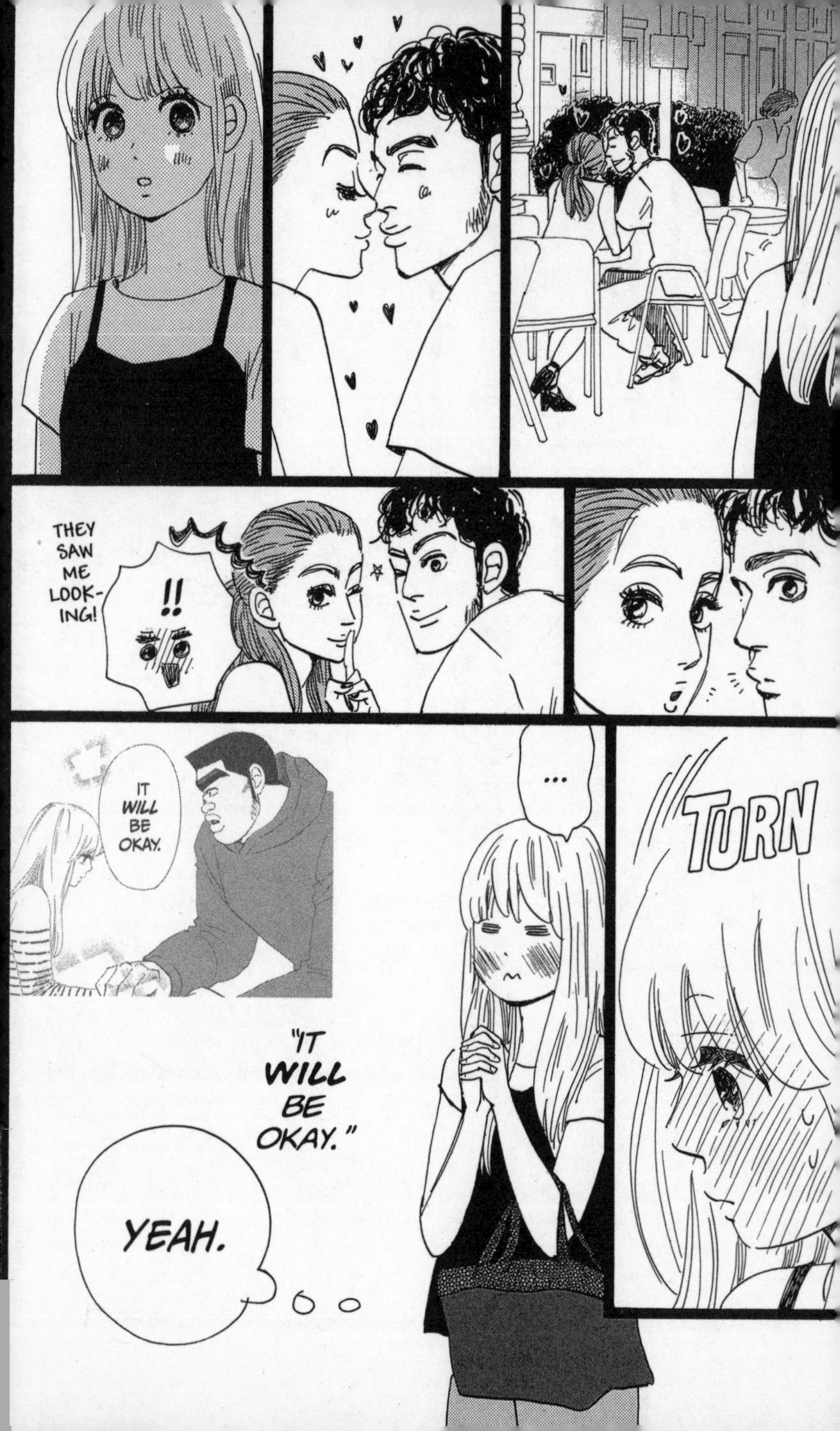
THEY SAW ME LOOKING!
!!
TURN
...
IT WILL BE OKAY.
"IT WILL BE OKAY."
YEAH.

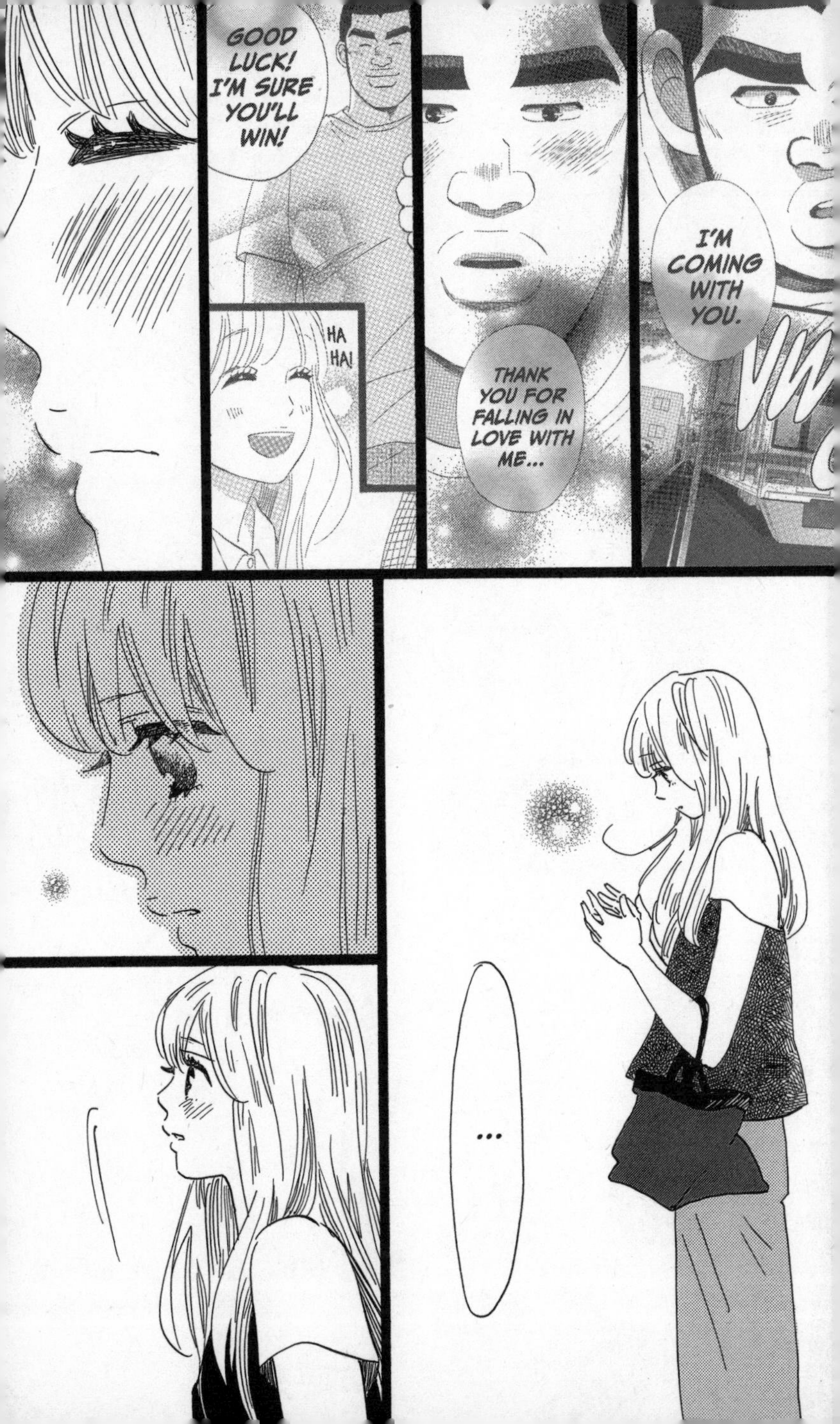
I'M COMING WITH YOU.
THANK YOU FOR FALLING IN LOVE WITH ME...
GOOD LUCK! I'M SURE YOU'LL WIN!
HA HA!
...

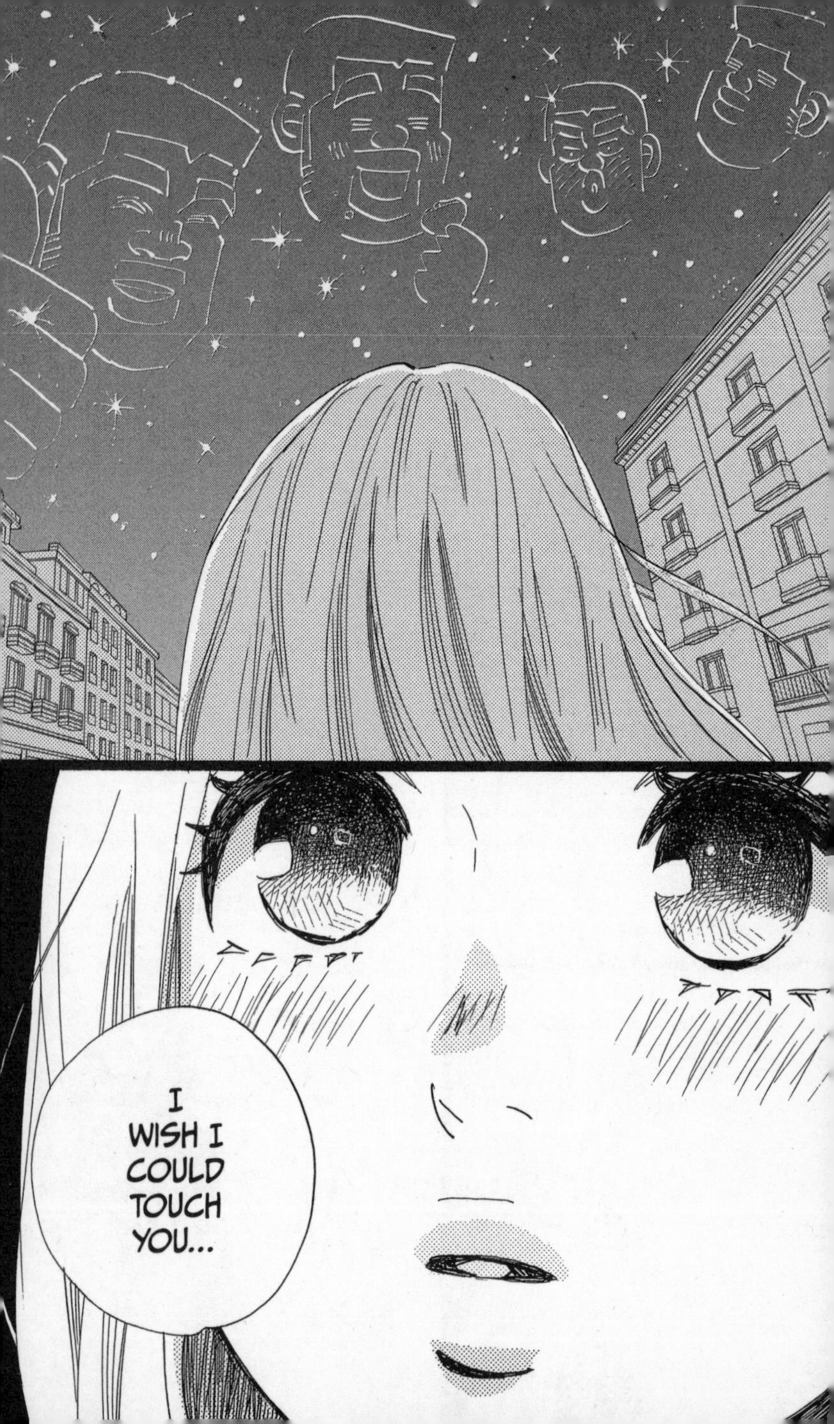
I WISH I COULD TOUCH YOU...

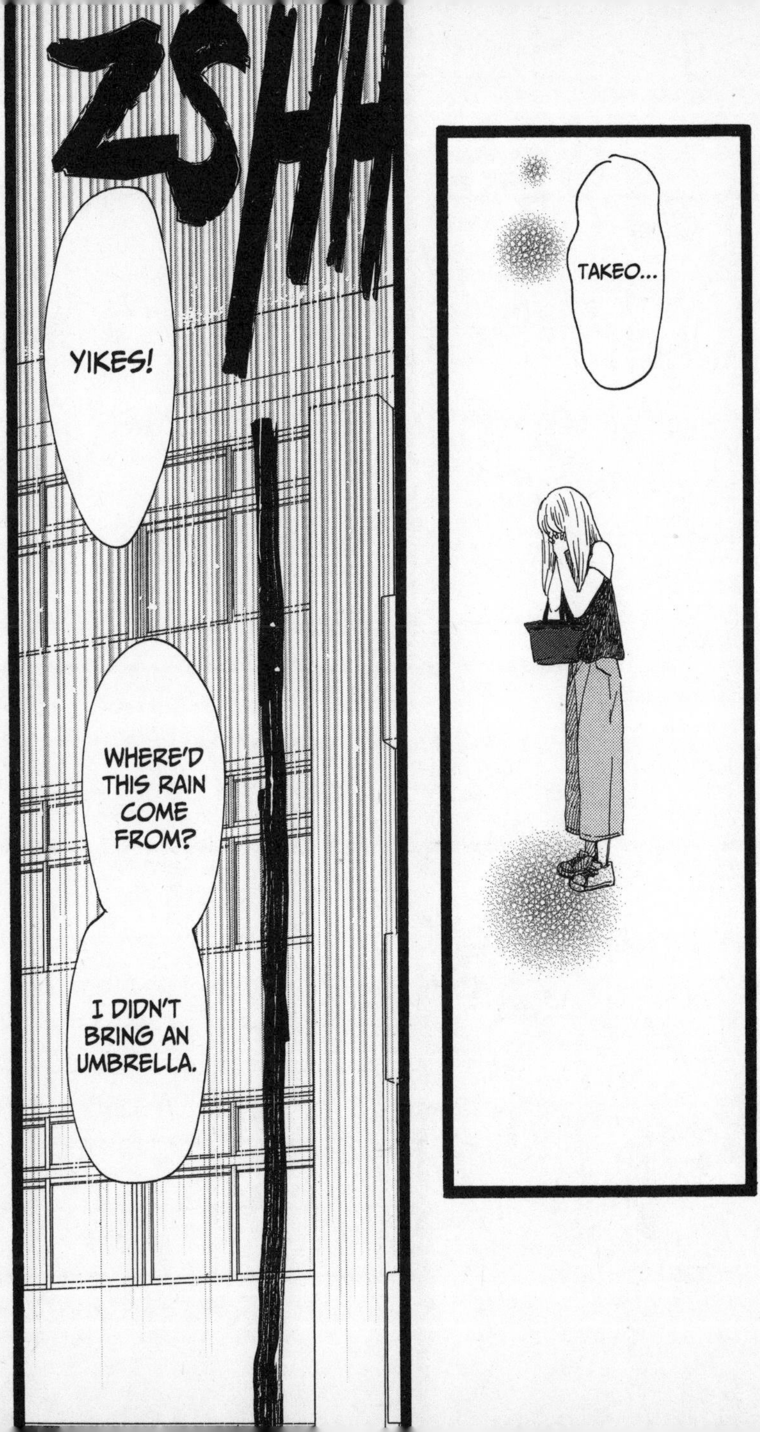
TAKEO...
ZSHH
YIKES!
WHERE'D THIS RAIN COME FROM?
I DIDN'T BRING AN UMBRELLA.

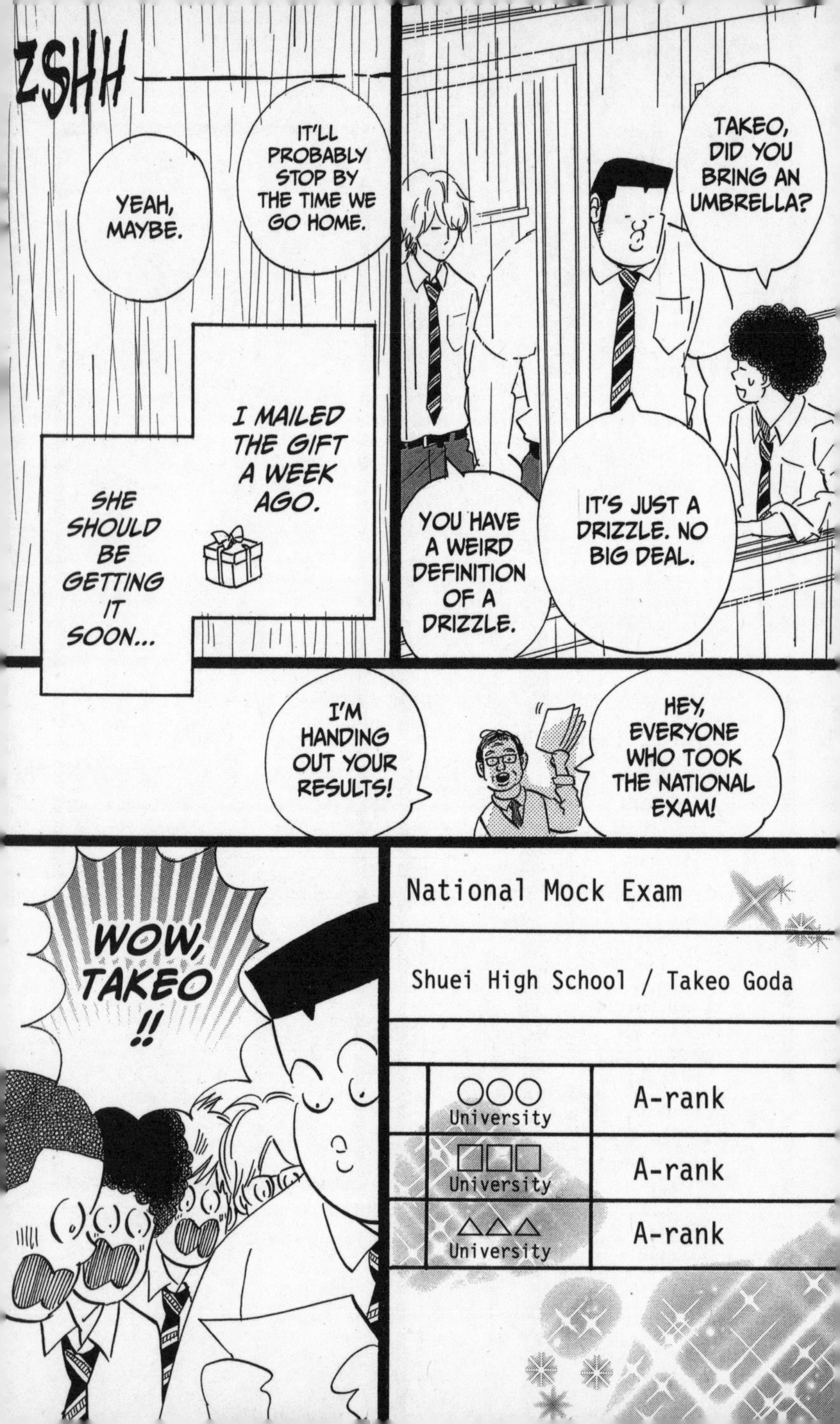
TAKEO, DID YOU BRING AN UMBRELLA?
IT'S JUST A DRIZZLE. NO BIG DEAL.
YOU HAVE A WEIRD DEFINITION OF A DRIZZLE.
ZSHH
IT'LL PROBABLY STOP BY THE TIME WE GO HOME.
YEAH, MAYBE.
I MAILED THE GIFT A WEEK AGO.
SHE SHOULD BE GETTING IT SOON...
HEY, EVERYONE WHO TOOK THE NATIONAL EXAM!
I'M HANDING OUT YOUR RESULTS!
National Mock Exam
Shuei High School / Takeo Goda
○○○ University
A-rank
□□□ University
A-rank
△△△ University
A-rank
WOW, TAKEO!!

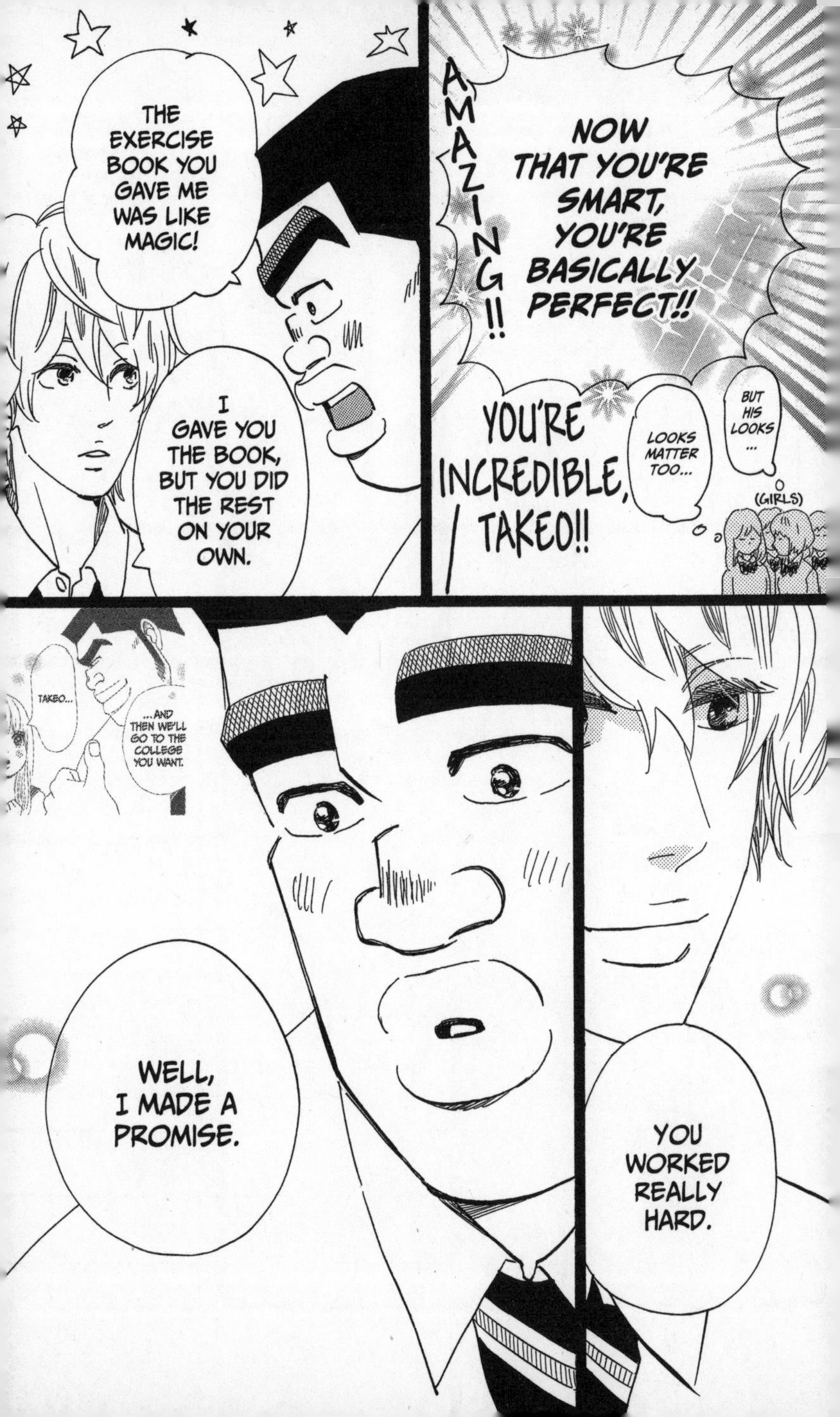
NOW THAT YOU'RE SMART, YOU'RE BASICALLY PERFECT!!
AMAZING!!
BUT HIS LOOKS...
LOOKS MATTER TOO...
YOU'RE INCREDIBLE, TAKEO!!
(GIRLS)
THE EXERCISE BOOK YOU GAVE ME WAS LIKE MAGIC!
I GAVE YOU THE BOOK, BUT YOU DID THE REST ON YOUR OWN.
YOU WORKED REALLY HARD.
WELL, I MADE A PROMISE.
...AND THEN WE'LL GO TO THE COLLEGE YOU WANT.
TAKEO...

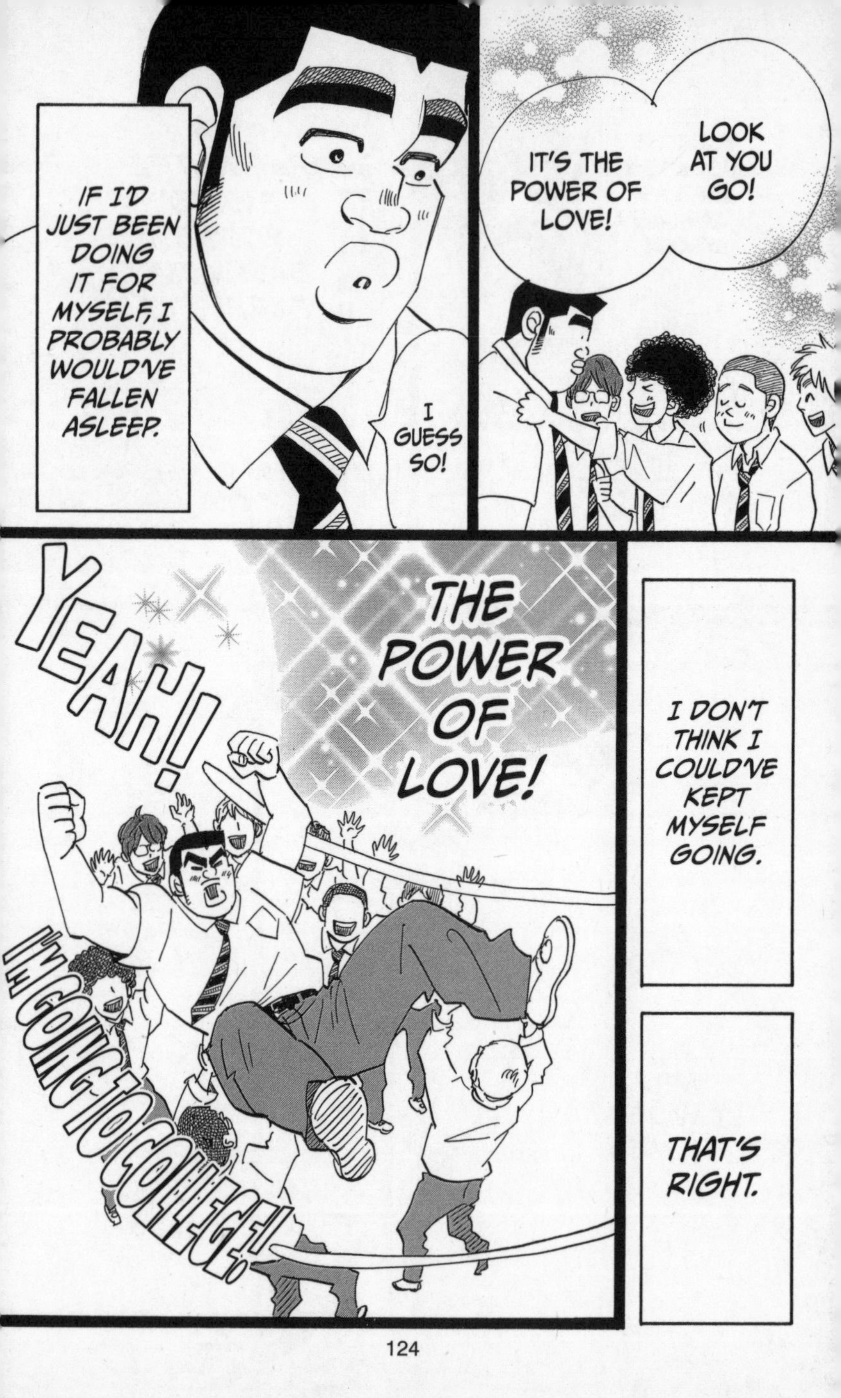
LOOK AT YOU GO!
IT'S THE POWER OF LOVE!
I GUESS SO!
IF I'D JUST BEEN DOING IT FOR MYSELF, I PROBABLY WOULD'VE FALLEN ASLEEP.
I DON'T THINK I COULD'VE KEPT MYSELF GOING.
THAT'S RIGHT.
THE POWER OF LOVE!
YEAH!
I'M GOING TO COLLEGE!

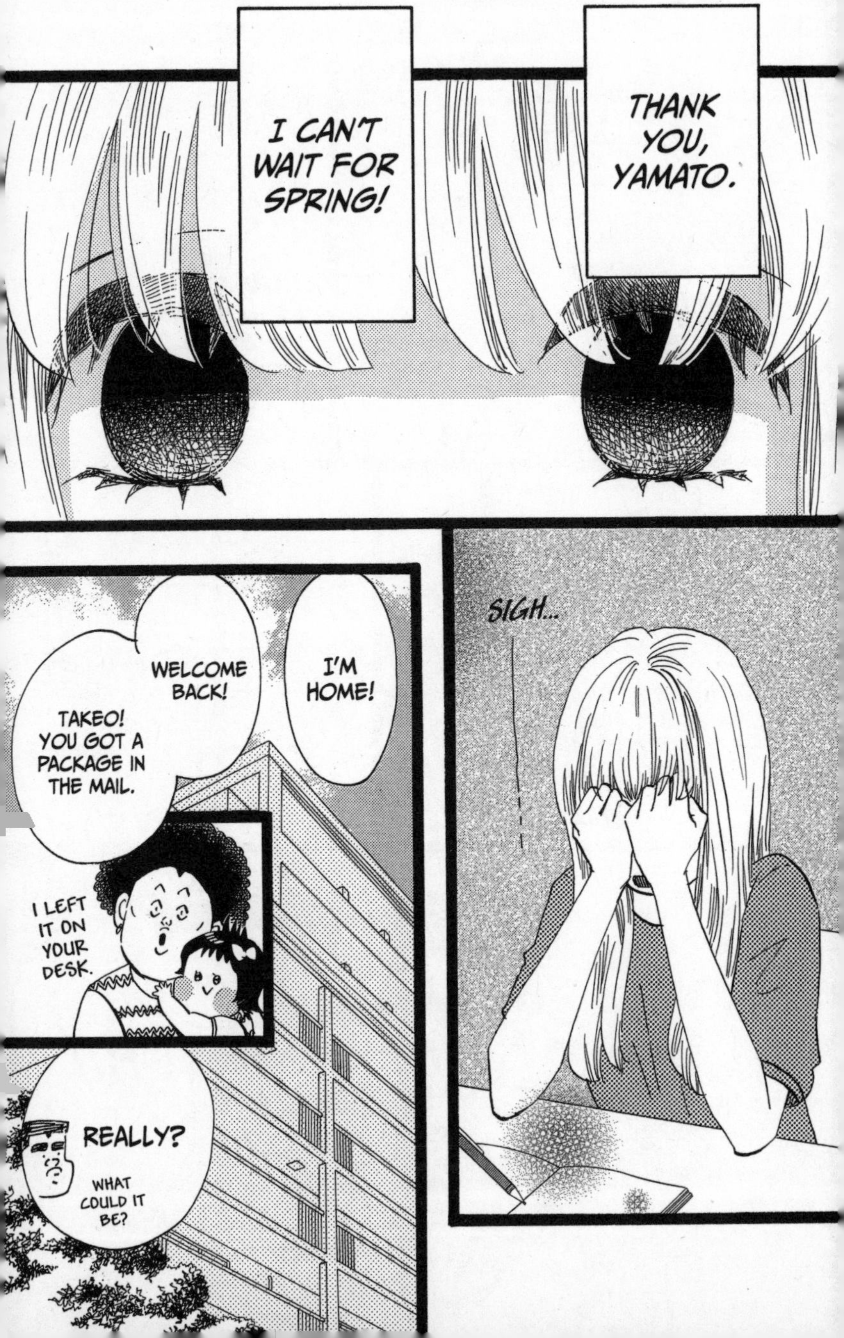
THANK YOU, YAMATO.
I CAN'T WAIT FOR SPRING!
SIGH...
I'M HOME!
WELCOME BACK!
TAKEO! YOU GOT A PACKAGE IN THE MAIL.
I LEFT IT ON YOUR DESK.
REALLY?
WHAT COULD IT BE?

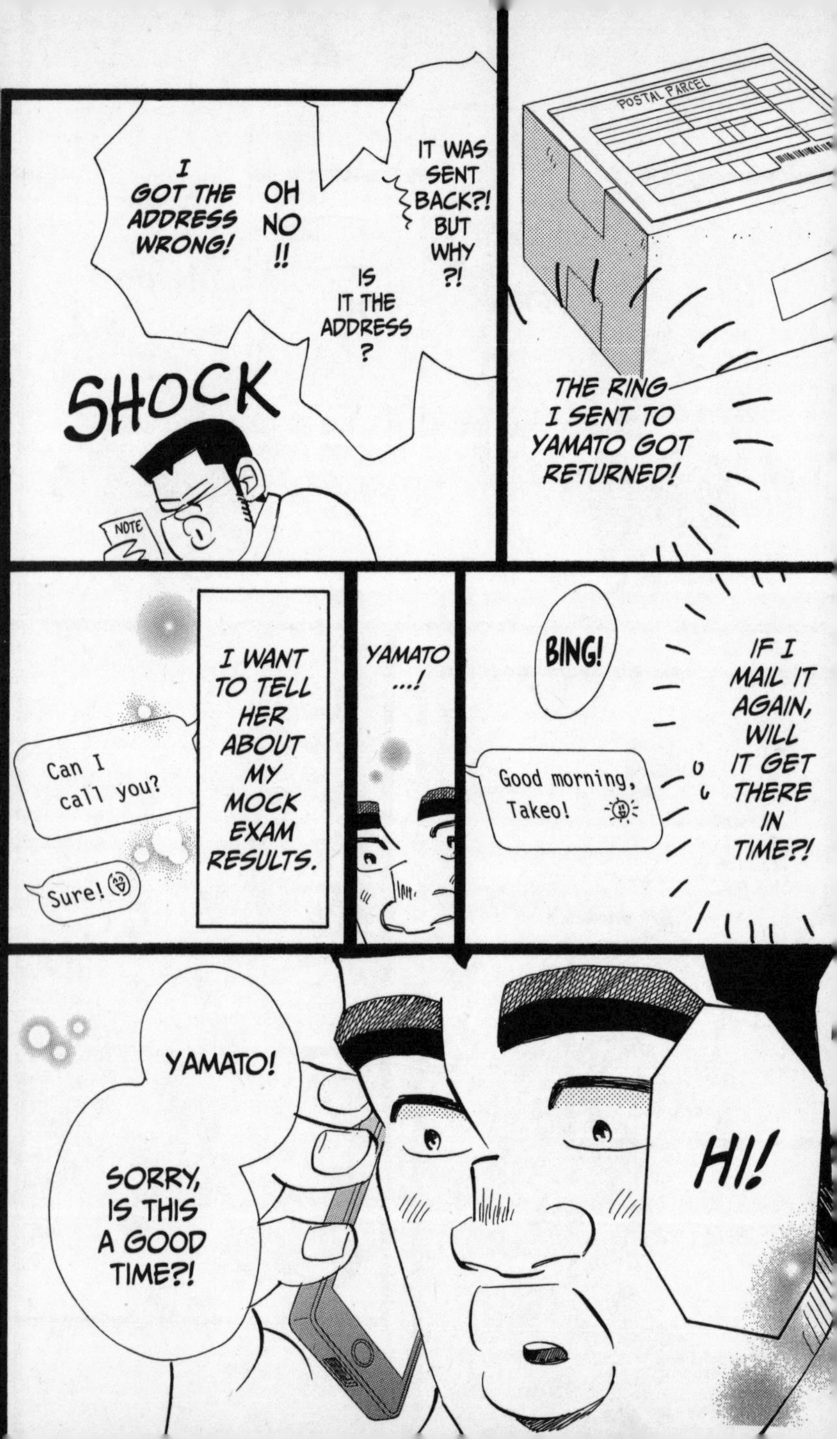
POSTAL PARCEL
THE RING I SENT TO YAMATO GOT RETURNED!
IT WAS SENT BACK?! BUT WHY ?!
IS IT THE ADDRESS ?
OH NO !!
I GOT THE ADDRESS WRONG!
SHOCK
NOTE
IF I MAIL IT AGAIN, WILL IT GET THERE IN TIME?!
BING!
Good morning, Takeo!
YAMATO ...!
I WANT TO TELL HER ABOUT MY MOCK EXAM RESULTS.
Can I call you?
Sure!
HI!
YAMATO!
SORRY, IS THIS A GOOD TIME?!

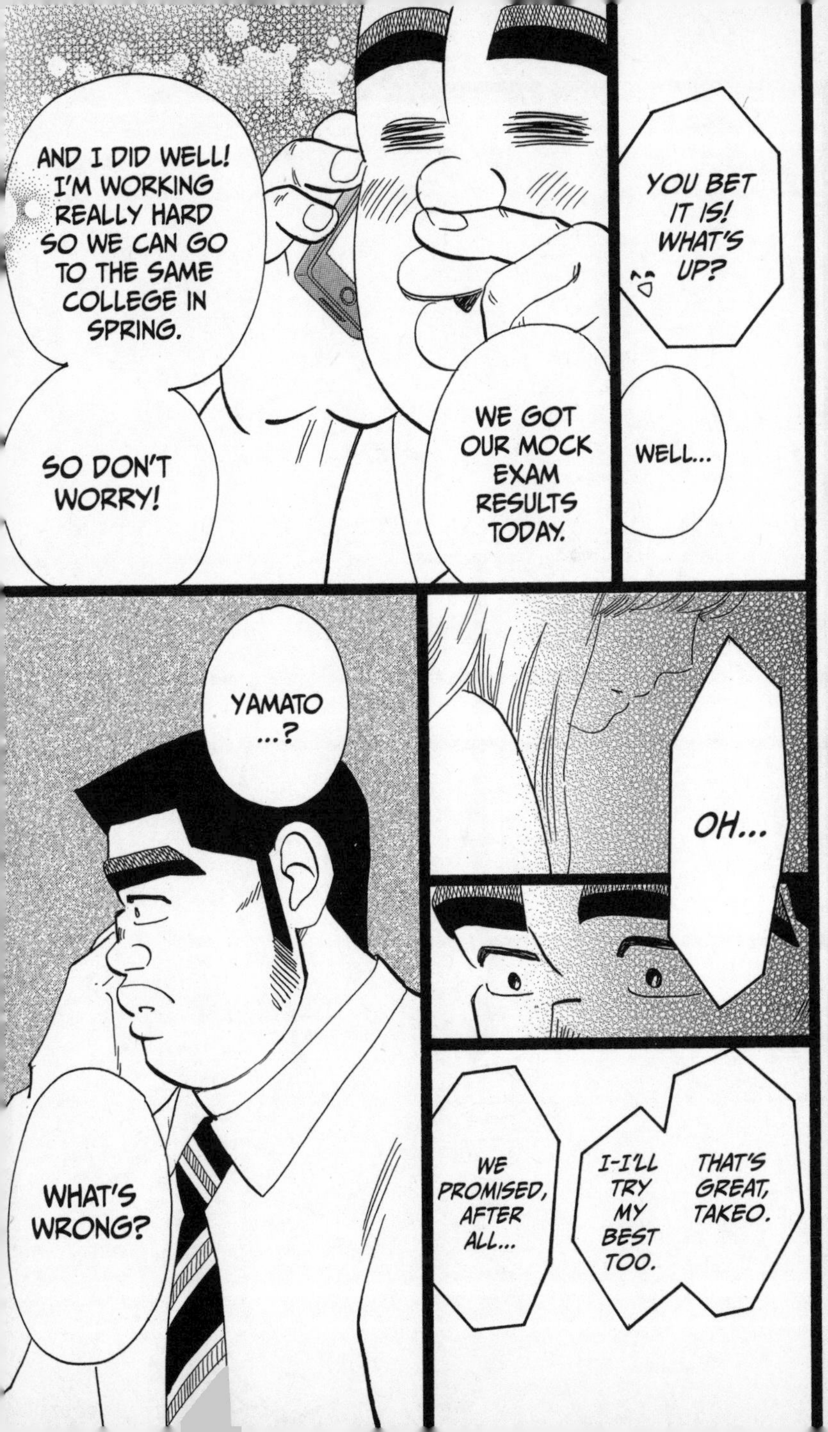
YOU BET IT IS! WHAT'S UP?
WELL...
WE GOT OUR MOCK EXAM RESULTS TODAY.
AND I DID WELL! I'M WORKING REALLY HARD SO WE CAN GO TO THE SAME COLLEGE IN SPRING.
SO DON'T WORRY!
OH...
THAT'S GREAT, TAKEO.
I-I'LL TRY MY BEST TOO.
WE PROMISED, AFTER ALL...
YAMATO ...?
WHAT'S WRONG?

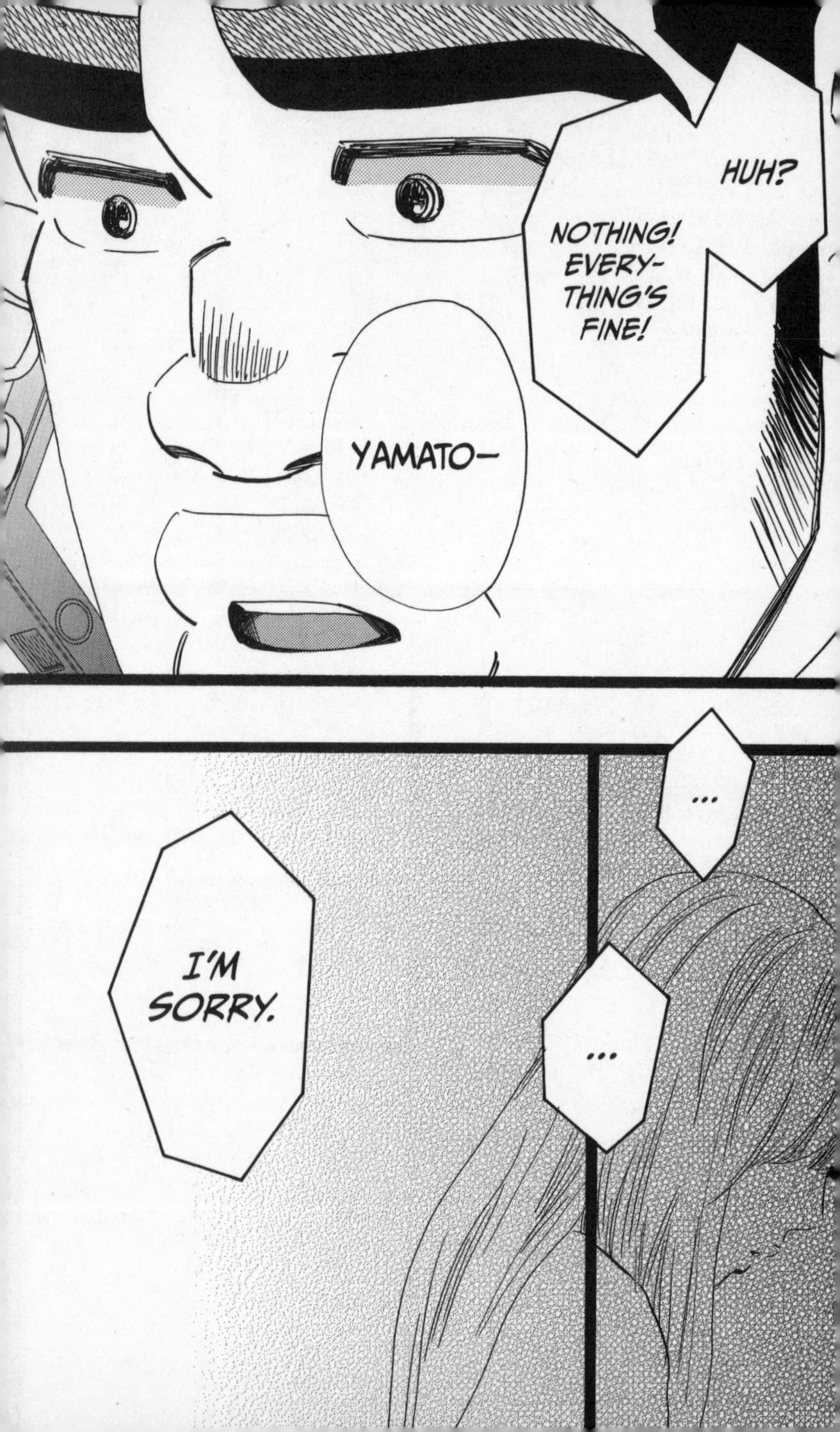
HUH?
NOTHING! EVERY-THING'S FINE!
YAMATO—
...
...
I'M SORRY.

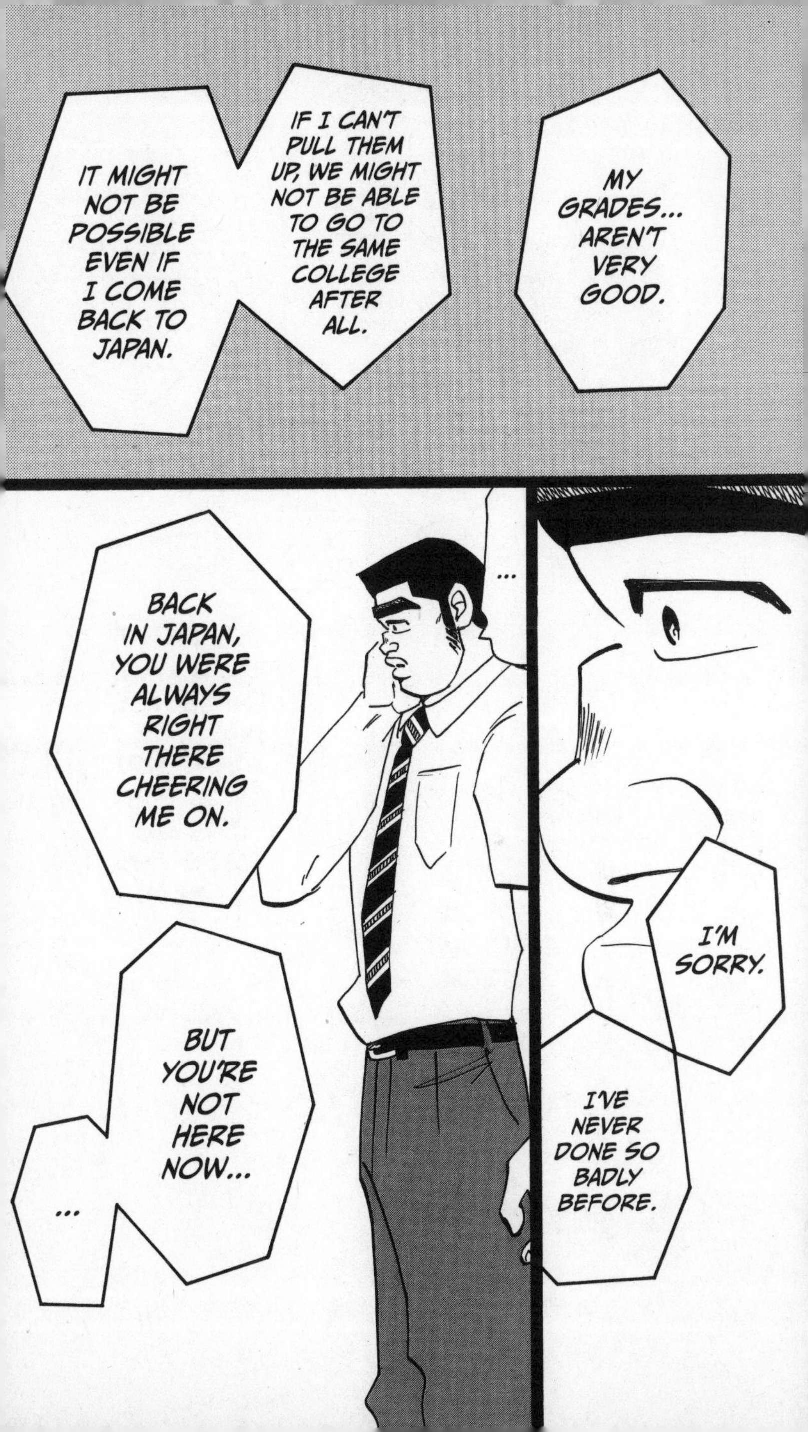
MY GRADES... AREN'T VERY GOOD.
IF I CAN'T PULL THEM UP, WE MIGHT NOT BE ABLE TO GO TO THE SAME COLLEGE AFTER ALL.
IT MIGHT NOT BE POSSIBLE EVEN IF I COME BACK TO JAPAN.
I'M SORRY.
I'VE NEVER DONE SO BADLY BEFORE.
...
BACK IN JAPAN, YOU WERE ALWAYS RIGHT THERE CHEERING ME ON.
BUT YOU'RE NOT HERE NOW...
...

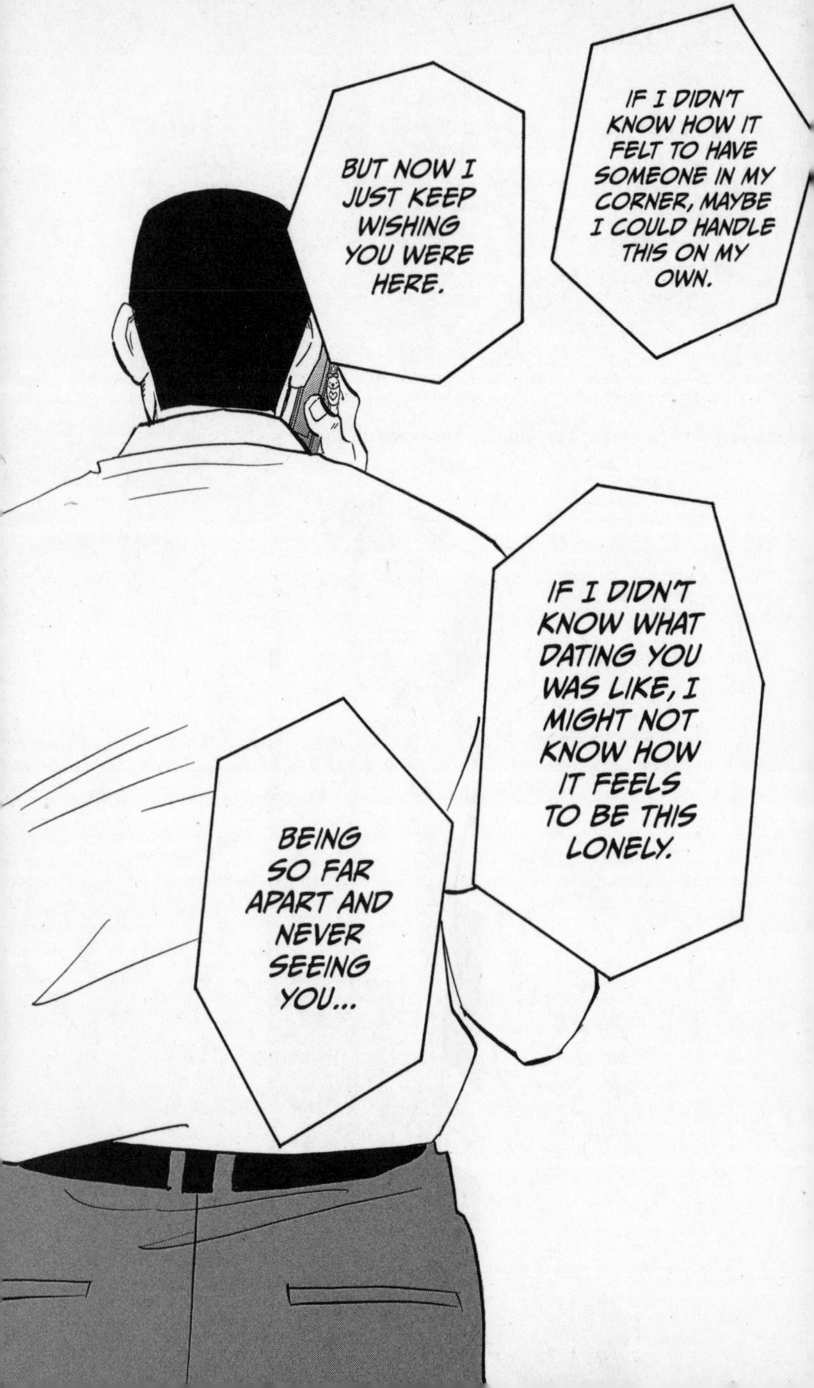
IF I DIDN'T KNOW HOW IT FELT TO HAVE SOMEONE IN MY CORNER, MAYBE I COULD HANDLE THIS ON MY OWN.
BUT NOW I JUST KEEP WISHING YOU WERE HERE.
IF I DIDN'T KNOW WHAT DATING YOU WAS LIKE, I MIGHT NOT KNOW HOW IT FEELS TO BE THIS LONELY.
BEING SO FAR APART AND NEVER SEEING YOU...

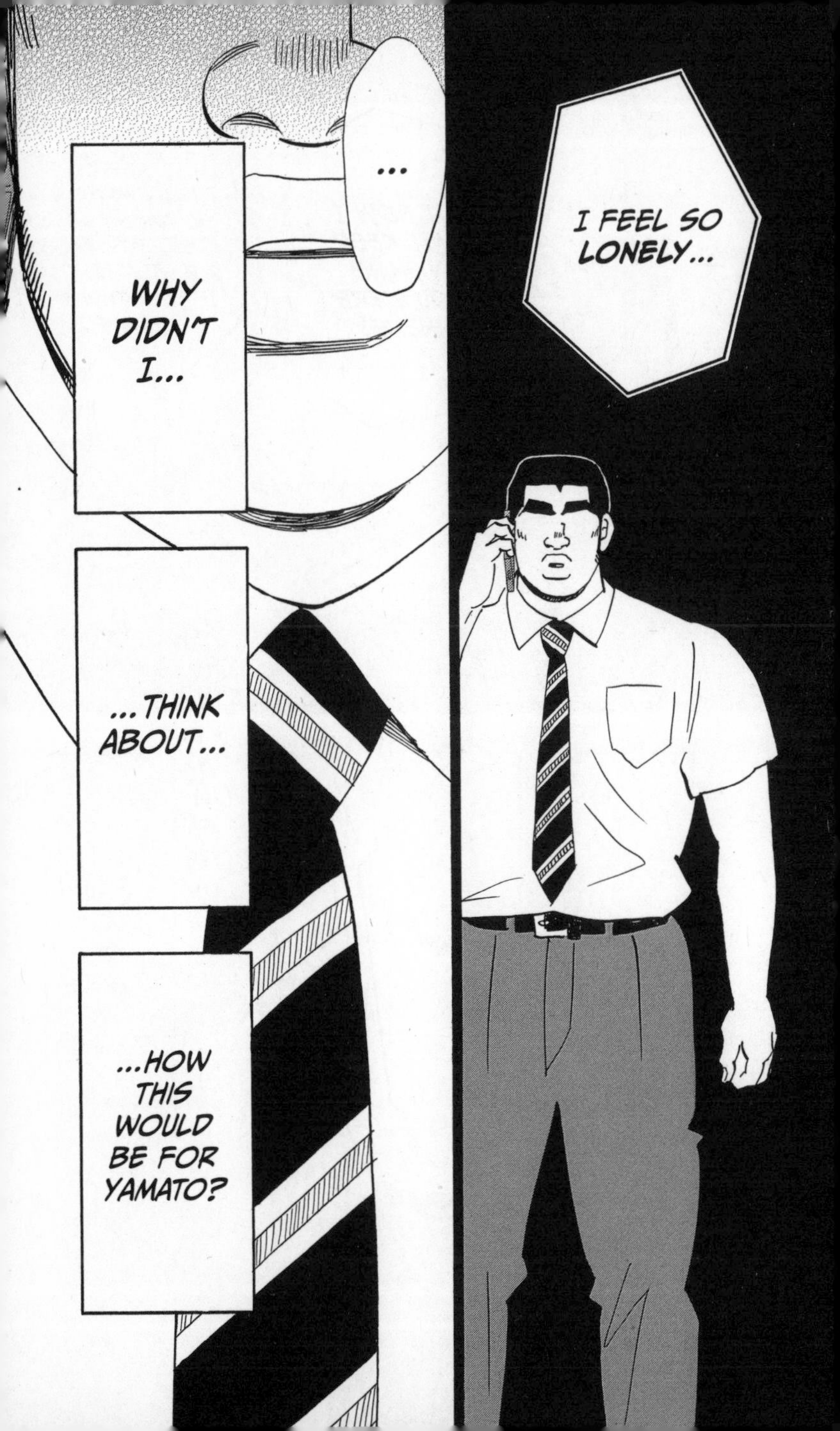
I FEEL SO LONELY...
...
WHY DIDN'T I...
...THINK ABOUT...
...HOW THIS WOULD BE FOR YAMATO?

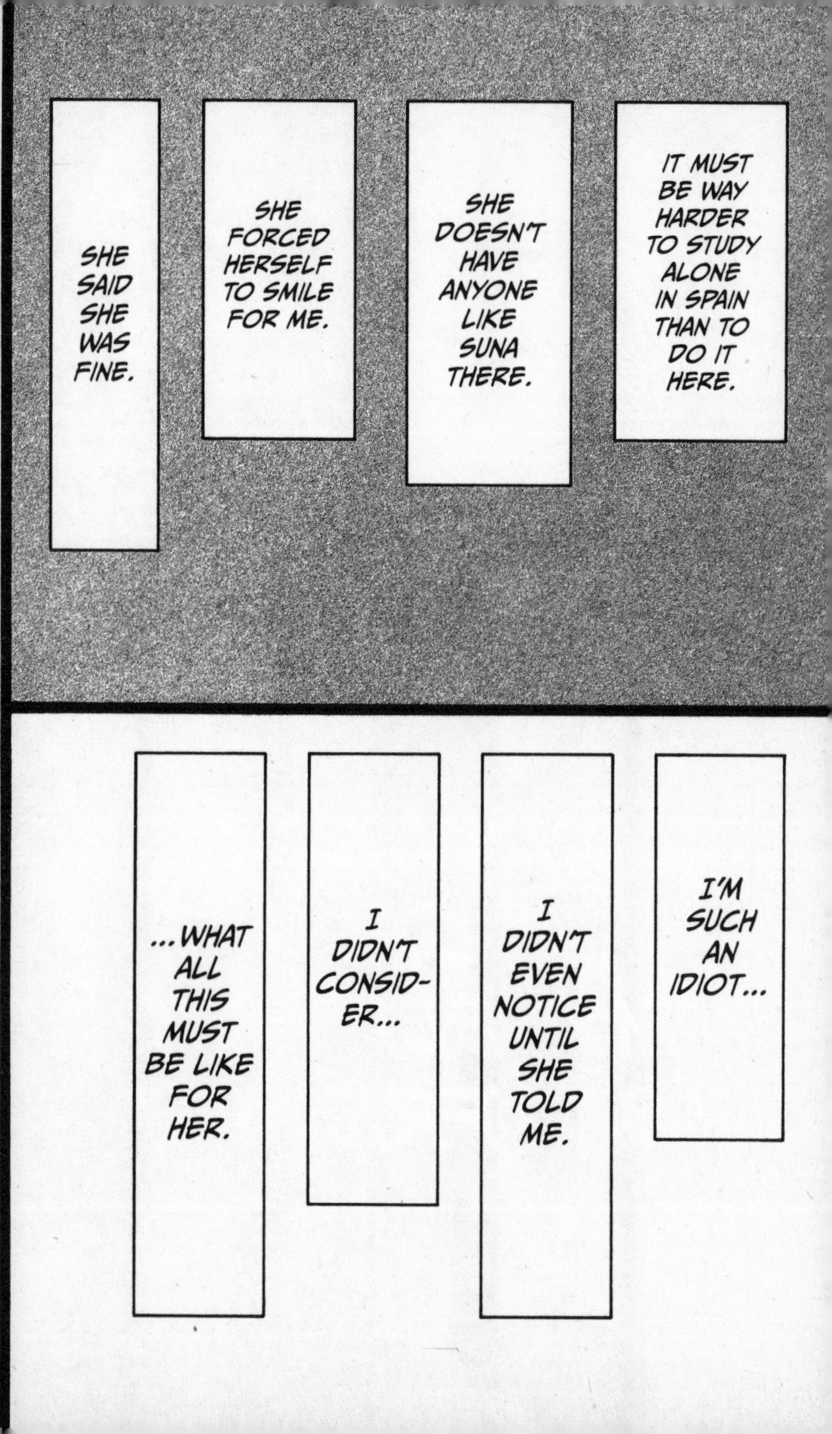
IT MUST BE WAY HARDER TO STUDY ALONE IN SPAIN THAN TO DO IT HERE.
SHE DOESN'T HAVE ANYONE LIKE SUNA THERE.
SHE FORCED HERSELF TO SMILE FOR ME.
SHE SAID SHE WAS FINE.
I'M SUCH AN IDIOT...
I DIDN'T EVEN NOTICE UNTIL SHE TOLD ME.
I DIDN'T CONSIDER...
...WHAT ALL THIS MUST BE LIKE FOR HER.

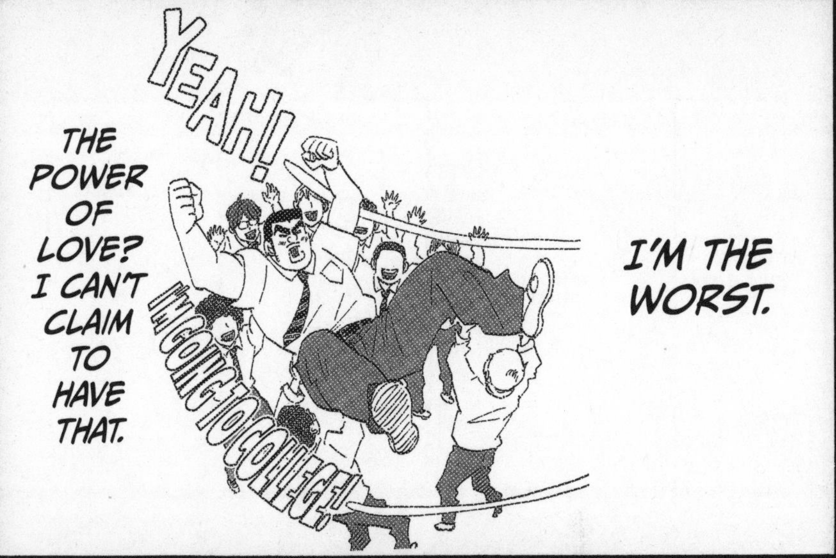
I'M THE WORST.
YEAH!
THE POWER OF LOVE? I CAN'T CLAIM TO HAVE THAT.
I'M GOING TO COLLEGE!

HOW CAN I CALL MYSELF HER BOYFRIEND?

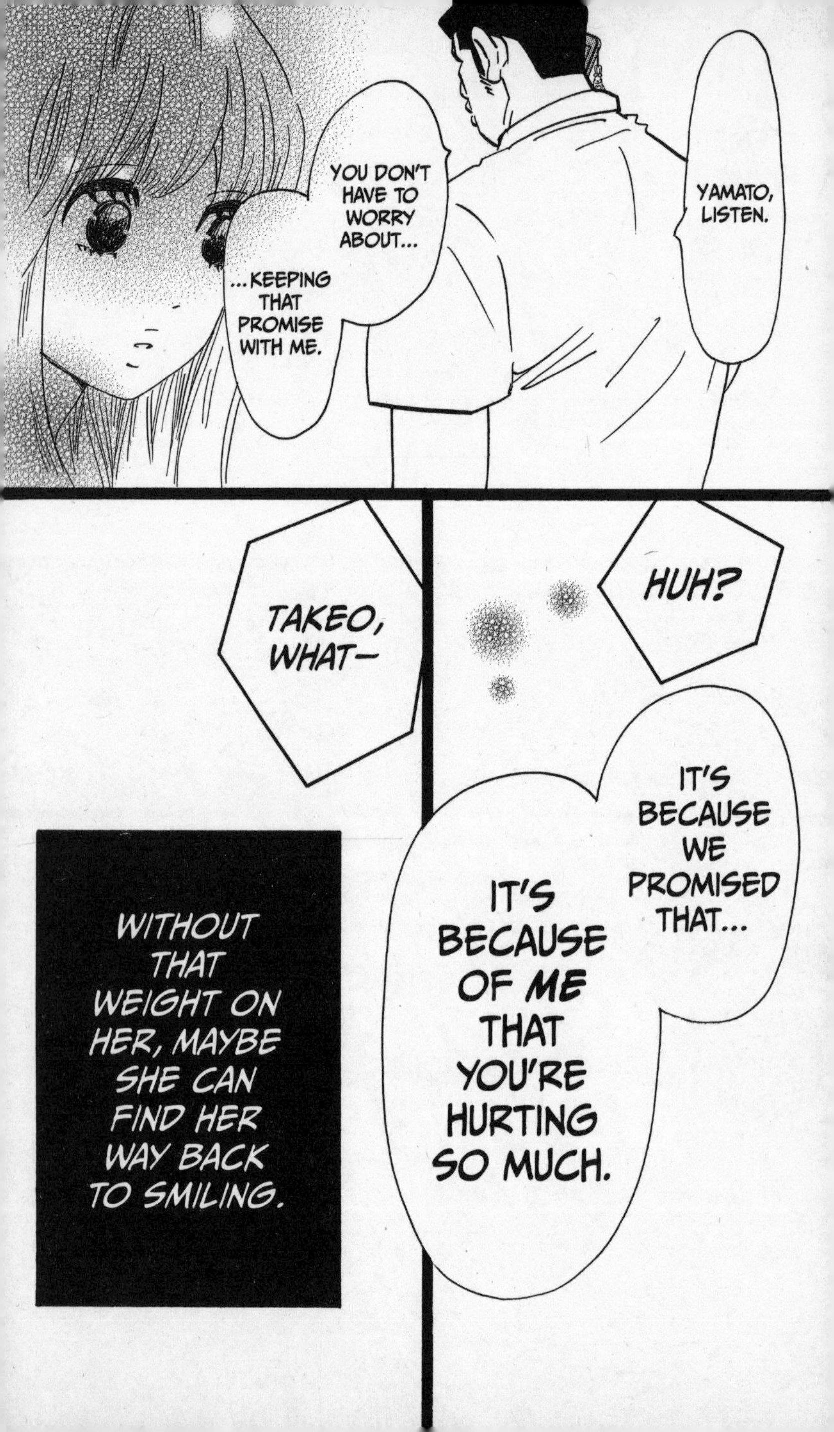
YAMATO, LISTEN.
YOU DON'T HAVE TO WORRY ABOUT...
...KEEPING THAT PROMISE WITH ME.
HUH?
IT'S BECAUSE WE PROMISED THAT...
IT'S BECAUSE OF ME THAT YOU'RE HURTING SO MUCH.
TAKEO, WHAT—
WITHOUT THAT WEIGHT ON HER, MAYBE SHE CAN FIND HER WAY BACK TO SMILING.

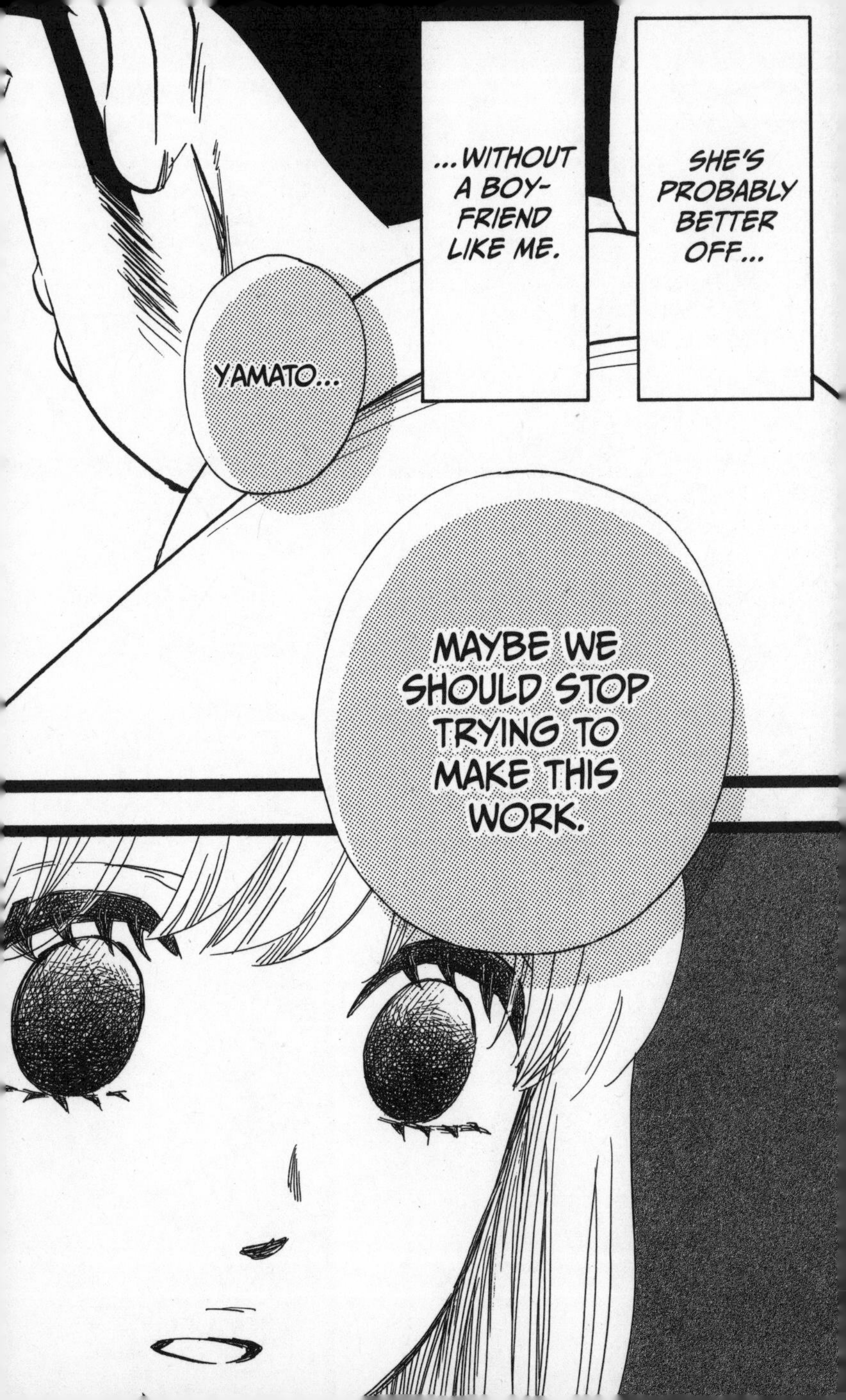
SHE'S PROBABLY BETTER OFF...
...WITHOUT A BOY-FRIEND LIKE ME.
YAMATO...
MAYBE WE SHOULD STOP TRYING TO MAKE THIS WORK.

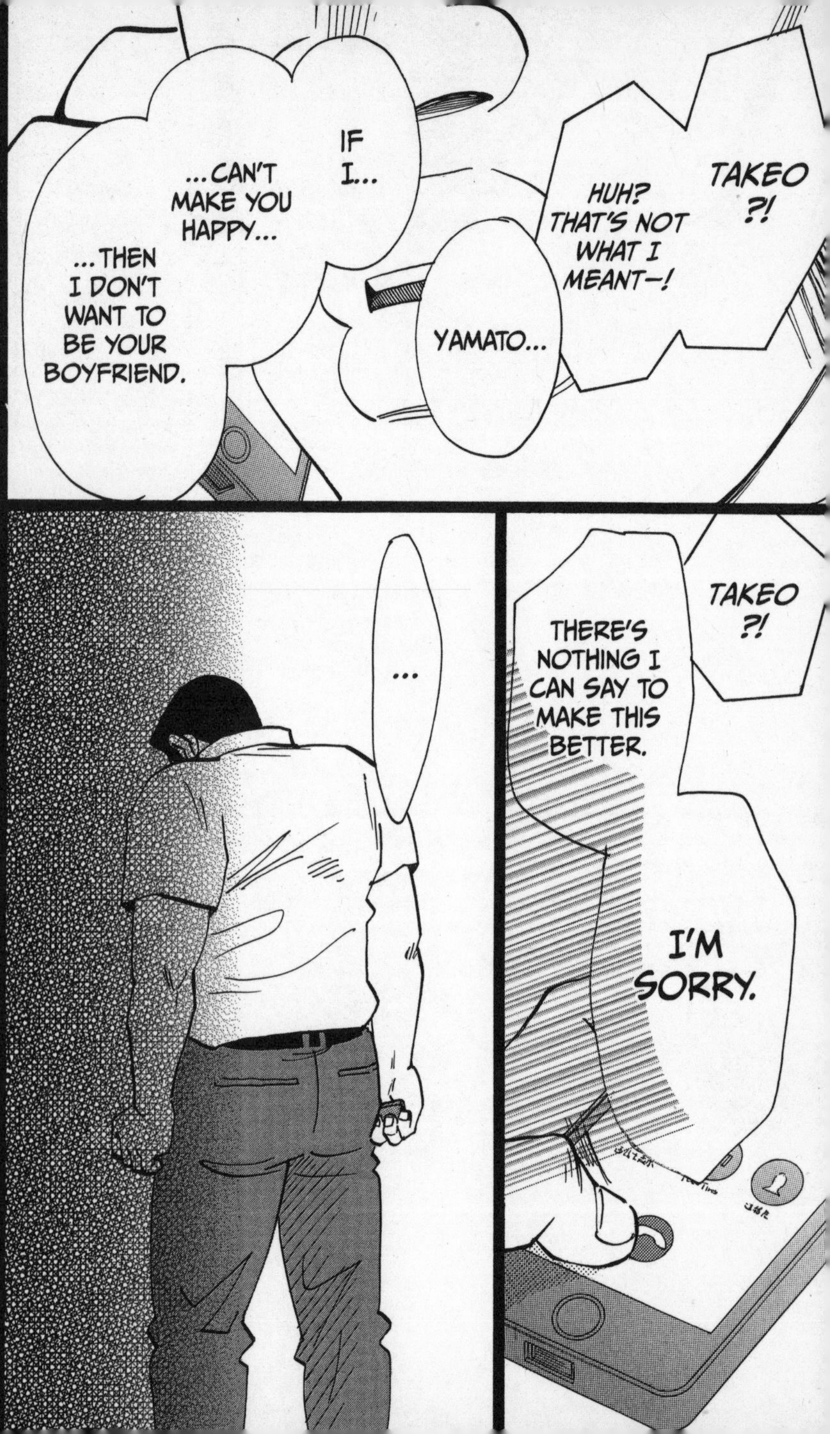
TAKEO ?!
HUH? THAT'S NOT WHAT I MEANT—!
YAMATO...
IF I...
...CAN'T MAKE YOU HAPPY...
...THEN I DON'T WANT TO BE YOUR BOYFRIEND.
TAKEO ?!
THERE'S NOTHING I CAN SAY TO MAKE THIS BETTER.
I'M SORRY.
...

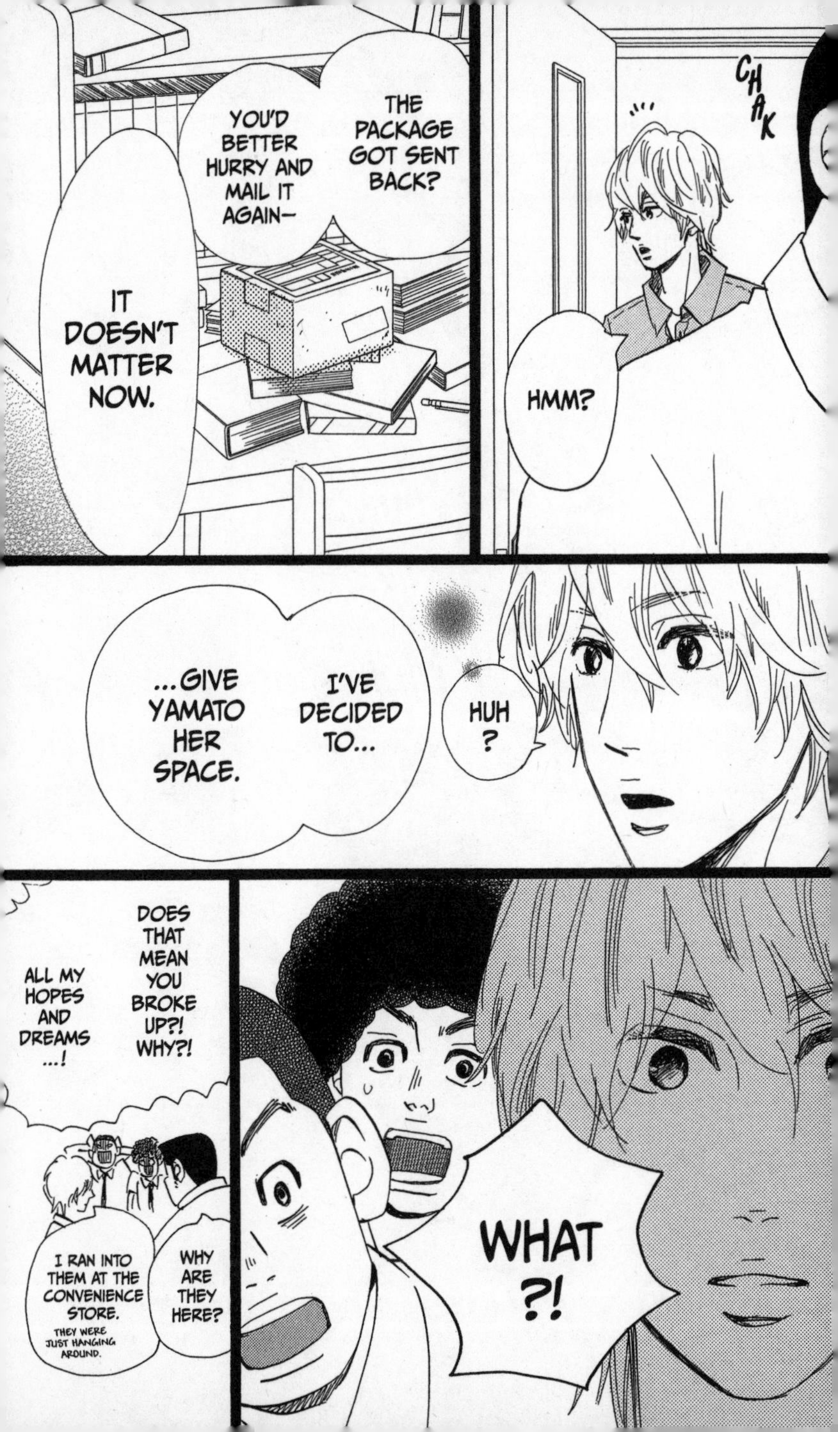
CHAK
HMM?
THE PACKAGE GOT SENT BACK?
YOU'D BETTER HURRY AND MAIL IT AGAIN—
IT DOESN'T MATTER NOW.
HUH?
I'VE DECIDED TO...
...GIVE YAMATO HER SPACE.
WHAT?!
DOES THAT MEAN YOU BROKE UP?! WHY?!
ALL MY HOPES AND DREAMS...!
WHY ARE THEY HERE?
I RAN INTO THEM AT THE CONVENIENCE STORE.
THEY WERE JUST HANGING AROUND.

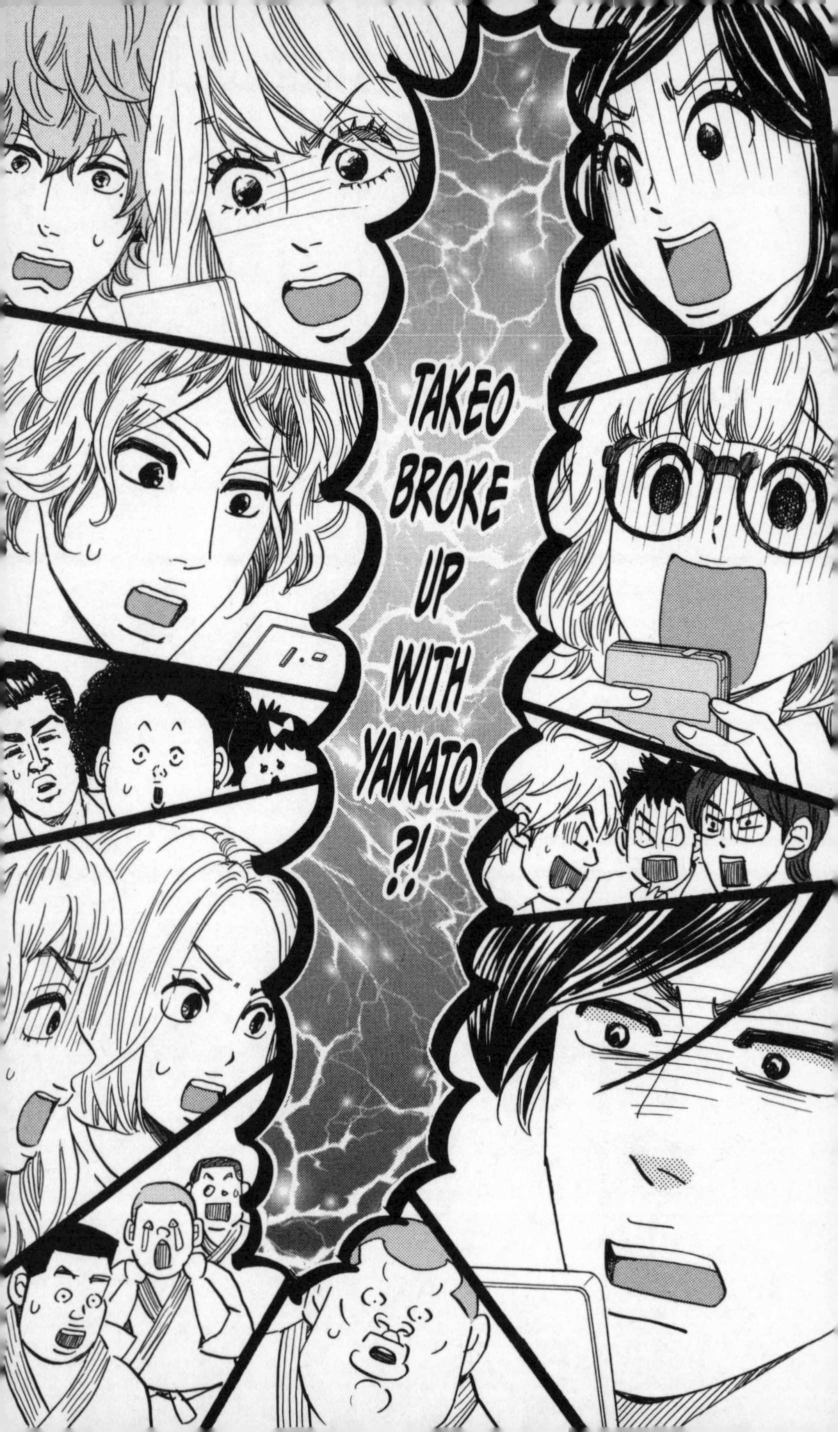
TAKEO BROKE UP WITH YAMATO ?!

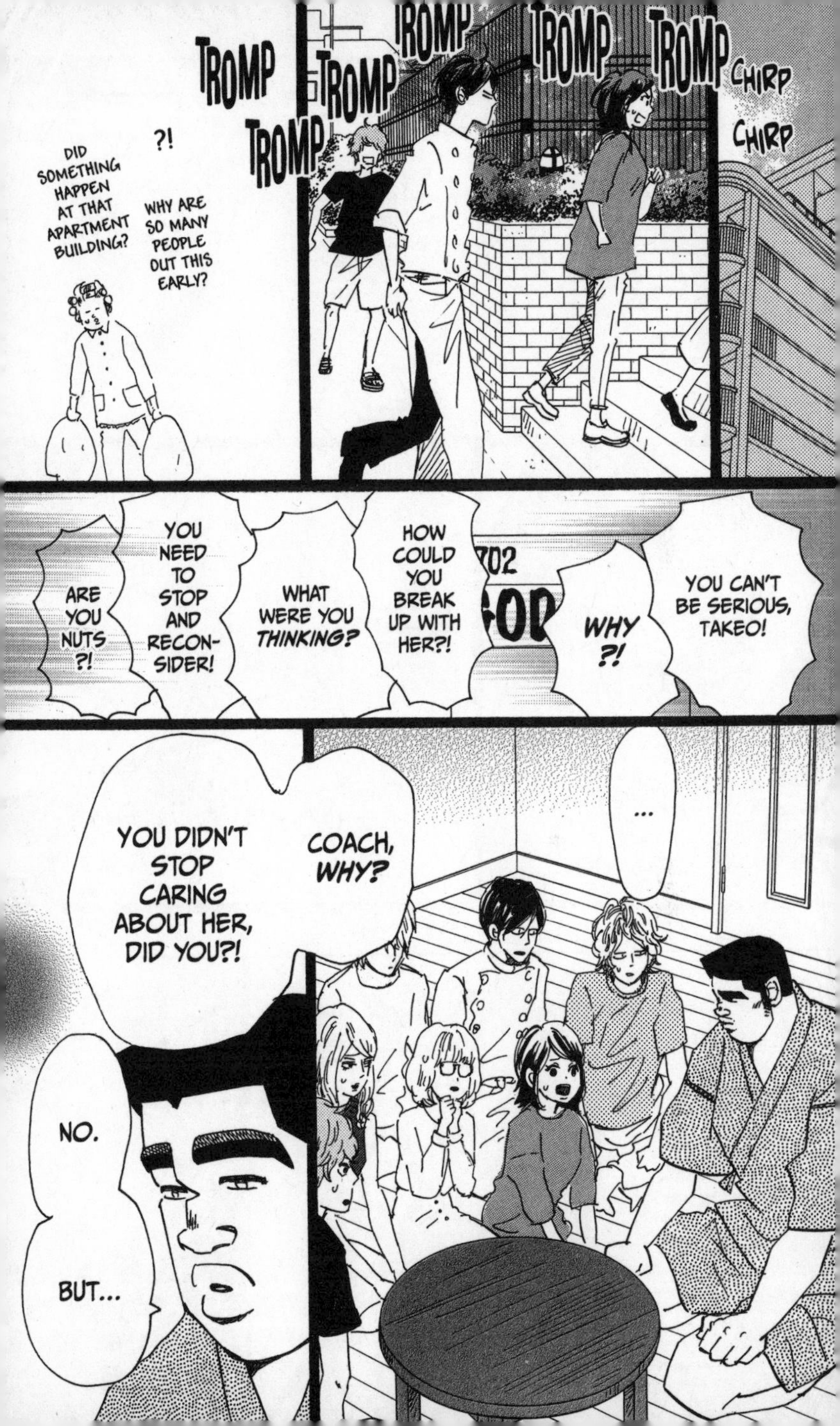
CHIRP
CHIRP
TROMP
TROMP
TROMP
TROMP
TROMP
TROMP
?!
WHY ARE SO MANY PEOPLE OUT THIS EARLY?
DID SOMETHING HAPPEN AT THAT APARTMENT BUILDING?
YOU CAN'T BE SERIOUS, TAKEO!
WHY ?!
702
HOW COULD YOU BREAK UP WITH HER?!
WHAT WERE YOU *THINKING?*
YOU NEED TO STOP AND RECONSIDER!
ARE YOU NUTS ?!
...
COACH, *WHY?*
YOU DIDN'T STOP CARING ABOUT HER, DID YOU?!
NO.
BUT...

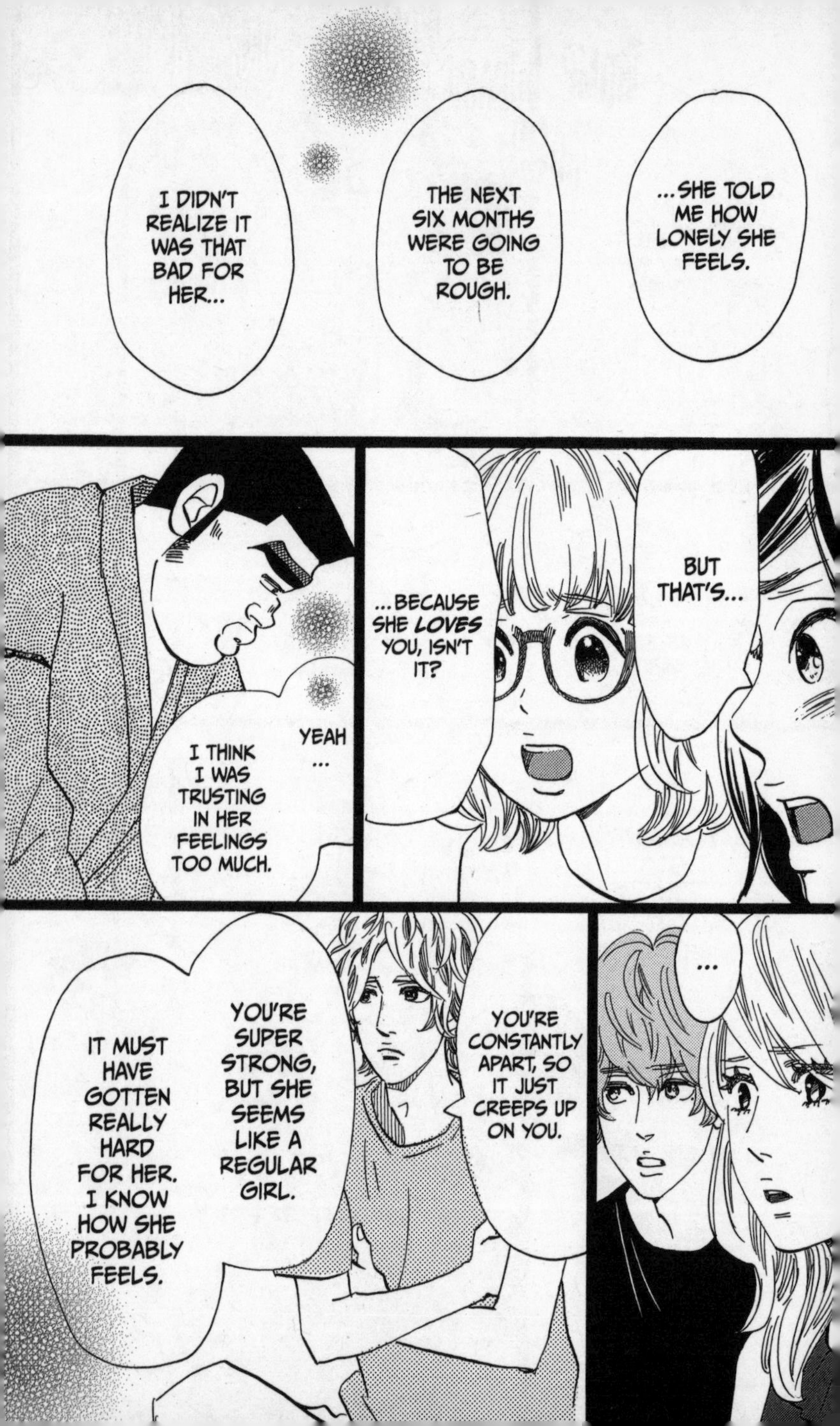
...SHE TOLD ME HOW LONELY SHE FEELS.
THE NEXT SIX MONTHS WERE GOING TO BE ROUGH.
I DIDN'T REALIZE IT WAS THAT BAD FOR HER...
BUT THAT'S...
...BECAUSE SHE *LOVES* YOU, ISN'T IT?
YEAH ...
I THINK I WAS TRUSTING IN HER FEELINGS TOO MUCH.
...
YOU'RE CONSTANTLY APART, SO IT JUST CREEPS UP ON YOU.
YOU'RE SUPER STRONG, BUT SHE SEEMS LIKE A REGULAR GIRL.
IT MUST HAVE GOTTEN REALLY HARD FOR HER. I KNOW HOW SHE PROBABLY FEELS.

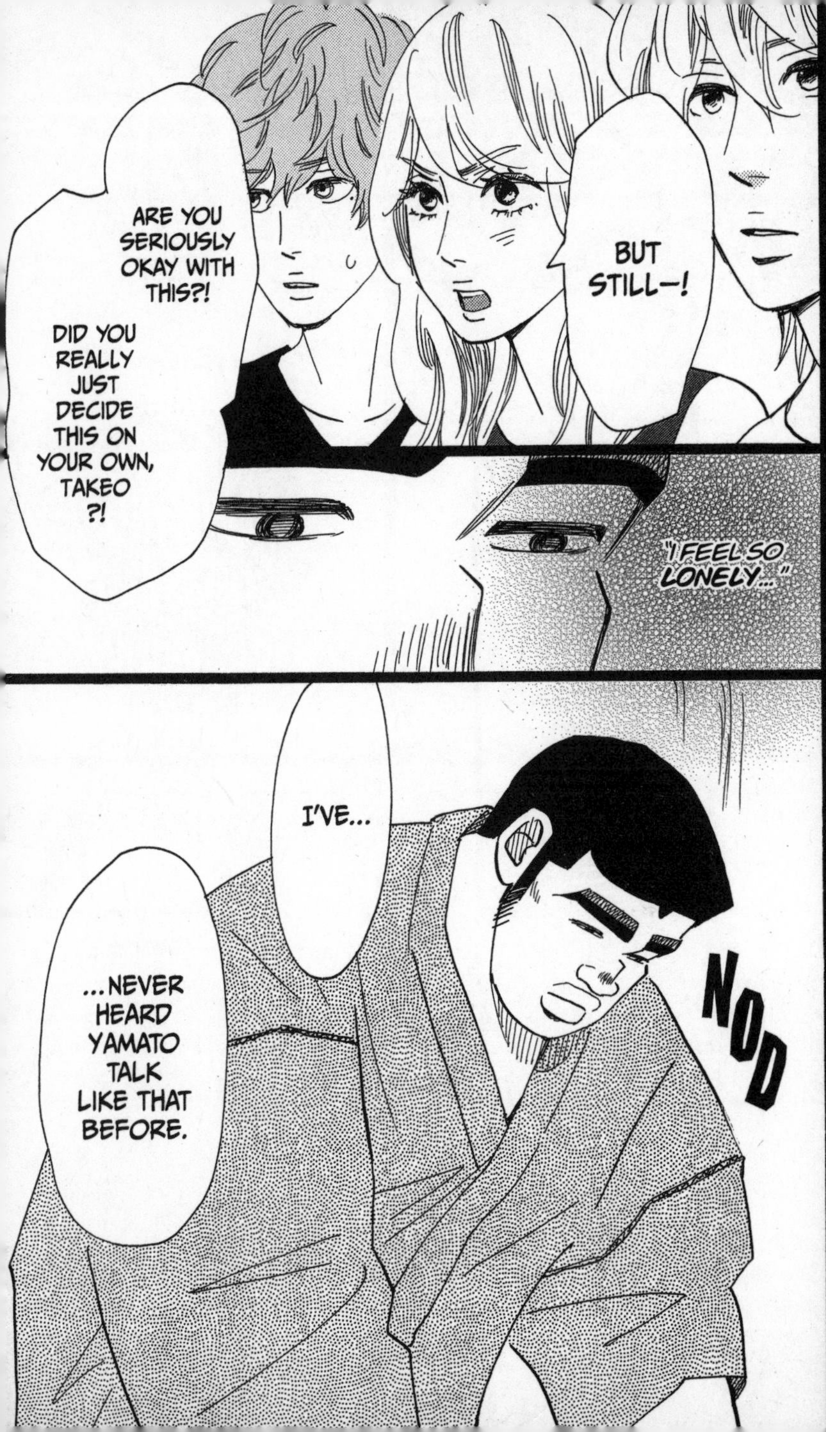
BUT STILL—!
ARE YOU SERIOUSLY OKAY WITH THIS?!
DID YOU REALLY JUST DECIDE THIS ON YOUR OWN, TAKEO?!
"I FEEL SO LONELY..."
I'VE...
NOD
...NEVER HEARD YAMATO TALK LIKE THAT BEFORE.

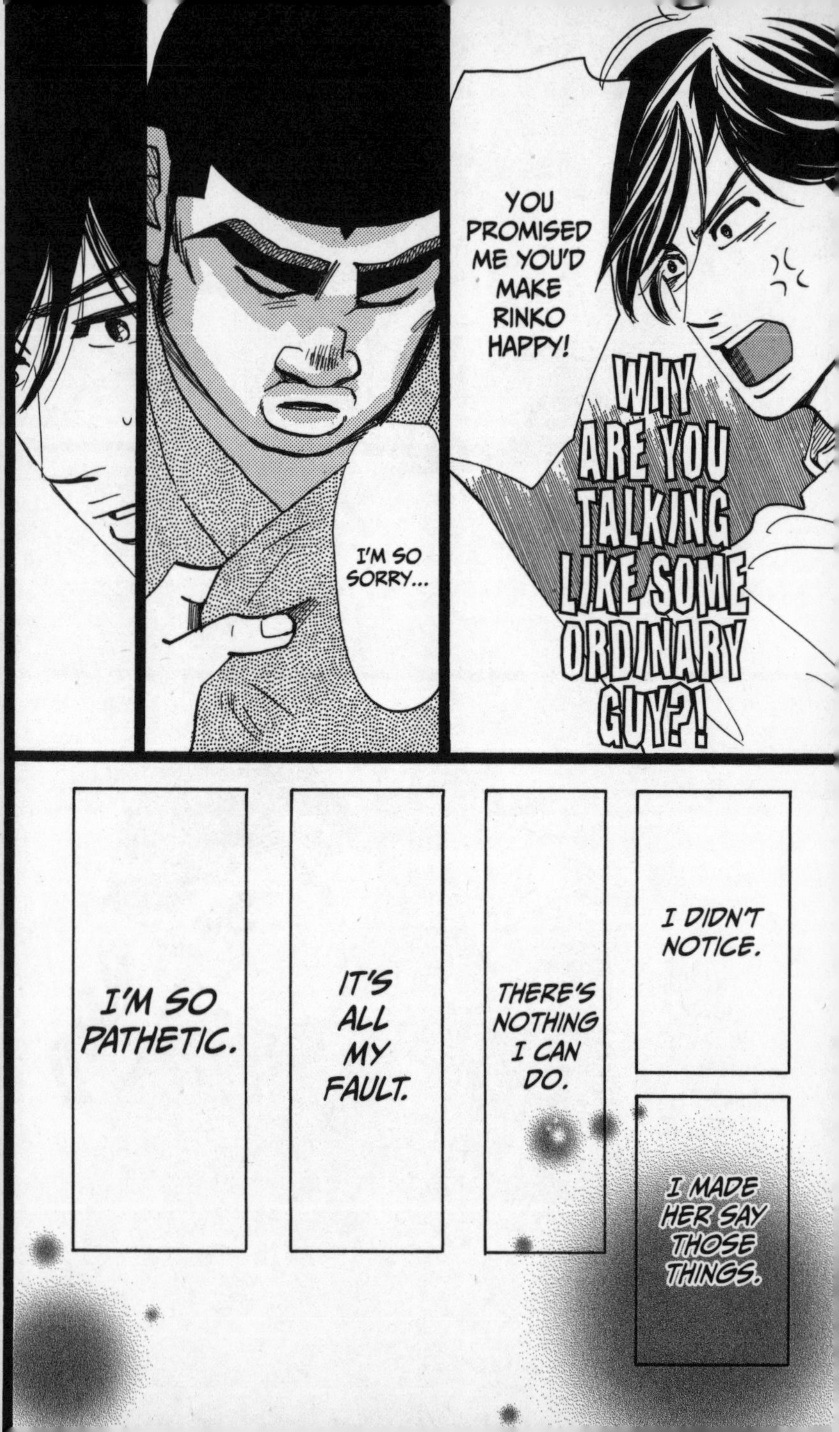
YOU PROMISED ME YOU'D MAKE RINKO HAPPY!
WHY ARE YOU TALKING LIKE SOME ORDINARY GUY?!
I'M SO SORRY...
I DIDN'T NOTICE.
I MADE HER SAY THOSE THINGS.
THERE'S NOTHING I CAN DO.
IT'S ALL MY FAULT.
I'M SO PATHETIC.

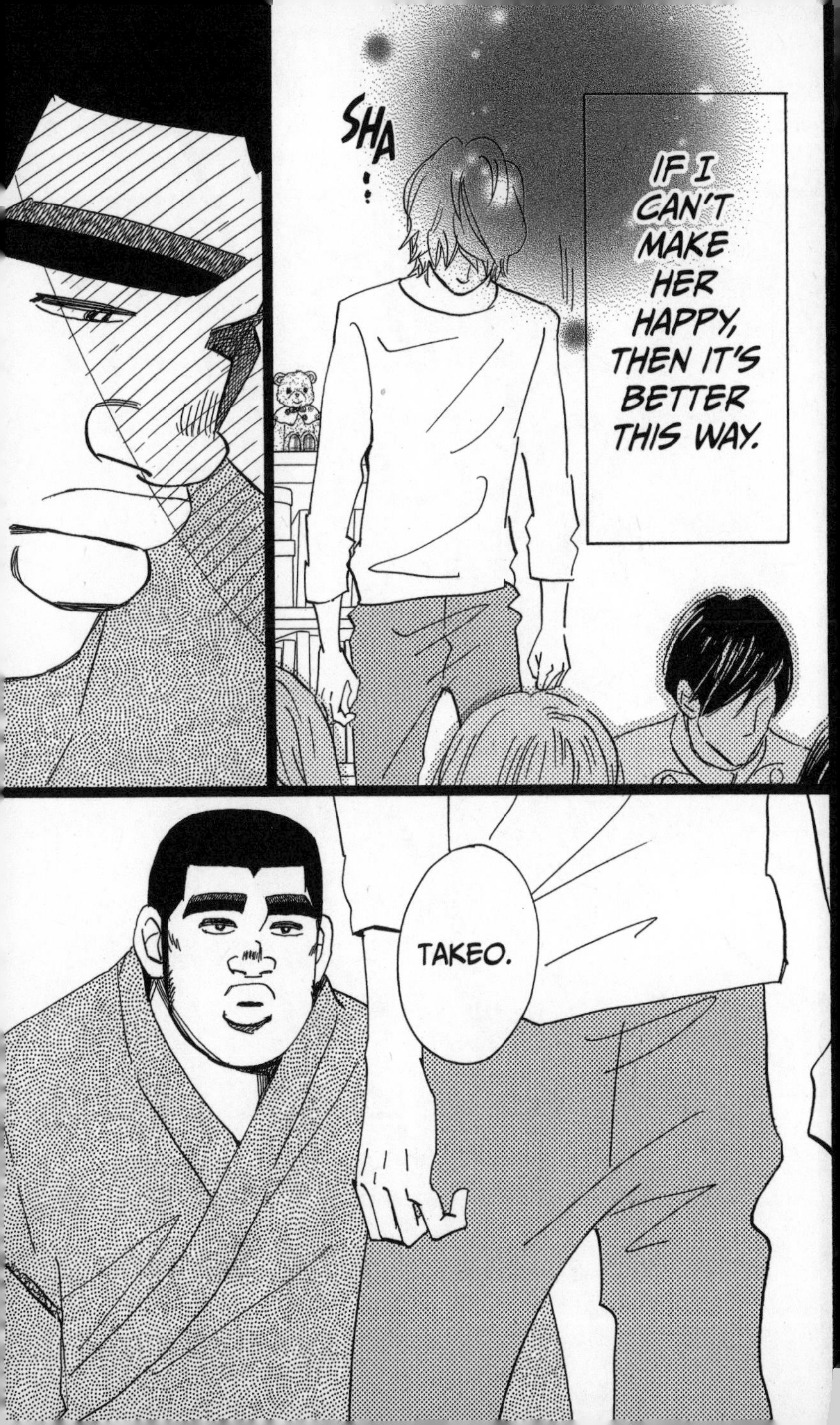
IF I CAN'T MAKE HER HAPPY, THEN IT'S BETTER THIS WAY.
SHA
TAKEO.

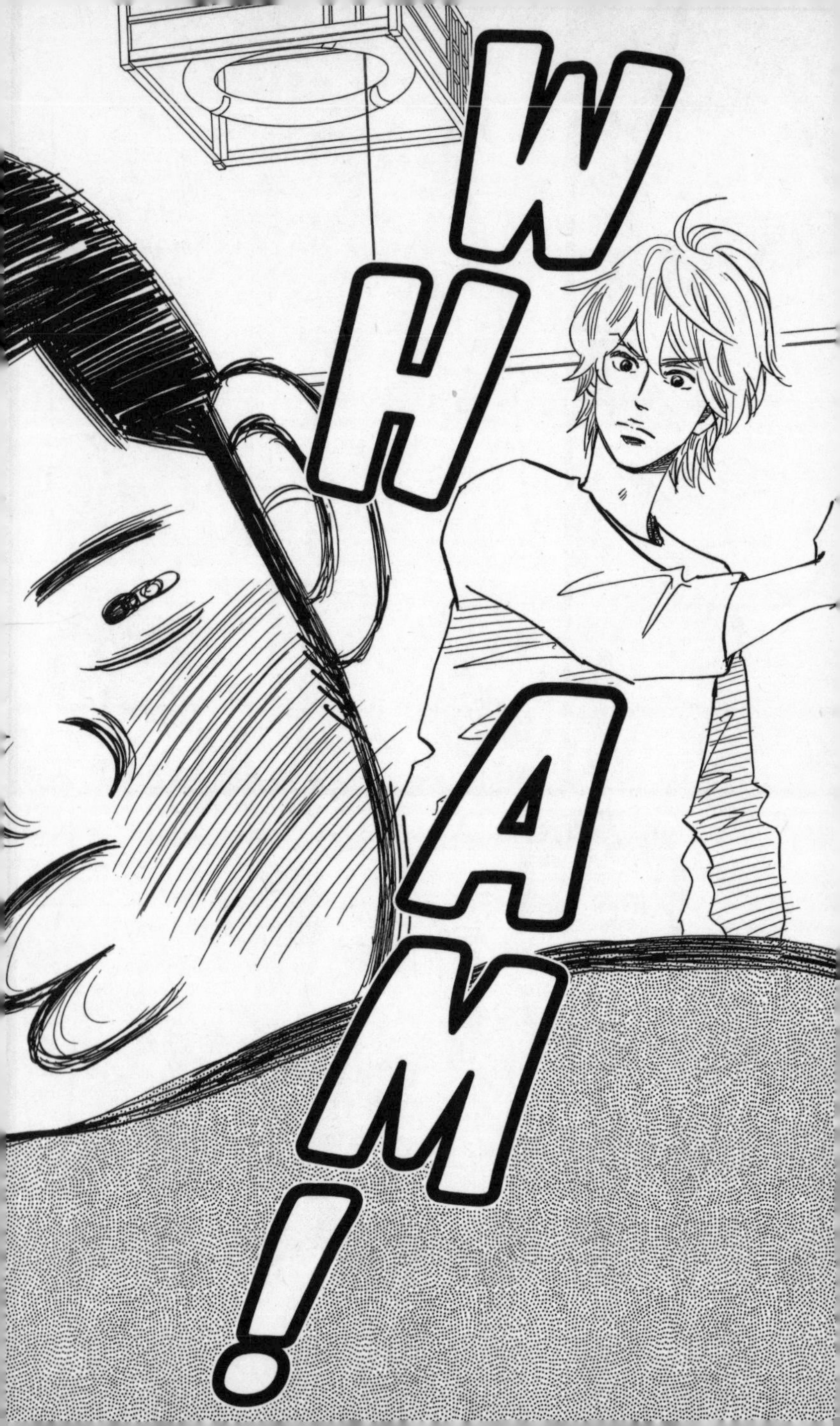
WHAM!

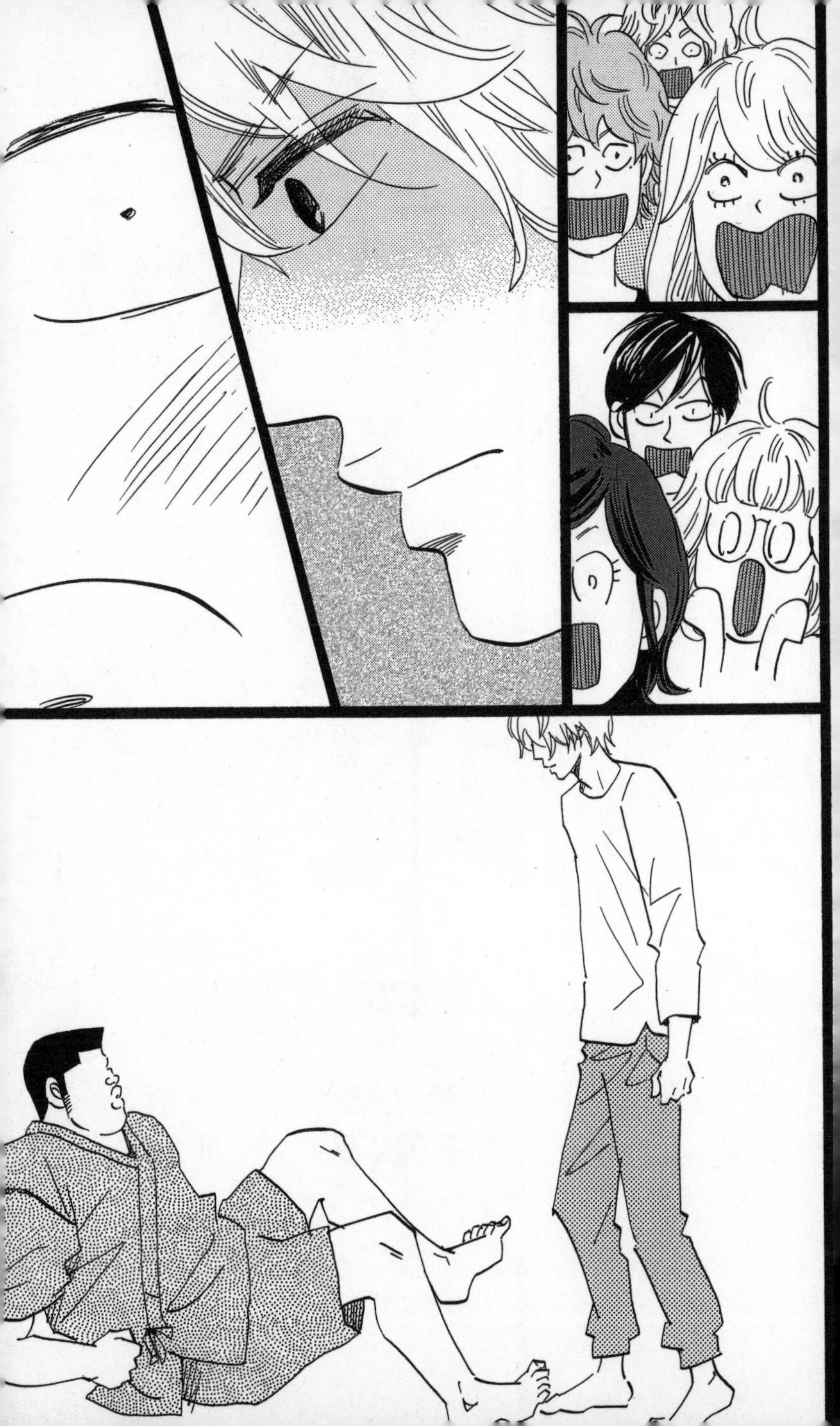

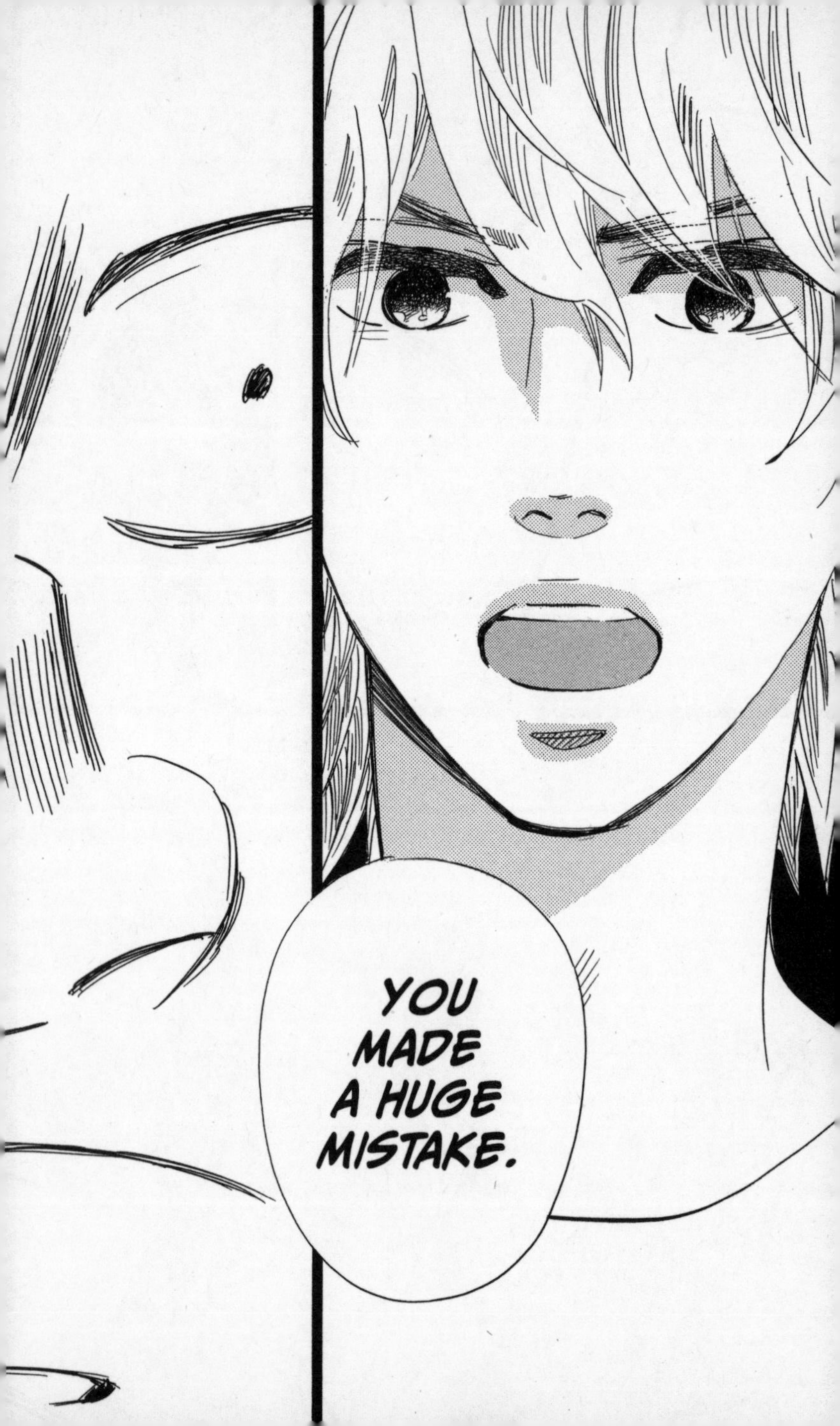
YOU MADE A HUGE MISTAKE.

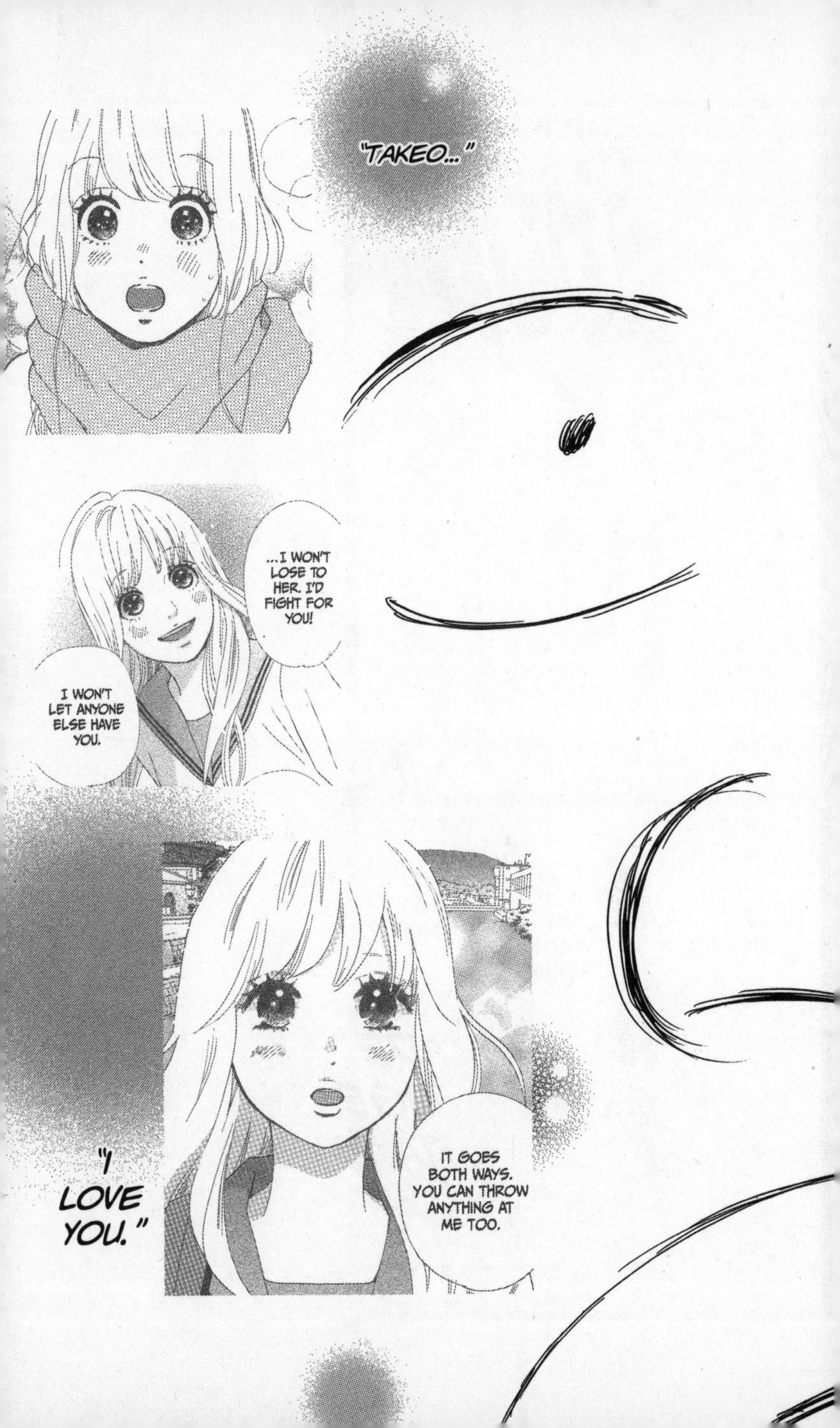
"TAKEO..."
...I WON'T LOSE TO HER. I'D FIGHT FOR YOU!
I WON'T LET ANYONE ELSE HAVE YOU.
IT GOES BOTH WAYS. YOU CAN THROW ANYTHING AT ME TOO.
"I LOVE YOU."

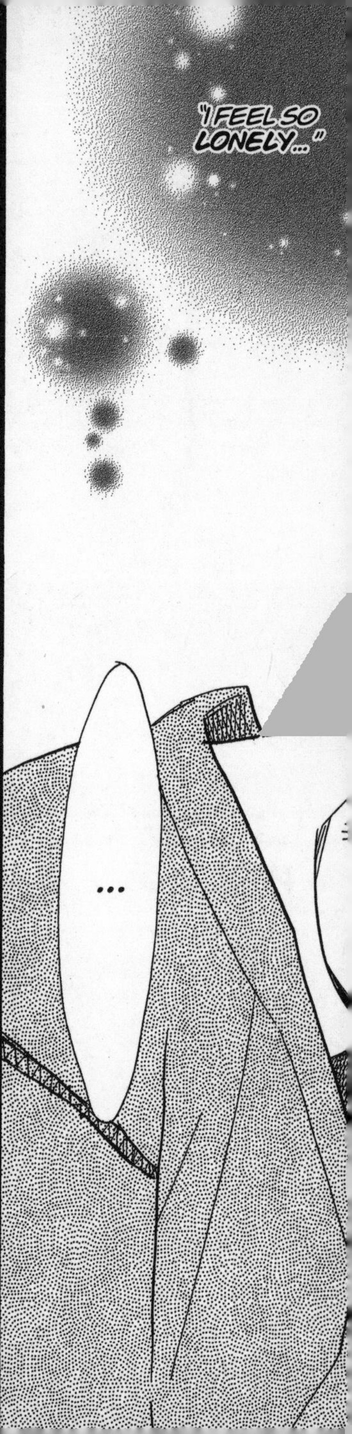
"I FEEL SO LONELY..."
...

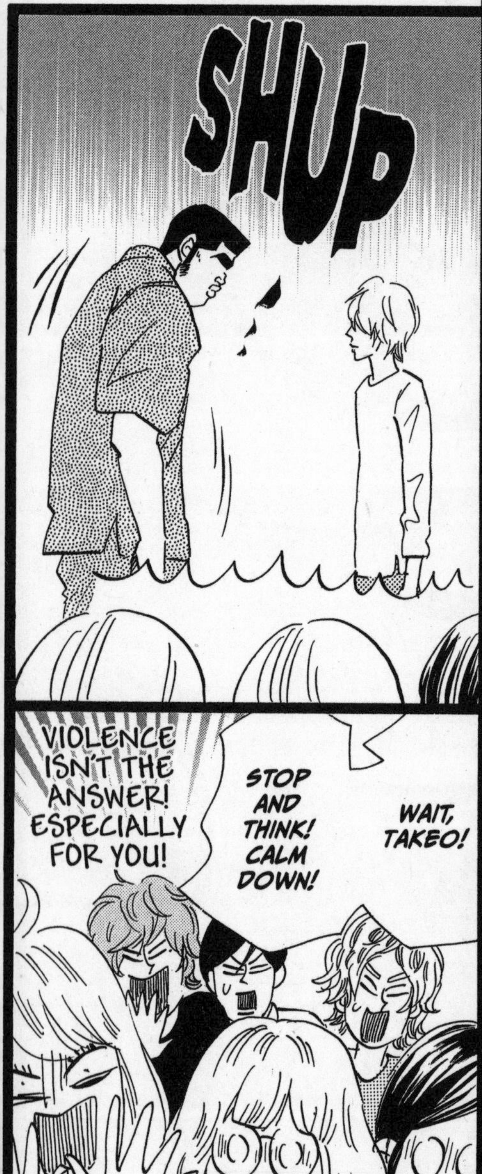
SHUP
WAIT, TAKEO!
STOP AND THINK! CALM DOWN!
VIOLENCE ISN'T THE ANSWER! ESPECIALLY FOR YOU!

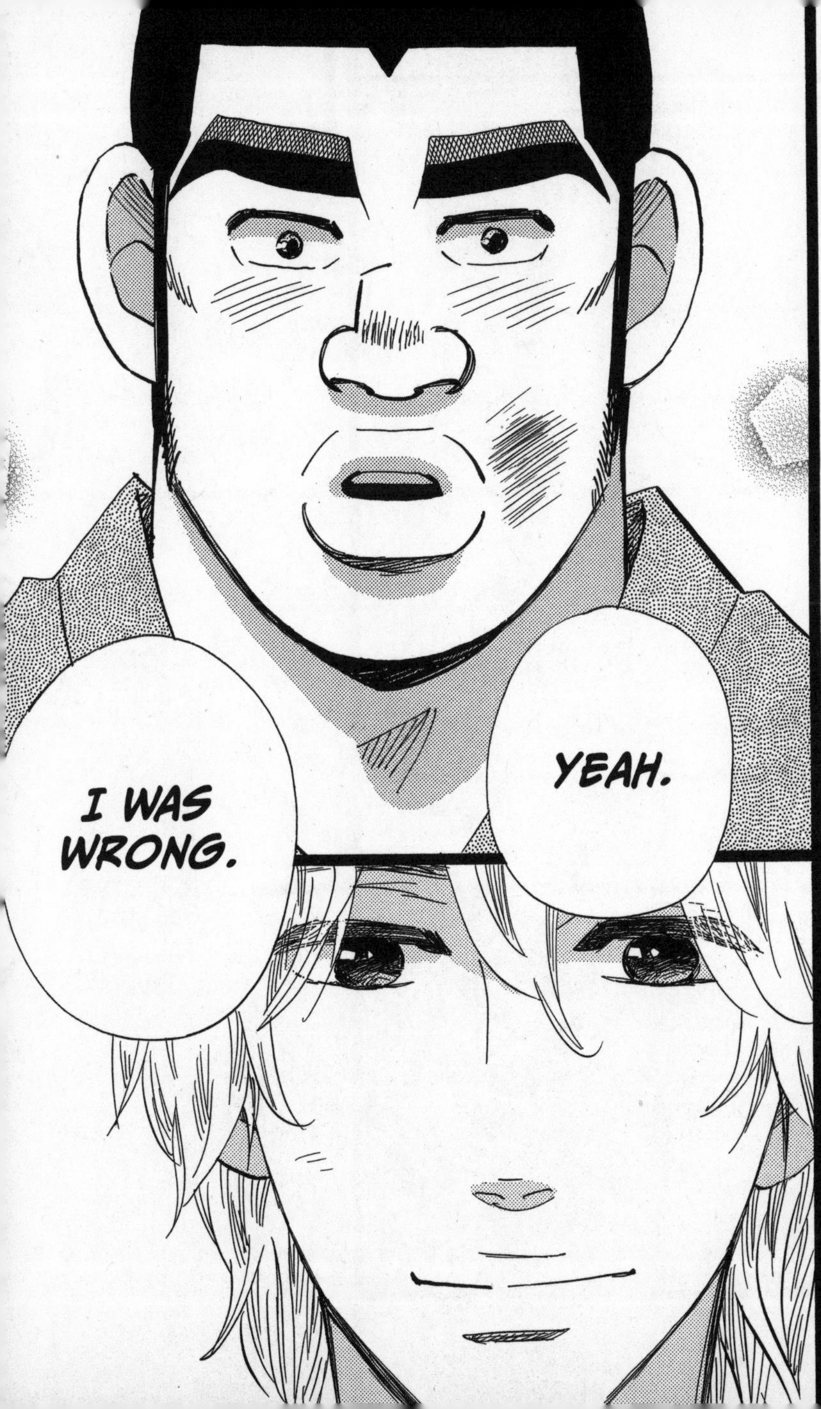
YEAH.
I WAS WRONG.

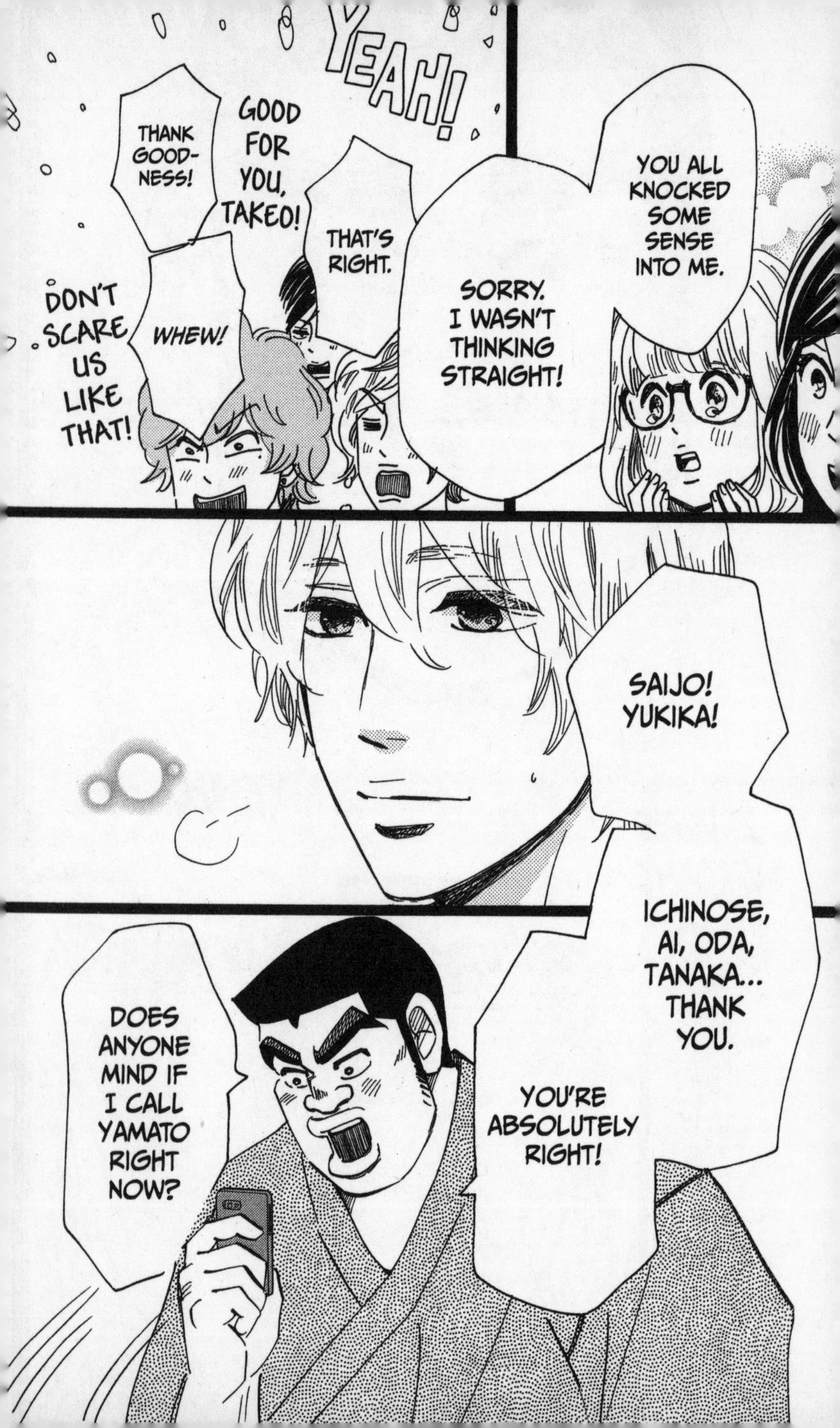
YOU ALL KNOCKED SOME SENSE INTO ME.
SORRY. I WASN'T THINKING STRAIGHT!
YEAH!
GOOD FOR YOU, TAKEO!
THANK GOODNESS!
THAT'S RIGHT.
WHEW!
DON'T SCARE US LIKE THAT!
SAIJO! YUKIKA!
ICHINOSE, AI, ODA, TANAKA... THANK YOU.
YOU'RE ABSOLUTELY RIGHT!
DOES ANYONE MIND IF I CALL YAMATO RIGHT NOW?

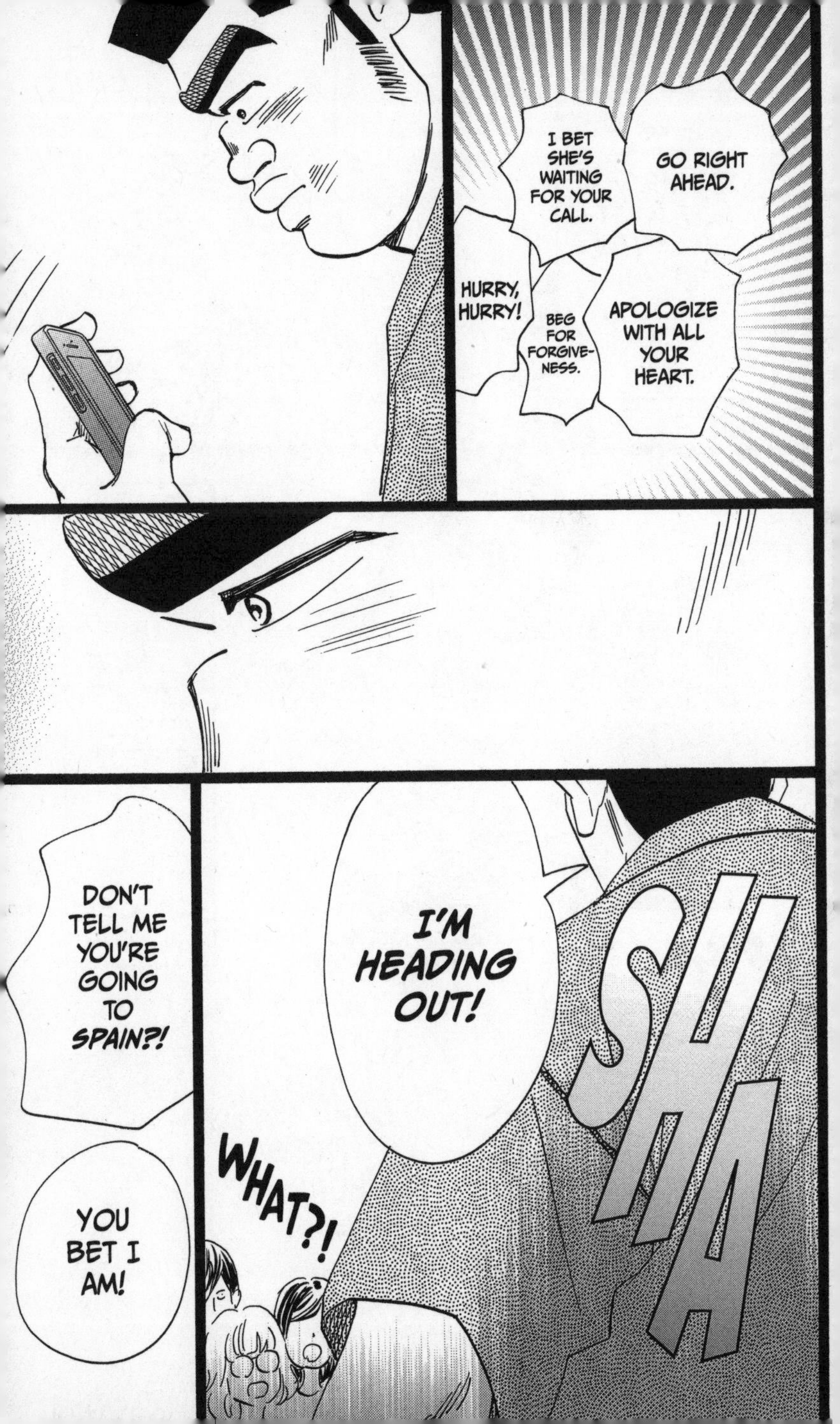
GO RIGHT AHEAD.
I BET SHE'S WAITING FOR YOUR CALL.
APOLOGIZE WITH ALL YOUR HEART.
BEG FOR FORGIVE-NESS.
HURRY, HURRY!
I'M HEADING OUT!
SHA
WHAT?!
DON'T TELL ME YOU'RE GOING TO SPAIN?!
YOU BET I AM!

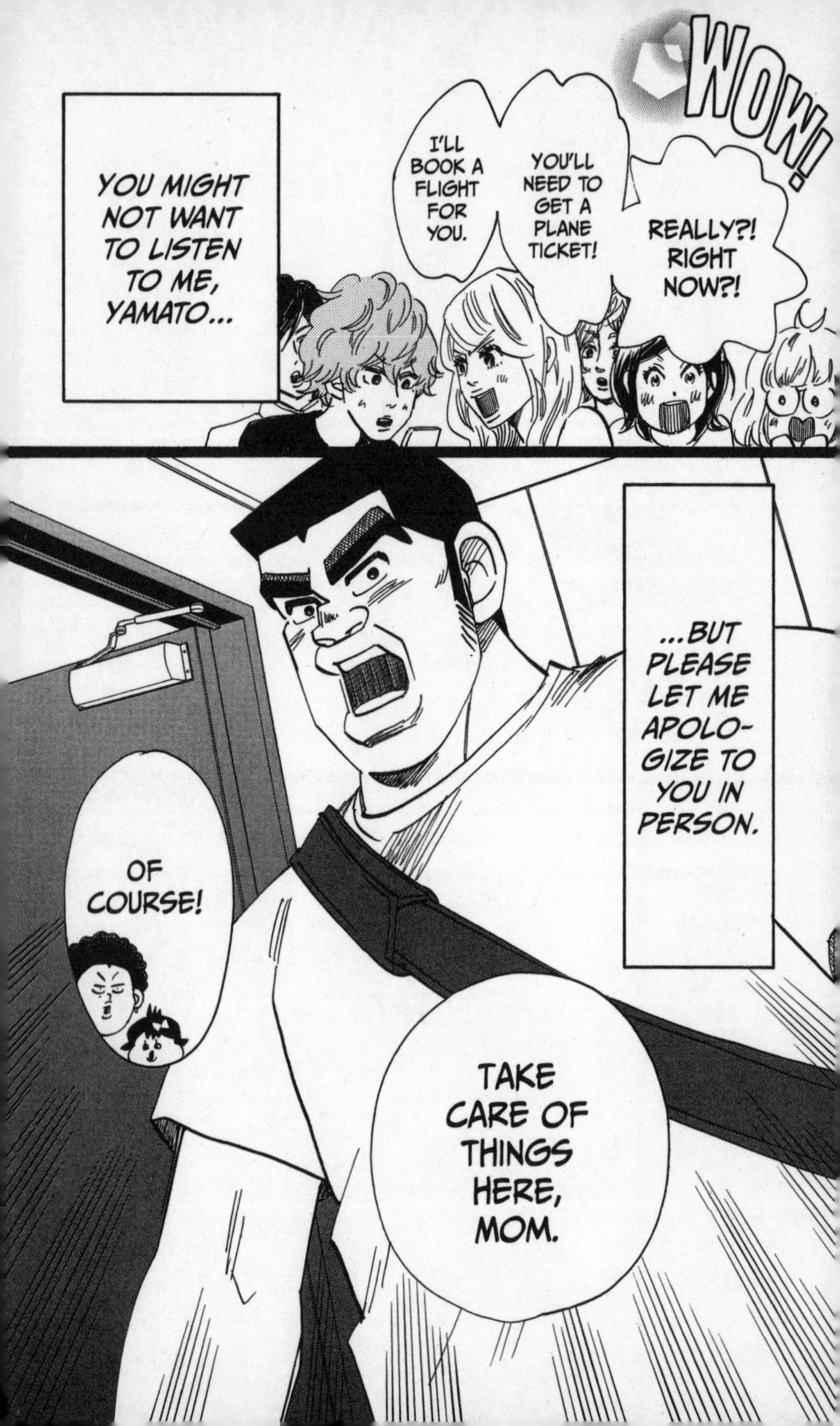
WOW!
REALLY?! RIGHT NOW?!
YOU'LL NEED TO GET A PLANE TICKET!
I'LL BOOK A FLIGHT FOR YOU.
YOU MIGHT NOT WANT TO LISTEN TO ME, YAMATO...
...BUT PLEASE LET ME APOLOGIZE TO YOU IN PERSON.
OF COURSE!
TAKE CARE OF THINGS HERE, MOM.

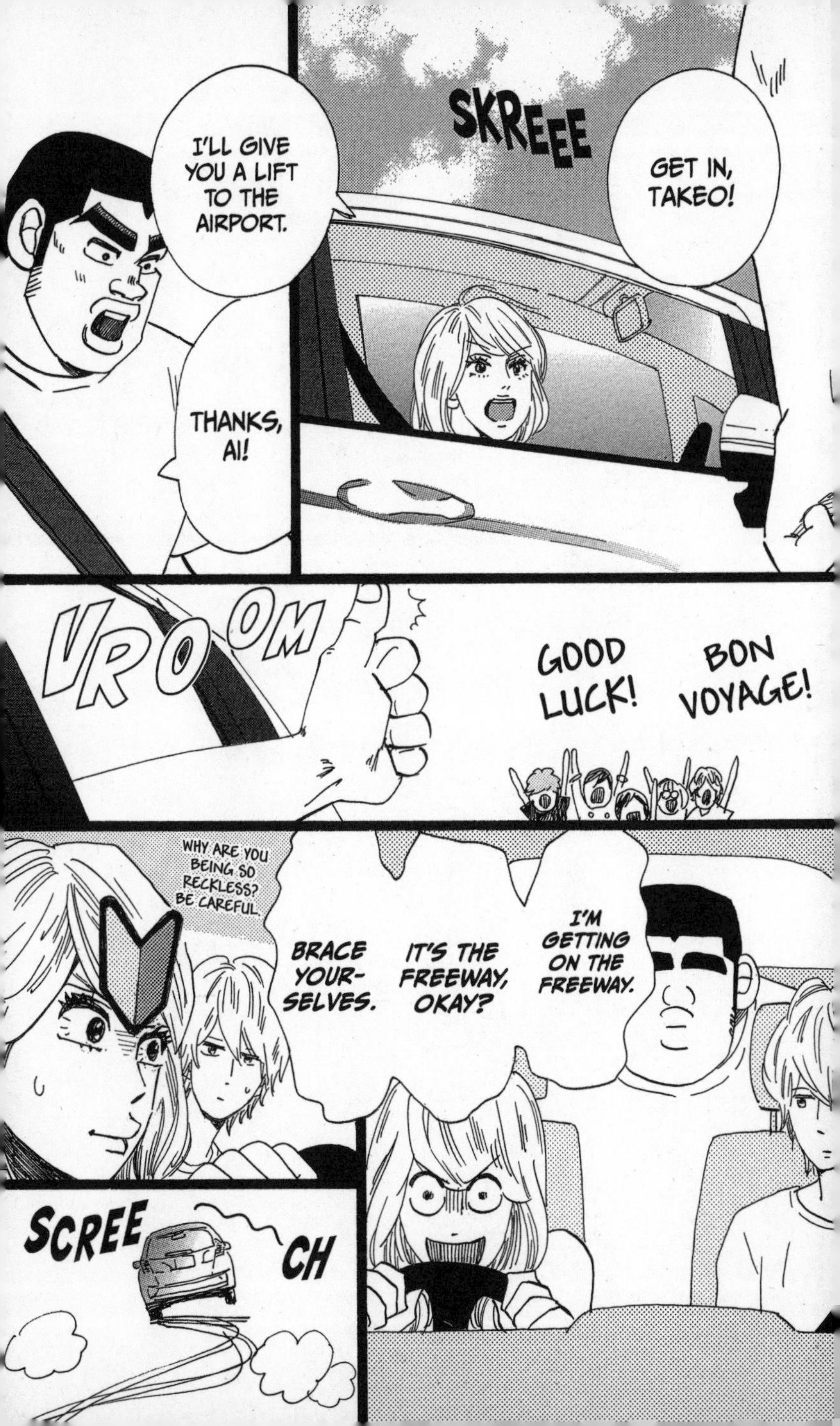
SKREEE
GET IN, TAKEO!
I'LL GIVE YOU A LIFT TO THE AIRPORT.
THANKS, AI!
BON VOYAGE!
GOOD LUCK!
VROOM
I'M GETTING ON THE FREEWAY.
IT'S THE FREEWAY, OKAY?
BRACE YOUR-SELVES.
WHY ARE YOU BEING SO RECKLESS? BE CAREFUL.
SCREECH

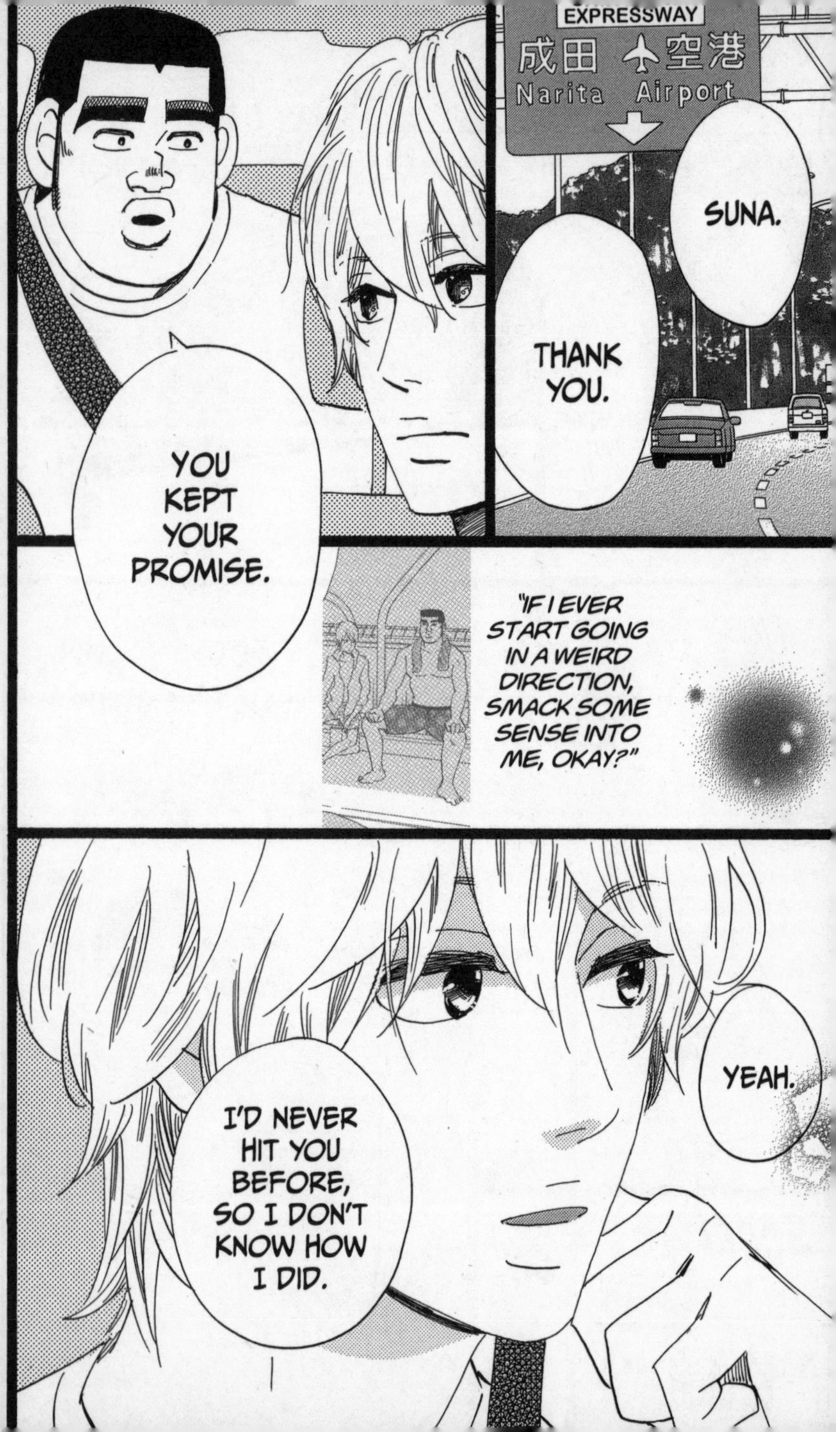
EXPRESSWAY
成田 空港
Narita Airport
SUNA.
THANK YOU.
YOU KEPT YOUR PROMISE.
"IF I EVER START GOING IN A WEIRD DIRECTION, SMACK SOME SENSE INTO ME, OKAY?"
YEAH.
I'D NEVER HIT YOU BEFORE, SO I DON'T KNOW HOW I DID.

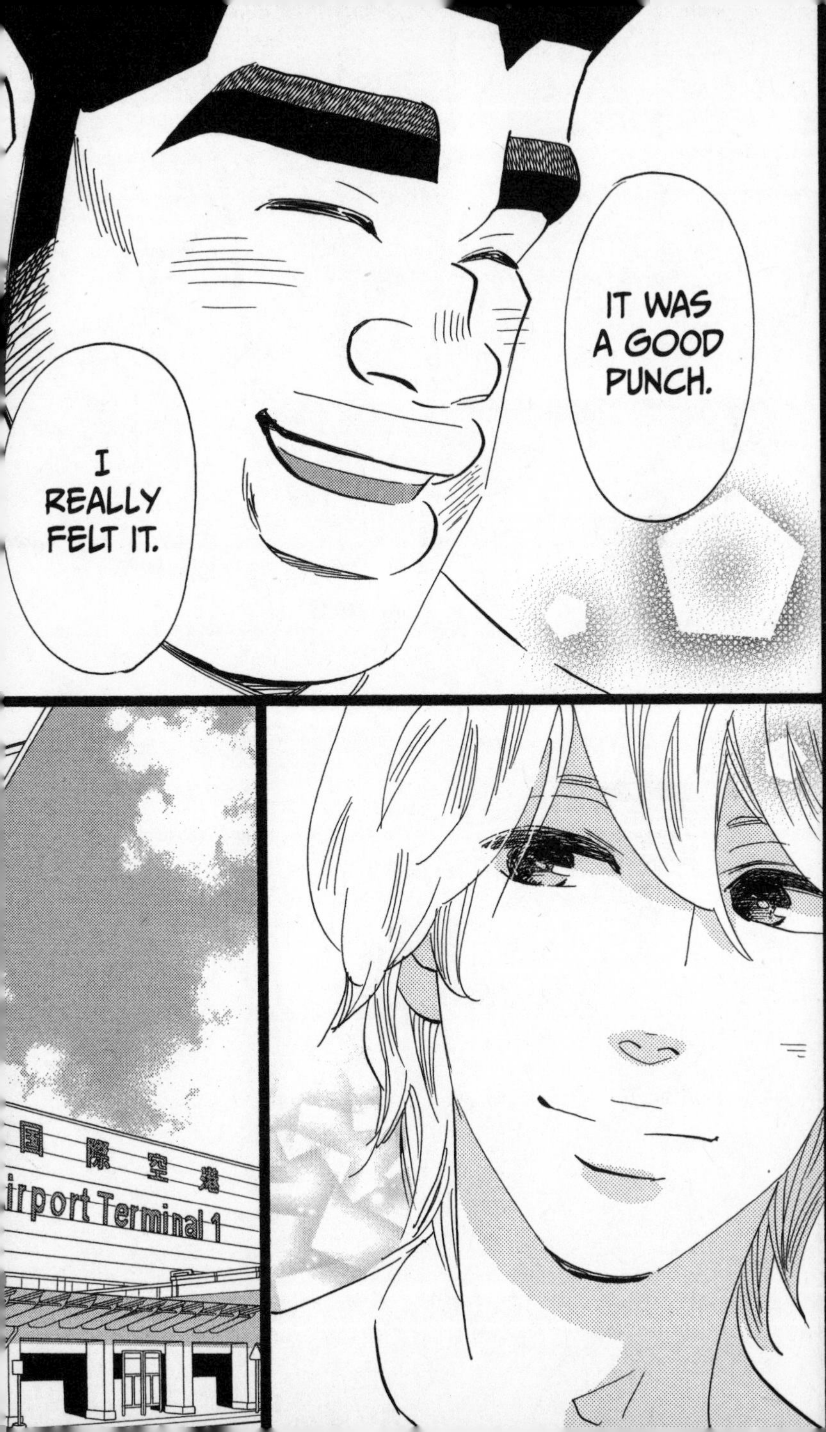
IT WAS A GOOD PUNCH.
I REALLY FELT IT.
国際空港
irport Terminal 1

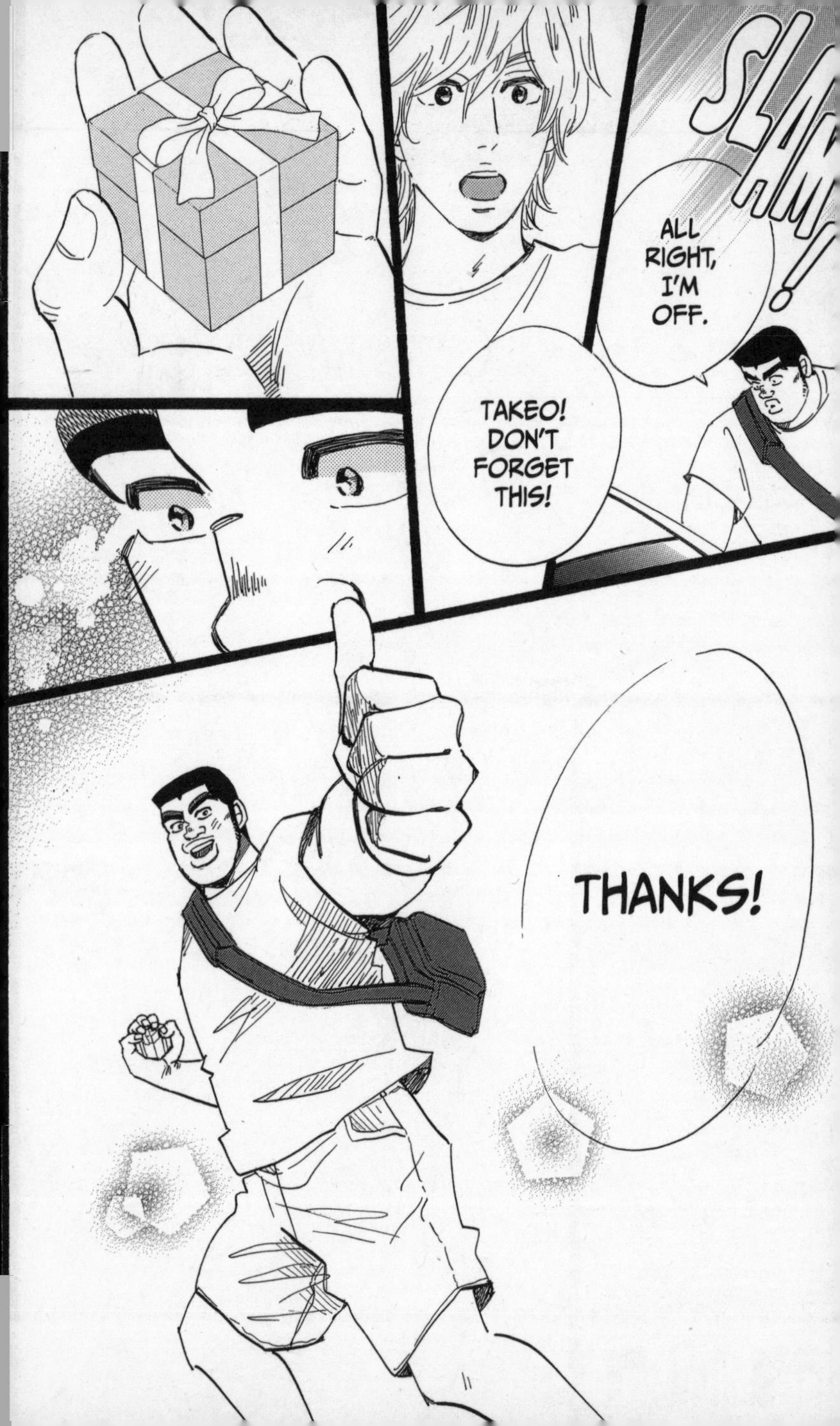

SLAM!
ALL RIGHT, I'M OFF.
TAKEO! DON'T FORGET THIS!
THANKS!

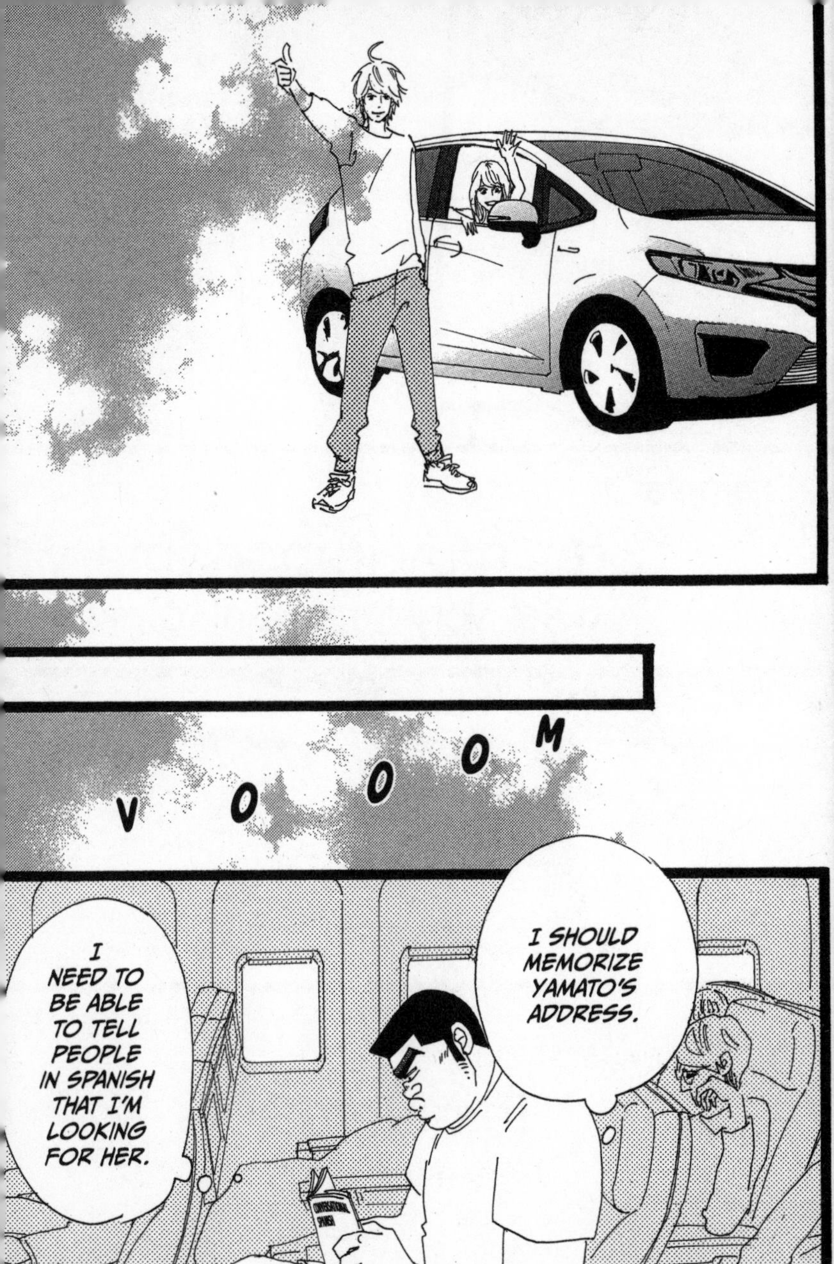
VOOOOM
I SHOULD MEMORIZE YAMATO'S ADDRESS.
I NEED TO BE ABLE TO TELL PEOPLE IN SPANISH THAT I'M LOOKING FOR HER.

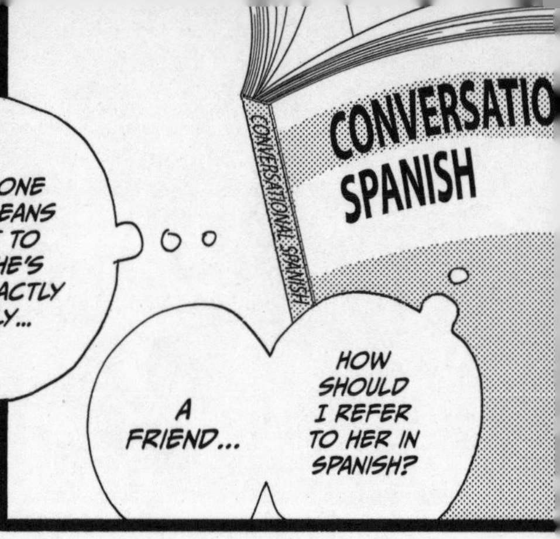
CONVERSATIONAL SPANISH
CONVERSATIO SPANISH
HOW SHOULD I REFER TO HER IN SPANISH?
A FRIEND...
SOMEONE WHO MEANS A LOT TO ME. SHE'S NOT EXACTLY FAMILY...
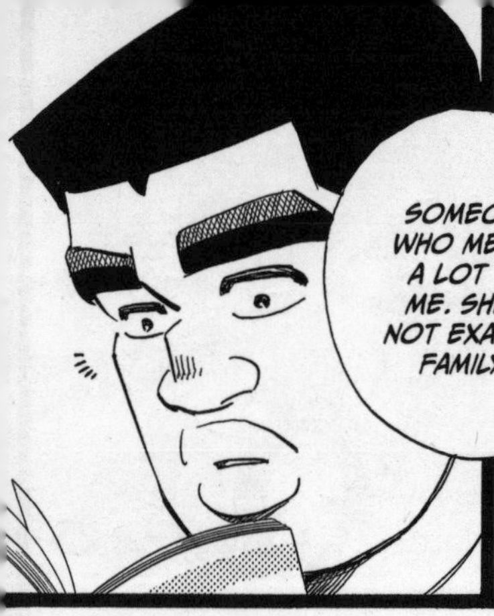

Example

Eres muy importante.

You are very important to me.

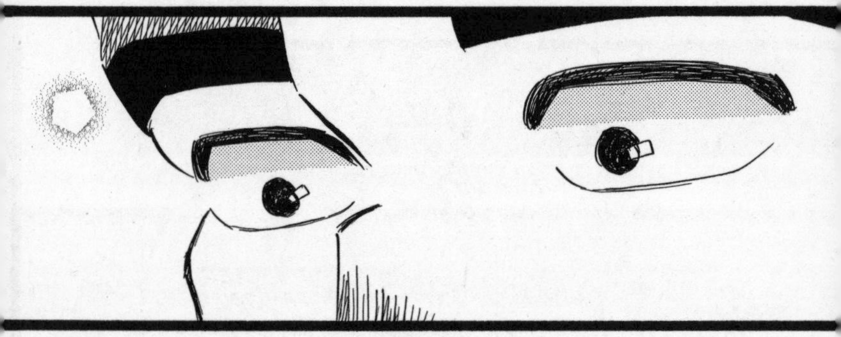

Similar expression

Te quiero.

I care for you.

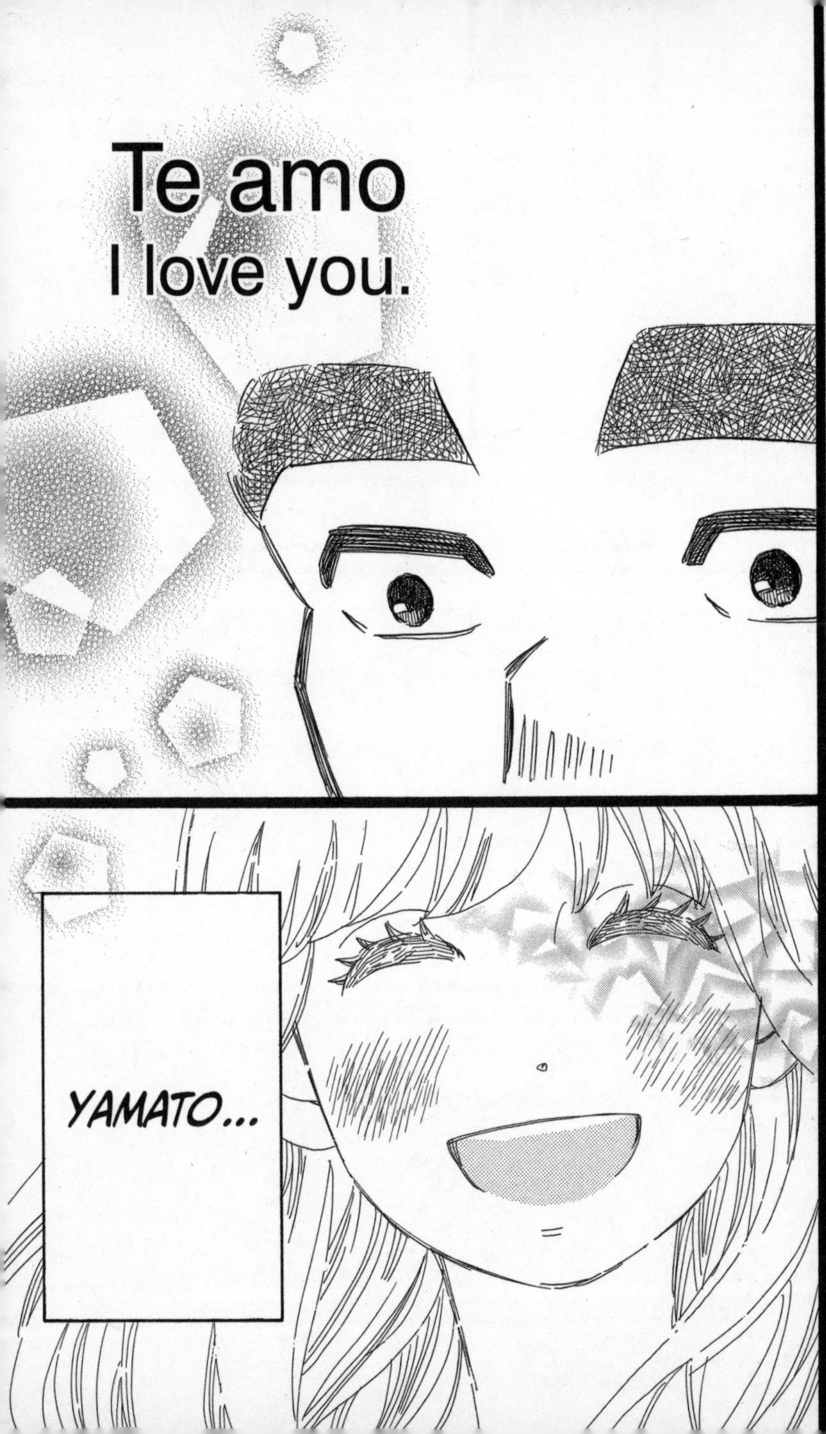
Te amo
I love you.
YAMATO...

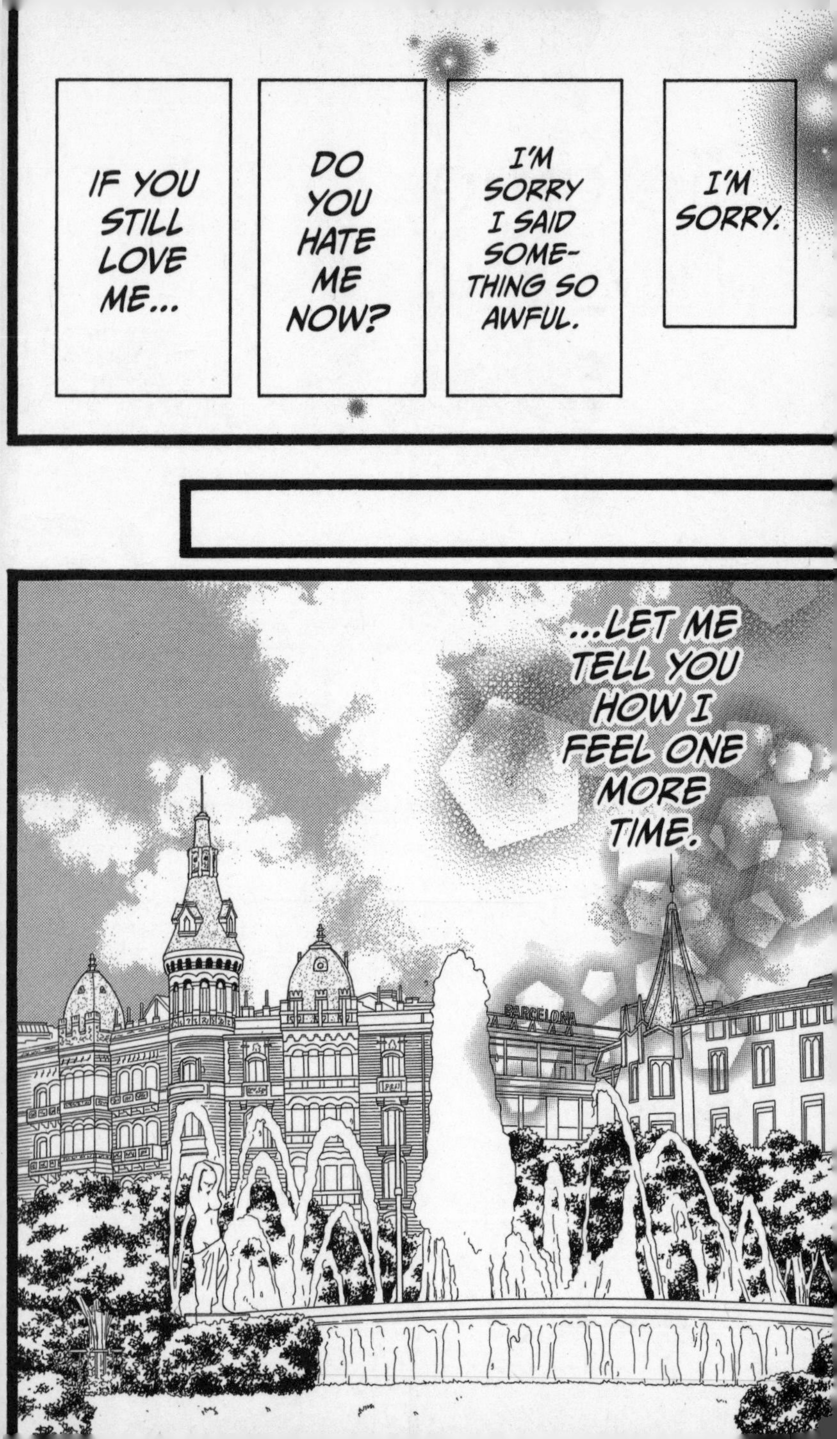
I'M SORRY.
I'M SORRY I SAID SOME-THING SO AWFUL.
DO YOU HATE ME NOW?
IF YOU STILL LOVE ME...
...LET ME TELL YOU HOW I FEEL ONE MORE TIME.
BARCELONA

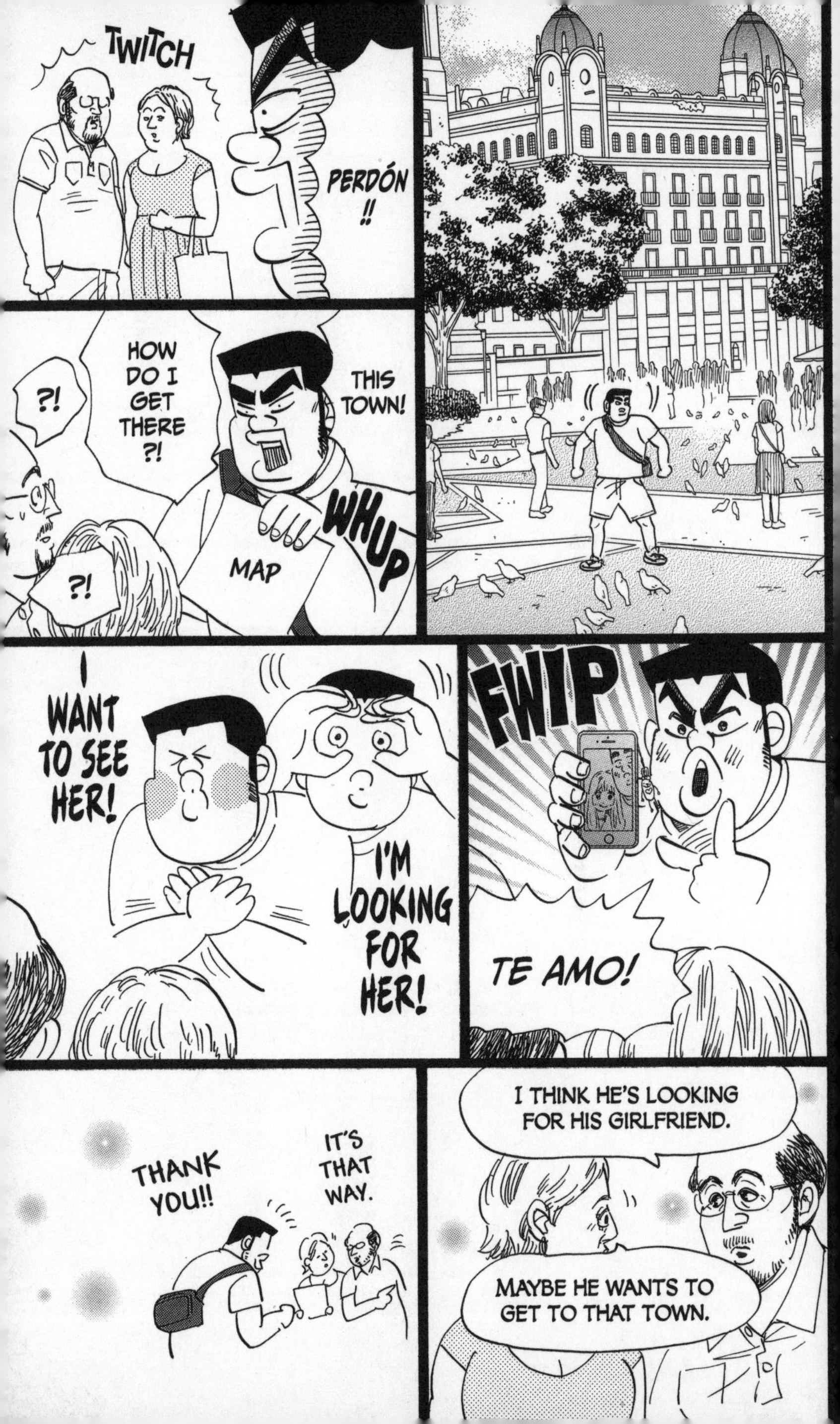
PERDÓN!!
TWITCH
THIS TOWN!
HOW DO I GET THERE?!
?!
WHUP
MAP
?!
FWIP
TE AMO!
I'M LOOKING FOR HER!
I WANT TO SEE HER!
I THINK HE'S LOOKING FOR HIS GIRLFRIEND.
MAYBE HE WANTS TO GET TO THAT TOWN.
IT'S THAT WAY.
THANK YOU!!

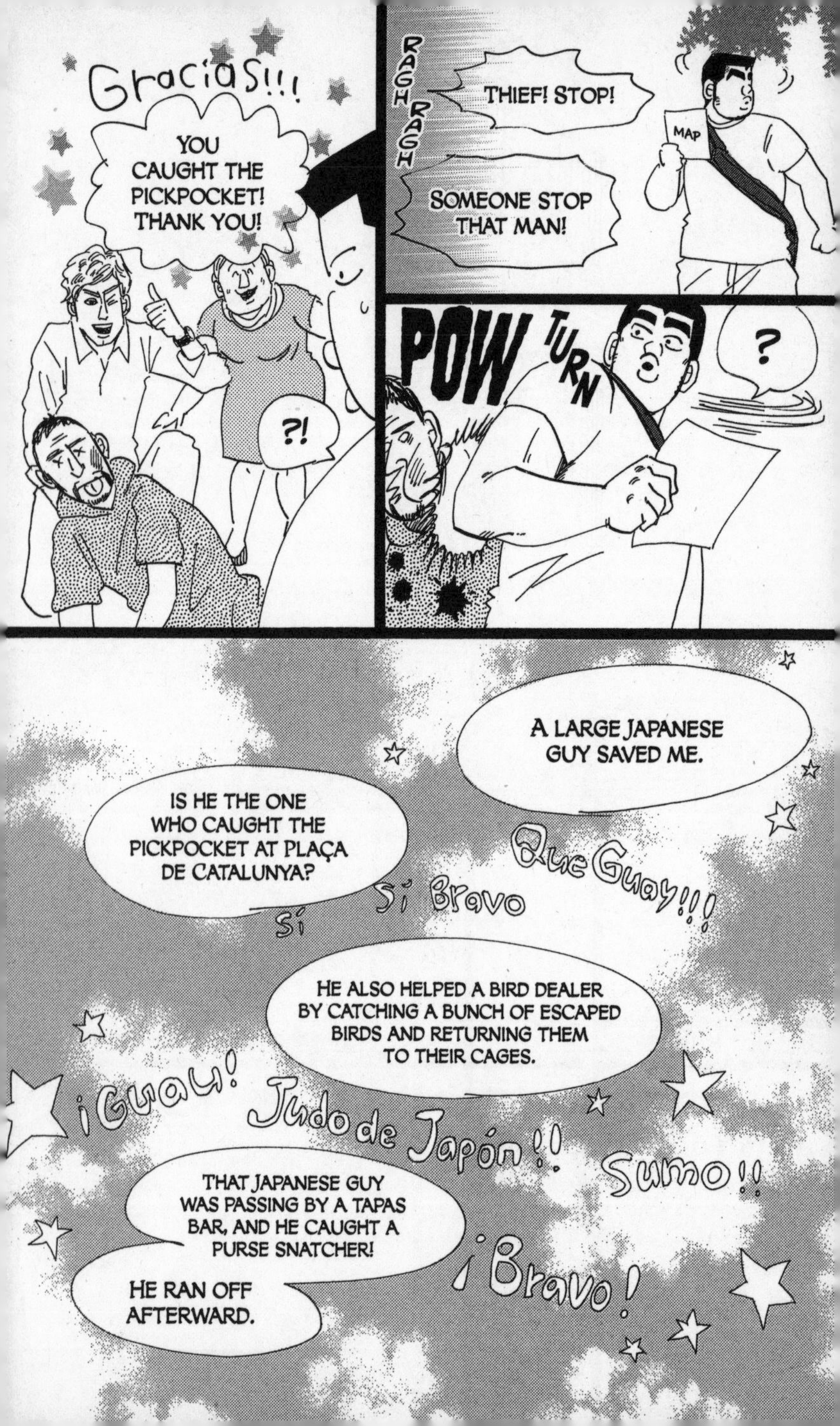
MAP
THIEF! STOP!
RAGH RAGH
SOMEONE STOP THAT MAN!
?
TURN
POW
Gracias!!!
YOU CAUGHT THE PICKPOCKET! THANK YOU!
?!
A LARGE JAPANESE GUY SAVED ME.
Que Guay!!!
IS HE THE ONE WHO CAUGHT THE PICKPOCKET AT PLAÇA DE CATALUNYA?
Sí Bravo
Sí
HE ALSO HELPED A BIRD DEALER BY CATCHING A BUNCH OF ESCAPED BIRDS AND RETURNING THEM TO THEIR CAGES.
Sumo!!
Judo de Japón!!
¡Guau!
¡Bravo!
THAT JAPANESE GUY WAS PASSING BY A TAPAS BAR, AND HE CAUGHT A PURSE SNATCHER!
HE RAN OFF AFTERWARD.

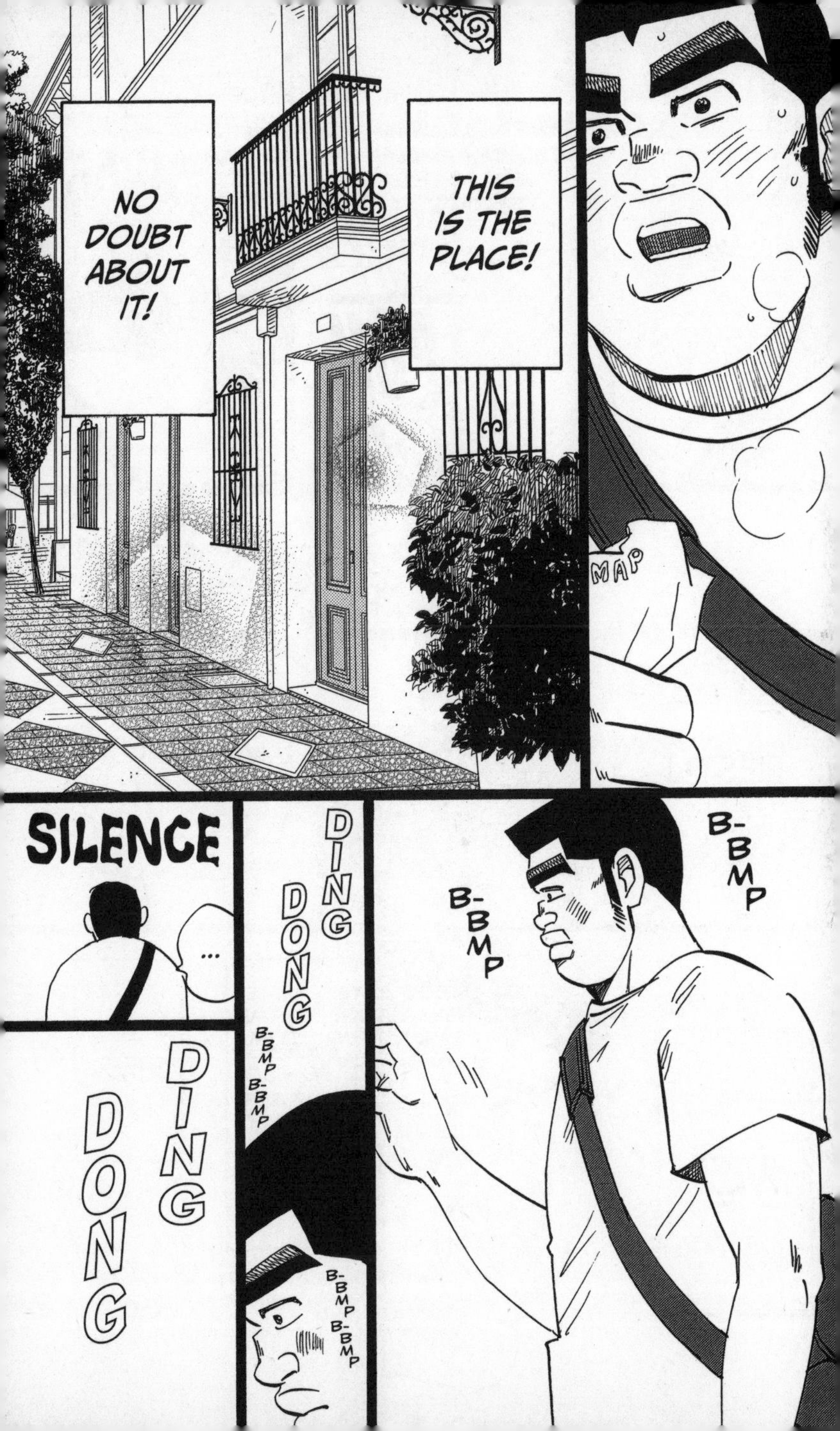
MAP
THIS IS THE PLACE!
NO DOUBT ABOUT IT!
B-BMP
B-BMP
DING DONG
B-BMP
B-BMP
B-BMP
B-BMP
SILENCE
...
DING DONG

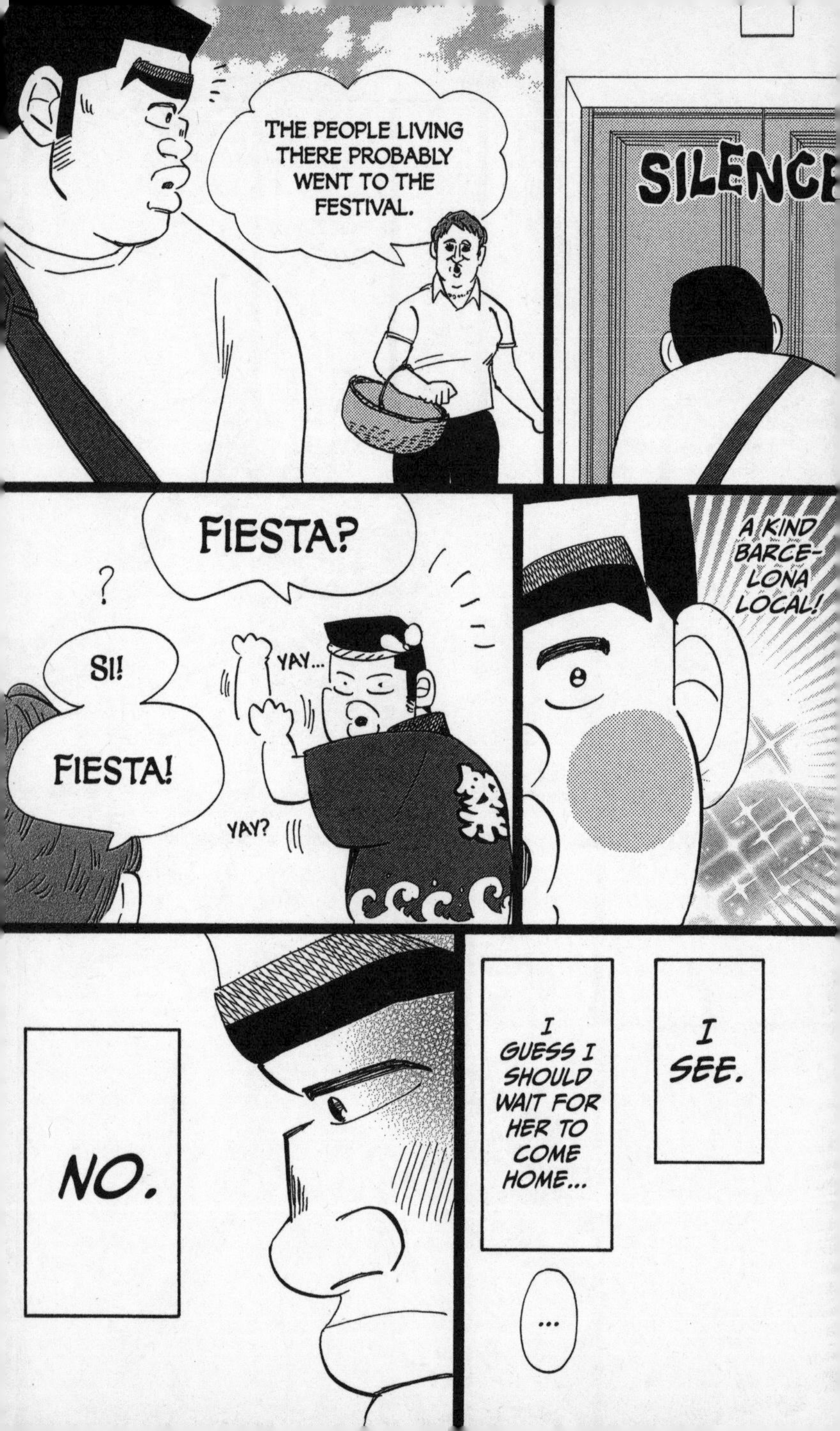
SILENCE
THE PEOPLE LIVING THERE PROBABLY WENT TO THE FESTIVAL.
A KIND BARCELONA LOCAL!
FIESTA?
YAY...
SI! FIESTA!
YAY?
I SEE.
I GUESS I SHOULD WAIT FOR HER TO COME HOME...
...
NO.

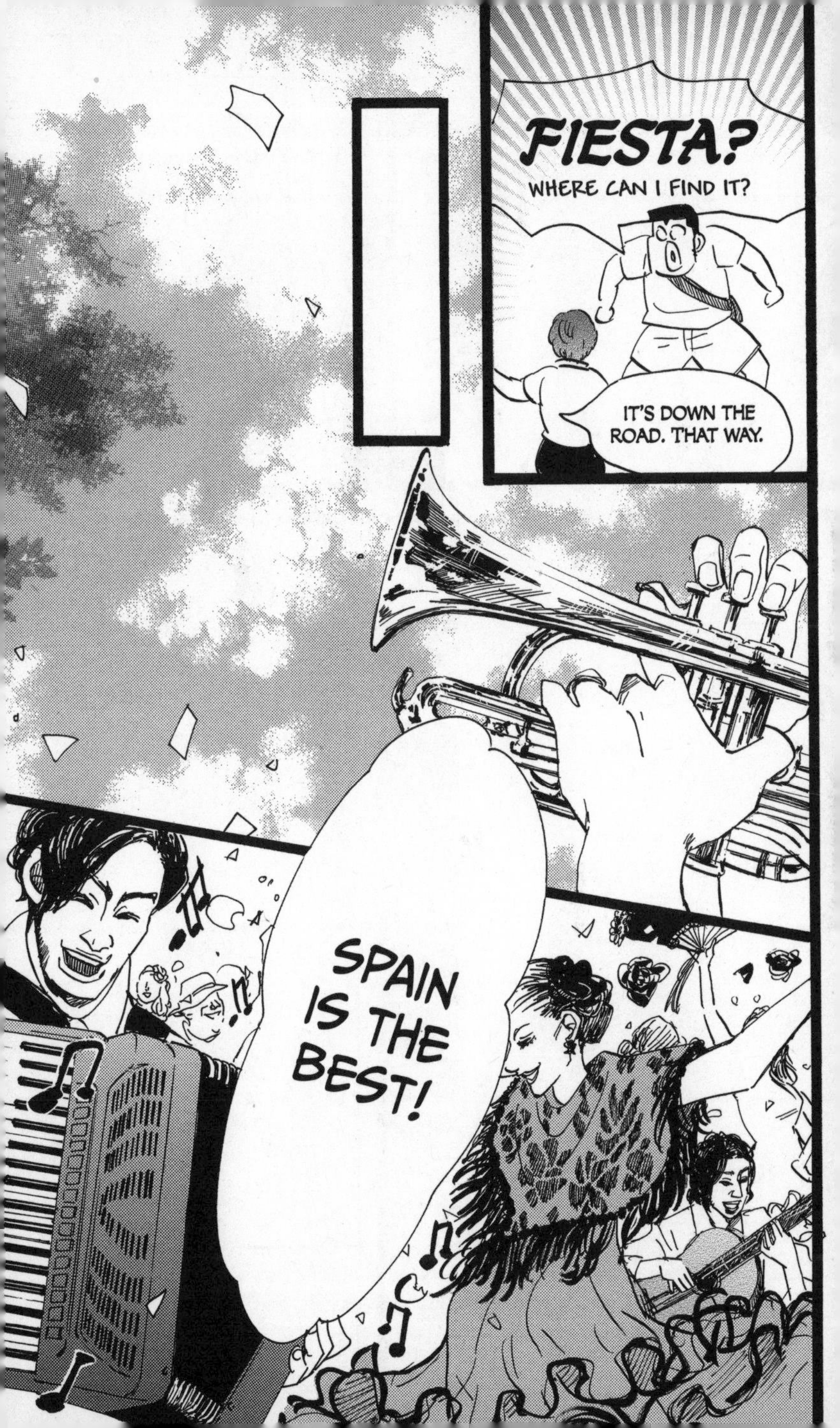
FIESTA?
WHERE CAN I FIND IT?
IT'S DOWN THE ROAD. THAT WAY.
SPAIN IS THE BEST!

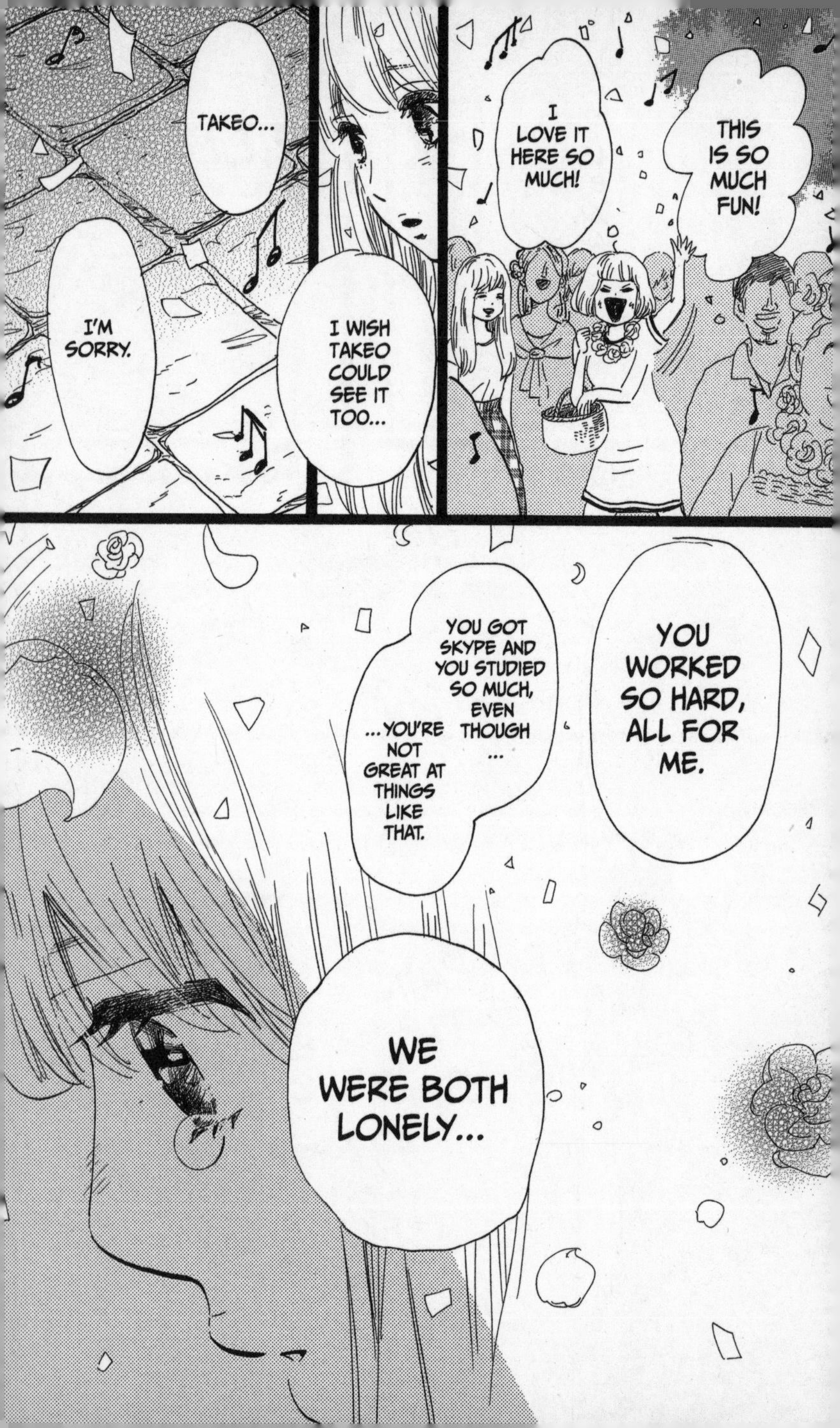
THIS IS SO MUCH FUN!
I LOVE IT HERE SO MUCH!
I WISH TAKEO COULD SEE IT TOO...
TAKEO...
I'M SORRY.
YOU WORKED SO HARD, ALL FOR ME.
YOU GOT SKYPE AND YOU STUDIED SO MUCH, EVEN THOUGH...
...YOU'RE NOT GREAT AT THINGS LIKE THAT.
WE WERE BOTH LONELY...

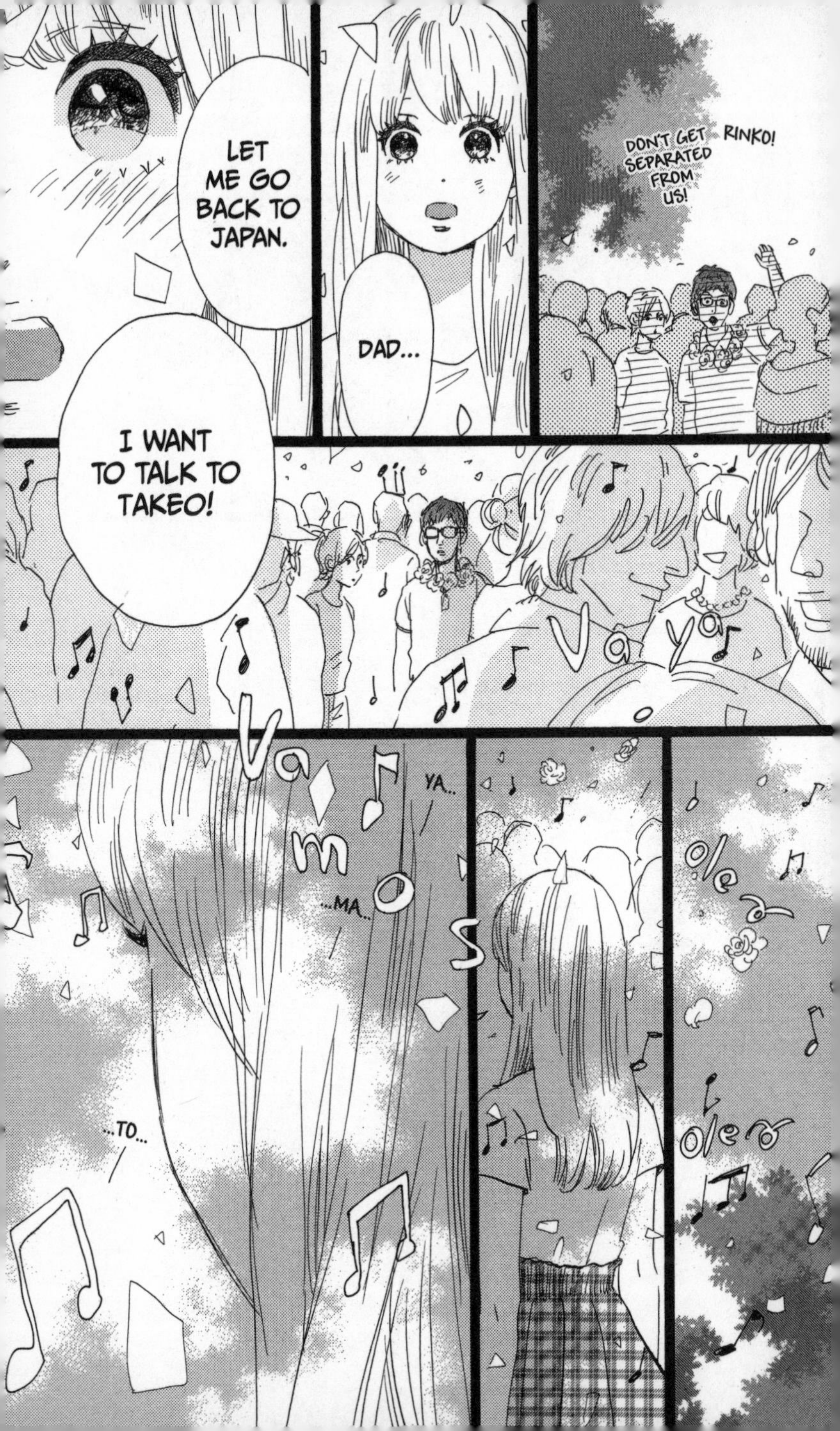
RINKO!
DON'T GET SEPARATED FROM US!
DAD...
LET ME GO BACK TO JAPAN.
I WANT TO TALK TO TAKEO!
Va ya
ole
ole
YA..
...MA..
...TO...
Vamos

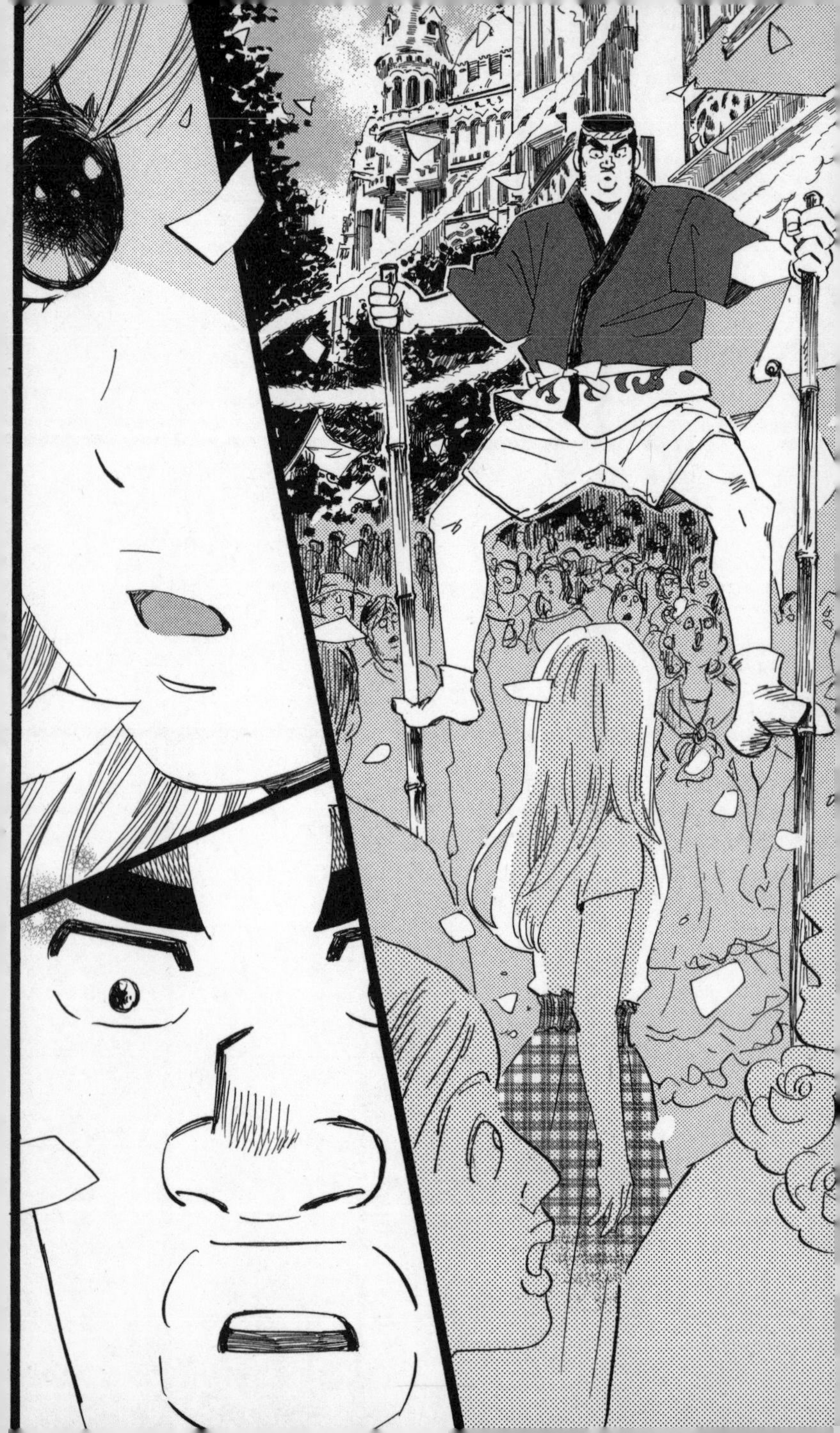

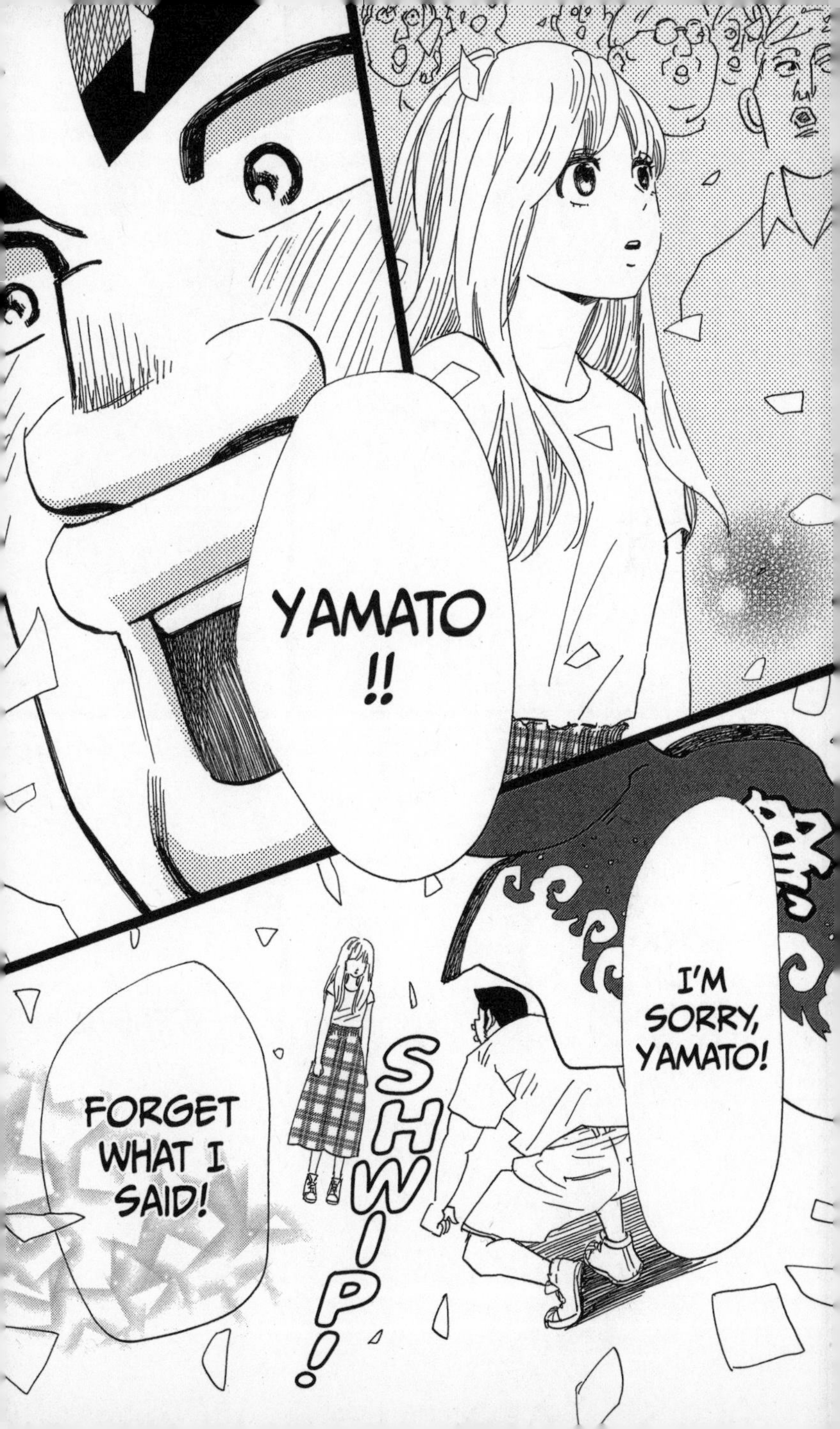
YAMATO!!
I'M SORRY, YAMATO!
SHWIP!
FORGET WHAT I SAID!

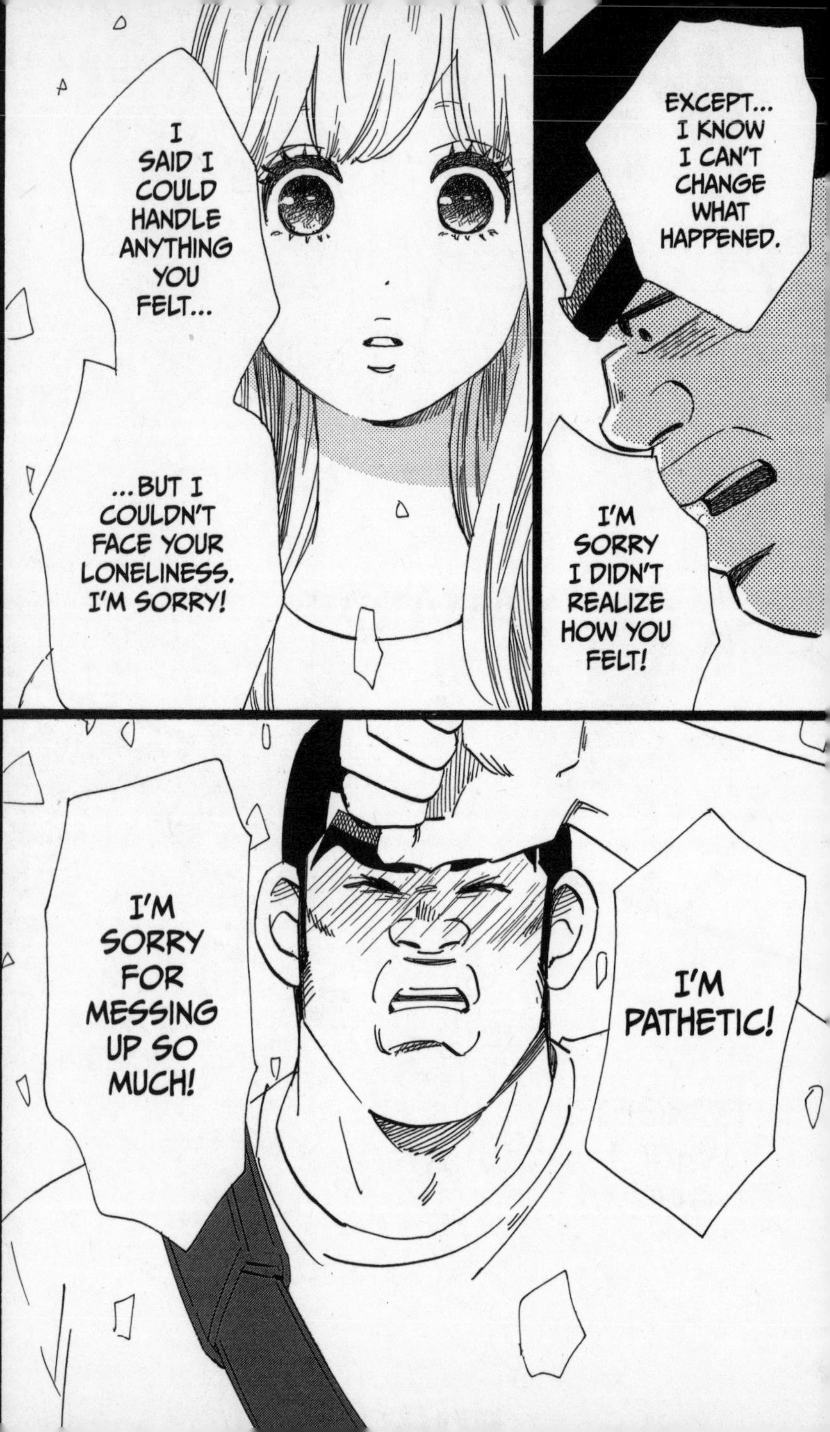
EXCEPT... I KNOW I CAN'T CHANGE WHAT HAPPENED.
I'M SORRY I DIDN'T REALIZE HOW YOU FELT!
I SAID I COULD HANDLE ANYTHING YOU FELT...
...BUT I COULDN'T FACE YOUR LONELINESS. I'M SORRY!
I'M PATHETIC!
I'M SORRY FOR MESSING UP SO MUCH!

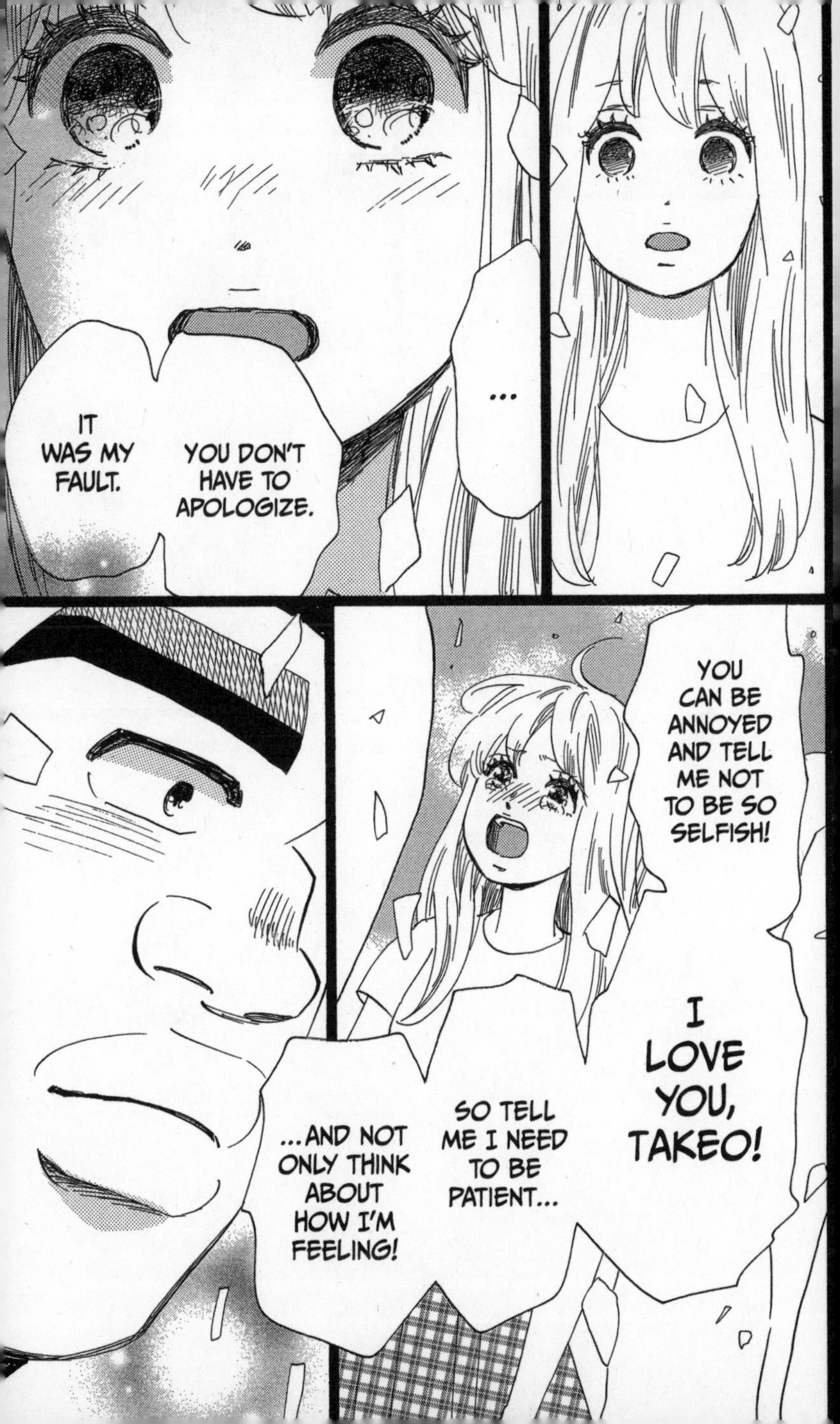
...
YOU DON'T HAVE TO APOLOGIZE.
IT WAS MY FAULT.
YOU CAN BE ANNOYED AND TELL ME NOT TO BE SO SELFISH!
I LOVE YOU, TAKEO!
SO TELL ME I NEED TO BE PATIENT...
...AND NOT ONLY THINK ABOUT HOW I'M FEELING!

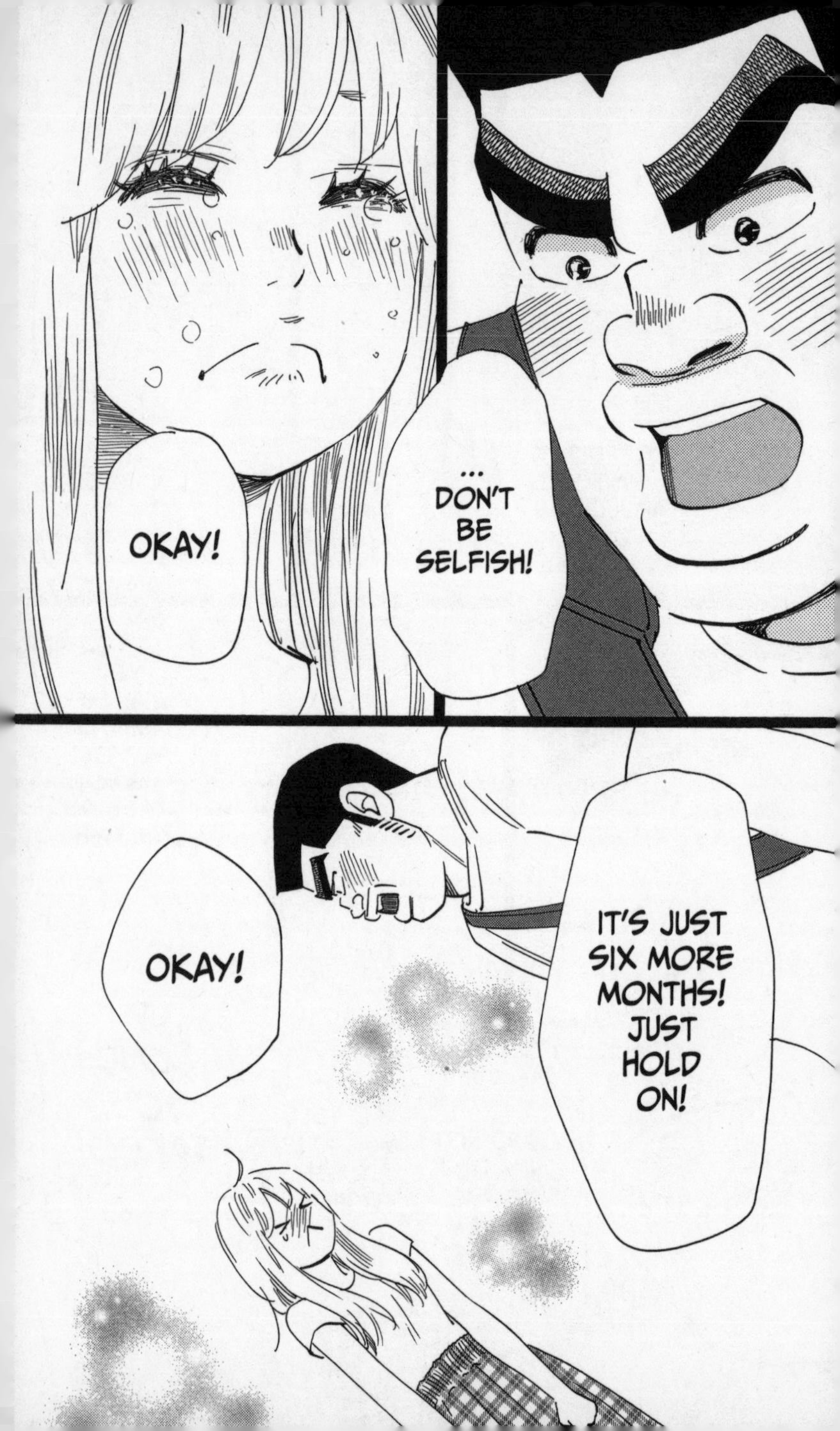
... DON'T BE SELFISH!
OKAY!
IT'S JUST SIX MORE MONTHS! JUST HOLD ON!
OKAY!

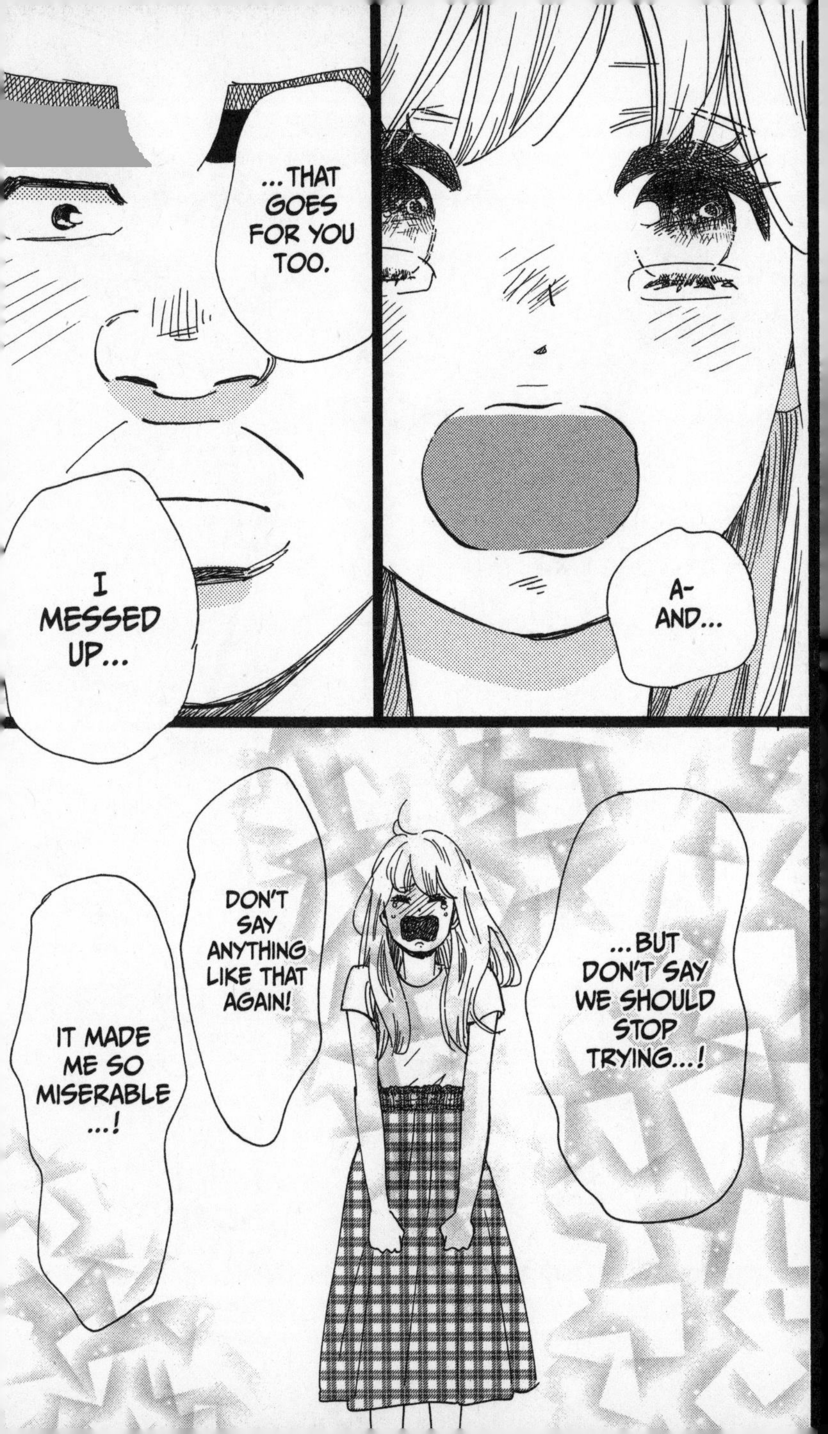
A- AND...
...THAT GOES FOR YOU TOO.
I MESSED UP...
...BUT DON'T SAY WE SHOULD STOP TRYING...!
DON'T SAY ANYTHING LIKE THAT AGAIN!
IT MADE ME SO MISERABLE ...!

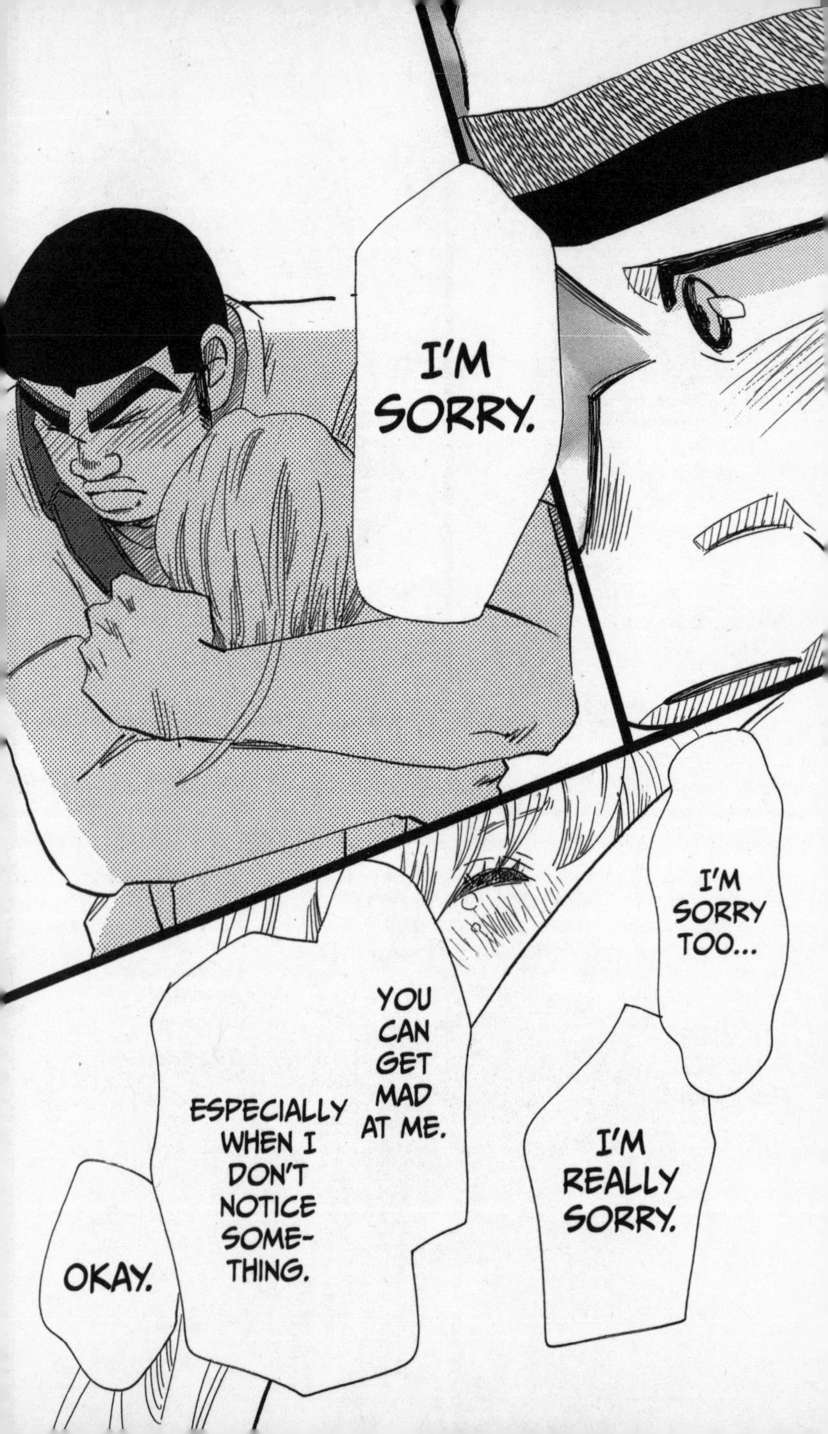
I'M SORRY.
I'M SORRY TOO...
I'M REALLY SORRY.
YOU CAN GET MAD AT ME.
ESPECIALLY WHEN I DON'T NOTICE SOME-THING.
OKAY.

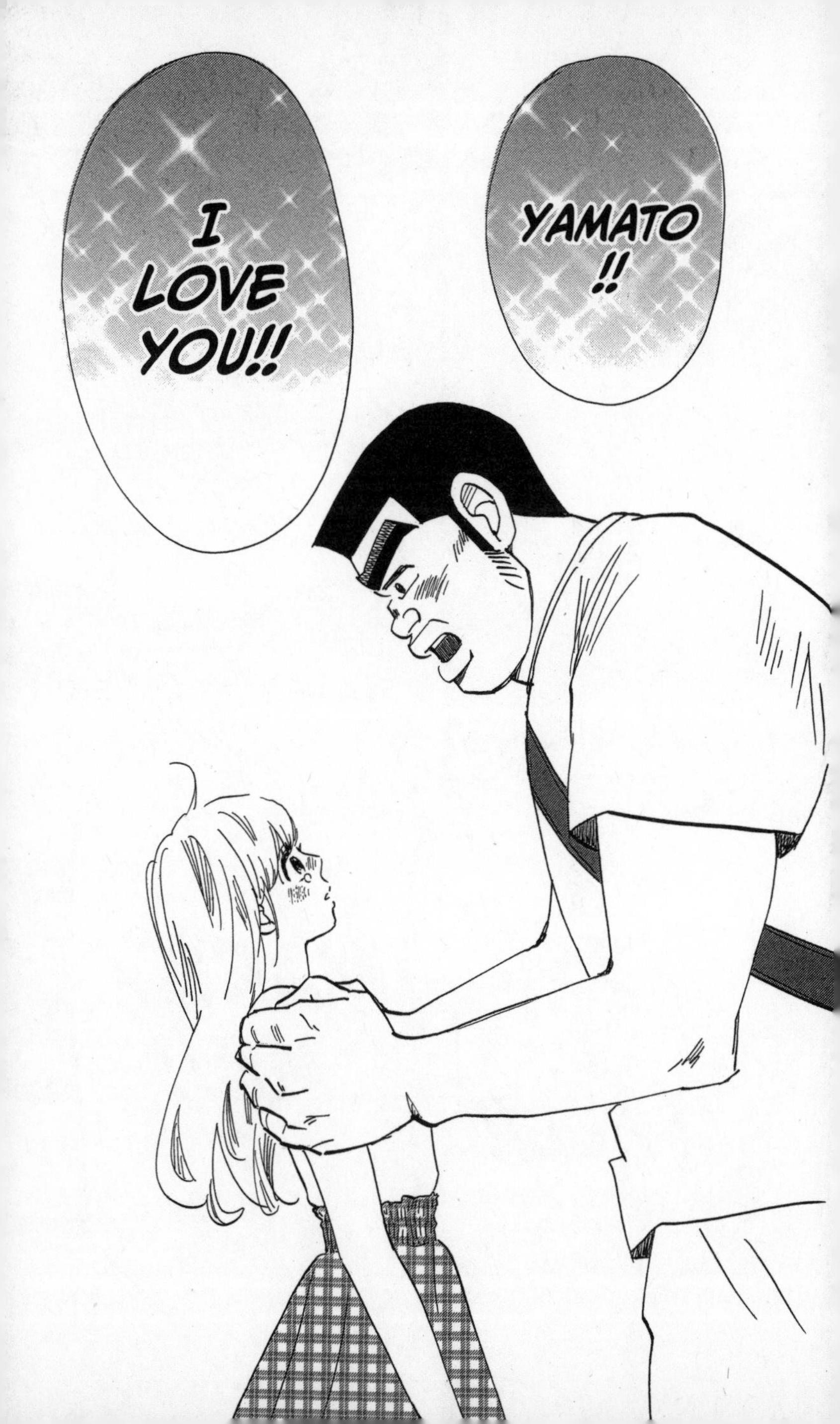
YAMATO !!
I LOVE YOU!!

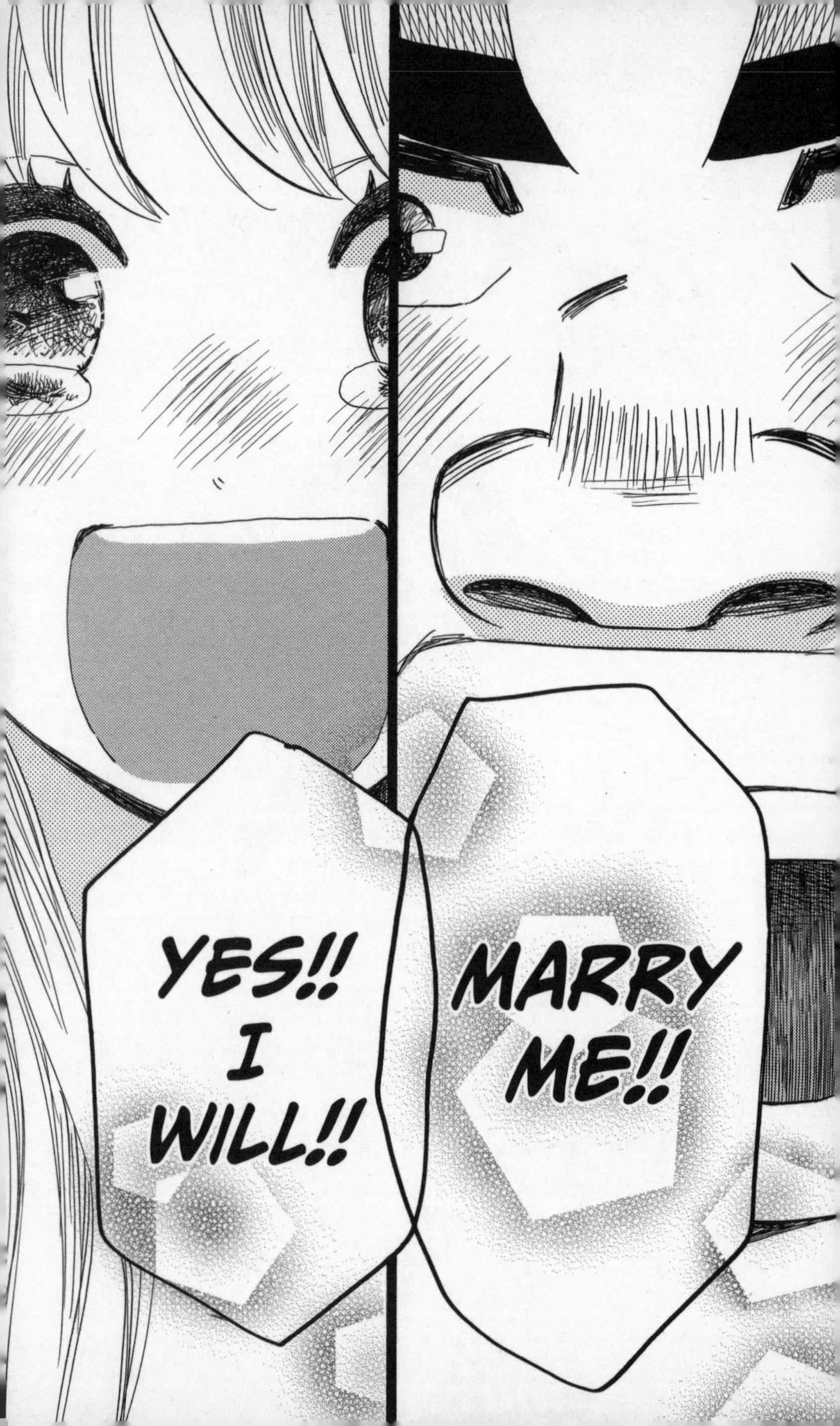
MARRY ME!!
YES!! I WILL!!

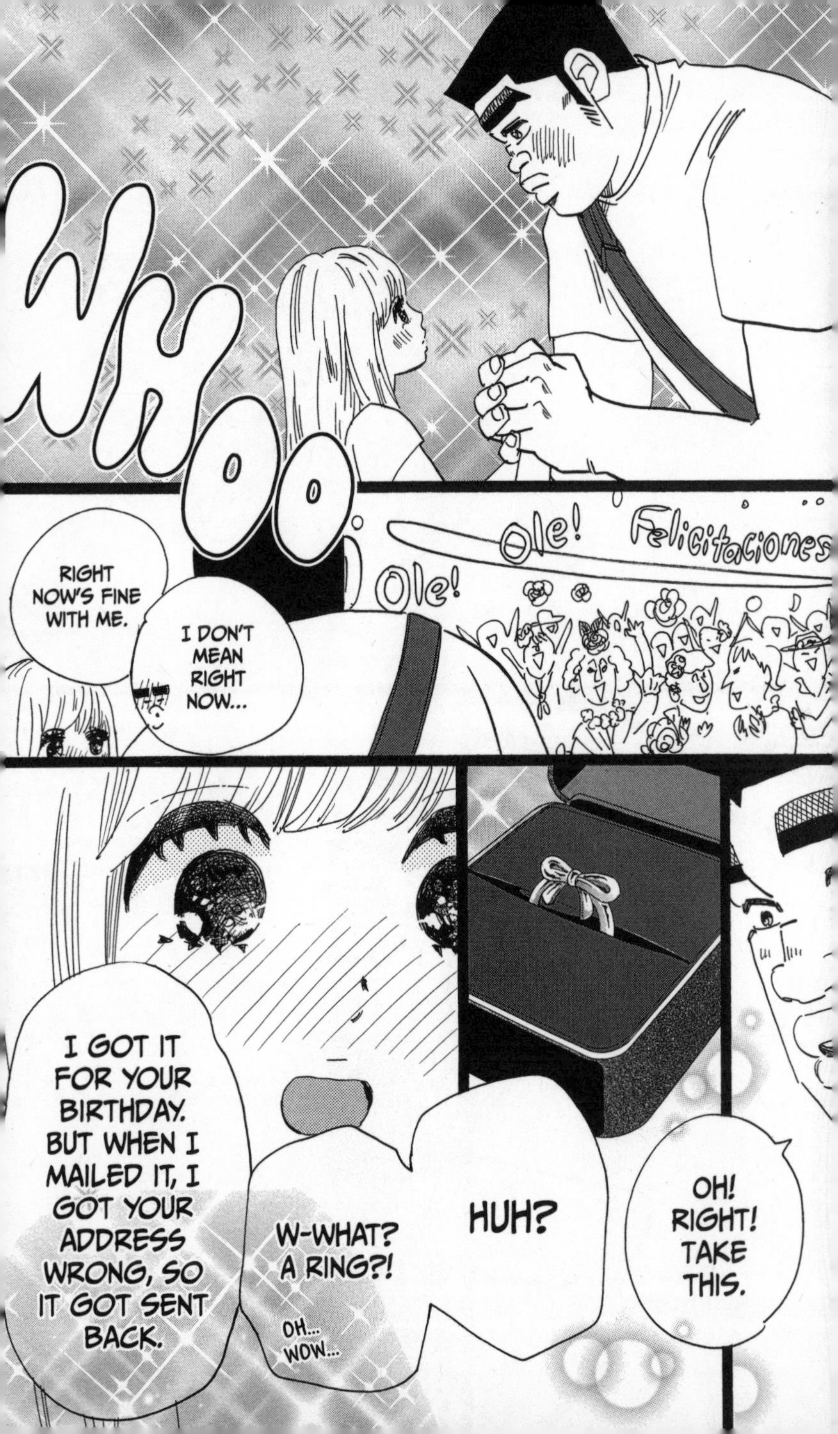
WHOOO
Felicitaciones
Ole!
Ole!
I DON'T MEAN RIGHT NOW...
RIGHT NOW'S FINE WITH ME.
OH! RIGHT! TAKE THIS.
HUH?
W-WHAT? A RING?!
OH... WOW...
I GOT IT FOR YOUR BIRTHDAY. BUT WHEN I MAILED IT, I GOT YOUR ADDRESS WRONG, SO IT GOT SENT BACK.

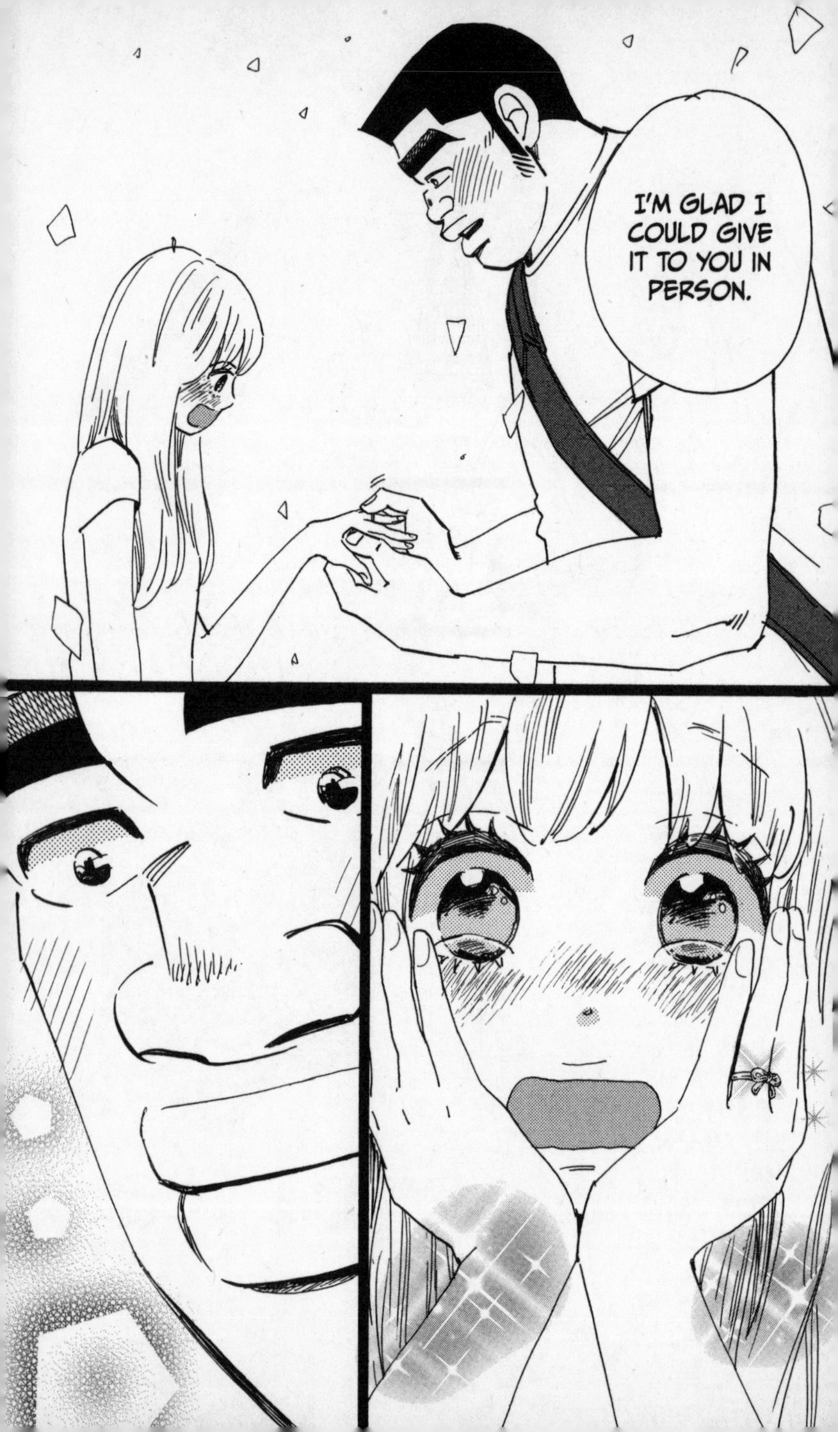
I'M GLAD I COULD GIVE IT TO YOU IN PERSON.

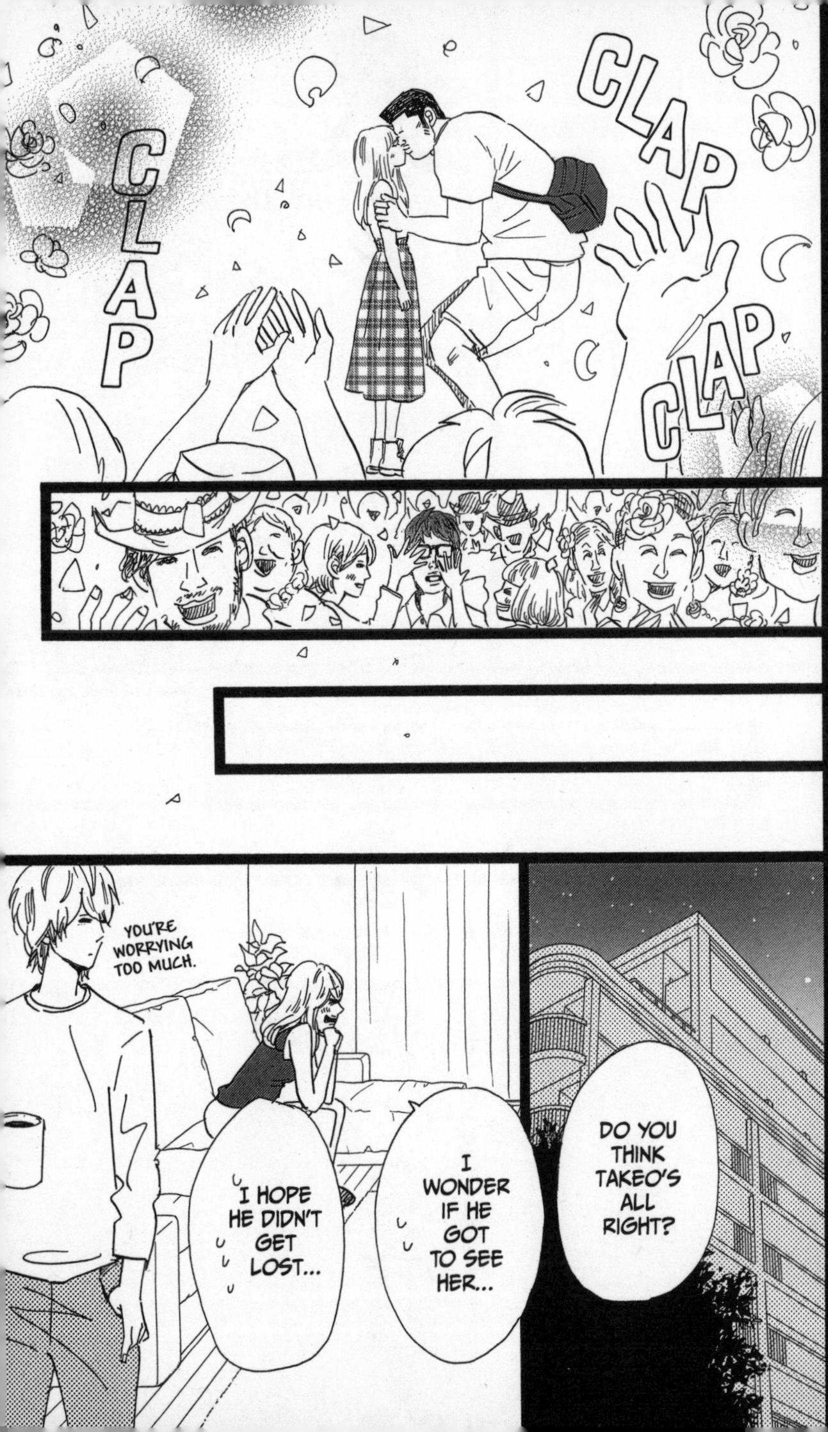
CLAP
CLAP
CLAP
DO YOU THINK TAKEO'S ALL RIGHT?
I WONDER IF HE GOT TO SEE HER...
I HOPE HE DIDN'T GET LOST...
YOU'RE WORRYING TOO MUCH.

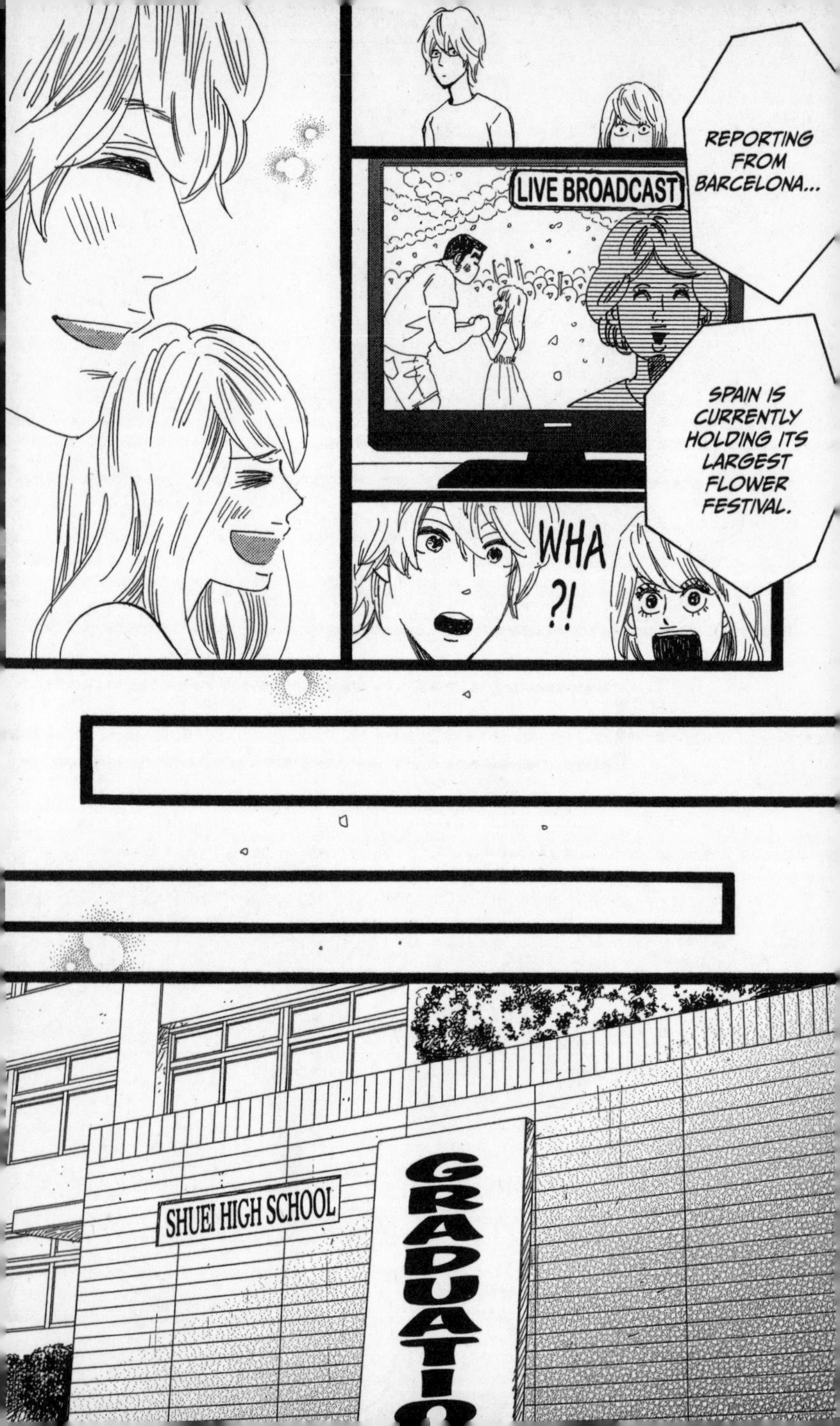
REPORTING FROM BARCELONA...
LIVE BROADCAST
SPAIN IS CURRENTLY HOLDING ITS LARGEST FLOWER FESTIVAL.
WHA ?!
GRADUATIO
SHUEI HIGH SCHOOL

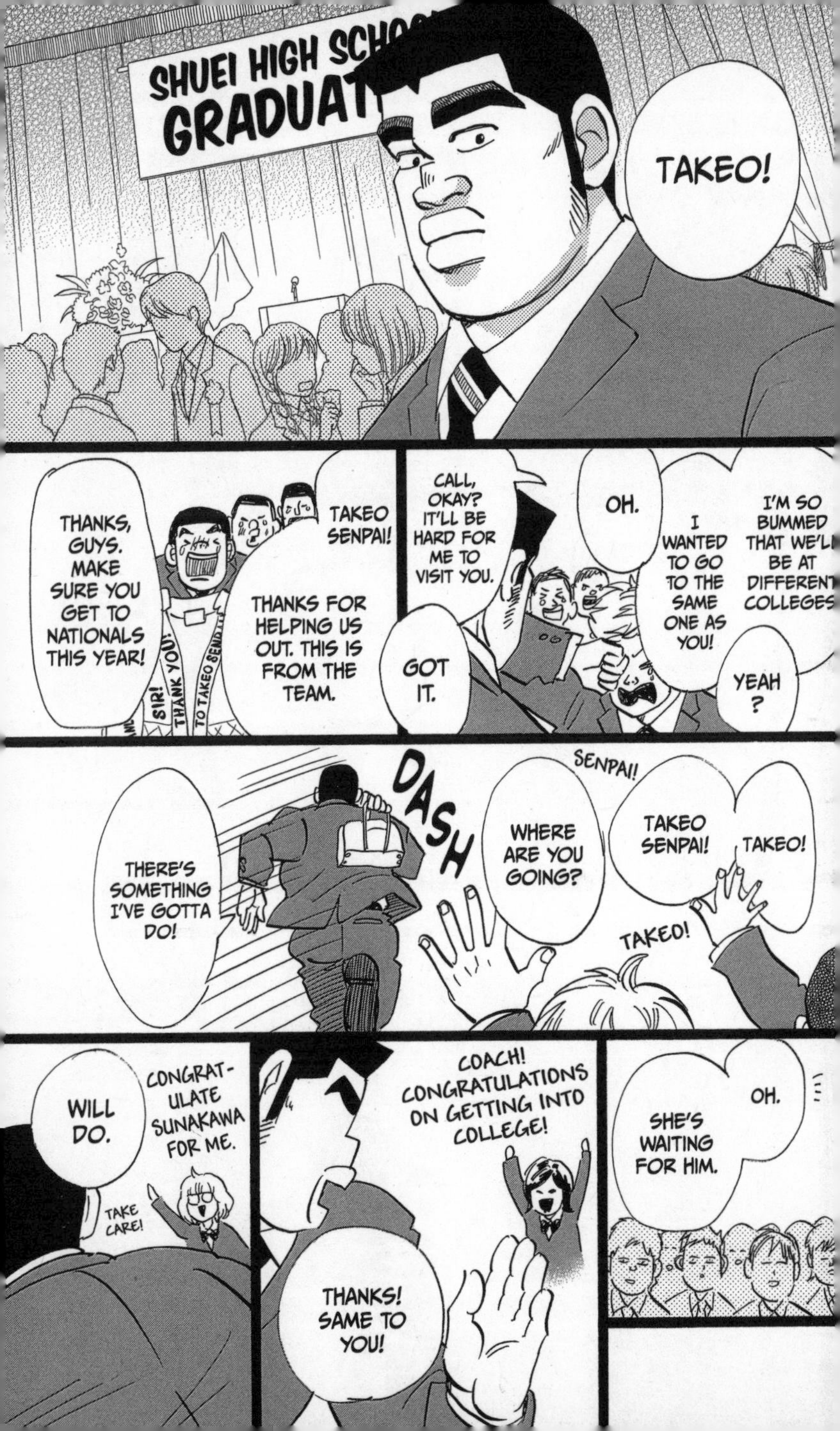

SHUEI HIGH SCHO
GRADUAT
TAKEO!
I'M SO BUMMED THAT WE'LL BE AT DIFFERENT COLLEGES
OH.
I WANTED TO GO TO THE SAME ONE AS YOU!
YEAH?
CALL, OKAY? IT'LL BE HARD FOR ME TO VISIT YOU.
GOT IT.
TAKEO SENPAI!
THANKS FOR HELPING US OUT. THIS IS FROM THE TEAM.
THANKS, GUYS. MAKE SURE YOU GET TO NATIONALS THIS YEAR!
THANK YOU!
SIR!
TAKEO!
TAKEO SENPAI!
SENPAI!
WHERE ARE YOU GOING?
TAKEO!
DASH
THERE'S SOMETHING I'VE GOTTA DO!
...
OH.
SHE'S WAITING FOR HIM.
COACH! CONGRATULATIONS ON GETTING INTO COLLEGE!
THANKS! SAME TO YOU!
CONGRAT-ULATE SUNAKAWA FOR ME.
TAKE CARE!
WILL DO.

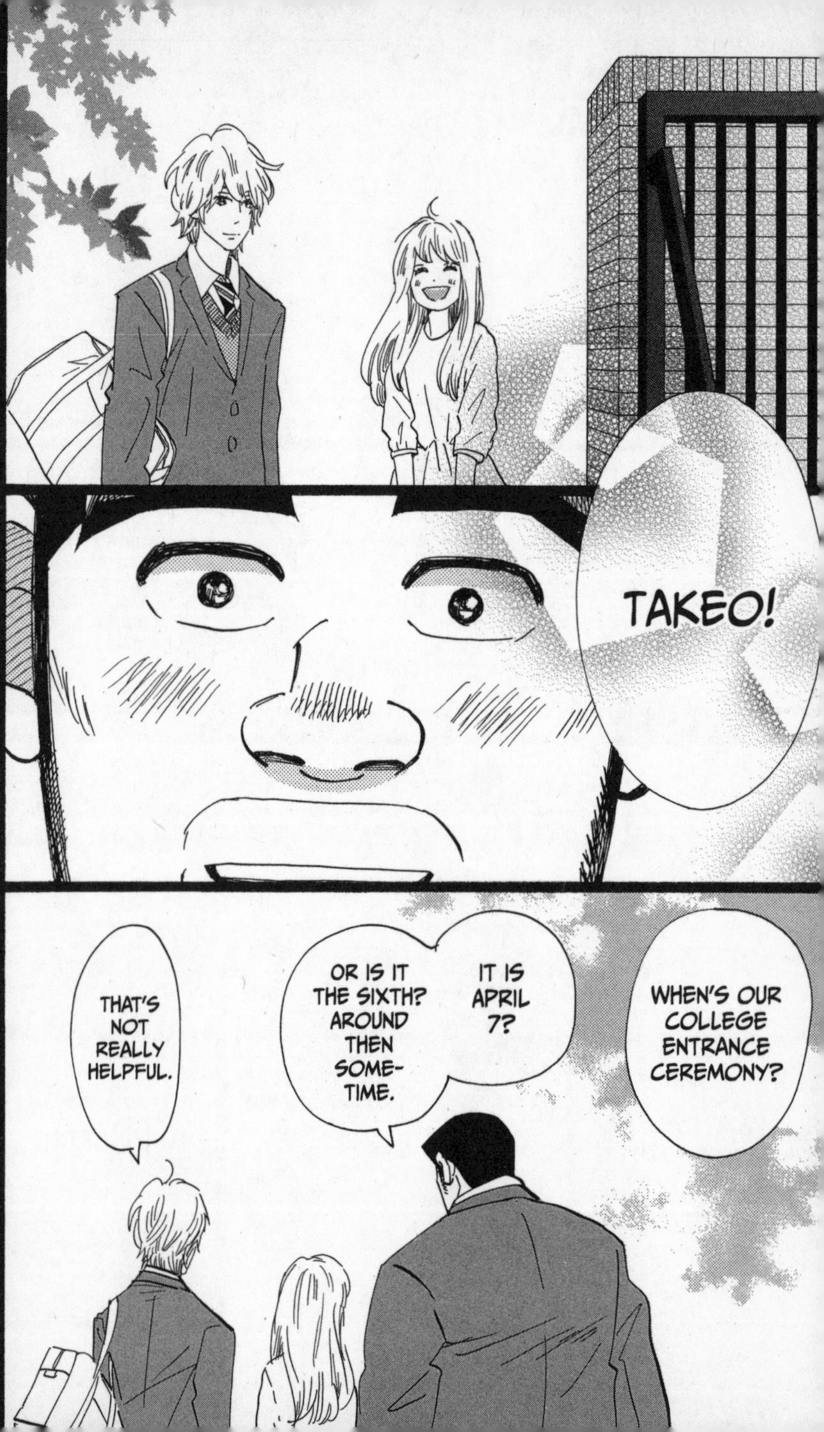
TAKEO!
WHEN'S OUR COLLEGE ENTRANCE CEREMONY?
IT IS APRIL 7?
OR IS IT THE SIXTH? AROUND THEN SOME-TIME.
THAT'S NOT REALLY HELPFUL.

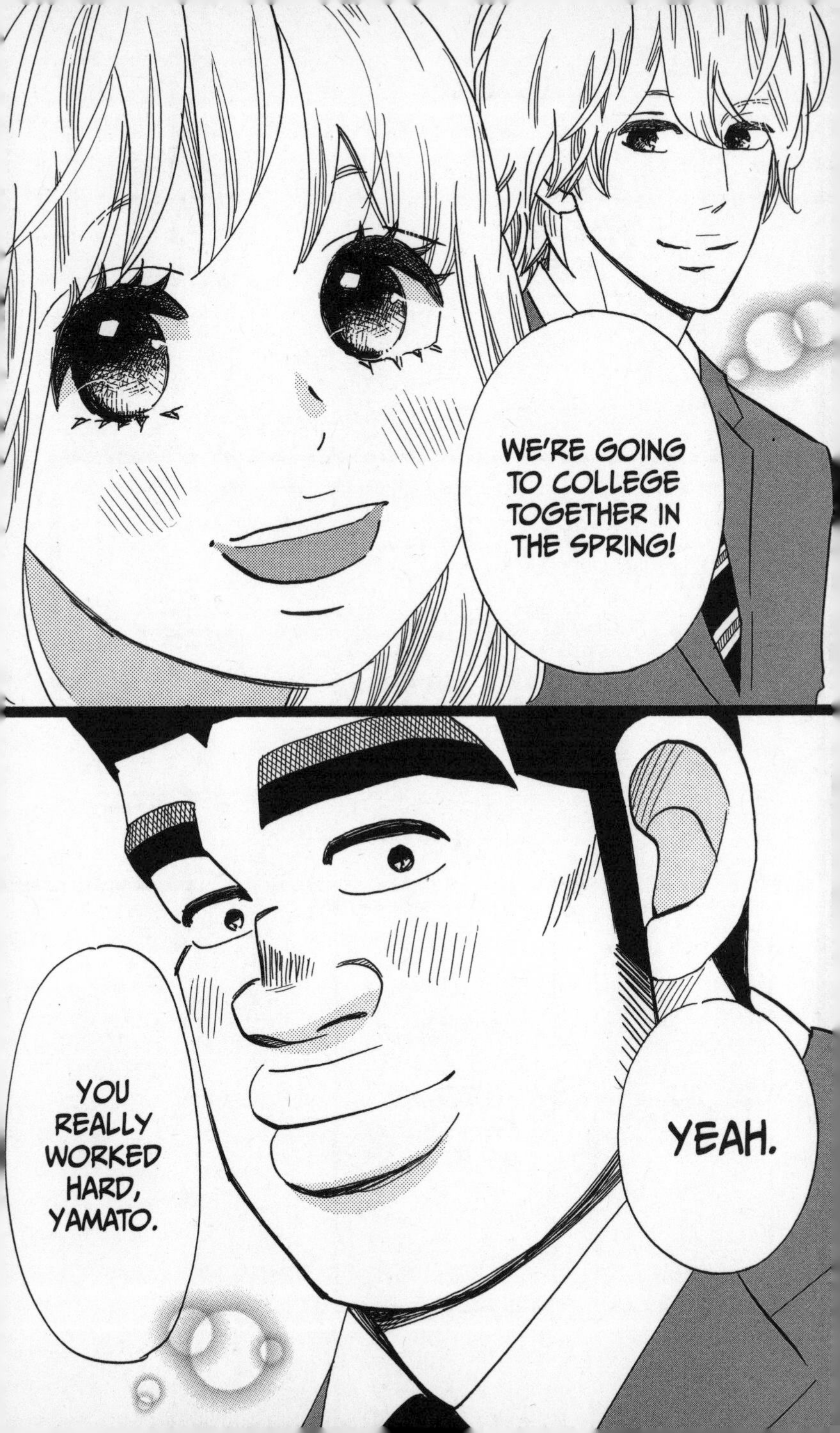
WE'RE GOING TO COLLEGE TOGETHER IN THE SPRING!
YEAH.
YOU REALLY WORKED HARD, YAMATO.

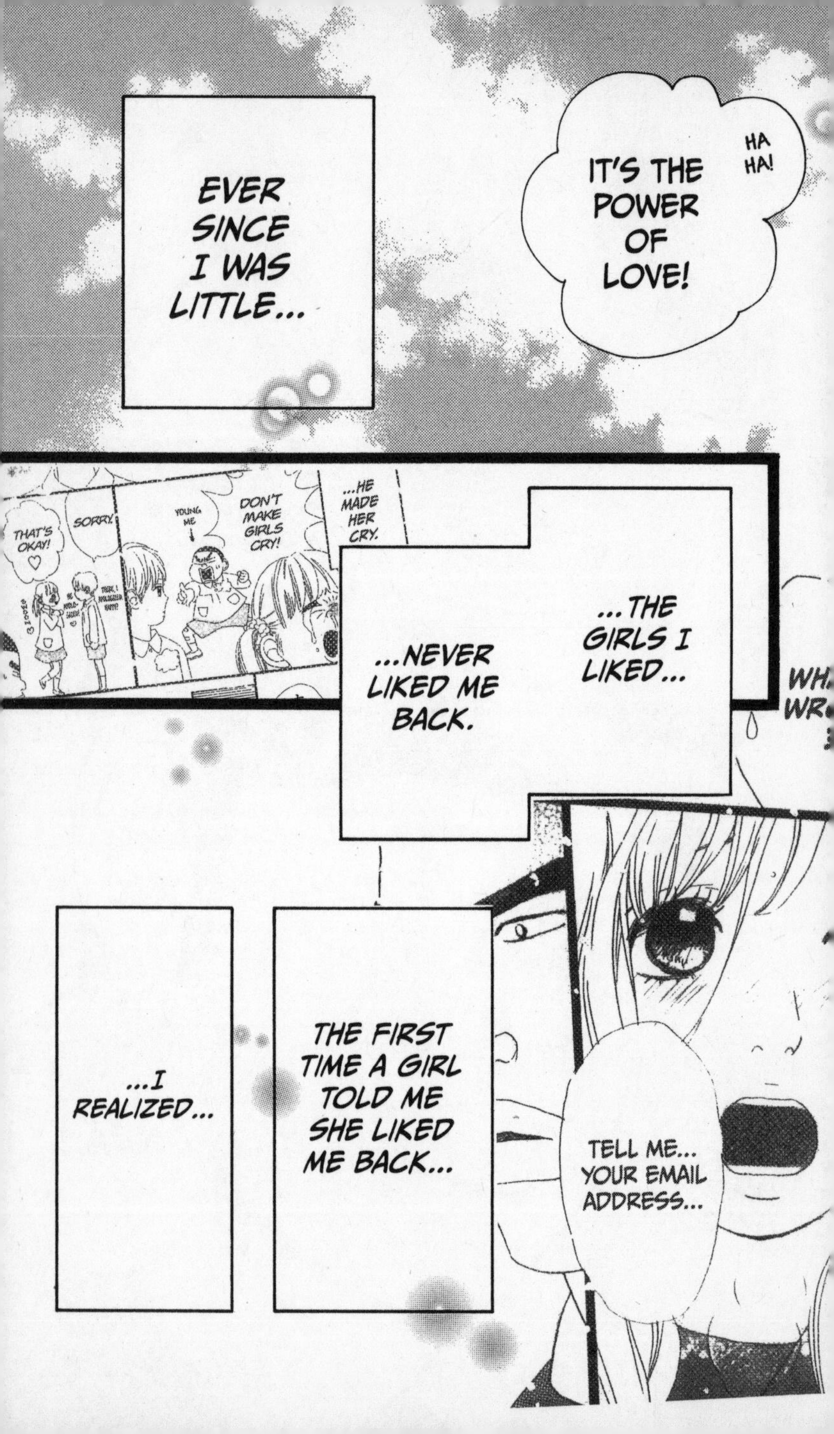
HA HA!
IT'S THE POWER OF LOVE!
EVER SINCE I WAS LITTLE...
...THE GIRLS I LIKED...
...NEVER LIKED ME BACK.
...HE MADE HER CRY.
DON'T MAKE GIRLS CRY!
YOUNG ME
SORRY.
THAT'S OKAY!
TELL ME... YOUR EMAIL ADDRESS...
THE FIRST TIME A GIRL TOLD ME SHE LIKED ME BACK...
...I REALIZED...

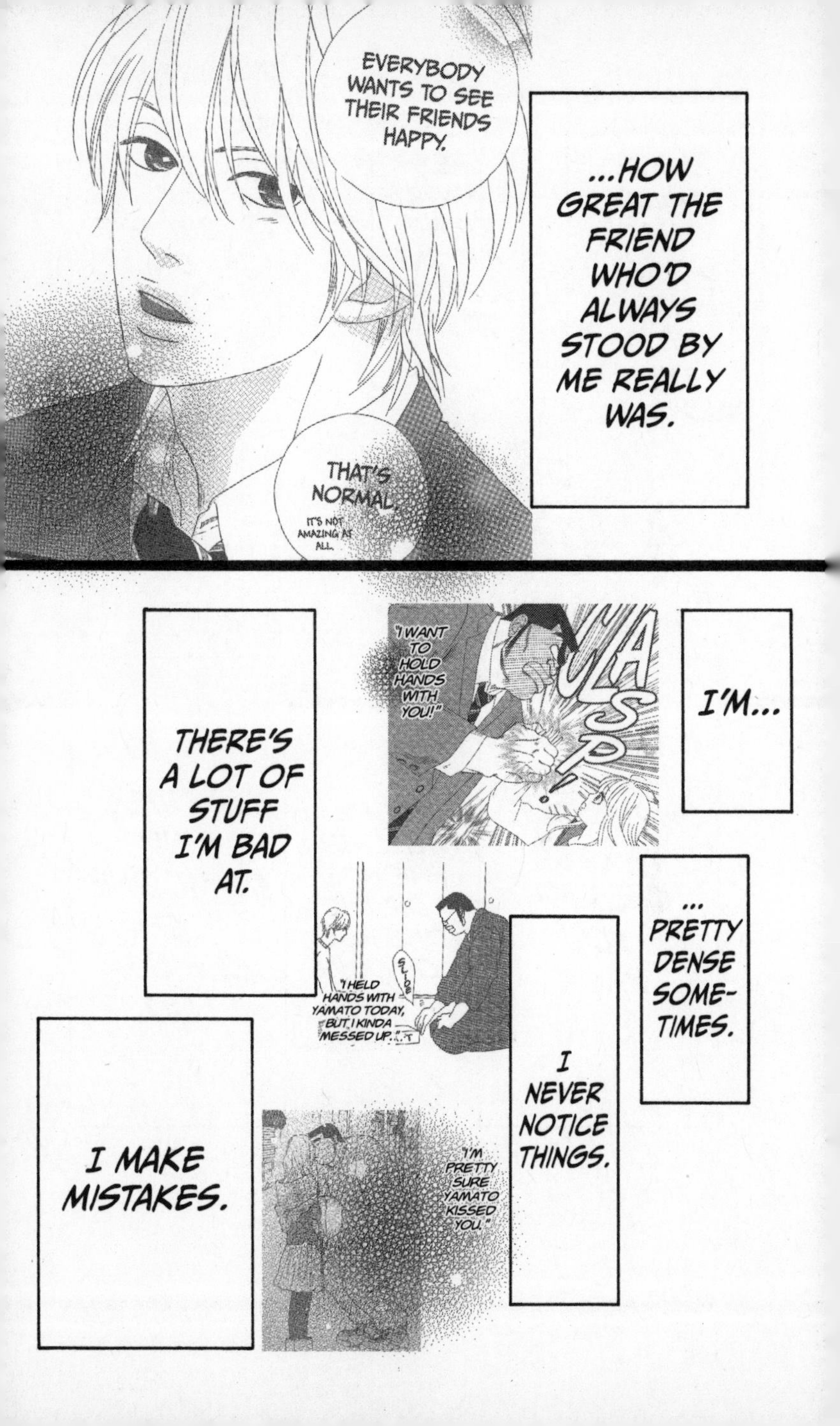
...HOW GREAT THE FRIEND WHO'D ALWAYS STOOD BY ME REALLY WAS.
EVERYBODY WANTS TO SEE THEIR FRIENDS HAPPY.
THAT'S NORMAL.
IT'S NOT AMAZING AT ALL.
I'M...
"I WANT TO HOLD HANDS WITH YOU!"
...PRETTY DENSE SOME-TIMES.
THERE'S A LOT OF STUFF I'M BAD AT.
SLIDE
"I HELD HANDS WITH YAMATO TODAY, BUT I KINDA MESSED UP..."
I NEVER NOTICE THINGS.
"I'M PRETTY SURE YAMATO KISSED YOU."
I MAKE MISTAKES.

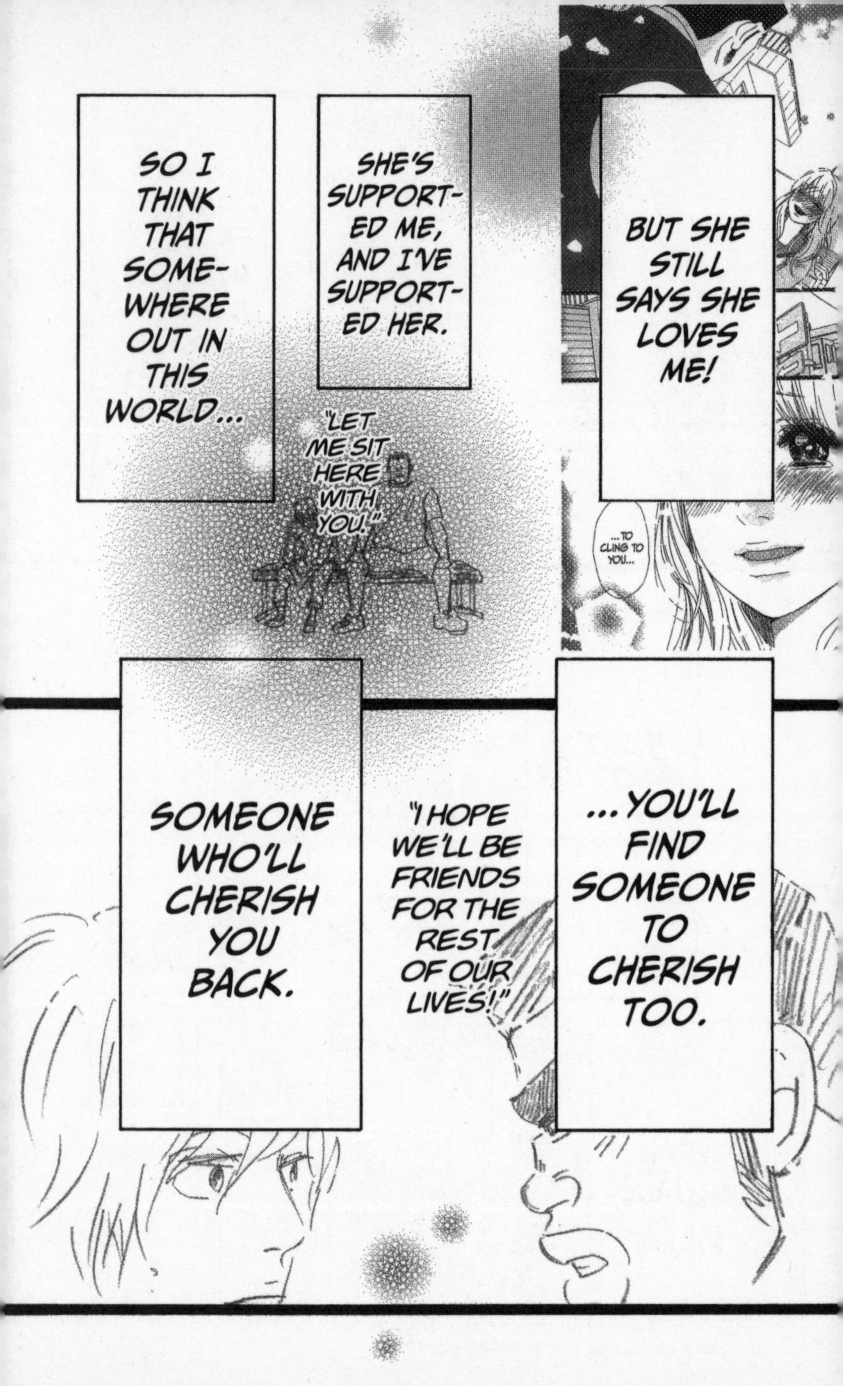
BUT SHE STILL SAYS SHE LOVES ME!
...TO CLING TO YOU...
SHE'S SUPPORT-ED ME, AND I'VE SUPPORT-ED HER.
SO I THINK THAT SOME-WHERE OUT IN THIS WORLD...
"LET ME SIT HERE WITH YOU."
...YOU'LL FIND SOMEONE TO CHERISH TOO.
"I HOPE WE'LL BE FRIENDS FOR THE REST OF OUR LIVES!"
SOMEONE WHO'LL CHERISH YOU BACK.

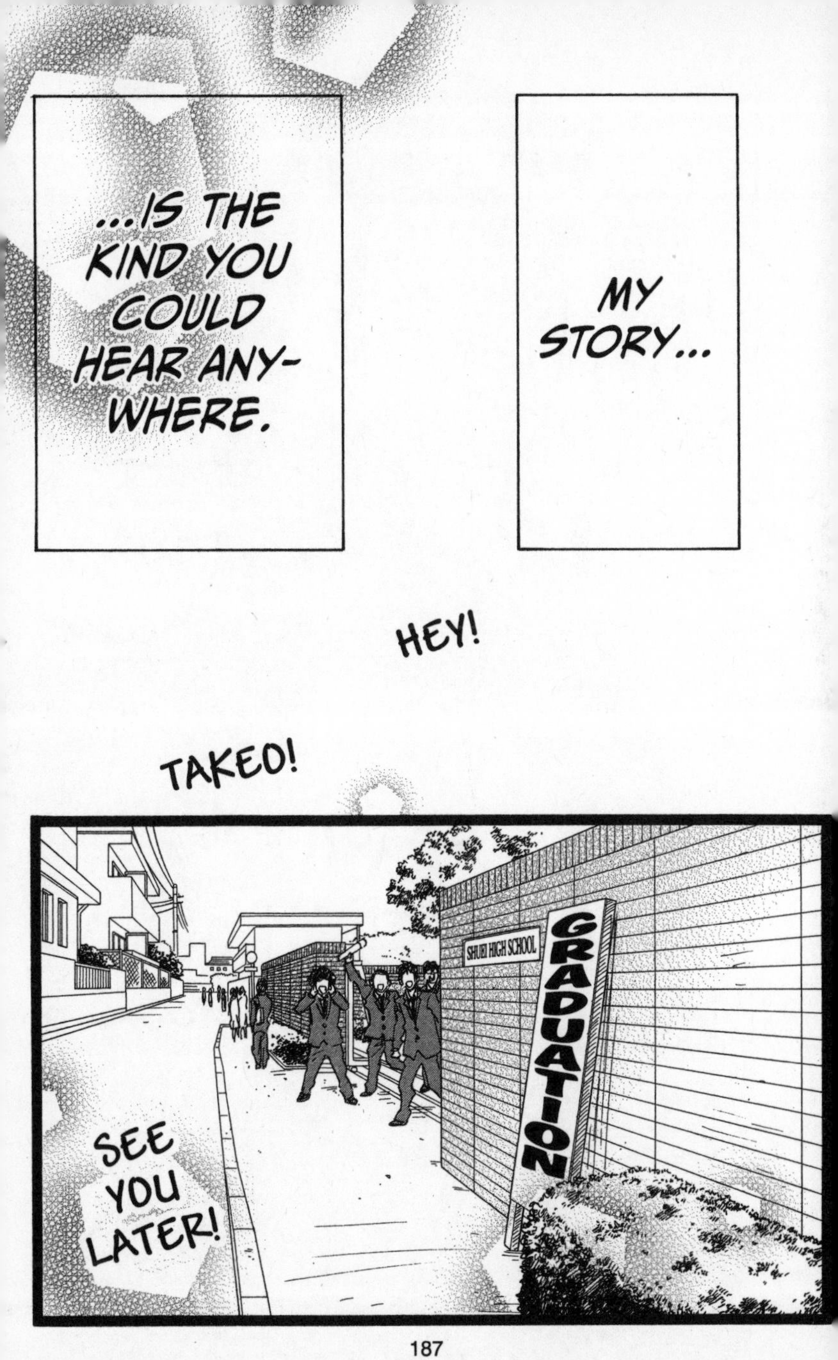
MY STORY...
...IS THE KIND YOU COULD HEAR ANY-WHERE.
HEY!
TAKEO!
SHUEI HIGH SCHOOL
GRADUATION
SEE YOU LATER!

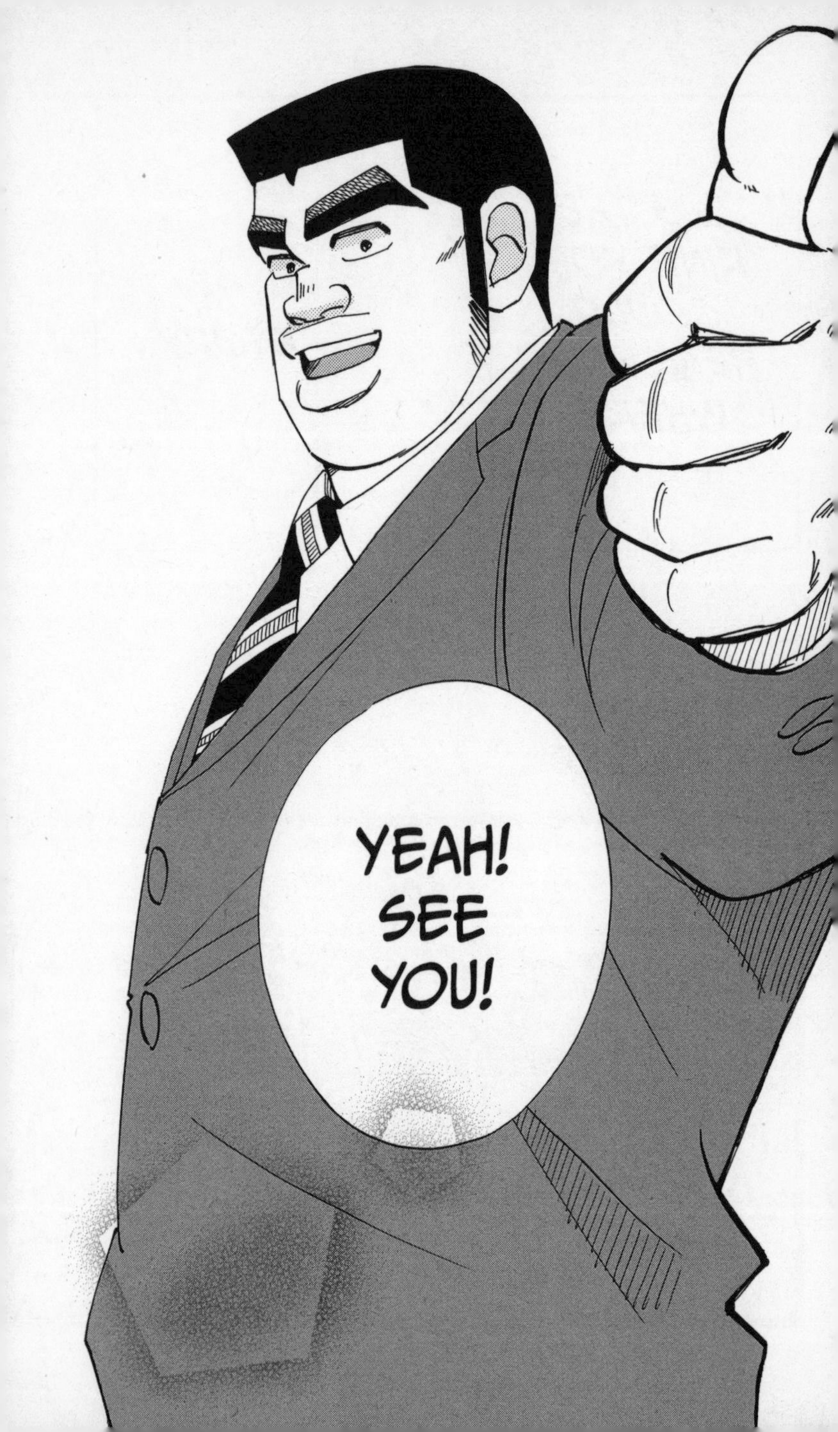
YEAH! SEE YOU!

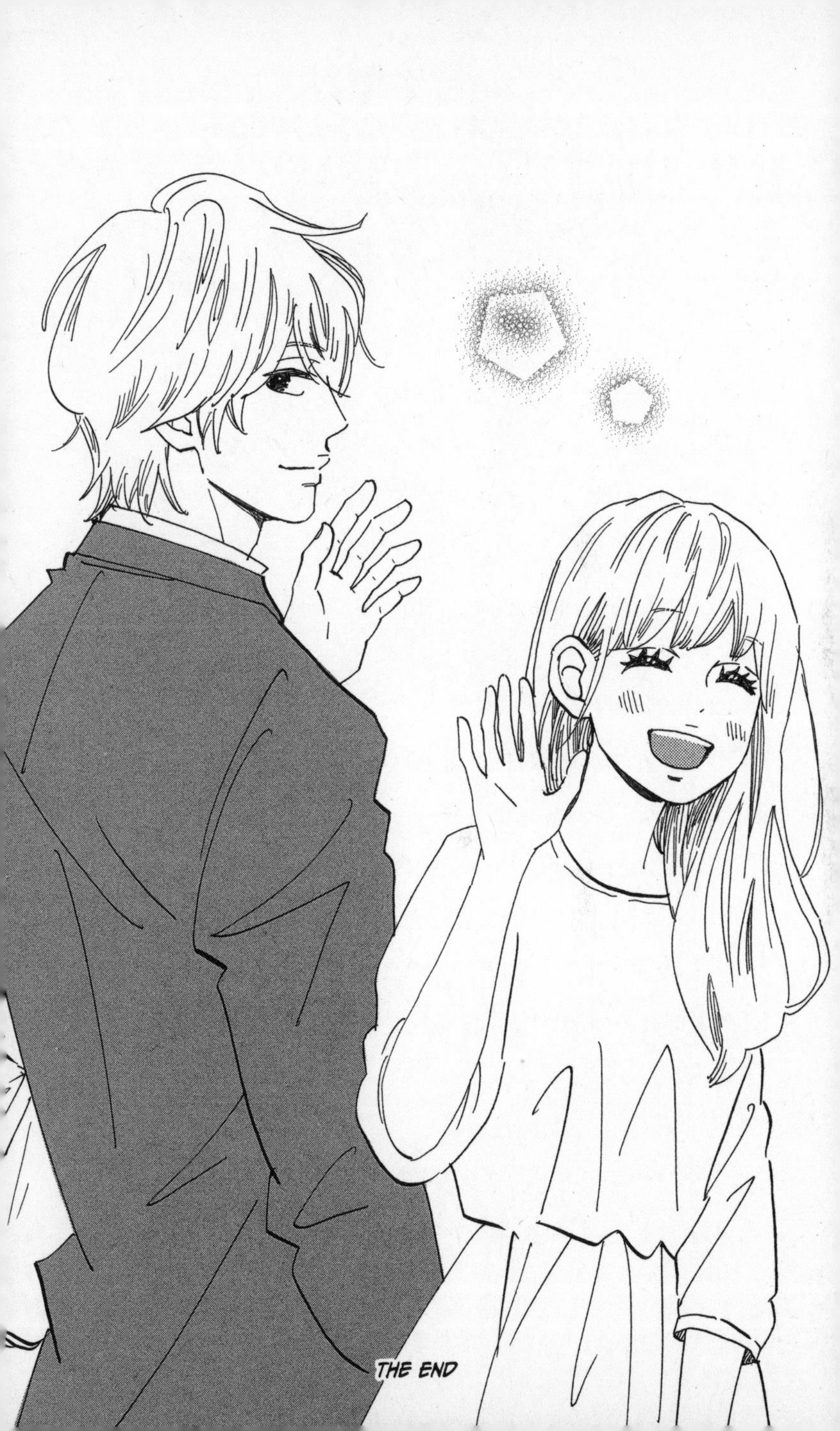
THE END

VOLUME 13

THANK YOU VERY MUCH!!

We've reached the final volume.
Five years ago, *My Love Story!!* was
published as a one-shot comic. I never
expected to be illustrating it for so long,
but I've always enjoyed drawing Takeo.
Thanks to Takeo and his friends, I've met
and talked to all kinds of people. It's been
an incredibly special experience and
has really touched my life.
I'm a huge fan of Kawahara Sensei's,
and working with her was a joy. I'd like
to thank all of our readers for
sticking with us. I'd also like to
thank our editor.
And finally, I'd like to
thank my assistants Asai,
Osawa, Kisaragi and Hayashi!

Bye Bye♡
-Aruko
August 2016

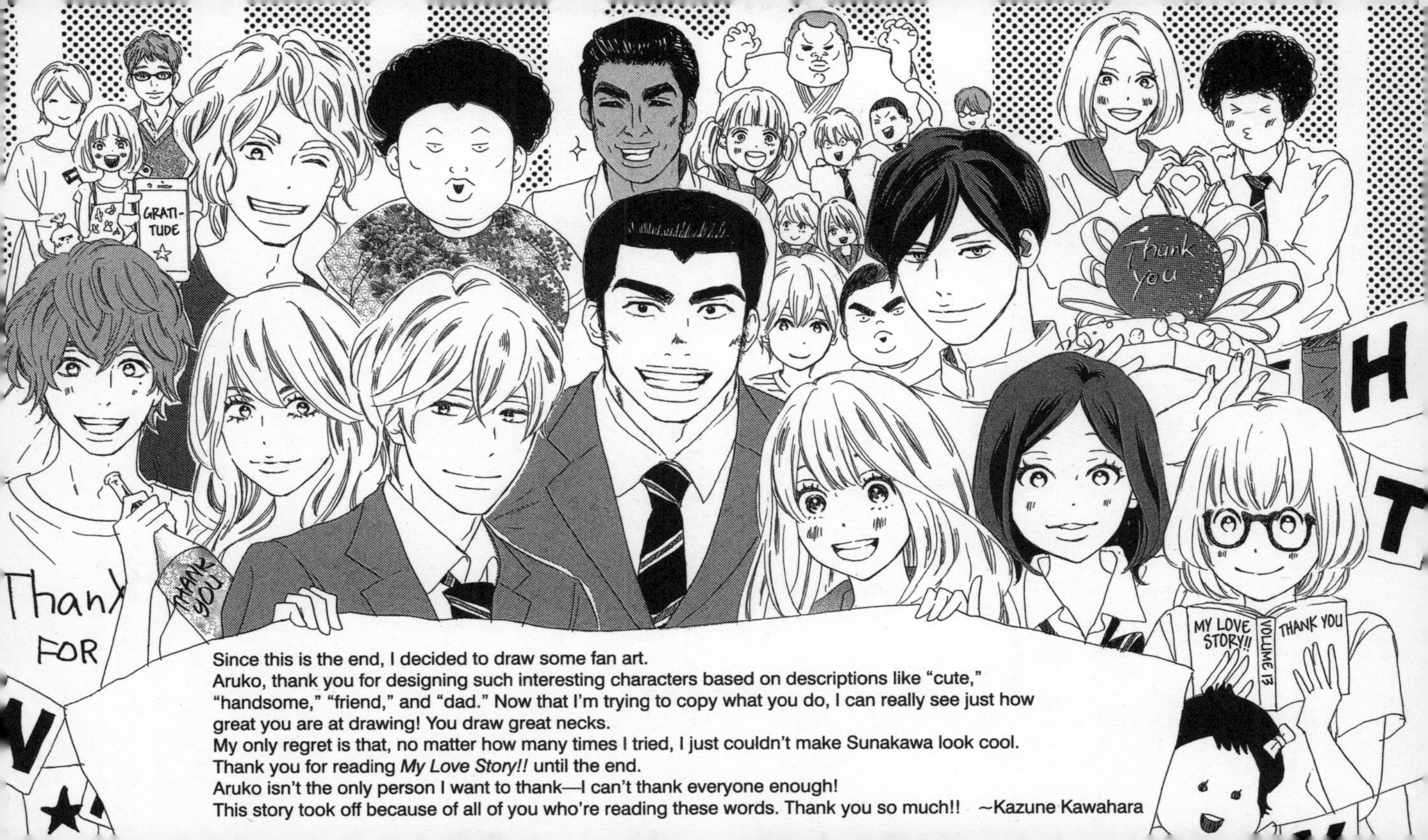

GRATI-
TUDE
Thank
you
H
T
Thank
FOR
THANK
YOU
MY LOVE
STORY!!
VOLUME 13
THANK YOU
Since this is the end, I decided to draw some fan art.
Aruko, thank you for designing such interesting characters based on descriptions like "cute," "handsome," "friend," and "dad." Now that I'm trying to copy what you do, I can really see just how great you are at drawing! You draw great necks.
My only regret is that, no matter how many times I tried, I just couldn't make Sunakawa look cool.
Thank you for reading *My Love Story!!* until the end.
Aruko isn't the only person I want to thank—I can't thank everyone enough!
This story took off because of all of you who're reading these words. Thank you so much!! ~Kazune Kawahara

It was so fun working on this series, and I was always pleased with the feedback I received. I'm really glad that I could share this experience with Aruko. In the end, it felt like one long festival. I'm sad that it's over, but I think it might be nice to write more of this story someday. This series is full of many great memories. Thank you very much for reading!
– Kazune Kawahara
Ⓚ

ARUKO is from Ishikawa Prefecture in Japan and was born on July 26 (a Leo!). She made her manga debut with *Ame Nochi Hare* (Clear After the Rain). Her other works include *Yasuko to Kenji*, and her hobbies include laughing and getting lost.

KAZUNE KAWAHARA is from Hokkaido Prefecture in Japan and was born on March 11 (a Pisces!). She made her manga debut at age 18 with *Kare no Ichiban Sukina Hito* (His Most Favorite Person). Her best-selling shojo manga series *High School Debut* is available in North America from VIZ Media. Her hobby is interior redecorating.

This time, for the cover, I scattered sesame seeds. My editor and a skilled photographer came to my workplace to take a picture of Sesame Takeo! The photo session was a lot of fun. I asked my designer to do a lot of things to create this wonderful final product. What do you think? Thank you for helping us reach the final volume. I hope we can meet again. (^O^)
– Aruko
Ⓐ

MY LOVE STORY!!

Volume 13
Shojo Beat Edition

Story by **KAZUNE KAWAHARA**
Art by **ARUKO**

English Adaptation ♡ **Ysabet Reinhardt MacFarlane**
Translation ♡ **JN Productions**
Touch-up Art & Lettering ♡ **Mark McMurray**
Design ♡ **Fawn Lau**
Editor ♡ **Amy Yu**

First published in Japan in 2011 by SHUEISHA Inc., Tokyo.
English translation rights arranged by SHUEISHA Inc.

Printed in the U.S.A.

Published by VIZ Media, LLC
P.O. Box 77010
San Francisco, CA 94107

10 9 8 7 6 5 4 3 2 1
First printing, September 2017

www.viz.com

PARENTAL ADVISORY
MY LOVE STORY!! is rated T for Teen and is recommended for ages 13 and up. This volume contains suggestive themes.
ratings.viz.com

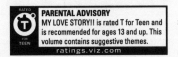

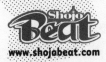

www.shojobeat.com

High School DEBUT

By **Kazune Kawahara**

When Haruna Nagashima was in junior high, softball and comics were her life. Now that she's in high school, she's ready to find a boyfriend. But will hard work (and the right coach) be enough?

Find out in the *High School Debut* manga series—available now!

Honey
So Sweet

Story and Art by *Amu Meguro*

Little did Nao Kogure realize back in middle school that when she left an umbrella and a box of bandages in the rain for injured delinquent Taiga Onise that she would meet him again in high school. Nao wants nothing to do with the gruff and frightening Taiga, but he suddenly presents her with a huge bouquet of flowers and asks her to date him—with marriage in mind! Is Taiga really so scary, or is he a sweetheart in disguise?

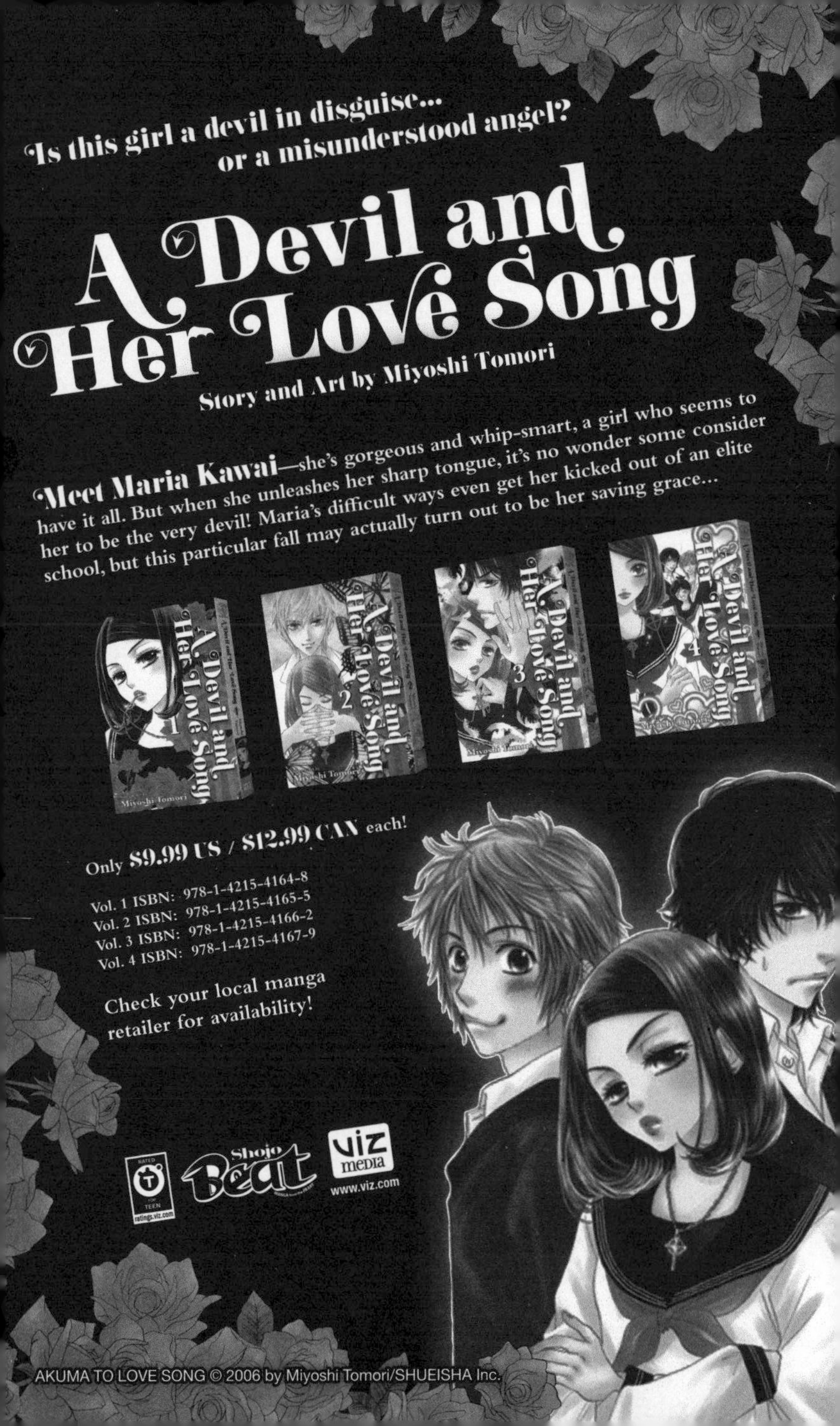
Is this girl a devil in disguise...
or a misunderstood angel?
A Devil and Her Love Song
Story and Art by Miyoshi Tomori
Meet Maria Kawai—she's gorgeous and whip-smart, a girl who seems to have it all. But when she unleashes her sharp tongue, it's no wonder some consider her to be the very devil! Maria's difficult ways even get her kicked out of an elite school, but this particular fall may actually turn out to be her saving grace...
Only $9.99 US / $12.99 CAN each!
Vol. 1 ISBN: 978-1-4215-4164-8
Vol. 2 ISBN: 978-1-4215-4165-5
Vol. 3 ISBN: 978-1-4215-4166-2
Vol. 4 ISBN: 978-1-4215-4167-9
Check your local manga retailer for availability!
RATED T FOR TEEN ratings.viz.com
Shojo Beat
VIZ media
www.viz.com
AKUMA TO LOVE SONG © 2006 by Miyoshi Tomori/SHUEISHA Inc.

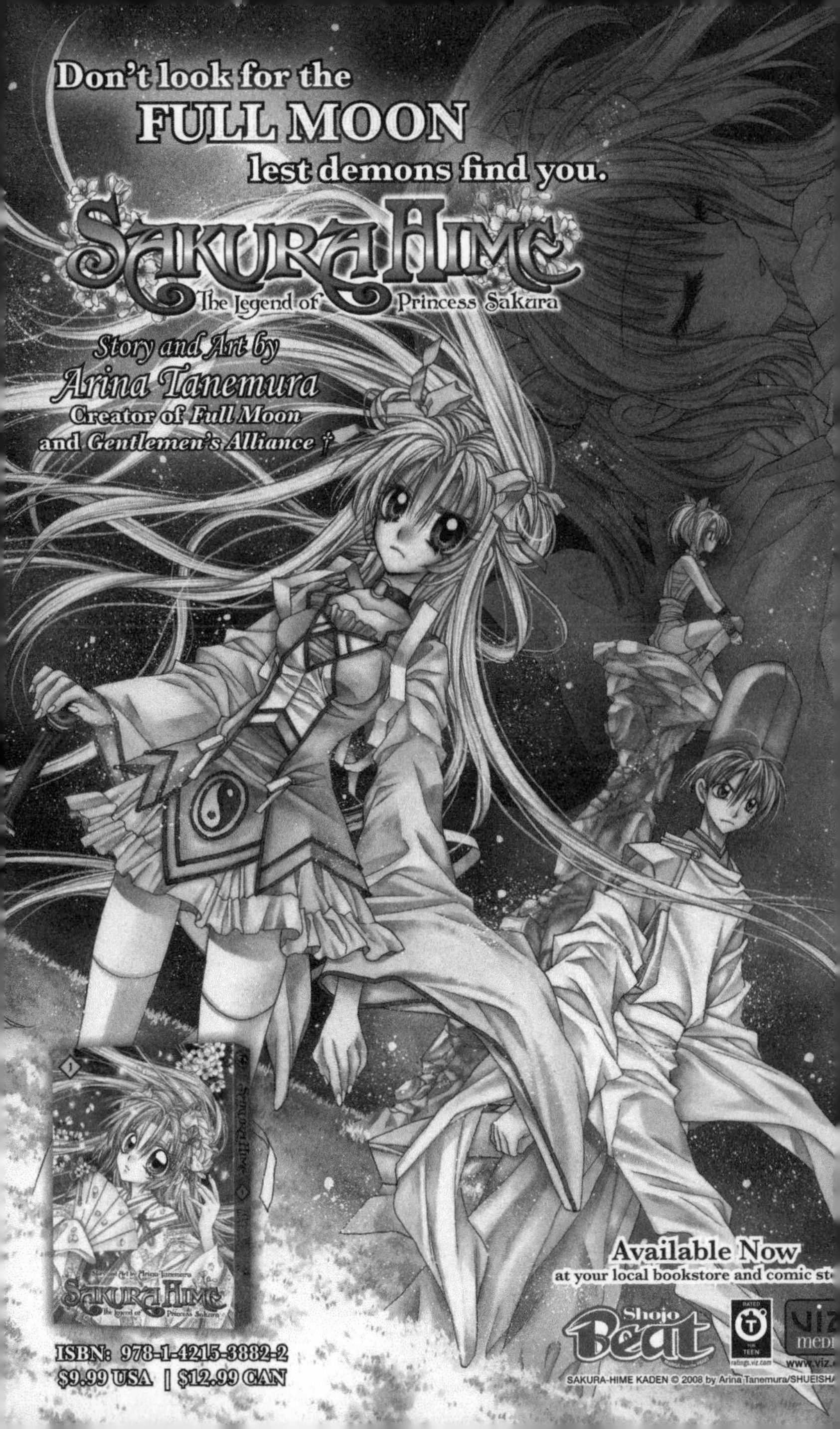

Don't look for the
FULL MOON
lest demons find you.
SAKURA HIME
The Legend of Princess Sakura
Story and Art by
Arina Tanemura
Creator of Full Moon
and Gentlemen's Alliance †
Available Now
at your local bookstore and comic
Shojo Beat
TEEN
ISBN: 978-1-4215-3882-2
$9.99 USA | $12.99 CAN
SAKURA-HIME KADEN © 2008 by Arina Tanemura

You may be reading the **wrong way!!**

IT'S TRUE: In keeping with the original Japanese comic format, this book reads from right to left—so action, sound effects, and word balloons are completely reversed. This preserves the orientation of the original artwork—plus, it's fun! Check out the diagram shown here to get the hang of things, and then turn to the other side of the book to get started!

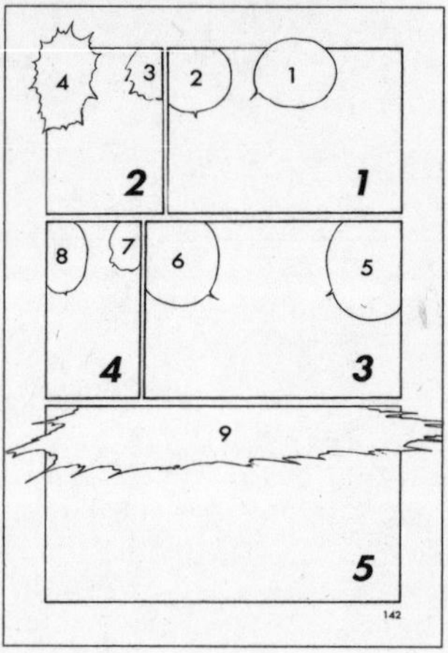
1
2
1
3
4
2
5
6
3
7
8
4
9
5
142

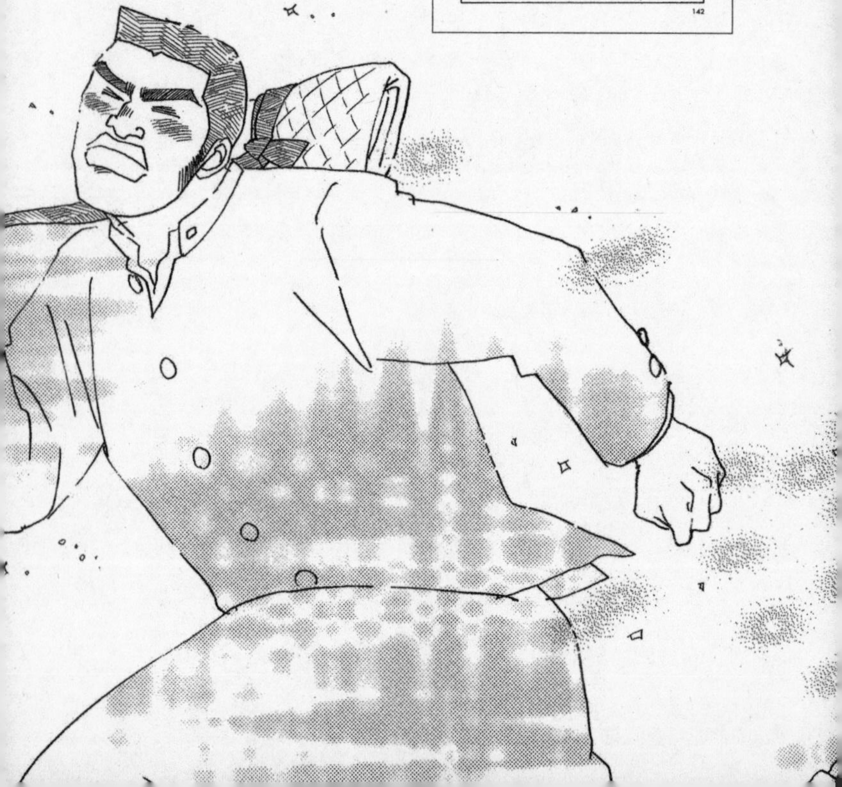